Diarmaid Ferriter is Professor of Modern Irish History at University College Dublin. His previous books include *The Transformation of Ireland 1900–2000* (2004), *Occasions of Sin* (2009), *Ambiguous Republic* (2012), *A Nation and not a Rabble* (2015), *On The Edge* (2018) and the international bestseller *The Border* (2019), all published by Profile Books. He is a regular broadcaster on radio and television and a columnist for the *Irish Times*. He was elected a m⎯⎯ of the Royal Irish Academy in 2019.

Praise for *Between Two Hells*

'*Between Two Hells* is a ⎯⎯⎯⎯⎯⎯⎯⎯ ⎯⎯⎯⎯⎯⎯ ⎯⎯⎯⎯ War and its impact on Ireland ⎯⎯⎯⎯⎯⎯⎯⎯⎯⎯⎯ ⎯wing half-century, rich in insights in ⎯⎯⎯⎯⎯⎯⎯⎯⎯ ⎯⎯en experienced and responded to the calam⎯⎯⎯ ⎯⎯⎯t and the tawdry violence that followed. This absorbing ⎯⎯dy begs the question of why Irish politics did not develop along left/right, urban/rural lines, akin to those seen in other newly independent states' *Irish Times*

'Simply outstanding ... *Between Two Hells* takes us closer to the messy truth behind independent Ireland's birth pangs than ever before ... Ferriter has richly earned his reputation as one of Ireland's leading historians' Andrew Lynch, *Irish Independent*

'Original and arresting ... By the time of the Treaty, the Irish revolution had cost 2,850 lives, almost 1,200 of them civilians. Ireland paid a high price in a conflict with issues that resonate more than a century later' Henry Patterson, *Sunday Times Ireland*

'Meticulously researched, judiciously balanced and unflinching ... breaks new ground' *Sunday Business Post*

'Excellent ... Diarmaid Ferriter, Ireland's best-known and most prolific historian ... enriches lucid and judicious accounts of events and personalities with fresh archival evidence' Cormac Ó Gráda, *BBC History Magazine*

ALSO BY DIARMAID FERRITER

The Border: The Legacy of a Century of Anglo-Irish Politics

On the Edge: Ireland's Offshore Islands: A Modern History

A Nation Not a Rabble: The Irish Revolution, 1913–23

Ambiguous Republic: Ireland in the 1970s

Occasions of Sin: Sex and Society in Modern Ireland

*Judging Dev: A Reassessment of the Life and Legacy
of Eamon de Valera*

The Transformation of Ireland 1900–2000

BETWEEN TWO HELLS

THE IRISH CIVIL WAR

DIARMAID FERRITER

P

PROFILE BOOKS

This paperback edition first published in 2022

First published in Great Britain in 2021 by
Profile Books Ltd
29 Cloth Fair
London
EC1A 7JQ
www.profilebooks.com

Copyright © Diarmaid Ferriter, 2021

3 5 7 9 10 8 6 4 2

Typeset in Garamond by MacGuru Ltd
Printed and bound in Great Britain by
CPI Group (UK) Ltd, Croydon, CR0 4YY

The moral right of the author has been asserted.

All rights reserved. Without limiting the rights under copyright reserved
above, no part of this publication may be reproduced, stored or introduced
into a retrieval system, or transmitted, in any form or by any means (electronic,
mechanical, photocopying, recording or otherwise), without the prior written
permission of both the copyright owner and the publisher of this book.

A CIP catalogue record for this book is available from the British Library.

ISBN 978 1 78816 175 6
eISBN 978 1 78283 510 3

Dedicated with love to my parents, Vera and Nollaig

Contents

INTRODUCTION:
FAITH, REASON AND BETRAYAL

In September 1922, at the height of the Irish Civil War, Eamon de Valera sought to explain to a confidante, Mary MacSwiney, why he could not share her uncompromising republicanism:

> Reason rather than faith has been my master ... I have felt for some time that this doctrine of mine ill fitted me to be leader of the republican party ... nature never fashioned me to be a partisan leader ... For the sake of the cause I allowed myself to be put into a position which it is impossible for one of my outlook and personal bias to fill with effect for the party ... every instinct of mine would indicate that I was meant to be a dyed-in-the-wool Tory, or even a Bishop, rather than the leader of a revolution.

De Valera was the president of Sinn Féin and the most high-profile figure to oppose the acceptance of a compromise Anglo-Irish Treaty with Britain that brought an end to the War of Independence and created a twenty-six-county free-state dominion rather than the desired Irish Republic. Yet he was clearly struggling to make common cause with those on the same side of the Treaty divide as him, but who 'keep on the plane of Faith and Unreason and maintain that position consciously'.[1]

As a conflict, the civil war was small-scale, but the rhetoric it generated was grandiose. Fought between two blocs of the republican movement over a treaty that had fairly broad public support, it was coloured by regional disparities, the creation of a new National

Army by the leaders of the new pro-Treaty provisional government, and a recalcitrant Irish Republican Army (IRA), particularly strong in Munster and labelled the 'Irregulars' by its opponents, who were increasingly forced to rely on guerrilla tactics. As a military contest it was almost over by the end of 1922. Resulting in the region of 1,300 fatalities, it has garnered the labels 'Brother Against Brother' and 'Green Against Green'.[2] A century on from the war, however, those labels are inadequate; there were numerous shades of colour and men had no monopoly on the division. Neither is the faith/reason dichotomy satisfactory. While civil war opponents did much to contrive narratives that emphasised these contrasts, in reality the war was never as clear-cut as either side pretended or came to believe. In the words of writer George Russell (AE), both sides embraced 'the one-dimensional mind ... beaten by the hammer of Thor into some mould or shape when they cling to one idea'.[3] The challenge at its centenary is to discard that hammer to do justice to its various contours and colours.

De Valera's despondent words in 1922 seemed to suggest a vindication of the assertion earlier that year of his nemesis in London, Winston Churchill, secretary of state for the colonies and one of the negotiators of the Treaty, that 'Mr de Valera may gradually come to personify not a cause but a catastrophe'. He added ominously that the provisional government seeking to implement the Treaty 'must assert itself or perish and be replaced by some other form of control'.[4] It was a typical Churchillian bullying flourish communicated to Michael Collins, chair of the provisional government, the IRA intelligence master turned Anglo-Irish negotiator who had signed the Treaty with reluctance. It was also a reminder of the British shadow that hung over Ireland in 1922; that the civil war was not just an internal Irish matter. With the British-assisted attack on anti-Treaty IRA members in Dublin in June 1922 that began the civil war, was it Churchill's policy rather than an Irish policy that 'had effectively triumphed'?[5] And could the Irish general election that same month, during which pro-Treaty candidates prevailed, be seen as fair and free, given the lingering British pressure?

De Valera, Churchill and Collins were central to the gestation of Ireland's civil war; two of them not only survived this turbulent period but went on to achieve iconic status, seen by their supporters twenty years later when ensconced in power as representing the destiny of their respective nations. Collins, killed during the civil war at the age of thirty-one, became its most high-profile victim.

As Collins came into his own in the aftermath of the signing of the Treaty, de Valera experienced disdain both from anti-Treaty militants, who distrusted what they regarded as his moderation, and from his pro-Treaty opponents, who regarded him as dangerously subversive. It was this falling between stools that created the greatest dilemma of his sixty-year career in politics. While he could not or would not accept the Treaty, he was also, as evidenced by the Mac-Swiney letter, uncomfortable with the republican purists and was floundering. Ronan Fanning has suggested this was because, having been 'swaddled in the comfort blanket of four years of deference and obedience, de Valera tried to chart a course too subtle [suggesting, not Irish membership of the Commonwealth, but an 'external association' with it] to be understood by those less intellectually astute than he was'.[6]

Contemporaries were much less kind, seeing his opposition as solely about personal ambition and power rather than principle, placing the burden of compromise 'on his opponent's shoulders' – an unforgivable act with deadly consequences. It was deemed especially egregious from someone who had not even deigned to be involved, as the senior Sinn Féin leader, in the Treaty negotiations.[7]

Fanning's dismissal of de Valera's opponents is, however, too sweeping, implying a lack of depth and engagement with issues that most were deeply sincere about. Nor did anti-Treatyites have a monopoly on expressions of faith; the pro-Treaty IRA officer Michael Rynne recorded in his diary 'I support the Treaty from conviction ... I cannot retract my faith.' And that came at a personal cost: 'I stand to lose 50% of my friendships and 70% or so of my acquaintanceships.' At a dance in the Mansion House in March 1922, 'Cathal Brugha was there and I had to cut him [off] in no uncertain manner.'[8] Rynne grew weary of the sternness of those who 'adopt an air and tone of moral superiority to all lesser men'.[9] Brugha, who had been Sinn Féin minister for defence, was shortly to lie dead. But that both sides were still dancing, if awkwardly, in early 1922 is a reminder that the first half of that year still held out the possibility of avoiding war.

The reasons put forward for accepting the Treaty – that it offered substantive independence and could be a pathway to even greater autonomy in the future, or was a pragmatic compromise in the face of a much more powerful Britain and an alternative to renewed war – were persuasive to many. Others, however, were adamant that Ireland's plight could not be addressed through contemporary real-politik. Frank Gallagher, a trenchant opponent of the Treaty and an IRA Volunteer in Dublin, who spent decades after the civil war jus-tifying the anti-Treaty side, insisted Ireland was not land or people: 'Ireland is something else ... Ireland is the dead and the things the dead would have done ... Ireland is spirit.'[10] Likewise, it was asserted by Todd Andrews, who fought with the anti-Treaty IRA as a teen-ager, that 'our Ireland had in fact become a political abstraction'.[11]

Todd's son, David, who went on to have a successful career with the political party Fianna Fáil, founded by anti-Treatyites in 1926, argued decades later that 'the civil war had little to do with ideol-ogy. The choice of sides in the war had, in most cases, little to do with politics. Often it had more to do with personality clashes, the manoeuvrings of cliques and the readiness of troops to follow indi-vidual leaders.' This assessment too, seems to place the participants outside of their time, as if they were automatons, but they felt deeply; Andrews quoted the Belfast Catholic Sinn Féiner and subsequent Fianna Fáil stalwart Seán MacEntee: 'this was one of those periods when emotion overthrows reason'.[12]

Reason, it seems, also became ruthless for those running the pro-Treaty government. Just over two weeks after de Valera wrote his letter to MacSwiney, the provisional government introduced a public safety bill making the bearing of arms against the state punish-able by execution, to show, according to William T. Cosgrave, who replaced Collins as leader of the government, 'that there is a govern-ment prepared to take the responsibility of governing ... although I have always objected to the death penalty, there is no other way'.[13] The first executions took place on 17 November and there were to be seventy-seven by the end of the civil war, or eighty-three, if four men executed for armed robbery and two summarily shot by firing squad in Cork and Kerry before the legislation was passed, are included.[14]

Pro-Treaty political leaders articulated justification for this policy by reference to the existential crisis the fledgling state faced and the insistence that they were protectors of democracy. It is a contention that has proved convincing to some historians, but others are more sceptical; if 1922 was essentially about the 'birth of democracy', why was there such failure to find a political solution in 1922? In any case, Irish democratic culture predated the Treaty, 'so the vista of a heroic elite forcing democratic values down the throat of a recalcitrant society should not be taken at face value'.[15]

The battle to control the labelling and narrative of the war began during it. Cosgrave was adamant as he faced into 1923 that the Irish civil war was no such thing: 'I may say to call this "civil war" is a libel on civil war.'[16] It was, as he saw it, about defeating criminals, not soldiers. Those passionately opposed to him also dismissed the civil war label for different reasons. Muriel MacSwiney, whose husband Terence was one of the best known martyrs of the Irish War of Independence, was in Washington in September 1922 to push the anti-Treaty case and insisted 'the fight in Ireland is not in reality a civil war. England has only persuaded some Irish to help her.'[17]

But civil war it was, given that it involved armed conflict between Irish citizens and within their communities, parishes and even families, and the 'rhetorical battles' regarding the concept of civil war should not overshadow that. True, civil war experiences can be self-servingly shaped and distorted 'through language and memory' and by the 'conceptual heritage of civil war', but they are 'first and foremost a category of experience'.[18] Nor can the violence of civil wars be reduced to irrationality or pre-existing cleavages; rather it carries its own logic and amounts to 'a joint process created by the actions of both political actors and civilians', while non-combatants are not always just pawns trapped between rebels and the state.[19] The violence of the Irish civil war was, however, small in scale compared with other contemporary civil wars. There was little balance of power from 1922 to 1923; the provisional government had the backing of vested and 'moral interests'; republicans were beaten quickly because they had no proper military plan or enough public support. Partition, a reality since 1921 and which had created a six-county Northern Ireland to satisfy the demands of Ulster unionists opposed to an all-island Anglo-Irish settlement, 'saved the south from the most explosive internal problems subverting new states'.[20] But violence also marred the birth of Northern Ireland, and with one-third of its population nationalist and opposed to its creation, the northern backdrop to the civil war was not just a sideshow but a parallel and deadly conflict: over 500 people were killed there between 1920 and 1922.

In 2007 Charles Townshend argued, 'Ireland's violence was constrained by social mechanisms we do not yet fully understand.'[21] The Finnish civil war, fought from January to May 1918, killed up to 36,000; the Estonian War of Independence from late 1918 to early 1920 killed just under 12,000; the parallel Latvian equivalent resulted in 13,000 fatalities and the 1919–21 Hungarian 'red and white' terror caused about 5,000 deaths. Ireland was well down the fatality league table.[22] As elucidated by Anne Dolan, however, such figures are only one measurement ('a blunt and awkward instrument'); we need to be conscious of the nature as well as the extent of violence and also what Ireland had in common with other conflict zones as 'Ireland's wars came of the same mess of reasons found in every other place'. Perhaps also relevant was that Ireland was in a different 'zone of violence' and not part of the 'culture of defeat' after the First World War that prompted 'ultra violence' born of ethnic and religious tensions in other parts of Europe at that time.[23]

It might seem perverse to stress the need to factor in restraint in an analysis of the Irish civil war, given that we have got so used to quietly shaking our heads at its perceived viciousness, but a wider, comparative context suggests that might be required. Unlike in Ireland, a central question in the Finnish civil war was whether social justice should be prioritised over independence. In both countries,

> divisions emerged over who could further the nation's interests, but in Finland, these divisions had profound social dimensions. The victors interpreted their civil war in national terms, as a war

of liberation (*Vapaussota*) against leftist forces contaminated by their exposure to the Soviet Union. The left, in contrast, interpreted the war in social terms.

Finland was also more vulnerable geopolitically considering Russia, which made reintegration of the losers imperative.[24] Ireland was perhaps not in as much danger of reoccupation by Britain, but when that was deemed a possibility during the Second World War, it was an emergency that generated consensus among civil war opponents.

What also needs to be remembered is that in ways other than violence 'the Irish civil war was fully as destructive as most of its kind'.[25] Liam de Róiste, Cork Sinn Féin TD (MP) and pro-Treaty, decried that its opponents did not rely upon 'moral weapons' but the republicans did claim a monopoly of moral right, complicated in October 1922 by a pastoral from the Irish Catholic Bishops that denounced violent anti-Treaty republicans and justified their excommunication.[26] Given that some republicans based their opposition to the Treaty on the notion of 'faith', interpreting their movement religiously as guardians of the 'soul' of the Irish nation, and were intent on claiming a spiritual authority for their movement that transcended episcopal authority, the Bishops' move created serious tension, resulting in an acrimonious battle of words.

What is indisputable is that (from the perspective of the government) the pastoral 'gave a cloak of moral authority' to the executions that followed.[27] But there was little moral consistency. As Cork writer Seán O'Faoláin, who was a member of the anti-Treaty IRA, characterised it, the 'slick slogan' of some clergy that civil war outrages were perpetrated by those who forgot God 'was to be mocked at by Catholic murder, Catholic gun-fire and Catholic torch setting flames to the houses of Catholic people'.[28]

The resort to hunger strikes by interned republicans was another notable development that defined the civil war. They were also spiritual for some; as Ernie O'Malley, the IRA's assistant chief of staff who endured a forty-one-day hunger strike, put it in November 1923, 'the country has not as yet had sufficient voluntary sacrifice and suffering and not until suffering fluctuates will she get back her real soul ...

There is not enough of spirituality in our movement.'[29] Yet for all his ardent piety, O'Malley seemed incapable of or disinterested in defining 'people' or 'nation' or 'republic'.[30]

We need, nonetheless, to give sufficient weight to the emotional charge of 1922–3 and to 'bring the war back' to those who fought it, recognising that, in the words of Brian Hanley, 'any balanced discussion of terror in twentieth-century Ireland must identify all of its origins and agencies, not just those which conform to our own opinions and prejudices'.[31] Due to transformations in archival access, a growing interest in the depths of personal history and a weakening of the suffocation the more recent Troubles in Northern Ireland placed history writing under, we are much better placed to do emotion justice and be less judgemental. It is not the duty of the historian to 'lecture the people of the past on how they should have done better'.[32] The quest should be to understand and contextualise their positions, the lights that guided them and to humanise their dilemmas and the deadly consequences of their decisions, an approach that has been more apparent in some recent studies. David Fitzpatrick, the biographer of Harry Boland, killed in 1922 as an opponent of the Treaty, concluded Boland was 'at once a dictator, an elitist, a populist and a democrat ... whether we consider that he was driven by a laudable conviction in the inalienable rights of nations or a grotesque delusion, the sincerity of his struggle cannot be impugned'.[33]

Calton Younger did lecture the civil war's participants to an extent in his 1968 book *Ireland's Civil War*, in which he noted just how difficult it was to be specific about the causes of the war but was nonetheless clear that 'the Irish civil war ought to have been fought with words on the floor of the Dáil [the Irish Parliament] and it could have been'.[34] Perhaps it could have been in a fantasy post-Treaty Ireland, where the Dáil was the prime national and final arbiter, but that regard did not exist in 1922. Younger's account was regarded as favouring the pro-Treaty side. Eoin Neeson, too, in 1966, though clearly sympathetic to the anti-Treatyites, was of the view that nothing was achieved by the civil war that could not have been achieved by negotiation, though his book was at its strongest in describing the military engagements.[35]

Michael Hopkinson observed in his book *Green Against Green* in 1988 that 'it is hardly surprising that a bitter incestuous conflict in a small country, which saw neither compromise nor reconciliation at its end, has been extremely difficult for Irish historians to write about in a detached manner'.[36] Hopkinson also wrote of the difficulty of describing 'chaos. The war had an ill-defined beginning and end; the fighting was erratic, extremely confusing and highly regionalised.'[37] I have left the intense minutiae of military combat to others better equipped, but chaos had many forms in Ireland in 1922–3, and for far too many the civil war's afterlife was also cruelly disordered, a fracturing discussed in detail in the second half of this book. The conflict also spawned an acerbic civil war politics, 'that infused every part of it with such intensity that some parts of the country are uncomfortable with the memory of it still. Without taking full account of its bitterness it is questionable whether one can begin to understand the Irish civil war at all.'[38]

It is difficult to dispute the assertion of Charles Townshend that republicans during the civil war had a view of public opinion that 'was and remained generally dismissive'. While some gloried in it, the anti-Treaty republicans were faced with stark impediments; not just public opinion, but also the fact that 'there was no plan of campaign'.[39] But those who opposed them were well capable too of contemptuous disregard for the depth and sincerity of anti-Treaty sentiment.

Some young minds swayed during the conflict. Another Cork writer, Frank O'Connor, initially trenchant, became disgusted by the end of it and came to decry those who insisted 'the Irish Republic was still in existence and would remain so, despite what its citizens might think'.[40] Others, like the playwright Lady Gregory, found themselves with a foot in both camps; she told a priest after the end of the civil war: 'one should not be more angry with government or Republicans than with different sections of one's own mind, tilting to good or bad on one or the other side.'[41] Patriotism was both an expensive currency and a contested, confused concept in Ireland in 1922, and no side had a monopoly of it.

Female republicans generated some of the most heated rhetoric and ferocious responses during the conflict. Attitudes to republican women who endured great harshness dripped with contempt as the 'Furies' provoked a barely concealed misogyny.[42] These women were 'the women in men's clothing', as J. J. Walsh, a pro-Treaty minister, characterised them.[43] Warming to the culture of disparagement, the minister for home affairs (later justice), Kevin O'Higgins, referred to 'hysterical young women who ought to be playing five fingered exercises or helping their mothers with the brasses'.[44] While the Catholic Bishops decried 'decent' Irish boys who had 'degenerated' by taking up arms against the new state, the women who rejected that state were frequently dehumanised.

Yet others were neutral or indifferent, and some sympathies were kept secret or quiet amidst the cacophony of polarising rhetoric. Consider, for example, veterans of the 1916 Rising; of 572 people identified as active with the General Post Office garrison, where the rebels had their headquarters, the largest single portion, 41 per cent, were neutral during the civil war.[45] Liam de Róiste recorded in his diary in November 1922 that 'for the one person who is actively engaged in politics there are a hundred more who are only passively interested'.[46] There were numerous civil society organisations active in peace efforts and a Neutral IRA association established in December 1922, but there was also much evidence of tortured minds. Speaking in the Dáil in December 1921, P. J. Moloney, a Tipperary Sinn Féin TD and pharmacist who had come through a twenty-three-day hunger strike, the death of one of his IRA sons and the destruction of his home and business during the War of Independence, said simply 'we have been manoeuvred into a position where we have to choose between two hells'.[47]

Moloney opposed the Treaty and was to endure more hell – his two surviving sons continued to fight with the IRA and one of them was badly wounded – but then he opted out of politics in 1923, a move that 'most likely reflected not profound disillusionment, but the need to concentrate on rebuilding his life and business'.[48] Many, of course, had no commercial life to return to, yet while there were class dimensions to the polarisations of this period, and land hunger was a constant, there was no definite pattern relating support for the Treaty to class. Analysis of the TDs elected to the Dáil in 1918 or

1921 'disclose no significant distinguishing economic, social or familial factor that might explain the Treaty stance of individual TDs'.[49] There was still much tuppence halfpenny looking down on tuppence, however, and while some rebels liked to boast of their 'practical socialism ... poverty was only a political virtue when it was respectable', and the 'most glaring omission from the Dáil's membership was unskilled workers'. There were few references to class issues in the Treaty debate and the TDs were 'broadly representative of the upwardly mobile Catholic middle class but not of the mass of the population'.[50]

Many responses to post civil-war Ireland were 'both scathing and despairing'. As he faced death in the 1950s, Ernie O'Malley recorded that the British were no longer his enemies: 'each man finds his enemy within himself'.[51] This underlines that freedom had different meanings. The new state did not enshrine many of the ideals or objectives of the revolution but what did that mean in practice for the civil war generation and the afterlives of the rank-and-file soldiers who fought? We have more information than ever before on what they did and endured during the civil war and for those who survived it, how they fared in its aftermath, particularly because of the opening of the Military Service Pensions archive and the extensively documented post-war battles for status, recognition and material survival. There is a raw and exceptional intimacy on display in many of these files relating to claims for pensions, and historians are now in a position to investigate one of the underwritten themes of the civil war: personal trauma, both internalised and externalised, and its long, long reach.

The archive is also a reminder of luck and station in life: 'some of us were willing to throw up our employment when the call for recruits to the National Army came; they are now to be allowed to walk about without a penny to earn. Others were lucky to get back to their previous employment.'[52] The assertion of Fianna Fáil TD Oscar Traynor in 1935 that 'the man with the right [pension] claim will justify it and the other people will be unable to justify it' was far too neat and dismissive.[53] Michael D. Higgins, elected president of Ireland in 2011 and again in 2018, was far from alone in articulating a sense of betrayal. His father John applied unsuccessfully for a pension in 1934 and had to wait until a 1949 Act for an appeal process before being awarded a pension in 1956. Interned for almost all of 1923, he had been employed as a grocer's assistant earning £180 a year but on his release his employer refused to accept him back 'with the result that I was idle until 1 August 1924 when I got a position as junior assistant ... at a salary of £50 per year indoor. At the time very few people would employ an ex-internee.'[54] The indignity was compounded by the pension delay, just part of a disillusionment that led to his son angrily decrying in poetry

all that had in recent years
Befallen you.
All week I waited to visit you
But when I called, you had been moved
To where those dying too slowly
Were sent,
A poorhouse, no longer known by that name ...
Long before that, you had slept,
In ditches and dug-outs,
Prayed in terror at ambushes
With others who later debated
Whether De Valera was lucky or brilliant ...
Your eyes when you looked at me
Were a thousand miles away.
Now totally broken,
Unlike those times even
Of rejection, when you went at sixty
For jobs you never got ...
And all these things have been scraped
In my heart,
And I can never hope to forget
What was, after all,
A betrayal.[55]

As W. B. Yeats had recognised in 1923 'the country will not always be an uncomfortable place for a country gentleman to live in.'[56] But for those without a stake since they had 'taken the loser's side', a bleakness expanded and calcified.

Emigration was an inevitable consequence. Correspondence in 1935 in relation to a civil war Cork IRA brigade, for example, reveals that of thirty-five Volunteers who had been involved in an attack in Skibbereen in July 1922, eight were in the USA.[57] The widow of Patrick Doyle, a National Army soldier who fell from a lorry and developed fatal pneumonia in August 1923, told the military pensions administrators in 1928 that she was leaving the country for New York: 'I am leaving my child in charge of my mother.'[58]

Silence was also a legacy, and it was not necessarily ignoble. Despite his unashamedly tribal approach to civil war politics Seán Lemass, a young anti-Treaty IRA member in 1922 who eventually became Taoiseach in 1959, was determinedly mute about what had happened, including the sordid killing and mutilation of his brother Noel after the end of the civil war. Wary about commemorative flag waving, when asked about the civil war by journalist Michael Mills in 1969, he uncharacteristically welled up: 'Terrible things were done by both sides,' he finally said; 'I'd prefer not to talk about it.'[59] He was certainly correct in his assertion about joint responsibilities and as for the preference for silence, that was shared by many of his generation. But it is a conversation that should be opened up with the centenary of the civil war. It is also possible now to look at another controversial civil war legacy, the threatened mutiny in the army in 1924, as in 2019 the Department of Defence opened the files relating to the resultant inquiry that had been locked up for ninety-five years.

In 1924 Kevin O'Higgins, the Free State's minister for justice, addressing an audience at Oxford University, asked them to 'remember what a weird composite of idealism, neurosis, megalomania and criminality is apt to be thrown to the surface in even the best regulated revolution'.[60] His words underlined how skewed or selective versions of the civil war were being shaped from the outset, as were caricatures. O'Higgins was correct about the cocktail of vanity and brutality, but there were many other ingredients in the 'weird composite' – if it was weird at all – including sincerity, devoutness, despair, crushing sadness and poverty, elements elided in O'Higgins's determination to dehumanise his opponents by referring to their supposed 'savage, primitive passion'. William O'Brien, the austere labour leader and trade unionist, a TD in 1922–3 who accepted the Treaty, was also moved to melodramatic pronouncement in the aftermath of the civil war: 'the lack of magnanimity on the winning side and the criminal desperation of the losers constitutes a page of history which no unbiased Irishman can read without aching eyes and cheeks of shame'.[61] Such a regretful tone was understandable and deeply felt, but what mattered to the participants, and what should matter to historians, is what was felt at the time.

PART ONE

THE COURSE AND NATURE OF THE WAR

'To squeeze the republican fighters from every direction'

Chapter One

'NO ONE HAS EVER DEFINED
A REPUBLIC'

While the split in Sinn Féin was the dramatic and arresting Irish political story of 1922, the rupture was born of older problems. The challenge after the 1916 Rising in building Sinn Féin as a national movement was the need for 'the balancing of old and new' in the Sinn Féin hierarchy to include those who had opposed the Rising, during which 504 people died. While Sinn Féin delegates at the party's national gathering in Dublin in 1917 agreed to commit themselves to creating a republic, it was maintained that, once that objective had been achieved, the people would be free to decide on the form of government they wanted. This was an attempt to reassure the moderates, one of whom, Arthur Griffith, the founder of Sinn Féin, who did not take part in the Rising, ceded the leadership to Eamon de Valera, a commandant of one of the fighting forces during the rebellion. Fr Michael O'Flanagan, elected joint vice-president of Sinn Féin at that stage, was later keen to stress that 'the split was there from the start'.[1]

Historian Eoin MacNeill, who as chief of staff of the Irish Volunteers had tried to prevent the Rising, was also elected to the executive of the party in 1917. He was a 'republican bugbear', whom Michael Collins in 1917 wanted to see issuing a statement 'saying that he intends devoting himself solely to literature'. But there were, nonetheless, quite a few 'MacNeillites', and he received the highest number of votes in the election of members to the executive.[2] There was also room, however, for some of his strongest critics, including Constance Markievicz, the most high-profile female rebel, who had wanted MacNeill shot in 1916 for his perceived treachery.[3]

Between 1917 and 1921, 2,141 lives were lost in Ireland as a result of political violence; the War of Independence was fought between the IRA and British Crown forces between January 1919 and July 1921, when both sides accepted neither could inflict decisive defeat and agreed a truce. The same month Jan Smuts, prime minister of the South African Union, a self-governing dominion of the British Empire, was in London on imperial business. Part of his mission was to try to persuade de Valera to accept dominion status for Ireland within the Empire rather than insist on an Irish republic. De Valera claimed such a question was for the Irish people to decide and Smuts tellingly responded: 'The British people will never give you this choice. You are next door to them ... to you, the Republic is the true expression of national self-determination. But it is not the only expression.'[4]

This correspondence presaged what was to become a major controversy surrounding the Anglo-Irish treaty negotiated in 1921 between a Sinn Féin delegation and their British government counterparts led by prime minister David Lloyd George and including colonial secretary Winston Churchill, lord privy seal Austen Chamberlain and lord chancellor Birkenhead, from October to early December.

De Valera, however, refused to partake in the negotiations; to be uncontaminated by them, it seemed, would secure his position as symbol of the Republic, or one to rally the people in the event of resistance, or to act as a kind of 'final court of appeal to avert whatever Britain might attempt to pull over'.[5] He justified his selection of the Irish negotiating team (or plenipotentiaries, to give them their official title) on the basis that his choices, especially Michael Collins and Arthur Griffith, supposedly representing militants and moderates respectively, 'would form a well balanced team'.[6] But he also had his own 'external association' or 'Document no. 2' proposal, by which Ireland would be an independent country with a constitution stipulating that the source of all authority rested with the Irish people. Ireland would associate with the Commonwealth for defence purposes ('matters of common concern') and recognise the Crown as 'external' head of that Commonwealth. Yet he acknowledged he knew such proposals would probably be 'unacceptable to those whose political upbringing had been based on "separatism"'.[7] What precisely 'separatism' meant was not clear, and deliberate vagueness was also tactical; after all, Collins, in refusing to articulate a bottom line, had admitted to American journalist Carl Ackerman in 1920 'no one has ever defined a republic'.[8]

The British were, in the words of Lloyd George 'after a settlement – that was our objective'. They were particularly preoccupied with Empire, Crown and defence, but there was still an ambiguity as to what proposed dominion status for Ireland meant. The Irish delegation was, according to Michael Laffan, 'badly briefed'; in particular the negotiations were already under way 'before de Valera revealed to Griffith what his policy on the Ulster question should be'. This policy was that Ulster constituencies should be able to choose if they wanted to be ruled from Dublin and those in favour of remaining under Belfast rule could stay under the Northern Ireland Parliament, formally established in June 1921, which would be subordinate to a Dublin Parliament; what was regarded as 'essential unity' for Ireland.[9]

The Irish delegation was outmanoeuvred by the British in relation to a Boundary Commission clause in the Treaty, which they were led to believe would result in an alteration to the border, making the state of Northern Ireland unviable. They were deceived on that issue, not helped by their own naivety, but overall, the Irish delegates negotiated a measure of independence that some more than others believed was substantial: a dominion under the title Irish Free State (Saorstát). The contentious issues that came up for discussion during the negotiations included recognition of the right of Northern Ireland to self-government, a British military presence in Ireland and, most distressingly, the oath of allegiance to the British Crown to be taken by members of an Irish Parliament. Lloyd George threatened a swift resumption of 'immediate and terrible war ... within three days' if the Treaty was not signed.[10]

His bluff, if that is what it was, was not called. After a tortuous meeting at their headquarters, the Irish delegation signed the eighteen-article Treaty on 6 December, and in doing so not only formally reached a historic Anglo-Irish compromise, but also set the scene for a fatal division of the Irish republican movement. By 8 December, when the Sinn Féin cabinet met to discuss the Treaty, these differences could not be papered over. The controversy over the Treaty came to expose 'previously buried fault lines of ideology, political temperament and social outlook within Sinn Féin and also aggravated long-simmering personal and factional tensions within its leaders and activists' to the extent that 'Free Stater' and 'Republican' became pejorative terms, though that did not mean they represented a coherent ideology.[11] The cabinet split four to three in favour of the Treaty. Six days later the acrimonious debate on the Treaty began in the Dáil.

Christmas 1921 brought home to many just what was at stake, amplified by vocal Catholic Church support for the Treaty; the foundation of a new state for some of the Bishops would be the equivalent of 'the reaching of dry ground again' after the tumultuous War of Independence.[12] Cardinal Michael Logue, Catholic primate of all Ireland, suggested that opponents of the treaty did nothing but 'talk and wrangle for days about their shadowy republic and their obligations to it'. Logue insisted the Treaty granted everything that was necessary for the progress and welfare of the country.[13] Nor was public or media opinion with the anti-Treaty side; a survey of newspapers reveals that 'only the *Connachtman* in Sligo, the *Donegal Vindicator* and the *Waterford News* took an explicit anti-Treaty position in 1921'. Meanwhile, the *Kilkenny People* declared in hope that 'Ireland is too small for civil war'.[14]

Pro-Treaty TDs referred to it being 'the best rock from which to jump off for the final accomplishment of the Irish freedom', and their responsibility not to cause renewed war owing to their 'duty to the civil population', and that the contested oath would be to the Free State's constitution rather than the British Crown. It was not, maintained Collins, about whether 'the dead men would approve of it' but 'whether the living approve of it'.[15]

Some opponents of the Treaty maintained they were not republican 'doctrinaires' but believed in 'complete independence' from Britain; others focused on betrayal of the dead, the idea that the 'nation state' would be incomplete without Northern Ireland, and

British retention of three garrisoned Irish naval ports.[16] One of the key arguments of de Valera was that a Treaty signed under duress could not be binding; others cried slavery and coercion and abhorrence of the oath of allegiance.[17] There were six women TDs, all of whom voted against, and they were not just mouthpieces for the dead: as one of them, Ada English, a doctor imprisoned during the War of Independence, asserted, 'I have no dead men to throw in my teeth as a reason for holding the opinions I hold.'[18] Batt O'Connor, who was close to Collins, referred to the women 'mudslinging and name calling and spitting and frothing to the mouth like angry cats ... I think the Irish people will not be in a hurry again to elect women to represent them.'[19]

There was a parallel flurry of resolutions in favour of accepting the Treaty from local authorities, but ominously, the largest IRA division in the country, in Cork, rejected the treaty before the parliamentary vote and estimates suggest that nationally, up to 75 per cent of IRA members opposed it, though not all of them would take up arms against it. On paper, the IRA had a national membership of 112,650 in the autumn of 1921 and there was much incredulity within its ranks about the signing of the Treaty; it had not been prepared for compromise and local units had not been kept informed enough of what was going on in London. In any case, some IRA members regarded politics as moribund or irrelevant and saw themselves as 'in charge'. In historian Peter Hart's words, 'the guerrillas thought of themselves as sovereign ... they had brought the republic into being ... nobody else had the right to give it away.'[20] If the Dáil was going to jettison that declared republic, the IRA was not required to be answerable to it and, as Liam Lynch, a senior IRA commandant and soon to be chief of staff of the anti-Treaty IRA, stated emphatically, 'the army had to hew the way to freedom for politics to follow'.[21]

Frank Aiken, commandant of the 4th Northern Division of the IRA, suggested to Lynch an alternative: 'that he could do more for the Republic by propaganda than by fighting men of the old army'. According to Michael Fearon, also of the 4th Northern Division, Aiken had a preference for 'an ordered state of government', in the South so 'we could attack the north, with a chance of getting a united Ireland which was always the immediate job to us as northerners'.[22] But the lack of a coherent strategy was in some ways a more pronounced version of difficulties apparent during the War of Independence including limits to the control exercised by GHQ and the assertion of local autonomy, especially in Cork and Tipperary.

An informal meeting at the house of Seán T. O'Kelly, chief-whip to the anti-Treaty TDs in the Dáil, on 4 January 1922 was attended by both sides 'with a view to avoiding a split and dissipation of forces in the Dáil, the army and the country'. It was suggested that, if the Dáil endorsed the Treaty, 'the active services of president de Valera should be preserved for the nation. In this way every ounce can be got out of the Treaty.' A new provisional government, the nonsensical argument went, tolerated by a continuing Dáil from which it derived its powers, could operate and the army would remain as one, under the control of the provisional government and 'responsible to the Dáil'. O'Kelly maintained that Collins and Griffith agreed to this but de Valera 'at once turned down the proposals' and the others in turn spurned it.[23]

In London, Tom Jones, secretary to prime minister Lloyd George, wrongly predicted a vote in the Dáil in favour of the Treaty at seventy-five to forty-five against, while Andy Cope, the British civil servant who from the end of 1920 had been intensely involved in peace efforts and who was to remain in Dublin as the senior British civil servant until October 1922, forecast a 'landslide'.[24] When TDs voted on the Treaty on 7 January 1922 the result was sixty-four in favour and fifty-seven against ('rejection or ratification, they are both prongs of a devil's fork' noted Michael Rynne in his diary)[25]. De Valera resigned as president of the Dáil two days later to be replaced by Griffith, a reversal of the roles from October 1917.

Michael Collins chaired the provisional government appointed on 14 January to oversee the implementation of the Treaty; it also had to draft a constitution for the new state while, bizarrely, temporarily existing in tandem with a Dáil government led by Griffith, which was to fade away by April. Anti-Treatyites would not accept that the provisional government had legitimacy or had replaced the Dáil government. On 16 January the Lord Lieutenant, Viscount Fitz-Alan (Edmund Talbot), led British troops out of Dublin Castle, the historic seat of British power in Ireland. For Collins, this was 'the high point' of his career and was determinedly presented as a 'surrender', though 'the reality was much trickier' as legally the transfer involved 'devolution of authority by the Crown'.[26] Nonetheless, symbolically, it packed a punch. In Athlone, Seán Mac Eoin, who had commanded the North Longford IRA's flying column and was now pro-Treaty, heralded the taking over of Athlone Barracks by the pro-Treaty IRA with a celebratory banquet and a speech entitled 'From Khaki to Green'.[27] Whatever optimism and sense of tangible benefits the Treaty generated, however, were tempered by the 2nd Southern Division of the IRA renouncing the authority of the Dáil and declaring itself independent of IRA headquarters.

Richard Mulcahy, who had commanded the IRA during the War of Independence and was now pro-Treaty, sought a third way: a council 'to frame definite proposals for associating the IRA with the government elected by the Irish people', which fell flat. He then, much to the chagrin of Griffith, decided to call an army convention, which he paradoxically declared he did not want but urged the Dáil to allow.[28] The cabinet overruled this and Mulcahy tried to pretend in vain that the crisis would pass and 'the fundamental unity of the army will reassert itself'.[29] The following month, the growing disdain for politics was sharply expressed, ironically, in Parliament: 'the army is not concerned with majorities or minorities' declared Galway TD Liam Mellows, but 'with a question of honour, a question of principle and a question of right'.[30]

The Irish Republican Brotherhood (IRB), dating from 1858 and traditionally dedicated to a fully independent Irish republic through conspiracy and rebellion, also had a strong influence over the IRA and Sinn Féin, and there was overlapping membership between the three. It too, was split by the Treaty and ultimately 'disintegration was the result', but there was a parallel desire to use it as a mediating force during the civil war along with the hope by some members that it could be reorganised for their own purposes, whether pro- or anti-Treaty.[31] The female auxiliary of the IRA, Cumann na mBan, was also riven; at its convention in February of 482 delegates, 86 per cent were opposed to the Treaty. They remained a very public face and voice of implacable opposition as well as orchestrating protests against imprisonments; indeed, with over 12,000 Cumann na mBan members supporting the anti-Treaty side, 'much of the republican apparatus was run by women.'[32]

CHAPTER TWO

THE ULSTER ROCK

For all the ominous voices in the South, it was violence in Northern Ireland that was most pronounced in the first half of 1922. Historian Ronan Fanning has described how during the Treaty negotiations Northern Ireland prime minister James Craig had wanted to sit on Ulster 'like a rock' and give nothing away. That determination was also there in 1922 as the South slid towards conflict, and he had the comfort blanket of the British-financed Ulster Special Constabulary, originally established in October 1920 and which had a membership of over 30,000 by June 1922, organised into three classes: A, B and C, the part-time volunteer B Specials being the most notorious, trigger-happy and self-regulatory. The combined strength of the IRA brigades in the North amounted to 3,357 at the start of 1922.[1]

For all his public stridency, Craig was not absolutist about a long-term Northern Ireland: he met Collins in January 1922 at his own initiative 'to discover his future intentions towards Ulster. For three hours he was alone with Mr Collins and made it clear to him that for the present an all-Ireland Parliament was out of the question. Possibly in years to come – ten, twenty or fifty years, Ulster might be tempted to join with the South.' Collins said 'he had so many troubles in Southern Ireland that he was prepared to establish cordial relations with NI ... hoping to coax her into a union later.' Collins raised the issue of release of republican prisoners, but Craig saw them as 'trump cards' to be played in order to ensure that 'SF fulfil their promises to act in a friendly way'.[2]

In his dealings with the British coalition government Craig conveniently maintained that 'he could not take responsibility for what might happen in NI during the next six months if the special constabulary were not maintained'.³ Conservative Party leader Austen Chamberlain and the prime minister then spoke to Arthur Griffith (in London) about IRA activity in Ulster, insisting that if the provisional government could not 'control the situation ... we have not the least hope of being able to carry the Treaty'. Griffith 'felt himself imperfectly informed here and was going back to Ireland ... as he thought it better that he should be on the spot'. Chamberlain noted that he and Lloyd George 'both used grave – and even menacing – language to Mr. Griffith'.⁴ Kevin O'Higgins, pro-Treaty minister for economic affairs, remarked that the Irish in early 1922 were facing, again, a two-faced Lloyd George – at one moment 'with the beaming ingenious face of a boy', at another as 'a very very old fox'.⁵ He may have learned a few tricks from him, useful when he became minister for home affairs later that year.

Another note revealed the true extent of Craig's 'Ulsterisation' of the Irish problem and abandonment of his southern brethren: he was warned his provocative stances were dangerous as they would 'place in jeopardy the lives of southern unionists ... Craig said that he would confess that this was a point which had not occurred to him.'⁶ It was a telling forgetfulness; a substantial minority of Protestants (70,000) had been left on the 'wrong' side of the border, including in Cavan, Monaghan and Donegal, where one unionist resented the proposal that the 'three excluded counties' should retain 'honorary membership' of the Ulster Unionist Council: 'I do not see that any advantage could be gained by our remaining ... certainly not much has been done for suffering Protestants so far.'⁷

The result of the Collins and Craig January meeting was a pact that would involve an end to the boycott in the South of goods from Northern Ireland and a commitment that the Catholic minority in the North would be afforded protection. But militancy trumped diplomacy and in response to the arrest of members of the Monaghan Gaelic football team, some of whom were IRA men, on their way to Derry, the IRA kidnapped forty-two loyalists. A unit of A Specials then crossed the border and clashed with the IRA in Clones, suffering four constables killed and further kidnaps by the IRA. Churchill told the provisional government: 'the credit of your government depends upon your action in this matter'.[8] Chamberlain's account of a meeting with Craig recorded Craig's insistence that he would 'arrest a similar number of known and "poisonous" Sinn Féiners resident in the North and use them as hostages' if the loyalists were not released. Chamberlain told him he 'could not keep so grave a communication to myself' and needed to talk to cabinet.[9]

Collins spoke out of both sides of his mouth in relation to Northern Ireland during this period; he established a 'shadowy' new body, sometimes referred to as 'the Ulster Council', to secretly authorise a northern IRA offensive in an attempt both to destabilise the North and to achieve unity of purpose in the IRA. But he also sought to de-escalate IRA actions to coincide with political negotiations and was at pains to stress to the British government in February his 'several efforts to prevent acts of violence', in view of the impending executions of three men in Derry prison. When they were reprieved, he told London he had conveyed to 'leading men on the border ... to ensure against any untoward incident' and guaranteed the safety of men captured by the IRA. In parallel, he expressed alarm that Special constables 'are mobilising for action against our people in the North East area. This action can only be carried through under cover and by support of your troops.'[10] Ugly manifestations of that included a mixture of Royal Irish Constabulary and Specials attacking the home of Belfast publican Owen MacMahon and killing him and three of his sons, along with one of his employees: 'you boys say your prayers', they were instructed before their execution.[11]

The combination of the IRA's campaign and the Specials' free-for-all proved 'disastrous for the Catholic population of Belfast'.[12] Violence and mayhem in Belfast left as many as fifty dead by the end of February. Within a few weeks, Northern Ireland's minister for home affairs Dawson Bates announced 'we are at war with the Irish Republican Army'. Collins telegrammed Churchill on 6 March 1922: 'total death roll from eleventh Feb now amounts to 48 and 198 wounded while total casualties since Orange Pogrom beginning July 1920 number 257'.[13] Bates's department remained concerned about raids by the IRA and 'men imported from the IFS [Irish Free State]' as well as locals: 'in some cases inside our border we have been obliged to blow up bridges' for self-protection and he made the case to Churchill for 'all articles of equipment which are required to equip our forces to protect our people'.[14] He got them.

What had been recognised privately in March 1922 was that the government in Northern Ireland 'has succeeded in assuming the military functions specifically reserved to the British government simply by calling their forces "police" … things can't be left to drift', but 'in the absence of any deliberate policy or effective measures on the part of the British government to keep the border intact it is difficult to impute blame to the government of Northern Ireland'.[15]

On 30 March a second pact between Collins and Craig was signed, Collins committing to prevent IRA activity in the North and Craig to release political prisoners. On the back of the agreement it was ludicrously asserted that 'peace is today declared' and that 'IRA activities [would] cease in the six counties'.[16] But less than three months later Wilfrid Spender, secretary to the Northern Irish cabinet, declared that the provisional government had 'not only not co-operated with the government of northern Ireland to the extent which was foreshadowed in the pact but has taken steps to obstruct our government to try and prevent its proper recognition'.[17]

The sectarian impulses in Northern Ireland and the deafness of the north–south dialogue had been reflected in up to sixty deaths in March. Bates was soon equipped with a Special Powers Act, effective from 7 April, that gave him the power to take 'all such steps as may be necessary for preserving the peace and maintaining order', essentially transferring to the Northern Ireland executive powers that had rested with the military authorities under the 1920 Restoration of Order in Ireland Act and 'rather than claiming the special powers as necessary to prevent violence, the government soon heralded emergency law as critical to maintaining Northern Ireland's political structure'.[18] It suspended habeas corpus (judicial hearing before imprisonment) and permitted flogging of offenders found in possession of arms and the death penalty for bomb throwing. On 23 May the Northern Ireland government declared republican organisations illegal following the killing of unionist MP William Twaddell.

The IRA near the border had reason to believe its focus would remain northwards: of the 3rd Cavan Brigade of the 5th Northern Division, for example, it was noted in February 1922 'entire brigade mobilised for border'.[19] Maurice Donegan was appointed as OC of the 2nd Donegal IRA Brigade in early 1922 and Liam Deasy of the 1st Southern Division of the IRA claimed his appointment was part of an agreed policy between Liam Lynch and Collins by which Lynch hoped that 'a clash in the North may avert the civil war here'. As Donegan put it, in May 1922 he was ordered to go north 'under the direct instructions of the Executive Council who had agreed with the Beggar's Bush authorities [Beggar's Bush Barracks in Dublin had been handed over by the British to the pro-Treaty IRA in early February and became the new National Army's headquarters] that we go up there – in other words to start the war again. We started trouble on the spot as best we could ... it was fairly badly organised. As a matter of fact a good number had gone Free State.'[20]

It was worse than 'badly organised'; it was a fiasco and hopelessly uncoordinated. Leading Ulster Sinn Féiner Cahir Healy, interned in Belfast on the prison ship *Argenta*, complained in July that he and his fellow prisoners had got no 'light or leading' from the South; should they, he wondered, be looking to Dublin?[21] The previous month Stephen Tallents, the imperial secretary for Northern Ireland, had gone to Belfast. His findings suggested from 6 December 1921 to 31 May 1922 there were 73 Protestant and 147 Catholic civilians killed, the result of deep sectarian divisions, a great 'social cleavage' between Catholics and Protestants, and fear of the Boundary Commission, with violence fuelled by 'close co-operation with sympathetic organisations in the south' and 'terrible unemployment in Belfast'.[22] That month, as the civil war began in earnest in Dublin, fires, bombs, looting and shooting raged in Belfast: few were safe on the mixed streets: 'at 10.30 a.m. Annie Brennan, 6 years, RC, 33 California St received a gunshot wound in the shoulder outside her own house, RC area. Shot believed to have been fired from the protestant end of California St.'[23]

Senior military figures in Belfast attributed twelve murders to the IRA in May and June, including that of William Twaddell, and continued to insist there were 'links between the IRA in the six northern counties and Beggar's Bush, Dublin' – proof that the Dublin government was 'fully cognisant' of the IRA's northern divisions. IRA activity had, it was maintained, become 'much more intensive'.[24] By that stage however, the reality was an IRA offensive that had 'collapsed in ignominy'.[25] That summer an Ulster Vigilance Committee, formed to discourage the employment of Catholics, also ensured that those deemed to be 'employing Sinn Féin gunmen or their friends' were notified 'that all such must be cleared out ... or you will be shot and your place burned to the ground'. The same threat went to those 'making purchases of Guinness, porter, stout etc. from Dublin made by Sinn Féin gunmen'.[26]

There were also attempts to foist refugees from Northern Ireland on southern families in April and May 1922, who were told by armed men 'to billet some Belfast refugees'. The unwilling landlords included Justice W. E. Wylie, who had been a (conflicted) prosecutor at military tribunals after the 1916 Rising and had stood up to the British government subsequently about the need to engage seriously with Irish republicans. Wylie complained that armed men had threatened his wife to prepare rooms for a woman and three children; they were, said Wylie, 'copying the conduct which turned them into refugees'. Minister for home affairs Eamon Duggan assured him he 'deplored this occurrence', though some in the South allowed them to stay. As for those who had been forced from jobs or houses in Northern Ireland, southern government departments claimed lack of both funds and powers to assist them.[27] Many of them drifted back over the border in late 1922, 'among the clearest losers in the revolutionary period ... abandoned by all sides'.[28]

The sense of abandonment endured.

Chapter Three

'ONLY PUTTING OFF THE EVIL WAY'

In contrast to their unionist counterparts, when Sinn Féin met in the Mansion House in Dublin on 22 and 23 February, all it could manage was a fudge, with Collins and de Valera agreeing to delay an election by three months, the idea being that by then a new constitution could be unveiled to the public. That, it seemed, would offer an opportunity both for Collins to attempt to unify the army and for de Valera to keep pushing his third way, 'yet three months was a long time to allow events to drift, and with a divided elite and a confused authority structure, whereby the revolutionary Dáil government partially overlapped with the Provisional Government what transpired on the ground fed into unease about the direction of events'.[1] An estimated unemployment figure of 130,000 did not help, while militarists who had fought the War of Independence and had made scant transition to civilian life cared little for the views of politicians, even if, like de Valera in March, those politicians made reckless, inflammatory predictions that the IRA 'would have to wade through Irish blood, through the blood of the soldiers of the Irish government, and through, perhaps, the blood of some of the members of the government in order to get Irish freedom'.[2] This gave the impression that violence by a minority might be legitimate, 'provided a majority comes to approve it at some later stage', a position at odds with de Valera's private correspondence.[3] But it was his public utterances that cast the longer shadows, including his contention that 'the people had never a right to do wrong'.[4]

Provisional government ministers also had to face continuing impatience in London. Part of this had to do with the struggle to draft a constitution that would satisfy the British cabinet and Treaty sceptics. A committee appointed to mould it, nominally chaired by Collins, was dismally split and produced three different versions. Eventually, it was to incorporate the oath of fidelity to the king. In late February a measure of the imbalance at an Anglo-Irish conference in London was that there were eleven British representatives but only three Irish. Griffith was chastised for the failure of the provisional government to control events in Ireland and he in turn rejected the British interpretation of the attempts at compromise, suggesting of the IRA that 'on the whole they had acted in accordance with the view that they would leave politics alone'.[5]

Condescension continued to reign, with the cabinet refusing to acknowledge the dexterity involved in trying to prevent the complete rupture of the Irish republican movement. As Chamberlain saw it, the English people viewed the Treaty as a 'clear issue' but not so the constitution, and they 'feared that the provisional government would get themselves involved in detail which would obscure the big issue'.[6] They even raised Collins's comment that the Vice Regal Lodge, home to the Crown's representative in Ireland, 'would make an admirable cancer hospital'. That 'was a joke', retorted Eamonn Duggan, minister for home affairs: 'Jokes were so dangerous' responded Chamberlain.[7] They were also in very short supply.

British army strength in Ireland in October 1921 had stood at 57,000 and three phases of evacuation were planned. Churchill was more concerned that, given the uncertainty, 'complete evacuation' of British troops 'could not be justified'. Griffith replied that this would only exacerbate the difficulties for the government, to then be told 'it had never been proposed that all the troops should go'.[8] A few weeks previously the major general commanding the Dublin district had spoken with a provisional government contact who told him 'the biggest blow struck at the provisional government's prestige had been the suspension of the evacuation of imperial troops'.[9]

By the end of February, fourteen counties had been evacuated but Churchill announced a temporary suspension at the end of May. Churchill, it was noted the previous month, also 'attaches great importance' to the retention of a senior naval officer in Queenstown, Cork 'until the situation in southern Ireland has cleared, a matter probably of three or four months'.[10] It was mid December before a full clear-out had occurred and the remaining 5,500 soldiers departed. According to Richard Mulcahy 'the incubus of occupation that has lain as a heavy hand on the country for years has been removed'.[11] 'Years' was quite an understatement.

By March most of the Royal Irish Constabulary, policing Ireland since 1822, was gone, though it retained a presence in Dublin with formal disbandment at the end of August. This set the scene for the emergence of a new police force, the Civic Guard (later An Garda Síochána). Michael Staines, its first commissioner, faced a mutiny in May 1922 due to divisions over the Treaty and resentment at senior police roles being occupied by ex-RIC men. A government commission of inquiry into the mutiny carried out by two civil servants ('we find that undoubtedly a mutiny of a grave and dangerous character broke out') boldly recommended the force be largely unarmed: 'we consider that initial mistakes were made ... by arming all the men thereby creating a militaristic instead of a peace outlook'. Another recommendation was that politicians should not serve in it: 'no elected representative of the people should have been appointed to any position whatever'. This meant Staines, a TD, could resign as commissioner. It also suggested 'too extensive use was made of the RIC ... but the main cause of this disaffection was undoubtedly the propaganda from outside the force'.[12]

Excluding politicians from leading it did not solve the problem of its hierarchical nature and relationship with government. While, before he left his post, Staines made a memorable and noble prediction – 'the Civic Guard will succeed not by force of arms, or numbers, but on their moral authority as servants of the people' – its creation did not mark as radical a departure from the discredited RIC as some claimed. In truth, the structure of policing remained highly centralised and political.[13]

It was the increasing military standoffs between pro- and anti-Treaty IRA groups in relation to seizures of barracks, however, that were more urgent; while compromise was reached in Limerick to avert conflict, the IRA planned for its convention, which Griffith announced on 16 March would be banned. The prohibition was ignored and the convention took place in the Mansion House on 26 March (and resumed on 9 April), with delegates reaffirming their allegiance to the Republic and the IRA placed under the control of an executive council. The 220 delegates represented fifty-two of the IRA's seventy-two brigades. At the same time, Collins was being hailed at a public meeting in Waterford attended by an estimated 12,000 people as 'the man who won the war'.[14]

Though Liam Lynch became IRA chief of staff and was not seen as an extremist, the more militant Rory O'Connor, who had been director of engineering for the IRA during the War of Independence, became the most high-profile spokesman of the anti-Treaty officers and was a member of the new sixteen-strong executive. At an ominous press conference on 22 March he insisted it would be within the power of the republican army to prevent an election, claiming that 'if a government goes wrong it must take the consequences'. He also mentioned that armies had overthrown governments in many countries, and when asked if he was proposing a military dictatorship, he replied: 'You can take it that way if you like.'[15]

The following day he backtracked on these comments, but that was hardly convincing; there was such confusion even among executive members and 'the Executive never fused into an effective unit ... it never had a common mind or a common policy'.[16] In old age, Peadar O'Donnell, a member of the IRA executive in 1922, and a militant socialist, who was to spend much of the next two years in prison, would look back and decry that 'we were a very pathetic executive, an absolutely bankrupt executive. All it did was oppose the Treaty. It had no policy of its own.'[17]

Some British intelligence was wide of the mark in relation to these developments and currents; a naval district intelligence officer in Queenstown suggested the IRA split was 'practically entirely bluff' and that they were only giving the impression of being at loggerheads so they could join forces and declare a republic when the Crown forces had left the country: 'the extremists are quite confident that England is too occupied in other directions'.[18]

In truth, the anti-Treaty IRA was already, through raids and robberies and the destruction of infrastructure and communications, especially railways and suppression of newspapers, demonstrating its power to destabilise and intimidate. The Dáil was informed that between 23 March and 19 April there had been 331 raids on post offices.[19] A report of the Ministry for Home Affairs decried 'the operation of armed bands ... trains are being held up and goods stolen, business premises are being raided and large quantities of goods being removed by force and large money levies are also being made of proprietors of business premises.'[20] Law and order was strained to the extent that twenty-five Bank Of Ireland branches were raided on 1 and 2 May, for example, netting the robbers a total of £156,000.[21]

Some on the pro-Treaty side continued to cling to their delusions. Seán Mac Eoin maintained in a private letter on 10 April that the army split would 'right itself in the course of a few weeks because it has taken one oath, an oath to the Republic and will never take another. There shall never be such a thing as a Free State army ... I will sacrifice anything for a united armed manhood of Ireland.'[22] Such resolve was to dissipate quickly as Mac Eoin was appointed General Officer Commanding (GOC) of the Western Command in the new National Army two months later.

Anxiously watching events unfold was Mary Spring Rice, a member of the original Anglo-Irish committee that arranged gunrunning in 1914 for Irish nationalists. Naturally optimistic, her mind was darkened by the impending civil war. Her letters to her cousin from the family estate at Mount Trenchard, Foynes, in County Limerick were detailed as she struggled with the fallout from the Treaty divide. The Foynes Sinn Féin club voted nine to six against the Treaty, but its Cumann na mBan branch voted eleven to two in favour, which surprised her. That was not the only surprise: 'curiously enough the East Limerick Brigade [of the IRA] who did so much more fighting than the West Limericks are almost all pro-Treaty'.[23] Her preference was to stay supporting de Valera if he would enter Parliament. In March 1922 she spent 'three miserable days' mulling over whether to join Cumann na Saoirse, a new pro-Treaty women's group established as a result of the Treaty split in Cumann na mBan, which she did: 'no one can be enthusiastic about the Treaty, but on the whole I believe it will get us independence with less bloodshed and quicker than the other way'.[24] Cumann na Saoirse's inaugural meeting in Dublin was attended by 700 women who were told to be proud of their position as 'the bedrock of the Irish nation'.[25]

When she travelled to Dublin in May 1922 Spring Rice was told by a pro-Treaty IRA officer that a civil war 'won't last more than a week: all their best men have come over to us'.[26]

The same officer also referred to 'a small military despotism holding up the country', a reference to anti-Treaty forces under the command of Rory O'Connor, who had occupied the Four Courts in the centre of Dublin city in mid April to establish military head-quarters, an extraordinary show of defiance. Churchill in response authorised the supply of 600 rifles and 34 Lewis guns to the provisional government. Andy Cope recognised that the Four Courts, an eighteenth-century architectural gem and whose complex housed the Public Record Office, was 'probably the finest building in Dublin and its records are invaluable'.[27] He also noted 'The PG want us to leave the whole position to them. I agree with them,' but Churchill two days later responded, 'I do not understand why they do not ring them round and starve them out.'[28] There were numerous things Churchill did not understand but Cope recognised that the provisional government did 'not want dramatic effects and funeral orations'.[29] Churchill had written secretly to William Brodrick, the Earl of Midleton, former Conservative MP and champion of the southern Irish Protestant minority, to tell him the provisional government needed to be 'helped in the right way and not in the wrong'.[30]

The same month the Lord Lieutenant, Viscount FitzAlan, at the Viceregal Lodge was puzzled that the '40 communists' in the Four Courts were tolerated; if they had occupied the 'law courts in London they would not have been allowed to stay'. Nonetheless, he did not want the cabinet fussing about his safety and worrying that he would be kidnapped: 'I told them this was absurd and contrary to their own policy of keeping the flag flying here.' Nonetheless his movements were restricted; he could visit Fairyhouse racecourse but not attend Mass: 'in this so-called Christian country it appears to be safe for me to go to the races and not to church'.[31]

Midleton also wrote to King George V with a bleak analysis,

referring to plunder, looting and the 'selection of Protestant victims for murder', in retaliation for Catholics killed in Belfast. The king concluded 'the Provisional Government seems to be paralysed'.[32] Midleton also contended that 'the provisional government are still unaware that in three months they have lost 50% of their prestige'.[33] He also vented his prejudices to Churchill in June: Ireland was different from England, he maintained, because 'the people are exceedingly ignorant' and were inexperienced when it came to political organisation (quite the opposite was true): 'the Irish are morally cowards ... the powers of the senate [designed to ensure minority, especially Protestant concerns were heard] will be the only defence against extravagances.'[34]

The Constitution was a sore point for Midleton and ministers 'had given a private undertaking to consult us about the Constitution when it was ready', which seems to have happened as he had a draft of it by 10 May.[35] But Midleton was to remain exasperated that the ministers he met regularly would not listen: 'the government have a vague war policy but absolutely no civil policy'; they would not concentrate on 'constructive projects' being too preoccupied with propaganda and 'resent all advice as interference'.[36]

Efforts at compromise had continued, including by the adroit Lord Mayor of Dublin, Laurence O'Neill, and the Catholic Archbishop of Dublin, Edward Byrne. O'Neill, who had hosted the Sinn Féin convention in 1917, supported the provisional government, while Byrne's 'instincts were cautious ... an adapter to political developments rather than their architect'.[37] In chairing a conference between both sides at the Mansion House in April Byrne told them he had no desire to interfere in politics, but only to prevent war; or, as he put it privately, to ensure that the antagonists 'might at least keep their hands off each other'.[38] The anti-Treaty IRA was adamant that no election could be held under a British threat of war and that the IRA would be accountable only to an independent elected executive, while the Labour movement suggested the appointment of a Council of State. Such measures were anathema to the provisional government and its crucial insistence was reported in the *Freeman's Journal*; the government 'has now cast upon it the duty of seeing that the people of Ireland who are and must be the sovereign authority shall be free to vote their approval or disapproval of the Treaty'.[39]

Some Cork officers on the IRA executive were opposed to what they regarded as the dangerous trenchancy of their peers and were willing to talk peace with the provisional government. On 1 May, five anti-Treaty IRA leaders issued an 'army officers statement' declaring that civil war would be 'the greatest calamity in Irish history', arguing for IRA reunification and urging the formation of a government comprising both sides of the Treaty divide. This statement was dismissed by the IRA executive, but on 4 May a political truce of sorts was agreed between pro- and anti-Treaty sides, leading to a further meeting in mid May with the focus on the possibility of an 'agreed election', and on 17 May there was acceptance of the idea of a joint panel of pro- and anti-Treaty candidates being nominated relative to their existing strength in the Dáil. Crucially, 'third party' candidates would also be permitted to contest the election. On 20 May this was approved by the Dáil and subsequently by a convention of Sinn Féin.

The Dáil committee established to arrange the election, having had six 'prolonged' meetings, suggested that nominated pro- and anti-Treaty candidates 'would go before the electorate without public speeches, without public meetings' and would agree 'no issue is being determined by the election'. For the anti-Treaty side, unyielding republican TD Kathleen Clarke maintained these meetings were useless as 'the other side were more concerned with committing us to an acceptance of the Treaty'.[40] The government's attorney general, Hugh Kennedy, also let it be known privately that he thought the pact was a mistake, as 'you cannot have a coalition provisional government consisting of pro-Treaty and anti-Treaty members. Every member of the provisional government must accept the Treaty in writing.'[41] In Foynes, hearing the talk of the pact from a distance, Mary Spring Rice was overly optimistic but also craving a chink of light: 'what a mercy it is. It may be only putting off the evil way but at any rate it will put down the hooliganism.'[42] But for much of the next few months it was a case of 'no more news but many rumours'.[43]

The response from London to the pact was furious and slowed the evacuation of British troops from Ireland. Conferences on Ireland at the Colonial Office in London became ever more tense, the pact election being derided as a 'farce' by Churchill, to which opinion it was retorted that the alternative was 'turmoil and bloodshed'. Kevin O'Higgins employed the Bolshevik scare (one of Churchill's tropes also), insisting 'red flag elements were taking advantage of the situation'.[44] But Churchill insisted disingenuously that 'it was a fair point for England to make that in all the horrors Irishmen – not Englishmen – were now involved'.[45]

In correspondence with Churchill in June, Lloyd George mixed frankness with imperial delusion and nods to his liberalism. He was still concerned about Ulster ('divides British opinion at home ... consolidates American opinion against us') on the grounds that Britain was being manoeuvred into 'giving battle on the very worst grounds which could possibly be chosen', that of the border. In relation to the awaited Irish Constitution, if it did not satisfy the imperial connection 'we could carry the whole world with us in any action we took' (the grandstanding of the prime minister clearly equalled that of Churchill at times).[46] He was disgusted there were 9,000 British army troops in Ulster while they were also 'half maintaining and wholly equipping another force of 48,000 Specials' (an exaggerated figure) for a tiny area ('not one sixth of that of the Free State and only one third of its population'). He also warned that the focus had to remain on the constitution and empire because 'if you come down from that height and fight in the swamps of Lough Erne you will be overwhelmed', another version of Churchill's complaint in 1914 about progress on the Ulster question getting stalled in 'the muddy byways of Fermanagh and Tyrone'.[47]

Lloyd George also observed that, in two years, '400 Catholics' had been killed 'without a single person being brought to justice ... it is our business as a great empire to be strictly impartial in our attitudes towards all creeds ... our prestige depends on maintaining a stern impartiality'.[48] If war came out of 'the trouble at Pettigo and Belleek' it would be costly and strangling and 'make us look rather ridiculous'. Against Lloyd George's advice, Churchill had ordered an attack on Pettigo in Donegal where a large force of IRA was supposedly preparing an assault on Derry and Strabane; instead 'we found

23 Free Staters on Free State territory in Pettigo, of whom seven were killed and 15 captured'.[49]

While Churchill had averred in December 1921 that 'we do not wish to continue [to be] responsible one day longer than is absolutely necessary', necessity was defined according to his satisfaction.[50] The accusation of the anti-Treaty side that the threat of British interference continued to loom large was far from baseless; the military sub-committee of the British Provisional Government of Ireland Committee was asked in April 'to consider the reports received from Ireland and to consider such action as may be thought desirable. All members are requested to bring the latest information as to the position of troops, ships, stores of arms, explosives and equipment'.[51]

The question of the Constitution continued to generate fraught distrust in the weeks leading up to the outbreak of civil war. Midleton wanted Churchill to use his influence to get rid of the proposed Article 45, which gave people the power to initiate legislation as it would be used for 'popularity hunting intentions to get rid of the [oath of] allegiance or the senate'.[52] Midleton was actually given considerable autonomy on deciding on the election of senators but he was concerned that his advice was sought only in relation to the senate.[53] In response to British alarm that the constitution would eschew imperial references, Griffith assured Lloyd George that those who drafted the constitution were Treaty supporters and that amendments could be inserted to 'reconcile its terms with those of the Treaty'.[54]

The general election campaign became bitter to the point that on 14 June an exhausted Collins seemed to repudiate the pact at a speech in Cork: 'I am not hampered now by being on a platform where there are coalitionists, and I can make a straight appeal to you ... to vote for the candidates you think best of.' The following day he was more circumspect: 'support the agreement that has been made in the spirit it has been made'.[55] When polling took place on 16 June, pro-Treatyites won fifty-eight seats and anti-Treatyites thirty-six (38.5 per cent and 21.2 per cent of the vote, respectively) with Labour, which accepted the Treaty, winning seventeen seats, Farmers seven and independents six, while four candidates were returned for Trinity College. It has been asserted that the pact held in all but two constituencies, but only thirty-seven of the 142 seats were uncontested and 'the fact that transfers under the STV [single transferable vote; proportional representation] system were generally made within the two Treaty sides where there was a second pro- or anti-treaty candidate to receive them endorses [the] view that it was impossible to hold an election in 1922 that would not be seen as a plebiscite on the Treaty'.[56] Perhaps many electors also saw it as a choice between war and peace, and an impressively hefty portion of the vote went to non-Sinn Féin candidates.

On the same day as the general election the new Constitution was published; the original draft had virtually ignored the Treaty with no mention of the oath of allegiance or the Crown, but the British had amended it on the grounds that if it conflicted with the Treaty it would be 'void and inoperative'. Collins's hope of using the Constitution as a 'private promise' to sway republicans, having already asked the IRB to trust his strategies, had been 'wishful thinking, based [more] on his intense desire to satisfy his co-ideologists than on any realistic expectation of how the already suspicious British government would react'.[57] While there was much distaste about the oath, what was often overlooked was that the principle of power resting with the people was intrinsic to the document.

As far as Collins was concerned on 11 June, the British government was determined to 'load the dice against us at every turn'.[58] But he chose instead to blame his Irish political opponents, naively declaring that if they had not stoked British suspicions 'we could have got a Gaelic constitution based on the fact of our freedom and our general authority, that the British would have to acquiesce'.[59] It was yet another reminder of the balance of delusion between both sides. Richard Mulcahy, who had insisted the Dáil had to be 'the sole body in supreme control of the army', was still backing the northern IRA efforts to destabilise Northern Ireland. He also remained involved with ongoing attempts to achieve a unified Army Council and a minister for defence acceptable to both sides – the IRA executive wanted to choose the chief of staff – and negotiating with the Four Courts occupiers, all to no avail. Tom Barry, the famed IRA commander from Cork during the War of Independence, who estimated anti-Treaty national IRA strength 'did not exceed 8,000 men' (the provisional government and later historians estimated it at *c.*13,000, equipped with 6,780 rifles), made an attempt at another anti-Treaty IRA convention on 18 June to switch the focus by putting forward a motion to declare war on Britain which was only narrowly defeated.

The assassination of Sir Henry Wilson in an audacious killing on his London doorstep by two freelance IRA men, Reginald Dunne and Joe O'Sullivan (both British Army First World War veterans) on 22 June brought the focus back to the Four Courts. Wilson, former Chief of the Imperial Staff of the British army, now military adviser to the Northern Ireland government, was a hate figure for republicans. The insistent message from London was that the occupation of the Four Courts had to end. Lloyd George told Collins 'documents have been found upon the murderers ... which clearly connect the assassins with the Irish Republican Army' and 'the ambiguous position of the IRA' could no longer be 'ignored or tolerated'.[60] The dramatic assertion of documented IRA involvement in Wilson's killing was quietly dropped at the murder trial and was more an effort at leverage; the Home Secretary informed Lloyd George 'we have no evidence at all to connect them, so far as the murder is concerned, with any instructions from any organised body'.[61]

Lionel Curtis, the Colonial Office adviser on Irish affairs who had served as a secretary to the British delegation during the Treaty negotiations, admitted to Lloyd George they had nothing 'to connect the murder of Wilson with Liam Mellows', now an IRA executive member who was part of the Four Courts garrison.[62] Wilson's killers were executed, despite an appeal by the Irish attorney general Hugh Kennedy that the authorities consider what had 'goaded' these men to kill; that the circumstances of the case were 'outside of the ordinary rut of the criminal law' and that executions would 'disaffect those who have shown a will to peace in the North notwithstanding terrible provocation'.[63]

More intriguing was whether Collins had an involvement, but there was no proof of that and the killers seem to have taken matters into their own hands, believing Wilson was responsible for sectarian murders in Northern Ireland.[64] Whether sloppy talk from Collins in previous years might have been a factor, however, or the idea that

Wilson's killing was vaguely planned during the War of Independence, cannot be wholly discounted.[65] But surely from Collins's perspective, the timing was woeful. Two days after Wilson's killing, a 'very secret' copy of a proclamation by Nevil Macready, who had commanded the British forces in Ireland during the War of Independence and remained after the Treaty to oversee the evacuation of British troops, noted that he had 'received instructions to clear the Four Courts' and take its occupants into British custody: 'these instructions have been carried out ... we would have preferred to leave the responsibility for dealing with this course of anarchy to the Provisional government, had not special reasons for prompt action arisen.'[66]

The instructions, however, had not been carried out. Keith Jeffery points out that Macready, while a friend of the slain Wilson, 'deliberately delayed acting on orders from London to deploy British forces against the republican-occupied Four Courts on the sensible grounds that this would plunge Ireland and Anglo-Irish relations into deep crisis'.[67] It signalled greater nuance than his political counterparts. As he observed, 'Panic and a desire to do something, no matter what, by those whose ignorance of the Irish situation blinded them to possible results, was at the root of this scheme.'[68]

Churchill insisted in Parliament on 26 June that

firmness is needed ... Mere paper affirmations, however important, unaccompanied by any effective effort to bring them into action, will not be sufficient ... The time has come when it is not unfair, not premature, and not impatient for us to make to this strengthened Irish Government and new Irish Parliament a request, in express terms, that this sort of thing must come to an end. If it does not come to an end, if either from weakness, from want of courage, or for some other even less creditable reasons, if it is not brought to an end and a very speedy end, then it is my duty to say, on behalf of His Majesty's Government, that we shall regard the Treaty as having been formally violated that we shall take no steps to carry out or to legalise its further stages, and that we shall resume full liberty of action in any direction that may seem proper and to any extent that may be necessary to safeguard the interests and the rights that are entrusted to our care.[69]

The same day, an extra layer of defiance was added with the kidnapping of J. J. O'Connell, the deputy chief of staff of the pro-Treaty forces, by the Four Courts garrison. Facing pressure from within and without, the provisional government issued an ultimatum to the Four Courts garrison on 28 June to evacuate. It was ignored, and the shelling of the building began the civil war. It was commenced before the convening of the Dáil, suggesting a waning of democratic sentiment, but the argument that the alternative was British intervention is convincing.[70] Writing to his wife from City Hall in Dublin, where government ministers were temporarily staying, Kevin O'Higgins suggested the move against the Four Courts garrison was 'inevitable'; the situation 'is sad enough' but 'absolutely necessary'.[71] The next day, Kathleen O'Connell, de Valera's secretary, carried dispatches between anti-Treaty IRA posts in Dublin ('directly under fire on a couple of occasions'). Ironically, given the carrier, they were full of macho bravado, as in this one from Rory O'Connor: 'The boys here are glorious and will fight for the republic to the end. How long will our misguided former comrades outside attack those who stand for Ireland alone? 3 casualties so far, all slight.'[72] O'Connell was to remain resolutely faithful to de Valera, who re-enlisted as a private in his previous unit, a battalion of the IRA's Dublin Brigade, but remained in hiding for most of the civil war.

CHAPTER FOUR

THE CALL TO ARMS

On the British side, there was some sensitivity about their role in the commencement of the fighting. Churchill wrote to Cope on 1 July hoping the provisional government would not 'indulge in recriminations' about his declarations in Parliament. He was concerned the Irish could maintain such interventions 'nearly stopped them acting by our tactless remarks after they had already made up their minds spontaneously'. That the provisional government had begun 'to act with resolution' was more important than 'the question of who ordered it'.[1] That was conveniently self-serving, seeking to disentangle Churchill from fires he had stoked, as had so often been his wont. The British continued to rely on the lazy assertion that opponents of the Treaty were 'extreme terrorists' and 'a discredited faction of fanatics', whose leading spirit was 'a perverted Englishman', a reference to Erskine Childers, the London-born former British civil servant and naval intelligence officer turned ardent republican.[2]

After two days enduring the assault of British eighteen-pounder field guns the Four Courts garrison surrendered, though not before fires and explosions ('a thunderous roar, deeper in sound than any gun') destroyed many precious records housed in the building, including nineteenth-century national census returns (1821–51), chancery records dating back to the fourteenth century and Crown land grants. The northern block of the Four Courts complex, used by the anti-Treaty garrison as their headquarters, was a building that stood to the east of the Public Record Office.[3] The complex also housed the Records Treasury, where the archives were stored, its holdings amounting to an estimated 12 million individual records.[4] On the day after the Four Courts was attacked its clerk Con

Curran was awaiting a reply concerning mines believed to have been set within the complex; as soon as he got in after the explosion his account made for bleak reading: 'nothing is recoverable ... in complete ruin', and it was small comfort that 'the indexes under the counter seem undisturbed'. The Royal Society of Antiquaries had written to Rory O'Connor to stress the value of the material; Curran had also told him weeks before that it would be 'inexcusable' to destroy such records: 'he made no reply'. A call went out for papers that had scattered and floated, 'however fragmentary or damaged'.[5] Those documents, so many now 'charred fragments of paper', had 'fluttered down into the streets for hundreds of yards around'.[6] Those who had fired from outside, however, were hardly cherishers of the documentary records either: 'The cultural vandalism involved in the destruction was not deemed significant by those inside or outside the Four Courts ... Free State gunners lobbed hundreds of shells into the Four Courts.'[7]

Civilians were already victims of a battle for control of Dublin, as in 1916. Patrick Cosgrave, a fourteen-year-old messenger boy, was killed by a bullet behind the Four Courts, while eighteen-year-old William Doyle was shot outside the nearby Ormond Hotel where he worked; at least eight civilians were killed in the crossfire on 28 June.[8] For the next few days fighting shifted to Sackville Street, where anti-Treaty forces occupied prominent buildings; by 5 July the fighting there had come to a close. Cathal Brugha, the former Sinn Féin minister for defence, was shot while refusing to surrender (a 'glorious rush into the jaws of death' declared republican 'war news')[9] and died two days later. His former close friend Piaras Béaslaí concluded 'his leonine courage was accompanied by an almost taurine obstinacy', while Collins was moved to assert, 'At worst he was a fanatic, though in what has been a noble cause. At best I number him among the very few who have given their all.'[10]

A defiant note was found in Brugha's pocket maintaining that if all bullets and money were spent and if surrounded by English enemies the demand to 'come into our empire' would be rejected.[11] Yet that too was more propaganda than truth, given that Brugha was not 'unreconstructed', in the sense that he was willing to accept de

Valera's alternative of external association and was shouted down by Rory O'Connor and Liam Mellows decrying such 'moderation'.[12] Nonetheless, he became 'a totem for violent republicanism', a reminder of the civil war legacy of lost nuance and contortion.[13] After his death, Michael Rynne privately recalled Brugha's 'hatred' of Collins and concluded 'his breath of life was as much hate as love'.[14] Brugha had decried a media that maintained Collins was 'the man who won the war'.

As Brugha died, the city centre was badly shaken and 'much of its main street was levelled in the war's first week'. While the main fighting there was quickly over, the week's battle still took about eighty lives, at least thirty-six of which were civilian, and yet two-thirds of Dublin's fatalities came after June and July and 'the city remained a conflict zone until at least the end of April 1923'.[15] Civilian responses at the outset in Dublin underlined the difficulties for the IRA. The *Irish Times*, while unionist in sympathy, was hardly inaccurate in observing that while there was a 'vociferous quality' to the support for the 'Irregular cause', it was also apparent that 'its mainspring was sentiment and personal ties of kinship ... for every vehement harangue there were twenty silent and stolid opponents.' The destruction of the north-eastern side of Sackville Street – 'the Hamman and Granville hotels were smashed by artillery shells and burnt out by fire, as were many of the houses behind them' – was an ugly reminder of both business and civilian losses.[16]

The provisional government quickly issued a call to arms, beginning a process that saw more than 55,000 troops in the new National Army by the end of the war, with roughly 25 per cent of its officers post-truce IRA; by early July a force of 20,000 had been authorised.[17] Collins was appointed commander-in-chief of this army, leaving the running of government to Cosgrave, with Richard Mulcahy as chief of staff and minister for defence. Collins noted that 'the conduct of the war is vested in a war council consisting of 3 members' – himself, Mulcahy and Eoin O'Duffy, who had commanded the IRA's Monaghan Brigade during the War of Independence, but O'Duffy, now deputy chief of staff of the National Army, then left for Limerick and 'the war council of 3 never functioned as a definite body of 3 acting together'.[18] As senior government figures took up military positions, the Dáil was prorogued from 30 June until 9 September. This has been described as a 'relentless process of centralisation'.[19] John Regan has also convincingly argued that Collins's devotion to constitutionalism in 1922 has been exaggerated, given that he was commander-in-chief of the National Army at the same time as he was president of the Supreme Council of the IRB, making it difficult to claim with certainty that 'the Treatyite regime was independent of the IRB executive'.[20]

The lack of legal relationship between the Treatyite government and the army during the civil war was another anomaly.[21] The government also feared that anti-Treatyites would appeal for justice to the Dáil courts that had been established by Sinn Féin during the War of Independence to supplant the British administration of justice, and that, given their lineage, they would be more sympathetic to republicans. The Dáil Supreme Court was abolished in July as the decree that had established the courts was rescinded without approval of the Dáil. The minister for foreign affairs, George Gavan Duffy, resigned in protest, fuming that the government had abolished the court rather than deal with applications for habeas corpus.

The British supply of arms greatly assisted the provisional government and, as Churchill saw it on 20 July, it was requesting a surprising number of munitions. The Colonial Office noted 'the ample requirements in munitions of all kinds that we are providing from British army stocks', but Churchill found it 'difficult to understand that Free State troops are armed with Colt revolvers in such numbers' as to require 'so large a quantity of ammunition as one million rounds' (90,000 rounds had been supplied). But he did not want the provisional government ordering them from elsewhere.[22] One account suggests that by September 1922, 27,400 rifles, 6,606 revolvers and 246 Lewis guns had been supplied by the British.[23]

Nevil Macready remained a frank assessor of Ireland, ever ready to opine, and surmised that 'the PG were not putting their heart into the restoration of order'. By that stage in mid July there were 5,300 ('fighting') British troops in Dublin; Macready was in favour of their withdrawal but Churchill felt that was too premature, tellingly remarking that both the 'moral' control by the British government of the situation and their parliamentary position would be greatly weakened by withdrawal.[24] The same month Frederick Solly-Flood, the military adviser to the Northern Ireland government, had what he regarded as 'reliable' information that 'a quantity of the munitions of war supplied by the British forces to the forces of the PG for the ostensible reason of aiding them to suppress the republican forces, in reality finds its way back into our territory'. He wanted the provisional government to 'disclaim the IRA' in the North 'and to cease giving them assistance in any form'.[25] Collins was adamant at the height of the summer that more 'forceful action' was necessary in reacting to the shootings of Catholics in Northern Ireland and insistent that 'the guilt lies with the higher authorities and we must face that'.[26]

Of much more urgency, however, was devising a military strategy to win the civil war swiftly after taking control of Dublin and then nearby Wicklow, to where some republicans had escaped but where a coherent plan was still lacking, as appeared to be the case in Wexford too. While only seven of sixteen divisions of the IRA were loyal to the provisional government and its military GHQ, and the largest divisions, the 1st and 2nd Southern, were anti-Treaty, the IRA had no chance of victory, despite its rhetorical 'bombast', as it had made 'no adequate preparations for civil war'.[27] Thoughts by the IRA of working towards a move back to Dublin were therefore in vain, but it had earmarked Limerick as a crucial location for anti-Treaty southern and western units, with the intention to clear it of National Army troops, planning then to move towards Clare and Galway. But they failed in Limerick city, not helped by Liam Lynch signing a truce with National Army generals who in reality were just buying extra time and broke it, driving the IRA out in nine days.[28] There was heavy Limerick street fighting between those labelled by P. J. Ryan, a member of the National Army, as 'The Staters' and 'The Diehards', and Ryan, who could write with comic understatement and irony unusual for civil war chroniclers, regarded it as 'a disorderly rout' and lamented the young IRA men wasting 'the joyous years of youth' on their doomed cause. Ryan, however, was later to find his way back to the IRA, such was his hatred of de Valera in the 1930s.[29]

Waterford also fell to the National Army; in June there was deemed to be 'anarchy' in Waterford city and ultimately IRA 'indiscipline fatally undermined any prospects of successfully defending' it.[30] One of its young IRA holders, George Lennon, had notions of himself and his colleagues as liberators and defenders of integrity, but denting their confidence was not only the knowledge that former comrades would target them, but that those whose rights they claimed to be vindicating had more pressing material concerns. There had already been an agricultural labourers' strike in May after their wages were cut from £1.18s. to £1.10s. a week. On being told of striking labourers marching in a small Waterford town, Lennon and his charges went to quell the protestors:

> A dark glaring man, seemingly the leader, was standing in front of the farm labourers, his eyes staring at me.
>
> 'What is going on here, my man?' said I, in my best officer manner.
>
> '—— you,' said he.
>
> The Sergeant Major moved from my side and felled him with a blow. Some of the men broke ranks and knocked down a few of the strikers with their rifle butts. A pause and a boy rushed forward to confront me. Calling me by name he said bitterly, 'What is the matter with you? I thought you would be the last person in the world to do this to us.' We pushed the strikers back to the end of the street and held them there at the bayonet point ... I sat on a stone wondering what the boy meant. You and Us ... Then it began to dawn on me. No wonder they were mad ... men in green jackets were putting them back in their place. Poor landless men, people of no property ... It was almost a relief when the pro-Treaty forces attacked us.[31]

Those forces had an eighteen-pound field gun and by 21 July the only centre of IRA resistance left was the jail. While there were two National Army fatalities and one IRA, there were also at least six civilian deaths 'including a ten-year-old girl who was shot as she ran to get bread during a lull', while another fifteen-year-old girl had a leg blown off.[32]

Florence O'Donoghue, the Cork IRA man who was adjutant general of the anti-treaty IRA from March to June 1922 and a member of its army executive, attempted in vain to reunite the pro- and anti-treaty IRA factions and resigned in June, subsequently helping to form the Neutral IRA Association. He wrote to Liam Lynch in early July 1922: 'my sympathies are entirely with you ... but out of civil war will come, not the republic or unity or freedom or peace but a prolonged struggle in which the best elements in the country will be annihilated or overborne.' If the English returned, he would take up arms again but 'meantime I have to find the means of living'; a few months later he was appointed a rate collector for Cork County Council.[33] His wife Josephine, like Florence, a stalwart of the IRA's intelligence efforts during the War of Independence, also opted out of the civil war.

For those in the IRA intent on a forward republican march there were limited options. In Sligo, Brian MacNeill reported to the O/C of the 4th Western Division that 'the tactics in this area will have to be altered to the guerrilla form as attacks on enemy posts on a large scale are impossible for the following reasons: (a) too expensive in ammunition (b) strength of enemy posts (c) more effect can be gained by ambushing them when passing between posts'.[34] In August, the North Longford IRA flying column, in what was a strongly pro-Treaty county, had '18 rifles and a stone of war flour'.[35]

The battle for Cork city was short; indeed, it was not really a full-scale battle at all, which would suggest the appetite of former comrades to fight each other was dulled. But it was not just about the military environment; there had been strikes and soviets in the city in the spring and class tensions were paramount.[36] Lack of shipping, commercial dread of disruption and postponed construction led to the assertion 'enterprise is dead'.[37] The conveyors of news were also targeted, with the offices of the *Cork Examiner* and *Cork Constitution* attacked and machinery 'wrecked ... Cork is now without any paper or even the means to print one.'[38]

In the preceding months, sectarian murders in County Cork

had been pronounced, with the brutal killing of thirteen Protestant civilians in Bandon Valley over three nights as unknown IRA men targeted their unionist enemies. These generated much condemnation, including from Catholic and Protestant clerics, while Tom Hales, the former commander of the 3rd Cork Brigade of the IRA during the War of Independence and soon to resume his old role, threatened execution of IRA men involved in any repeat of such killings: 'in these months sectarian anxiety peaked in Cork as the county peered into the abyss of religious warfare'.[39]

The killings also offered Churchill an opportunity to express irritation at Collins's focus on violence in Belfast: 'when you feel moved to anger by some horrible thing that has happened in Belfast, it may perhaps give you some idea of our feelings in Great Britain when we read of the murder of helpless, disarmed Royal Irish Constabulary and now, this morning, of what is little less than a massacre of Protestants in and near Cork'.[40] The moral high ground was hardly the place for Churchill to occupy but he no doubt took pleasure in seeking to unseat Collins from it.

Peter Hart controversially asserted that 'Behind the killings lay a jumble of individual histories and possible motives. In the end, however, the fact of the victims' religion is inescapable. These men were shot because they were Protestants.' He added, however, 'many of these men had been marked out as enemies [of the IRA] long before April 1922'.[41] Narratives more sympathetic to the republicans have honed in on the idea that those killed were slain spies. Allegations of 'mass murder' in Cork during this period have been disputed and the reliability of contrasting accounts contested: supposition, rumour and various possibilities have stitched themselves into competing sermons; what is clear is that some IRA members were intent on acting without sanction from their supposed leaders; sectarianism (not divorced from what was happening in Ulster), lust for revenge (including for the killing of senior IRA commander Michael O'Neill in April) and anticipation of renewed conflict combined to create a lethal turmoil and a shameful chapter. What happened in Dunmanway was not, however, representative of a co-ordinated or widespread strategy.[42]

But neither was it the end of sectarian brutality, as revealed by the ongoing viciousness in the North, including the reprisal killing of six innocent Presbyterians in Altnaveigh, County Down, on 17 June by the 4th Northern Division of the IRA in Frank Aiken's command area, some of them murdered 'in the presence of their terrified relatives ... in one case an aged man and his wife, who tried to save him, were shot down.'[43] As well as sparking Protestant fury, these killings also repulsed some IRA members.[44] Civil war violence played a part in Protestant migration and displacement (between 1911 and 1926, the decline of the Protestant population in Ireland was 33 per cent, in contrast to only 2 per cent for Catholics), but it was one factor among many, including the departure of military families, police and civil servants and the effects of the First World War. However, the majority of Protestants remained in Ireland.[45]

In relation to the continuing advance of the National Army, Kerry IRA leader Tom McEllistrim recalled later that 'he knew the civil war was over once they left Limerick'. Humphrey Murphy, another Kerry IRA stalwart, declared after Limerick was lost: 'we will stop at nothing ... we will defend every town to the last ... you will have towns in ruins.'[46] Anti-Treaty republicans briefly took over Listowel and a young National Army soldier, Edward Sheehy, was shot through the heart; for his funeral, the firing party had to borrow guns from republicans, 'a last moment of brotherhood in North Kerry'.[47] Meanwhile, on 31 July, a high-profile casualty was Harry Boland, shot in Skerries; at the time, Aodh de Blacam, a key propagandist for Sinn Féin during the War of Independence and who opposed the Treaty and continued his propaganda efforts, recorded 'Boland is dead. He has gone to Cathal Brugha. He has joined the proud, majestical multitude.'[48] A later biographer characterised Boland, a close friend of Collins, as 'Loyal and sincere, intimate with the leaders of both factions ... he epitomised in his death the failure of the revolutionary ideal.'[49]

That vanquishing of common purpose was happening in many other ways also, away from the headline killings. Christy Ferguson, an apprentice boilermaker at the Inchicore railway works, was arrested in August 1922 for shouting 'Up the Republic' on the job. His intelligence officer interrogator at Wellington Barracks told him, "'I'll give you Up the ******* Republic, you ******* little Robert Emmet"', and then proceeded to grip him by the hair, bang his head off the wall, discharge his gun beside his head and threaten him with instant execution before being removed to solitary confinement for a few days: 'I am only a boy of eighteen years and was no match for these bullies.'[50] The same month, an official in the Irish Office in London had told the Irish attorney general Hugh Kennedy that he was sure, despite the trouble, it would not be a case of *Inter arma silent leges*[51] (among arms, the laws are silent). His conviction was misplaced.

Richard Mulcahy told Seán Mac Eoin in August what was needed from a National Army military perspective: 'we are simply going to break up what we have of an army if we leave it any longer in small posts and do not give it proper military training. We are also going to leave it at the mercy of any small band of Irregulars with a "punch" in them ... there should be no further postponement. It is absolutely necessary to have at our disposal central force enough to allow elasticity in our plans.'[52] A novel tactic was to use the sea to land National Army troops in Kerry and Cork on 2 and 8 August and 'Republican Munster did not have sufficient resources to forestall an amphibious assault.'[53] On 2 August the *Lady Wicklow*, with 450 National Army men under the command of Brigadier Paddy O'Daly, steamed into Tralee Bay; on board was twenty-one-year-old Niall Harrington, whose mind was not so much on glory as sea sickness: 'to step on to a companionway to a lower deck was to slither on vomit into an abyss of lost souls below, most of them having their first taste of what the sea has to offer'. But soon, as the IRA began firing, and 'with a roar, the Vickers gun of the armoured car, together with Lewis guns and rifles opened up from the deck of the *Lady Wicklow* with terrifying effect ... within half an hour of the ship's berthing, the first important foothold had been gained in the south'.[54]

In shifting attention to Cork, Emmet Dalton, GOC of the National Army's Eastern Command, who had personally led the advance on Wicklow, had been a strong advocate of these seaborne landings 'to squeeze the republican fighters from every direction'. While the advance by sea was regarded as audacious and effective, neither it nor Dalton's stewardship was as straightforward as propaganda claimed; there was discreet assistance from Britain's Royal Navy and Dalton was also frantic in his correspondence with Collins about lack of reinforcements ('I am at a standstill', he wrote on 11 August). He also expressed frustration at having to spend so much time in Cork meeting dignitaries, dealing with civil issues and the constant quest to recapture government revenue seized by the IRA.[55] Banks in Cork were instructed not to pay over money to republicans, which worried Liam Lynch as the IRA needed the funds 'badly'.[56]

By 11 August, the anti-Treaty forces had lost possession of Fermoy in Cork; as the last town they held, its capture precipitated a move back to guerrilla tactics for the IRA, but they did not seem willing to confront their own weaknesses. Seán Lehane, OC of the 1st Northern Division, wrote to Ernie O'Malley in September from Donegal suggesting that because of the 'B+T [Black and Tan] methods of the Free Staters themselves and the growing demoralisation matters are slowly turning in our favour'. Yet at the same time he stated baldly 'the civilian population is practically 90% Free State'.[57]

O'Malley also complained that the 'route line to the North is absolutely useless. It takes nearly a week for a dispatch to reach Dundalk.' Indeed, O'Malley spent most of these months venting his frustration at IRA tardiness, while also bemoaning the fact that 'training has been absolutely neglected'.[58] If the IRA had a strategy it was perhaps best summed up by Con Moloney, the adjutant general of the IRA, who acknowledged in September that it could not be victorious: 'the most we can hope for is to keep the ball rolling, gathering speed at the same time but taking care not to overreach ourselves until such time as the enemy had enough and we will be able to strike a hard bargain'.[59] There was no unanimity on that; as O'Malley, by then assistant chief of staff of the IRA, wrote from the field HQ of the Northern and Eastern Command: 'the men are scattered and the equipment and armament poor'; nonetheless 'peace talk and peace negotiations must be definitely hit on the head'.[60]

CHAPTER FIVE

LOST LEADERS

The death of Arthur Griffith on 12 August was a shock on both sides of the Irish Sea. Andy Cope was worried that effusive sympathy from Britain about the demise of Sinn Féin's founder might be 'turned by de Valera into a statement that Griffith was more acceptable to England than to Ireland'.[1] Lloyd George was kinder than many of Griffith's compatriots, writing to Collins of Griffith's 'single-minded patriotism, his ability, his sincerity and his courage' along with his 'unremitting labours', but his tribute contained perhaps a warning: 'I trust his work will go on to complete success.'[2] He also wrote to Griffith's widow, Maud: 'I am certain that Ireland will always revere his memory.'[3] It did not, as Maud was bitterly to discover; while Griffith had his champions who insisted he was 'the prophet who gave his people a policy', they also lamented that he was 'crushed by the ingratitude and the fury of the fratricidal maniacs'.[4] Minister for local government Ernest Blythe had already decided Griffith was yesterday's man: 'he had played his part' and even if he survived civil war 'he would not be much use in the Dáil'.[5]

Griffith had, in effect, as W. B. Yeats put it, taken a 'vow of poverty' to prioritise his political work.[6] Maud's rows with her husband's colleagues 'turned much of her sorrow to rage'. By October 1922 the £100 she received from Dáil Éireann funds to meet the expenses of his death was gone and she was 'forced to beg' until a Griffith settlement bill 'limped into the Dáil', in February 1923, ensuring she would receive £500 annually, taxed. Maud was appalled that 'no honour or even a thought to a desolate woman has ever occurred to one of my husband's associates'.[7] In July 1923, almost a year after Arthur's death, she read of plans for a cenotaph to be erected in his [and Collins's] honour; she was not consulted in any way and 'wishes her husband's name erased from such a shameless show. It is more important to finish his grave ... all President Griffith wanted was rest. Respect it.'[8] Outside Leinster House, home to the Irish Parliament, the memorial was 'a sham. Made of wood and plaster and covered in cement, its medallions were merely painted to look bronze.'[9]

The fallout from Griffith's death was nothing compared to the impact of the killing of Michael Collins on 22 August at an ambush at Béal na Blá in his native west Cork, from a bullet fired by an IRA member. He had been touring Cork to liaise with his political and military networks and perhaps to persuade some of his opponents on to another path, or else because of deception about talk of possible peace.[10] His death inevitably created an intensification of the war and also led to W. T. Cosgrave assuming the position of chairman of the provisional government. Immediately after Collins's death – the result, it seems, of a shot from a skilled marksman – the myth-making was in full flow, with a statement from National Army headquarters suggesting 'forgive them' were his last words. The reality of the circumstances of his death – the worse for wear with drink and making a stupid military blunder by stopping to return fire – took second place to the conspiracy theories (many motivated by spite) and other imponderables. Clearly, 'an ordinary death just would not do'.[11]

It is much more likely that Collins's last words were the more prosaic 'Emmet, I'm hit,' these words being addressed to Emmet Dalton, in whose lap he died a few minutes later. Dalton, who outlived Collins by over fifty years, forever remembered that traumatic day and was certainly never willing to forgive; shortly before he died in 1978, at the age of eighty, he agreed to return to Béal na Blá for the making of a documentary, but he tersely dismissed a suggestion he might meet surviving members of the IRA ambush party from 1922: 'If their only claim to fame is that they shot at me from behind a wall, I don't want to meet the bastards.'[12] The anti-Treaty side's response to Collins's death was mixed; some were vexed by the purple prose of the eulogies, but for many soldiers and politicians 'this was also a very private kind of loss'.[13] De Valera had nothing to do with it, but Collins had amassed his fair share of enemies, including within the IRB.[14]

Once again, Lloyd George offered honeyed words layered with condescension, 'inexpressibly sad' about the demise of 'this gallant young Irishman ... endeavouring to restore ordered liberty to his country which stands sadly in need of it'. He hoped his death would be 'the last episode in this dark chapter ... in the life of that unfortunate land'.[15] Andy Cope told Lionel Curtis in the immediate aftermath of Collins's killing that he needed to stay in Dublin 'to show them we feel the loss almost as much as they do ... the present is a time for showing that we have a bond of sympathy not to be found between independent nations and I don't want to miss it'.[16] He surmised in relation to the funeral, 'there is no necessity for us to send flowers or wreaths'. Free State ministers, he also wrote, 'know I was on intimate terms with MC and they may think my absence from the funeral somewhat strange', but it was more politic to go to the cathedral only.[17]

For his part, Churchill was to write of Collins as 'an Irish patriot, true and fearless. His narrow upbringing and his whole life had filled him with hatred for England. His hands had touched directly the springs of terrible deeds. We hunted him for his life, and he had slipped half a dozen times through steel claws. But now he had no hatred of England.'[18] Paul Bew has suggested that Churchill shared with the Irish 'a temperamental affinity. His use of language was designed to stimulate rather than sedate', and that admiration of intensity of purpose and action 'linked him temperamentally' to Collins, with both sharing a 'similar manic depressive temperament'.[19] This assertion is far-fetched, not backed by convincing evidence and borders on psychobabble. Collins's biographer Peter Hart identified optimism as Collins's 'natural state', which alternated with 'bouts of brooding' brought on by overwork, illness and of course, the strain of the civil war, but he also observed that Collins and Churchill came to 'loathe each other, Churchill's posthumous compliments notwithstanding'.[20]

It is true that, as secretary of state for the colonies, Churchill did invest much in trying to get the Anglo-Irish Treaty bedded down, but it was not in the context of affinity. He certainly gazed more intently at the Irish question than many of his colleagues and at least, unlike some of them, he admitted, 'I cannot judge all the aspects of the situation from this end.'[21] But he was not the best reader of de Valera and suggested to Cope two days after the death of Collins 'the danger to be avoided is a sloppy accommodation with a semi-repentant de Valera. It may well be that he will take advantage of the present situation to try to get back to the position of a hunted rebel to that of a political negotiator. You should do everything in your power to frustrate this.'[22] He believed 'de Valera fanatics would unquestionably be swept out of existence' in a general election. What he did stress repeatedly was the need for resoluteness and constitutional methods to triumph, and, as always, he revelled in the sweeping declaration despite scant reason for it: 'firmness may easily make the life-sacrifice of Michael Collins a bond of future Irish unity'.[23] Churchill's actions in relation to Northern Ireland, however, would do anything but facilitate that.

After the platitudes had passed, and Collins was given a lying-in-state and funeral befitting his iconic status, it was quickly back to business. Republican propagandists had to melt a little: 'we acknowledge his bravery', but 'the war in which he has fallen was of his own making', while Churchill 'is the driving power behind this war'.[24] British concerns about the Irish desire to alter the Free State constitution had remained and in September Curtis told Churchill that Cosgrave had not been in London enough and

> does not seem to appreciate Parliament could not accept an amendment that would throw doubt on the all important principle that the constitution is governed by the Treaty ... if Cosgrave could be made to see now that he would be up against a very nasty position here he is more likely to show a stiff back in the Irish Parliament.[25]

Cosgrave was 'dangerously anxious' to obtain modification of the preamble of the constitution, seriously contentious, which made it subject to the Treaty: 'Irish sentiment feels that the Constitution is their own creation as contrasted with the Treaty and the pressure on Cosgrave to make [it] the governing instrument is extreme.'[26] As usual, Churchill preferred the direct approach, warning him not to give in to the 'extremists' on the question of the constitution: 'wreckers are always looking for these chinks'.[27]

Kevin O'Higgins seemed to posit the idea of 'chinks', in an interview for the *Morning Post* the following month in which he suggested, given the circumstances under which the Treaty was signed, that the Irish nation 'can publicly and without dishonour repudiate the Treaty'. O'Higgins sent a private message to Curtis, supinely offering deep regrets: 'he asked me to consider how inexperienced he was in public speaking', noted Curtis, who knew well how dubious that assertion was. Curtis resorted to indulging his inbuilt prejudices: 'this kind of Jesuitry comes far too easily to the Irish mind'.[28] O'Higgins had admitted in the Dáil the previous month that the constitution had 'the trappings, the insignia, the fiction and the symbols of monarchical institutions'.[29] By November 1922, two law officers confirmed for the new prime minister, Andrew Bonar Law, that there was 'nothing in the Constitution of the IFS as enacted by the Irish Parliament which violates the Treaty'.[30] It became operative on 6 December 1922 and the mission to take the king out of it had demonstrably failed.

British politics was also unstable during this period. Lloyd George was forced to resign in October, afterwards assuring Cosgrave that no action of his would compromise the Treaty, despite his resignation: 'we needed no telegram to assure us', purred Cosgrave.[31] His resignation came on the back of other foreign policy challenges fracturing his coalition government, including problems in Greece and Turkey and telegrams from the high commissioner in Iraq, a reminder that the Irish question was just one part of a complicated imperial jigsaw.[32]

A growing regard for Cosgrave had clearly developed on the British side. Curtis was impressed by the 'rapidity with which he transacts business ... he knows his own mind, decides rapidly and avoids all verbiage and irritating references to the past.' Cope was less sanguine, seeing the government as 'just muddling through', though believing it would prevail if the Dáil 'holds firm'. He also suggested, underlining the problems of military discipline, that 'The PG forces will have to be pulled up firmly both in leadership and on the part of officers and men.'[33]

Cope was also accurate in getting to the nub of the practical impact of Collins's death: 'there is a large body of opinion which wants to see the thing finished and not very particular which way'.[34] Churchill was more concerned about (inaccurate) reports that the PG forces were 'making no real headway against the Republicans' and that 'negotiations are on foot with Breen for an understanding or Truce'.[35] Dan Breen, a leading Tipperary IRA figure, had indeed been involved in attempts to achieve reconciliation between the two sides in early 1922 and certainly did not relish civil war, despite leading a column during it (though to little effect), but it was to be early 1923 before he renewed attempts to find a settlement.

Bill Kissane has suggested Collins's death also 'opened a window of opportunity to those who wanted to normalize relations with the Northern government'.[36] Two weeks before his death Ernest Blythe had advocated a 'friendly and pacific' policy towards Ulster and 'abandonment of all thought of force' as the longer unionists were assailed from the South the longer the British government would 'continue to lend them financial support'.[37] But Kissane also asserts that Collins's death 'removed the last person in the provisional government with a strong protective interest in Northern Catholics'.[38] Collins, some contemporaries believed, had an 'opposition to partition far more potent than his allegiance to the Treaty'.[39] A month after his death, Séamus Woods, commander of the IRA's 3rd Northern Division and its effective leader in Belfast, complained to Richard Mulcahy, who succeeded Collins as commander-in-chief of the National Army, that the attitude of the government 'is not that of the late General Collins ... the breaking up of this organisation is the first step in making partition permanent ... recognition of the Northern government, of course, will mean the breaking up of our division.'[40]

John Regan insists elements in the IRA wanted to initiate a border war, but 'the Treatyites frustrated what could easily be presented as an attempt to liberate Ulster', in order to protect their southern nationalist credentials and consolidate their own gains, with the implicit acceptance that partition was the price to be paid.[41] Perhaps they also wanted to avoid it as they were aware it would have been a calamitous campaign and strategically unwise; there were differing views, but Regan's thesis does hold some validity given the arrogant self-satisfaction of O'Higgins's response to northern nationalists. He told them in October what they needed was not Free State patronage but 'a great deal of strenuous voluntary work – just the same sort of strenuous work that brought the national position to the stage it has reached'.[42] The focus for the provisional government would remain firmly on the South.

CHAPTER SIX

RAW LADS AND THE NEW
BLACK AND TANS

The difficulties of the National Army combating their opponents in isolated areas was apparent in various regional command reports, including from Seán Mac Eoin, as the IRA derailed trains (declaring railway workers to be legitimate targets), held up post offices and blocked 'all roads between Sligo and Bundoran'. The blowing up of bridges caused particular disruption; a despairing Frank Dorr from Foxford Woollen Mills in Mayo complained in July 1922 that they had been 'completely cut away from the outside world' for the previous three weeks owing to the blowing up of the viaduct, railway line and bridge ('all done in the interests of Ireland, Moryah!'). There were 300 employed in the mills who were 'breadwinners for about 1800' but it had to close as nothing could be got in or out.[1] On the republican side, Con Moloney gave an insight into those he labelled the 'country people'; that after they had 'settled down to the inconvenience' of rail and road destruction they would 'improve Nationally', a curiously cold and abstract way of thinking.[2]

Yet there was a parallel dearth of confidence on the provisional government side, O'Higgins wondering how the new army of 'raw lads' could cope with their IRA opponents, which Kissane sees as bizarre, given that it took the pro-Treaty side 'just over a month to defeat the anti-Treaty IRA in conventional warfare'.[3] But the 'raw lads' were indeed problematic, as were the seasoned men, and the whole question of soldierly discipline and rules of war casts a long shadow over the conflict as 'an accumulating local viciousness' was manifest.[4] Neither group of combatants was adequately controlled.

Anglo-Irish aristocrat Ham Cuffe, the Earl of Desart, wrote to Midleton in October 1922 about a '2 hour' chat alone with Cosgrave: 'he impressed me favourably – an educated man ... quick and intelligent ... frank as to his difficulties, the weakness of his executive in many ways.'[5] Regarding the National Army, Cosgrave told Cuffe 'some were ruffians, but they were, as he was informed, gradually weeding these out ... one difficulty was that the best old soldiers were accustomed to serve under officers who were skilled and of a class they respected and that officers of this class they could not get.'[6]

Focus on the rank and file, however, avoided the issue of properly structured and disciplined leadership. Mulcahy was later to note that he took up the position of minister for defence in January 1922 as a member of the Dáil cabinet and not the provisional government: 'there was no formal definition of my responsibilities but I was entirely responsible for the army and the military situation generally.'[7] He also highlighted a memo from May 1922 suggesting the army staff 'generally is tending to a disintegration of outlook, particularly owing to the fact they are individually too much immersed in their own work and too deeply immersed in the detail of that ... there is no joint consideration by us of the work of the staff as a whole.'[8]

Gearóid O'Sullivan, lieutenant general of the National Army, was aware of reports that the army in the south-west was 'very badly disciplined, frequently mutinous, very inefficient from a military point of view, sometimes treacherous and except in certain barracks, dirty and slovenly.'[9] The problem of drunkenness was constantly emphasised. Free State propaganda throughout the war insisted acts of indiscipline were, in the words of Mulcahy 'utterly foreign to its spirit', while the IRA were deemed to be 'tending towards murder gang methods ... unpleasantly reminiscent of the days of the Black and Tan terror ... this is the people's war and the people must win', in contrast to the War of Independence which had been 'the Terror'.[10] But as Frank Shouldice, a 1916 veteran who refused to take part in the civil war, pointed out from Roscommon, the conduct of the National Army troops there was pitiful, 'very much under the influence of drink and absolutely incapable of carrying fire arms, not to mention effecting any discipline ... on a par with the Black and Tans whom indeed they out rival at times'. Liam de Róiste recorded in his diary a National Army 'not well disciplined' and 'very badly officered ... there are many grave abuses and complaints are frequent. There is laxity and looseness.'[11] Comparisons with the Black and Tans, the undisciplined force sent to Ireland during the War of Independence to augment the RIC and who indulged in brutality and reprisals, were made repeatedly throughout the conflict by both sides, and were not without foundation.

The IRA seemed well equipped in some parts and dominated, for example, north and west Mayo in November 1922: 'The Irregulars are now collecting in Mulranny and Districts and their strength is 575. They have 475 Lee Enfield rifles and 100 Mauser rifles and 57,500 rounds of ammunition, 4 Lewis guns and 3 Thompsons, each man carried two bombs.'[12] Provisional Government minister Desmond FitzGerald wrote to Mulcahy in December 1922 suggesting it was 'pretty evident that the Irregulars are getting stuff in from England in fairly large quantities' through shipping companies, while in the US, Free State envoy Timothy Smiddy noted that guns were 'easily procured' there, and in New York 'the dockers would help willingly to smuggle the guns out'.[13] There was also a need to divert British naval resources – trawlers and minesweepers – 'to deal with the smuggling of arms by Irregulars', but this was not deemed successful.[14] The British navy was seen by some as of more assistance to the pro-Treaty side than the British army soldiers still in Ireland, who were in 'a more difficult and delicate position'.[15] The navy, as Macready saw it, was working 'in very close conjunction under my advice'. Fed up as usual, and missing 'my old friend Henry Wilson', he lamented the 'ignorance of some people in Whitehall of the way in which we manage to keep the peace here'.[16]

Most of the correspondence in the Ernie O'Malley archive paints an altogether more bleak picture of the IRA's potential; in October, Seán Lehane wrote of the effectiveness of the Free State strategy in Donegal: 'the system here is large columns guard all the mountain passes and then 2 or 3 "mopping up" columns take the interior of the country and rake it for columns and stray volunteers ... a very effective means of tiring out our men.'[17] In Sligo, there was also a 'taking to the hills'; the area between Sligo town and Donegal was troubled, contested and mountainous, and while that allowed the IRA a degree of control of inaccessible areas it did not hold out the prospect of inflicting much damage.[18]

Commandeering by both National Army and IRA was also a constant theme (raids for money, clothes, bicycles, cigarettes, food, tea and sugar, which dribbled on after the formal fighting had ended),[19] as were the physical demands. A fifty-nine-page monthly operational report by General Tony Lawlor, second in command to Mac Eoin, on National Army operations in the west for December 1922 dwelt on want of food, clothing and sleep and 'what it means to pass several nights hungry, tired and cold ... the plan has been to allow no rest. To keep at them the whole time ... to force the pace'. But there was always the constant iteration of keeping up 'spirits' and exaggerated assertions of obedience, along with lamentations about what kind of war it was: troops 'have suffered and obeyed without murmur. If this was not a civil war the country would be crazy giving them socks, Xmas pudding.'[20]

For the republicans things were hardly cheerier, as remembered by Manus Moynihan in Kerry: 'a hard winter, sleeping out most of the time. We had little food and many people were unfriendly. At times we had to commandeer cattle for food.'[21] Seán Lehane wrote to Ernie O'Malley in October 1922; he didn't like leaving Donegal,

> but at the same time we are only part of an army and in my opinion we are funking fight here and stealing about from place to place like Criminals. I suppose it is only a matter of time until we are rounded up or more probably put out of action ... there is not a fighting chance, as the people are out of sympathy with us because we are strangers and they have friends they would help in the Barracks rather than us.

As for medical assistance, 'there is no doctor going to lose his job for us.'[22]

As the civil war progressed, Mary Spring Rice's diary gave an overview of the new communications difficulties and the complications of trying to 'get eggs away to England'. With the trains down, 'it seems the only way to Dublin is from Cork to Fishguard and thence by Holyhead', and when letters finally arrived 'we simply fell upon them and devoured them'.[23] There were also weeks where she was 'busy at the hay', with people 'plodding along' and trying to do their jobs, and there was 'no more news but many rumours' as they waited for those who cycled to Limerick city from Foynes (twenty-four miles) to return with updates.[24] The information deficit was constantly frustrating: 'no news and news now is the breath of life'.[25] As the IRA commandeered food or looked for shelter it created a dilemma: 'I thought on the whole I would tell a lie to help them escape. One's sympathies must always be with the pursued, I think, unless in the case of a murderer.'[26] Another crisis was the 'commandeering of horses' harness and traps by the Republicans. I can't arrange to hide 4 horses, the pony, 2 Traps, the side car and all the harness.'[27] Spring Rice was also troubled by the new texture of the civil war atmosphere: she met a friend, 'but I felt a kind of stiffness in his manner which said "I know you is a Free Stater", different from the old days before this hateful division'.[28]

For Spring Rice the burning of the military barracks in Foynes, as the IRA evacuated, was a quiet furnace: 'rather a strange sight, the IRA, waiting to see it well on fire before they went, standing around in their trench coats with their rifles and equipment slung on and all the villagers looking on, a curiously disinterested crowd of spectators expressing no emotion one way or the other'. The Free State troops had arrived and she heard stories of them looting too: 'what is one to believe?'[29] By September she could only record that 'this horrible civil war is poisoning everything and some people won't speak to each other … thousands of pounds of destruction being done instead of building up the country. One feels almost in despair sometimes.' She also asked herself the most pertinent of questions: 'This is the end of the first phase. What will the second be?'[30]

In October Spring Rice made a visit to Dublin where Kathleen Lynn, doctor, anti-Treatyite and council member of the Irish White Cross, established the previous year to distribute funds raised in America to relieve distress caused by the War of Independence, gave her republican prisoners' statements detailing brutality. Spring Rice was disgusted: 'One can't believe Irishmen would do that to each other.' She spoke to Desmond FitzGerald, who dismissed the concerns, but she was not convinced: 'one begins to think the Black and Tans were no worse than anyone else after all'.[31] There were other incidents that amplified those concerns; the previous month Liam Lynch had written to Ernie O'Malley of the 'most brutal' murder 'under the orders of [Emmet] Dalton' of Timothy (Tadhg) Kennefick, signaller with the 5th Cork Brigade.[32] He noted that Kennefick had been on his way home to his mother's funeral when stopped by a National Army patrol. Under censorship, contemporary newspapers reported he had been shot twice: 'it was believed he was shot while trying to escape'.[33]

It was a lot uglier than that and he was 'disfigured beyond recognition'. According to witness accounts

> the men beat him, tied his legs together onto the back of one of their trucks and proceeded to drive from the back roadway to Dripsey, through Coachford and onto Rooves Bridge. Dismounting at Rooves Bridge they gave him the martyr's death, shooting him twice into the face at close range, and dumped his body over the wall. Locals who witnessed the events and went searching for the body were alerted to his whereabouts by the braying of an ass standing near him. The inquest on 11 September 1922 in Coachford found that Free State troops had murdered Tadhg Kennefick. It is claimed that all inquiries thereafter were banned by the Government.[34]

FitzGerald, however, was a professional denier of such talk and writings in his role as manager of publicity for the pro-Treaty side (his wife Mabel was disgusted but they endured together) as well as minister for external affairs. He found himself involved in trying to discredit the republican credentials of former colleagues, including Seán MacEntee (though their friendship, too, endured long-term). Ministers were keen to use seized correspondence from republicans and to undermine them by leaking 'tit bits of these letters in a systematic, harassing way'.[35] In retaliation, republican propaganda hailed de

Valera as 'the colossus of his time ... he is an x-ray that sees through the purposes of men', while announcing 'General Macready is at the offices of the Provisional Government directing the campaign against the IRA.'[36]

FitzGerald kept a particular eye on the newspapers with Piaras Béaslaí, the chief press censor: 'all news with regard to the fighting should pass through Dublin or Waterford where we control the censorship'. The IRA fighters were not to be referred to as troops but called 'bands' or 'bodies' or 'armed men' and 'articles or letters as to the treatment of Irregular prisoners may not be published'. In addition, 'the term "provisional government" should not be used. The correct term is "Irish government" or simply "the government"'.[37]

But the IRA had its own crude methods of censorship. The editor of the *Freeman's Journal* was told that use of the term 'Irregular' or 'Irregulars' in the newspaper was unacceptable: 'a minimum fine of £1 will be imposed for each repetition of these terms and more drastic action' would be taken if the order was continually transgressed. Following the funeral of an anti-Treaty IRA man the military censor for the IRA Waterford Brigade told Edmund Downey, the editor of *Waterford News*, to use the headline 'Hero laid to rest' and the words 'remarkable manifestations of sympathy'.[38] Downey elaborated in a letter to Cosgrave about bullying by the IRA, which was anything but subtle:

> he came into the office with a revolver and said 'your paper has got to be produced as I say, not as you say' ... it is sufficiently difficult to produce a paper at all at the present time, but it is intolerable to be subjected, as we were in the Black and Tan era, from this class of thing from countrymen of our own. And what a reward for the six years of daily peril and the heavy losses we sustained in order to keep the flag flying in Waterford.[39]

By the end of July FitzGerald was arguing that censorship should be relaxed; newspapers already announced that what they published had been submitted to the censor, so 'the man in the street naturally gathers from this that the news served to him has been doctored'.[40]

Michael Collins agreed: 'at all times the censorship was too strict for my liking' and the government and army was now in control to the extent that 'the newspapers themselves may be trusted to do what's right if only they are spoken to occasionally'.[41] But there was no such smooth transition.

Busy on the opposite side propaganda wise was Dorothy Macardle, a teacher who had worked closely on anti-Treaty publications with Erskine Childers over the summer. Macardle complained of the censorship of a coroner's jury finding of the wilful murder of Patrick Mannion, son of an ex-police inspector, who had been involved in a planned attack on the headquarters of the National Army Intelligence Section at Oriel House in September 1922. It was thwarted, but Mannion was wounded in the leg and captured by National Army troops, dragged to a street corner by an officer and shot in the back of the head. Newspapers were told not to publish the details. Béaslaí's justification had nothing to do with the facts of the murder but was that Mannion was 'a "Truce Volunteer" who had never touched us while the Black and Tans were here'.[42] The IRA was also well capable of extra-judicial killings; two National Army officers, Tom and John O'Connor, sons of a prosperous farmer and grocer, were shot dead in their family home ('it appears that the two officers were sleeping') in September 1922 in what was described as an 'Irregular swoop' on Kenmare. Their parents were 'so affected with the awful shock of the loss and manner of death of their two sons that they are absolutely useless as far as carrying on the business of their shop and farm is concerned'.[43]

Even as the militarisation increased, people had other battles to fight, including over land. The report of the local government department in 1922 focused on the western seaboard and 'a state of affairs clearly bordering on famine. A most painful feature is that the native speaking population has suffered from economic pressure to an altogether disproportionate extent'. Relief of £16,000 was administered 'to ward off the imminent consequences of actual destitution', while in the towns, unemployment had become 'chronic' and was continuously revealed 'in the pulse of local government'. Rates were being withheld due to the 'unsettled conditions' but unemployment 'cannot be dealt with directly by the state alone'. Emigration was inevitable 'where no immediate remedy for unemployment is available'.[44]

John Joe Sheehy in Tralee recalled the various social tensions threading through the civil war: 'we had land trouble. People trying to enlarge their holdings. Anyone who could claim that an ancestor had been evicted put the boot in. There were too many trying to take advantage of things.'[45] This worried the Marquess of Lansdowne, who possessed thousands of acres and whose cherished mansion in Kerry was looted and burned. Loyalists, he maintained, were facing, 'the gradual but unrelenting confiscation of their property ... tenants are building on the expectation of a large measure of land purchase and confidently expect that when it comes to pass arrears will be wiped out ... the creditor has no redress.'[46]

There were also various attempts during the disturbed 1922 to revisit land settlements from an earlier period that were made 'under duress' and the Land Settlement Commission (LSC), established by Sinn Féin during the War of Independence, was 'overwhelmed with applications' and demands for protective orders.[47] The felling of trees, burning of straw, intimidation and hostility against substantial landowners were common complaints and tenants' associations were vocal in face of a government that insisted it 'has no funds for financing land purchase' but could only divide, fix prices and arbitrate.[48] In August 1922 the legal commissioner of the LSC noted that land courts were not functioning at that stage and 'under present conditions it is really impossible to know what to do in any case'.[49] An evicted tenants and land settlement association in 1922 insisted land was 'the most urgent issue that the government is called upon to face'; a new entity was demanded for the break-up of ranches and justice for those 'whose holdings were grabbed and are still held by the grabbers or their descendants'.[50]

Intimidation also had a sectarian dimension ('you bloody Protestant ... we will put decent Catholics in your husband's place') and given that over 90 per cent of the population of southern Ireland was now Catholic, there was undoubtedly a particular civil war plight for Protestants and a trend of 'minority persecution'. This co-existed with a more general urgency to define 'the other', whether as Protestant,

Loyalist, grazier (grazing farmers with large landholdings, also some-times called ranchers) or spy.[51] But the label 'ethnic cleansing' is far too exaggerated; it was a historic identification of Protestantism with 'usurping settler' rather than hatred of the minority religion. Protes-tant business owners were certainly targeted, including the Cleeve family in Limerick, who controlled swathes of the dairy industry and had a string of factories and creameries burned, and 1922 and 1923 were particularly fraught years for a nervy minority as reports from Church of Ireland local diocesan synods indicate.[52] Not all land grab-bing was by anti-Treatyites; the combination of 'anti-British hostility, sectarian enmity and local competition were bitterly entangled'.[53]

In February 1923 the Catholic Bishop of Cork, Dr Daniel Cohalan, acknowledged how 'Protestants have suffered severely during the period of the civil war in the south' and urged that 'charity knows no exclusion of creed'. A short time later, in May 1923, the Catholic Bishop of Killaloe, Dr Michael Fogarty, appealed to a higher sense of patriotism, noting that 'their Protestant fellow countrymen were persecuted and dealt with in a cruel and coarse manner'.[54]

Some of his Catholic flock felt likewise and parallel to land hunger was the experience of urban deprivation; charities in Cork in August 1922 highlighted 'very acute distress in many large areas' and a 'general collapse of everything vital to the life of the city'.[55] Reports from the adjutant general of the National Army in the midlands likewise referred to 'the present distress amongst unemployed' while nationally there were complaints of 'levies and forced collections imposed upon the civil population'.[56] The Catholic Archbishop of Dublin was told in November 1922 there were 'over 92,500 children under 14 living in conditions of overcrowding in Dublin'.[57]

Pockets of socialist militancy resulted in some fluttering of red flags. The flour mills in Cork were seized by workers and there was a six-week occupation of the Waterford gasworks by its employees, while their counterparts in Tipperary briefly ran a workers' soviet.[58] But overall it was a struggle for the Labour movement to influence events in 1922; although a general strike against militarism mobilised impressive numbers in April, it had little effect. The Labour Party accepted the Treaty, according to its election posters, as it was a 'Means to an End'.[59] The party played a vital role in providing a parliamentary challenge to political and military excesses and the trampling on workers' rights, but it was drowned out by the intensity of the civil war. In September a strike by postal workers further entrenched the government's hard line as later did the labourers' dispute in Waterford, when rural labourers were humiliated by military-backed farmers. The postal strike was, as the rhetorically acidulous postmaster general J. J. Walsh saw it, something to be 'smashed' as a 'salutary lesson to the general indiscipline' then supposedly rampant.[60] He also for years afterwards maintained that workers contributed to unemployment as they 'had not settled down to hard work ... the people of other lands have long since taken off their coats.'[61]

A government proclamation claimed the postal workers' strike was illegal: 'The Government does not recognize the right of civil servants to strike ... and the military was authorized to use force if warnings and arrests were not heeded.' Kevin O'Higgins told the Dáil 'Members must understand if this state is to be founded, if it is to live and flourish, it must be able to depend on loyal and constant service from its officials.'[62] In response, Labour's Cathal O'Shannon decried 'the scrapping of every principle of individual liberty' by the government.[63]

CHAPTER SEVEN

ESCAPE TUNNELS AND SHIT BUCKETS

As the conflict increasingly became one of guerrilla warfare from September 1922 official and unofficial reprisals gave 'substance to the charge' that 'their [the Free State's] project was essentially a neo-Colonial one' or deliberately designed to snuff out any prospect of reconciliation. It also meant that the more moderate politically, in terms of their literal interpretation of the Treaty, came to prominence and the idea of it being a 'stepping stone' to greater autonomy was abandoned.[1] De Valera was viewing the civil war, in his own words, 'as through a wall of glass, powerless to intervene effectively', because while his advice was sought he lacked control and was 'caught in Liam Lynch's slipstream'. He did meet Richard Mulcahy secretly in September but had little to bring to the table and could only aver that he was a 'humble soldier'. Mulcahy's colleagues were furious with him for attending the meeting and it nurtured a distrust that lingered.[2]

At the end of September the Public Safety Bill was introduced in the Dáil, making a number of offences, including the possession of arms, punishable by death. These sentences were imposed by military courts whose secretive nature caused widespread unease. An amnesty offer to republicans on 3 October gave them less than two weeks to surrender their arms and accept the state: 'a full amnesty and pardon should be offered to all those in arms against the State who, on or before 15 October, voluntarily deliver up all arms, ammunition etc. in their possession and all public or private property unlawfully held or occupied by them, and cease to take part in armed opposition to the Government'.[3]

This was, however, largely propagandistic. Kevin O'Shiel, barrister and adviser to the government, had suggested to Cosgrave on

28 September that, owing to the drastic nature of the emergency legislation, the amnesty offer could

> have a very good effect on public opinion, and would certainly lessen captious criticism of the New Bill ... Without an Amnesty the effect of the Decree might be to drive back into the ranks of the Irregulars large numbers of the luke-warm and timid who are only too anxious to seize every possible opportunity of escaping from their unpleasant commitments.[4]

The offer was spurned. At the same time, the IRA had authorised de Valera to establish a rival republican government, 'to be temporarily the Supreme Executive of the Republic and the State' until the people 'being rid of external aggression are at liberty to decide freely how they are to be governed', but it was just tokenistic, given that de Valera had such little sway over the militants. He was still intent on seeking peace on the basis of his external association idea, but also agreed that he and Lynch could jointly sign documents, hardly conducive to peace talk, and by December 1922 the correspondence between them about reprisals was tortuous.[5]

The imprisonment of anti-Treaty republicans was another long-drawn-out and bitter saga throughout the conflict, over the course of which there were about 13,000 republican internees. There was a standoff between prisoners and the military governor of Mountjoy Prison in Dublin, Diarmuid O'Hegarty, in July 1922 over the instruction that any resistance by the jail's 300 prisoners 'will render them liable to be shot down', including 'any prisoner who attempts to wreck his cell after transfer'. The prisoners demanded 'prisoner of war treatment' including 'our being kept in a camp under our own officers ... adequate medical supplies and three visits per week per man'.[6] Charlotte Despard, one of a number of female champions of the prisoners' demands, expressed the hope that the 'new Irish government will not emulate those other countries which have shocked civilisation in its treatment of prisoners ... these young men are not even allowed the clean garments necessary to health'. So fraught was the situation that a fifteen-year-old boy who went to Mountjoy with the mother of a prisoner and who whistled to attract the attention of the prisoner was 'without warning shot in the lungs'.[7] Ernest Blythe, holed up in government buildings, was impatient of the 'very finicky legal attitude' of George Gavan Duffy about 'captured Irregulars', making him 'a strange bird amongst us'.[8] In August 1922 the postmaster general in Drogheda had reported 'there were several daring attempts by females to convey arms and bombs to prisoners in barracks'; there were also 'arms being concealed in food parcels'.[9]

Kilmainham Jail in Dublin was also converted into a military prison and there were concerns about conditions in Limerick prison that were conducive to 'inefficiency, disease and escape'. A note to each minister noted that the 617-acre Lambay Island, off the coast of County Dublin, 'would be capable of accommodating 10,000 men'.[10] It surely could have become the real Irish republic if this proposal had been followed through, but it was deemed too expensive.[11]

More intriguingly, it was decided in September 1922 that the British government should be approached 'with a view to obtaining the use of the island of St Helena for the internment of captured Irregulars' and that the minister for external affairs should begin relevant discussions with Andy Cope. The *Irish Times*, having got wind of the proposal, placed its editorial tongue firmly in its cheek. The antiTreaty republicans might be welcomed by the natives as they could 'stimulate the flow of island trade ... a man may shout "Up the Republic" all day so long as he buys his cigars through the local merchant.' It was maintained in January 1923, however, that this project was 'not practicable'.[12] It was decided that Gormanstown in Meath, formally a training ground for police and Crown forces, could be converted to an internment camp at an estimated cost of £13,000. Preparations were also made to use the Curragh in Kildare, with the possibility of up to 12,000 incarcerations. The diets of the interned also came up regularly, as did disease and the 'danger of an epidemic'. In November 1922 Dublin Corporation established a committee to inquire into the treatment of prisoners and overcrowding and reported that the military authorities had refused them access. Government continued to deny any ill treatment of prisoners.[13]

Complaints about 'excessive overcrowding' of jails, however, were 'constantly received'.[14] O'Higgins responded by admitting 'deplorable congestion', in November 1922 but said also that 'the government could not have been expected to foresee that so many people would rise in arms against the first native administration we have had for centuries', adding the barb that 'it is probably a safe estimate to say that not 20% of those men were in arms against the British'.[15] This was propagandist nonsense given that up to 75% of IRA members opposed the Treaty and while there were, on the anti-Treaty side, 'Trucileers' who had joined after the War of Independence they certainly did not make up 80% of the anti-Treaty IRA.[16] The government estimated there were 8,338 prisoners in twenty-eight prisons by the end of 1922.

Seán Hayes, a Cork pro-Treaty TD, became military governor of Newbridge internment camp in Kildare; the governor's notebook held in his papers noted in October 1922: 'we cannot take any more prisoners ... we have actually 965 and 12 in hospital making total of 977.'[17] But by February 1923 there were 1,990 in the Newbridge barracks.[18] It seemed to be a leaky place of confinement judging by the amount of entries that refer to attempted escapes including those 'found to have escaped by means of a disused drain leading from central of tower to the Liffey' (the river running through Wicklow, Kildare and Dublin).[19] Two days later tunnels were discovered in two more blocks, while the following month another 'drain exit' had to be filled in and later the same month it was recorded 'tunnel discovered in "G" block underneath fireplace. It was about 7ft deep' and there were 'various implements for digging'.[20] In October 1922 149 prisoners escaped ('the largest prison break in Irish penal history') as a result of dogged tunnelling and only thirty-seven were recaptured.[21] But there was also the recording of concessions regarding letters, coal and heating to prevent further destruction of property, indicating the prisoners were not without bargaining power, though these concessions were temporarily withdrawn when they insulted guards with cries of 'murderers', likely a reaction to news of executions.[22]

In Kilmainham in August 1922 prisoners had complained of 'putrid' food and when the Dublin Corporation sworn inquiry (deemed 'illegal' by the government) went ahead it heard damning testimony of brutality and 'military savagery'. Maud Gonne and Hanna Sheehy Skeffington of the Prisoners' Defence Association were particularly vocal in decrying this.[23] After prisoners attempted an escape from Mountjoy in October 1922 that left three guards and one inmate dead an inquiry suggested more rigorous disciplining of internees was needed and 'if it is necessary to fire at a prisoner the shot should be fired to hit not to frighten'.[24]

Not everyone endured excessively harsh conditions; in New-bridge, while the diet was poor there was 'the luxury of a good wash and a bed to lie upon'.[25] Seán MacEntee recalled that Gormanstown was spacious and relaxed while for Jack Feehan in Hare Park intern-ment camp in Kildare until July 1924 'poteen came in cakes of Jelly'; there was drinking during a concert and the provision of dance classes: 'Mick Roth, who was an all-Ireland dancer from Kilkenny was the dancing instructor. We had everything in the world in the way of classes.'[26] Peadar O'Donnell recorded of Hare Park that 'we had a rather wonderful social life in our hut, and remarkable discus-sions were developed around the stoves each night'.[27] But Jack Comer in Tintown camp in Kildare had to sleep on concrete; he also recalled how 'the old lad with the shit bucket' used to smuggle dispatches in his cart, and 'poke the bottles out of the cart and send the messages'. There was also a certain hostility to visiting priests; some prison-ers refused the sacraments and even stole a wooden confessional.[28] Internment also created acute distress for families whose breadwin-ners were incarcerated and there was some tension in Dublin over the distribution of funds from the Irish Republican Prisoners Depend-ent's Fund, Paddy Brennan of the Dublin IRA complaining that some men would not parade unless the weekly donation was 'given to themselves' rather than direct to the families as was the stipulation.[29]

CHAPTER EIGHT

GOD'S LAW AND JOANS OF ARC

Irish republican women achieved equality at last in September 1922, when it was decided Kilmainham could be 'fitted up as a female military prison ... they are to be subject to the same prison regulations as men.' Richard Mulcahy informed his colleagues of 'a growing clamour for the arresting of women'.[1] There were eventually to be over 500 female prisoners and over ninety of them went on hunger strike.[2] Mary MacSwiney was the most high-profile prisoner and her three-week hunger strike in November 1922 generated widespread coverage at home and abroad.

MacSwiney, who first came to prominence as a suffragette, was one of six female Sinn Féin TDs in the Dáil in 1921, all of whom voted against the Treaty. A teacher and experienced public orator, she had harsh words for supporters of the Treaty on account of their 'gross betrayal' of the Republic; another weapon in her armoury was the ghost of her brother Terence, the Lord Mayor of Cork, who had died after a seventy-four-day hunger strike in Brixton prison in 1920. She was the keeper of his flame and her name carried weight because of that. For supporters, her protest underlined her purist republican credentials and the continuation of her brother's sacrifice; for her detractors, her hysteria and incorrigibility.

Part of this had to do with MacSwiney's reliance on sacred rhetoric and what she referred to as the 'sanctity of oaths'. Her stubbornness became a stick with which to beat her, but this was also because of her capacity to exercise considerable influence and generate embarrassment by directly challenging the new state and the Catholic Church as she chastised the Catholic Archbishop of Dublin, Dr Edward Byrne, for 'supporting one political side against another', which was clearly true. Byrne preferred to focus on her perceived breaking of divine law by embarking on hunger strike, and 'all who participate in such crimes are guilty of the gravest sins and may not be absolved nor admitted to Holy Communion'.[3] That contradicted the support the Catholic Bishops had shown for Terence MacSwiney in 1920, when they had publicly condemned his treatment.

MacSwiney retorted: 'I would not go to Holy Communion if I were in a state of sin ... Your Lordships are supporting one side against another ... supporting perjurers, job-hunters and materialists and driving away those who stand for truth and honour.'[4] She traded heavily on 'my sainted brother' and, never modest, compared herself to Joan of Arc before signing off as 'a devoted child of the Holy Church'. In response, Byrne noted 'with regard to your political beliefs, hopes and aspirations, I have nothing to say ... I too have ideals, many of them impossible of realisation' but that it was the Bishops' duty to 'guard and interpret the law of God – to point out what is right, to declare what is wrong'.[5] A medical report on Mac-Swiney on day seven of her strike, recommending 'immediate release', noted not just her physical state, but 'the unstable and highly strung mentality of the prisoner which renders a mental collapse as likely as a physical one'.[6]

But there was to be no spiritual collapse; MacSwiney was top of the republican faith class. P. S. O'Hegarty, a pro-Treaty civil servant, in his 1924 book *The Victory of Sinn Féin*, referred to such women as 'The Furies' and suggested they 'were largely responsible for the bitterness and the ferocity of the civil war'.[7] Politics or ideology as faith in 1922, it seems, came to be something to be despised and even mocked, but that was a poor reading of the mindset of the zealousness of that generation and their declarations, vulnerabilities, pieties, arrogance and aspirations that need to be seen in a broader European context; a product of that 'generation of 1914' who could be almost messianic in their rejection of the established order and very moved by images of martyrdom.

MacSwiney was adamant the IRA would not 'tolerate the subversion of the Republic', which has been translated as an assertion that the 'morally superior' should rule regardless of majority preferences.[8]

But the divisions of 1922 were not necessarily as clear-cut as that and there was a considerable reservoir of support for MacSwiney's stance, given the sacrifices and atmosphere of that era.

Cardinal Michael Logue also intervened, a reminder that for all the focus on the ire directed towards the anti-Treatyites by the Church, the government's relationship with that institution could also be tense. Logue wanted MacSwiney released but, in refusing, Cosgrave was adamant: 'the decision I convey to your Eminence is not open to revision'.[9]

Privately, Archbishop Edward Byrne also put pressure on Cosgrave: 'you will not, I think consider it undue interference on my part if I venture to give you my opinion'. While personally 'I have little sympathy for this lady and politically none', he did not want to see her die as it would lead to 'some taint of inhumanity' and enrage 'thousands of foreign and American sympathisers'. He also invoked the ghost of her brother and asked Cosgrave to 'pardon this intervention from a well-wisher of the Irish Free State.'[10] Cosgrave held firm, but what was equally revealing was his addendum: 'Your Grace may rest assured that far from the letter being an interference on your Grace's party, my government is only too happy at all times and particularly during these troubled times to receive your Grace's mature advice on the innumerable and complicated issues that confront us.' Cosgrave was especially pointed about the 'prominent and destructive part played by women in the present deplorable revolt'.[11] Liam de Róiste saw it differently: that Cosgrave could use the Bishops' concerns as an 'excuse' to release MacSwiney.[12]

Byrne was accurate about MacSwiney's capacity to complicate the government's efforts when it came to pro-Treaty diplomacy in the US. One of the challenges for Timothy Smiddy, the Dáil's economic envoy in the US in 1922, was to unite the now fractious Irish-American splinter groups, which required 'very great circumspection', and his task had not been helped by the arrival in March 1922 of pro- and anti-Treaty delegations, which 'means chaos and complete discrediting of [our] whole position'. Yet the truth was that at that point, 'the American papers are not interested in Irish affairs' and that general indifference combined with civil war made the hope that Ireland would be seen as 'first of the small nations' forlorn. Nonetheless, diplomats retained the not misplaced hope that Ireland would always find influence in the US as there was 'no other sphere in which we have equal opportunities for making ourselves seriously felt by England'.[13]

MacSwiney's hunger strike seemed to reinvigorate the anti-Treaty side there. Joseph Connolly, the consul general of Ireland in the US, believed that prior to the hunger strike the political activities of the Irish-Americans were 'dying quickly', but with the MacSwiney affair there was 'an old time revival of interest in the AARIR' (American Association for Recognition of the Irish Republic) and that to allow her 'to indulge her idea of heroic self-sacrifice was going to destroy our work', in the US.[14] A Brooklyn representative of the AARIR maintained 'millions of Americans will hold President Cosgrave responsible for murder if she dies'.[15]

On 28 November MacSwiney was moved to a nursing home, ostensibly on grounds of ill health, but not before she directly raised the question of gender with her opponents. When Tomás Mac Aodha of the Director of Intelligence Office of the National Army refused permission for her sister Annie to visit her, she responded, 'I am reluctantly forced to the conclusion that the action of your authorities in this matter is one of vindictiveness against women whose spirit you cannot break any more than you can kill the Republic for which they stand.'[16]

Michael Curran, the republican-minded secretary to Byrne's predecessor Archbishop William Walsh until he went to the Irish College in Rome in late December 1919, was critical of 'platitudes from theological manuals' regarding the MacSwiney hunger strike, suggesting they were politically rather than theologically motivated, and he used his position to assist the anti-Treatyites.[17] The MacSwiney affair underlined that the Catholic Church did not enjoy an uncontested authority during the civil war and there was no single current of opinion within it. Fr Walter McDonald of Maynooth College, for example, suggested episcopal claims to moral righteousness provided 'a very efficacious shield' to cover their real motive, which was political.[18] Cosgrave complained to Archbishop Byrne in July 1922 about the conduct of priests hostile to the National Army: 'clergymen, enjoying the faculties of the Dublin diocese ... have used their sacred positions as a shelter for treasonable acts.'[19] Kevin O'Higgins fumed about a Dublin priest who spoke to his congregation about the government-directed 'murder of the men who are fighting for the republic'.[20] There was also a list of priests sympathetic to republicans who were excluded by the government from visiting prisons, including eight Capuchins from Dublin's Church Street.[21] One of them, Fr Dominic O'Connor, was unabashedly anti-Treaty and encouraging of the IRA, while Fr Augustine Hayden married republicans and lectured on their behalf.

The notion that the Jesuits remained 'serenely above' the political tensions of the civil war is exaggerated; ambiguity from Rome left them with a measure of autonomy, and while the Irish provincial Fr John Fahy 'was known to have been a proponent of the Free State side', some of his contemporaries wavered. Others such as Edward Boyd Barrett were publicly anti-Treaty, indicating 'shades of republican dissent' within the Jesuits.[22]

A member of the IRA in Cork observed plaintively in a letter to George Gavan Duffy in October 1922, 'the priests keep up their persecution of our boys ... can nothing be done to make the priests give up politics for the time being?'[23] This came on the back of a joint pastoral letter from the Catholic Bishops threatening excommunication for those in arms against the state. The pastoral maintained anti-Treaty republicans 'have caused more damage to Ireland in 3 months than could be laid to the charge of British rule in so many decades'. Frank Gallagher, a stalwart republican prisoner, responded: 'this sentence alone should invalidate the pastoral as a serious document'; they were also using the sacraments, he insisted, 'as a political weapon'.[24]

Austin Stack, minister for finance in the anti-Treaty 'republican government', when writing to Joseph McGarrity, a key supporter of the anti-Treaty cause in America, maintained the Bishops' pastoral letter 'has fallen flat'.[25] Republicans came up with their own solutions; in Tralee in March 1923 there was a 'scene created by Cumann na mBan' at a church where 'in defiance of Bishops' edict excommunicating Irregulars, when priest had left altar at conclusion of night service, members of CnB proceeded to offer prayers for dead Irregulars'.[26]

Republicans also overestimated their capacity to influence the Church; Paddy Brennan of the Dublin IRA had spoken to John Hagan, the rector of the Irish college in Rome the month before the pastoral ('he is a republican, perfectly genuine, I think, but abhorring this war'). Brennan naively believed Hagan 'can silence the bishops and keep them silent'.[27] That was far-fetched and overestimated the extent to which the bishops were guided by external pressures. Civil war fighting was perhaps less intense than during the War of Independence in certain parts of the country because of the strong pro-Treaty disposition of many priests, in contrast to the more delicate balancing acts of 1919–21.[28] Some republicans felt crushed by the vehemence: 'what chance had we against this?' wondered Peadar O'Donnell: 'The sense of being overwhelmed and buried beyond all chance of being understood soused me almost insensible.'[29]

Archbishop Byrne was firm in not allowing 'my name to be used for republican propaganda' as correspondents appealed to him in the name of God.[30] An outraged Anna O'Rahilly, a prominent Cumann na mBan activist, demanded to know of Byrne in December 1922 'if it is with your approval that Father Farrell of Donnybrook refused me Holy Communion publicly on Tuesday morning last when I went to the altar?' Byrne responded by pointing her in the direction of the Bishops' pastoral.[31]

Bishop Cohalan of Cork was adamant that 'one who is Catholic, who already believes in the Catholic Church, in the teaching office of the Catholic Church, does not set up his own subjective speculations or judgements in opposition to the teaching of the Church or of its pastors, whom he is bound to obey.'[32] In November 1922, however, Bishop Hallinan in Limerick expressed concern to Cosgrave about the serious overcrowding in Limerick Prison, referred to by the deputy adjutant general in Portobello as a 'special request', and Cosgrave as his 'obedient servant' promised no effort would be spared.[33]

The following year Hallinan maintained it was appropriate for the clergy and bishops to intervene in politics because of the unique position of the Catholic hierarchy in Ireland and that the active leadership of the clergy had earned them the right to such power 'when natural [political] leaders [had] failed' the people.[34] But in his own diocese in Rathkeale during the civil war, because a priest, Canon O'Donnell, was for weeks advising his parishioners to obey the government, 'an Irregular went into the church with 2 bombs, avowing in very blasphemous language that he would "do for" the Canon. Some friend of the Irregular followed him into the Church and succeeded in getting him to leave, without perpetrating any outrage.'[35]

Liam de Róiste also had interesting reflections on religion during the civil war in his diary. A committed Catholic ('I put my hope and confidence in God'), he found the anti-Treatyites criticism of Bishops the height of arrogance (the republicans believed 'they alone are right in a wicked world') and noted 'the Churches are thronged these days while the Novena of prayer for peace is being offered'.[36] As people sought to get on with daily life and amusements in Dublin ('last evening I stood with a queue of hundreds waiting to get into a cinema. We could hear bombs or rifle shooting as we stood. It did not disturb ... the plain people live their lives in as normal a manner as possible') de Róiste was nonetheless disturbed: 'The Terror has left its influence on my mind. I know death is near so often that one asks oneself – what is the good of anything? God is perhaps teaching me a lesson – the vanity of human affairs.'[37] He found it sad that the voice of the Irish bishops 'is unheeded' and that there was such 'moral degradation' of large numbers of people.[38]

In January 1923 Conn Murphy, a founder member of the Irish language association the Gaelic League, who worked for the Post Office, was part of a republican delegation to Rome, sent to convince the Vatican to lift the excommunication order on IRA members. Murphy was there due to his reputation as a prominent Catholic lay person and his friendship with John Hagan, who as rector of the Irish College in Rome, could open Vatican doors. Conn was optimistic they could make an impression.[39] In correspondence with his wife he described visiting the Vatican galleries and the Sistine Chapel and also recounted a Neapolitan 'Punch and Judy' show: 'It was great gas.'[40] But at home his daughter Connie was in jail in Cork: 'I still find it hard to realise I'm here ... I little thought I'd be a heroine but generally one seems to be the one thing that one [tends] to avoid.'[41]

The Vatican visitation was taken seriously enough as two months later Monsignor Salvatore Luzio arrived in Ireland as a papal envoy and most of the Bishops and government representatives were extremely hostile to his visitation. Galway's Bishop Tom O'Doherty believed the idea of Luzio as a mediator in pursuit of peace was 'ludicrous'.[42] The Bishops were also concerned that the real purpose of Luzio's mission was to lay the ground for a permanent Vatican representation in Ireland, which they were indignant about, given its likely consequences for their much-prized independence.

Luzio, who had been a canon law academic at Maynooth from 1897 to 1910 before becoming a Vatican diplomat, referred to 'the coolness and suspicion' with which he was received; republicans, in contrast, 'thronged to him' and he recorded his belief that republicans were 'more religious' than their opponents. He met de Valera secretly but could not persuade him to call a ceasefire and enter the Dáil. Luzio was seen, however, to be generally open to republican views, prompting criticism from the *Freeman's Journal*. He was also privately critical of Kevin O'Higgins and the Irish bishops, allegedly complaining they saw themselves 'as 26 popes'.[43] He regarded Cosgrave's appointment of Protestants to the Senate as 'incredible in Catholic Ireland'. Cosgrave, for his part, found Luzio's mission 'in the highest degree embarrassing to the government ... scant respect shown by him to its dignity or authority ... serious mischief may flow from his actions.'[44] His cabinet colleague Desmond FitzGerald was dispatched to Rome to complain, speaking with Monsignor Pazzardo, secretary to the cardinal secretary of state.[45] Luzio was recalled shortly afterwards.

It was the women, however, who proved more troublesome than the Vatican men. In November 1922 Liam de Róiste had wanted Mary MacSwiney released on charitable grounds, but 'I do not regard her, or some of the other women engaged in public affairs, as normal beings, with normal human mentality. They are monomaniacs ... excepting Childers she is the most hated of that party ... there is a moral sore in the soul of Ireland and its enemies may rejoice.'[46]

Archbishop Byrne also had to wrestle with the incarceration of women other than MacSwiney. Conn Murphy outlined to Byrne how his two sons and daughter Constance (Connie) were imprisoned: 'a very grave responsibility for the arrest and imprison-ment of my daughter rests upon you'. As he saw it, Connie had been arrested for bogus reasons: 'You have deprived me and my family of the sacraments because of our active support of an armed republican movement on the ground that constitutional means for advancing our republican ideals are open to us. Your Grace must now be aware that such means are not open to us.'[47]

Another daughter, Kathleen, head of Cumann na mBan in UCD, the only one of his four children to remain at liberty, pointed out that her father, by March 1923 on hunger strike in Mountjoy, where he had encouraged others to do likewise, was 'a distinguished member of your flock who has done much in the cause of Catholicity'.[48] Byrne chose not to answer. Conn was fired from his civil service post after he wrote a letter to the national newspapers complaining that his eldest son, Feargus, had been so badly beaten by soldiers in the Curragh internment camp that he was unrecognisable. His wife Annie was feeling the pain of the material decline: 'with not a penny to bless ourselves with', and 'no one cares a pin ... I know we are down and out but I'm not going to let the world see it and if I have to rob a bank I'm going to be dressed.'[49] Connie was transferred to Kilmainham, from where she wrote letters to her father in Mountjoy.[50] She was not released until October 1923 after further incarceration in the North Dublin Union, where she was lonely, 'in an awful state of dirt' and 'perfectly lost' due to lack of letters.[51]

In November 1922, seventeen women in Mountjoy wrote to Byrne complaining of the 'tyranny which is being perpetrated by men who profess to be loyal sons of the church'.[52] Dorothy Macardle was another of the female prisoners. From wealthy stock in Dundalk, her father a prominent brewer, her family's activities reflected the mul-tiple allegiances of that era and two of her brothers served in the British army. Her arrest and imprisonment in November 1922 were turning points. Fired from her teaching job, she was now pursuing a path completely at odds with her background, and her politics put great strain on her personal and family relationships. On one level her embrace of militancy seemed total; she began 'to hone a literary record of the moral failings of those who accepted the Treaty' and believed imprisonment would 'accord her republican credentials'. But she feared having to engage in hunger strike and was conscious of those who seemed 'stronger as actionalists' than herself, nonetheless hoping 'I'll go out from this prison a better republican than I came in'.[53]

The republican women incarcerated in Mountjoy and Kilmainham and the North Dublin Union during the civil war were far from united; the faction Macardle identified with 'think the military should serve' while the more extreme 'think it should command'. She resented what she regarded as counterproductive aggression and was scared when Mary MacSwiney went on hunger strike, wondering if all prisoners must 'in loyalty hunger strike too?' She did briefly bear the hunger strike cross and the mental torments of hunger strikers featured heavily in her future writings while her accounts of violence against republican women 'had strong undertones of sexual aggression and assault'.[54] In January 1923 Macardle's father wrote to Cosgrave's secretary promising he would 'passionately undertake, as far as a father's influence could go' to impress on her that he was under a 'moral obligation that she will not, under any circumstances do anything that will militate against the interests of the Free State'.[55]

Macardle, however, did the exact opposite. She was apt to portray soldiers and officials of the Free State as morally reprehensible, sentiments that worked their way into *Tragedies of Kerry* (1924), her account of civil war atrocities. But she was also well capable of reinforcing gender roles through her propaganda, defining women according to their male relatives from whom they 'inherited the task and the tradition'.[56] Her biographer Leeann Lane argues that imprisonment was a central step in her development as a propagandist; she constructed 'a rigid binary of honour and integrity versus compromise and betrayal'. After her release this became her overwhelming focus; in her own words, she had 'an unlimited belief in the value of propaganda for the cause'.[57] This, of course, was true of the pro-Treaty side also.

CHAPTER NINE

PUBLIC SAFETY

On 17 November 1922 the first executions took place at Kilmainham Jail under the terms of the Public Safety Act when four anti-Treaty Volunteers were shot for possession of revolvers – Peter Cassidy, James Fisher, John Gaffney and Richard Twohig. The Labour Party leader Thomas Johnson decried the absence of public trial and legal aid for the four men (aged eighteen to twenty-two) and the worrying class bias: 'we say that the disadvantages of youth, social standing and education of the four men ought to have been taken into account and positive aid given to them to ensure they would not be handicapped as compared with men of greater experience and knowledge'.[1] Richard Mulcahy responded contemptuously to parallel concerns about the dearth of notice or information given to the mens' families: 'in the whole of this matter of trial the relatives are to be ignored and the press not allowed to be present in court'. The *Freeman's Journal* pungently observed, 'In 1916 the British military were humane enough to allow our soldiers to bid farewell to their relatives before they were executed.'[2]

Twohig was a nineteen-year-old blacksmith's helper on the Inchicore Railway works; his father James had died in the First World War in 1917 as a member of the Royal Inniskilling Fusiliers. His stepmother was later unsuccessful in an application for compensation as there was no provision for a stepmother to qualify as a dependent; she described herself as 'depending on him as I was the mother of four younger children and he himself was earning from three to four pounds per week'.[3] Bureaucrats did not see 'how the word mother can be stretched to include the word stepmother'.[4] Mary responded that she had reared Richard from the age of three 'and looked upon him as my own son. I also gave him to Ireland as a son. I often heard a lot of talk about British injustice, but as they look after cases such as mine and treat same very decent, I am very fortunate not to be totally depending on your charity.'[5]

On 24 November Erskine Childers was executed. He had been caught in possession of a small pistol that had been a present from Michael Collins. Four days later, Liam Lynch chillingly threatened 'very drastic measures' against those who voted for the Public Safety Bill as well as senators and judges and other 'aggressive Free State supporters' who should be 'shot on sight'.[6] The *Irish Times* mused on the fate of Childers in the context of the 'mysterious difference which sometimes, in ardent minds, perverts the ideal of freedom from a blessing into a curse. Erskine Childers was an idealist, a thinker of high thoughts and a brave man; that last tribute not even those who condemn most fiercely the work of his closing years need hesitate to lay upon his grave.'[7]

Childers's crime was also, it seemed, the widely promoted notion that 'latterly he was de Valera's right hand'.[8] When Andy Cope wrote to James Masterson Smith, under-secretary of state for the Colonial Office in August 1922 about 'that Beggar Childers' when Childers was visiting England, he wondered could he be 'picked up on a small charge and held in England for a few weeks ... at present his reputation over here is as low as it can be.'[9] A propaganda battle had also played out before his death over his characterisation as an 'Englishman' and the accusation that he had used his 'experience as a British Intelligence (spy) officer to destroy Ireland' with 'diabolical cunning', Childers rejecting this 'outstandingly wicked' slur.[10]

The basis for his execution was contested, as anti-Treaty lawyers were keen to test the legality of the military courts and Childers's solicitor attempted habeas corpus to prevent his execution. Master of the Rolls Charles O'Connor dismissed this: '*Suprema lex, salus populi* [the welfare of the people is the supreme law] must be the guiding principle when the civil law has failed.' By embracing civil war, 'which he himself has helped to produce' Childers had placed himself outside civil law and his recourse to it was brushed aside as hypocritical.[11] Other legal figures regarded this reasoning as poor and thought that an appeal, which his lawyers were still trying to get listed when they heard of his execution, 'would have raised arguments of substance'.[12]

Childers showed exceptional dignity and nobility by sharing cigarettes with and shaking the hands of the firing party preparing to execute him and, indeed, by impressing on his sixteen-year-old son, also Erskine, the need to forgive and work for reconciliation and avoid speaking publicly of these horrors of 1922. Renowned Gaelic scholar Douglas Hyde and others pleaded in vain that Childers should be spared because of the work he had done during the War of Independence, but what Hyde described as 'past services' were no safety net by that stage. Yet in contrast to the working class executed, Childers's friends were communicated with before his killing.[13]

Cruelties abounded for the families of the executed. When Thomas Cassidy pleaded for the return of the remains of his son Peter, the personal view of Mulcahy 'was that the remains should not be handed to the relatives' and the families were informed 'remains are being coffined and buried in consecrated grounds'.[14] The decision was denounced as a 'complete justification of precedent set by Black and Tan regime'.[15]

Thomas Johnson continued to consistently and courageously challenge the government throughout the era of executions and raised the issue of the callous treatment of relatives with Cosgrave, pointing out that for some parents, 'the first information they received of the trial or sentence of their sons was contained in the evening papers ... surely it is not necessary that parents should be made to suffer unnecessarily for the actions of their sons?' An unapologetic Cosgrave told him curtly that relatives would be 'advised by wire as soon as possible after the execution has taken place'.[16]

The militarisation of politics in 1922 and the cross over between the army and Dáil was manifest in the fact that by November there were fourteen TDs who were 'also otherwise employed in the paid service of the state', including eight in the army (among them Adjutant General Gearóid O'Suillivan, Seán Mac Eoin and Piaras Béaslaí), two in the civic guards (commissioner since September Eoin O'Duffy and superintendent Seán Liddy) and two military governors, Philip Cosgrave in Mountjoy and Seán Hayes in Newbridge detention barracks.[17] Cosgrave, the younger brother of William T. and imprisoned after the 1916 Rising, was Sinn Féin TD for Dublin North West. The civil war crushed him personally, especially the executions, and he was certainly not devoid of compassion, a reminder that not all those in positions of authority on the pro-Treaty side were steely and callous. As depression took hold he sought solace in drink, dying suddenly in October 1923 at the age of just thirty-eight.[18] As a result of his brother's death William, who was close to him, 'was not at all too well' and was persuaded to take 'a short holiday'.[19]

But weeks later, on 6 December, a year after the signing of the Anglo-Irish Treaty, the Irish Free State officially came into existence and Cosgrave became president of the Executive Council (prime minister). The following day Seán Hales, a pro-Treaty TD who had led the fight against the IRA in various Cork locations, was killed as a consequence of Liam Lynch's reprisal order. Hales was shot outside the Ormond Hotel in Dublin and there were 'four distinct wounds ... one on the left side of the neck, one in the left breast, one in the left thigh and on a finger on the left hand.'[20] In retaliation the government executed four republican prisoners, Rory O'Connor, Liam Mellows, Joe McKelvey and Dick Barrett ('one from each province'), who had been in prison since the attack on the Four Courts and therefore before the Public Safety Act had been introduced. They were executed 'without trial for acts committed by others. The new state was barely two days old and the Constitution guaranteed life, liberty, freedom of conscience and due process or at least trial by military court.'[21]

Kevin O'Higgins stoutly defended the executions:

> There are no real rules of war. They may be written in a book; they may get lip service from philanthropists. When war breaks out they are more honoured in the breach than in the observance. I have spoken to men who were through the late European war, and I could not come here to this Dáil and talk with any seriousness of the rules of war or the laws of war after what I heard from these men ... the safety and preservation of the people is the highest law.

Cosgrave's defence suggested the jackboot would now take precedence over all else: 'I know fully well there is a diabolical conspiracy afoot ... there is only one way to meet it and that is to crush it.'[22] In his response to the executions Thomas Johnson maintained, 'There was no pretence at legality. I am almost forced to say that I believe you have killed the new state at its birth.'[23]

Much was made of Mellows's supposed radicalism; from Mountjoy jail he had advocated a focus on 'the use to be made of unemployment, starvation, the postal strike and the desire for land', in order for the republicans to 'capture Irish labour'. His incarcerators sneered that the prison author of a radical manifesto had not 'in any previous phase of existence been an adherent of the gospel of state socialism'.[24] Mellows appreciated the need, according to his biographer Desmond Greaves, who believed Mellows was an appropriate 'symbol' of the Irish revolution, to bring the 'revolutionary petite bourgeoisie' of the republican movement into an alliance with the workers, but did not appreciate that they needed to lead it and be 'its base'.[25] Mellows's father had served in the British army until 1904 and had wished Liam to do likewise, but he ended up as a clerk before becoming heavily involved in the republican movement and acquiring arms for the IRA; he was unseated as a TD in 1922 but had been elected to the anti-Treaty IRA executive.

His fellow prisoner, socialist Peadar O'Donnell, was a heavy influence, as was James Connolly, the iconic Labour leader executed in 1916. O'Donnell regarded Mellows as having had unusual depth and richness of mind and in prison lamented his death: 'had there been such as he to assemble around there was a team of us left yet. Was there a Connolly left in Dublin?'[26] Ten years later Mellows's mother, Sarah, was granted a gratuity of £112 for her loss. It was spent on food and medicine; she lamented that 'had God spared him he would have been my breadwinner ... I may add my health has finally and for all time broken down and I am an invalid.'[27] His brother Herbert ('the two of us were like peas') was also interned for over eighteen months during the civil war as an IRA commandant and endured a forty-day hunger strike and was 'compelled to sleep on a bed that was saturated with that day's rain', which created serious health conditions

– 'nephritis, sclerosis, insomnia, stomach trouble, kidney disease' – and he died in 1942.[28]

Rory O'Connor had been a paving engineer for Dublin Corporation on an annual salary of £301 until 1919, when he went on leave, but the extent of his family's dependence on him – a mother and sister, 'an invalid brother and nieces and nephew whose sole income is the brother's life pension of £108 pa' – was disputed, as the mother was in possession of two adjoining properties in Rathgar; the mother later received a 'partially dependent' gratuity of £112.[29]

Two days after these executions seven-year-old Emmet McGarry, the son of Seán McGarry, a TD and captain in the National Army, was killed in a revenge attack on his Dublin home: 'there is assuredly a special heaven for such little martyrs' a newspaper declared at the time.[30] Kevin O'Higgins wrote to his cousin the same month blaming de Valera for much, and maintained that O'Higgins and his colleagues had the gift of compartmentalisation: 'even idealists have a duty to keep their feet on the ground and take stock of facts, particularly if the destinies of a country happen to be in their charge'.[31] The executions led to what Conn Murphy described as 'an appalling cowardly silence' from the Church. Although Archbishop Byrne objected in private ('unjustifiable from the moral point of view') the general episcopal silence was a simple succumbing to the advantages of realpolitik.[32] Free State propaganda in 1923 suggested that 'none but the feeblest of protests was evoked' by the executions on the part of a people who were 'the most sensitive in the world to the excesses of an executive government'; they accepted them as 'inevitable if Ireland was to be saved from a descent into Bolshevism'. The executions 'have saved many lives and shortened the conflict ... the government of Ireland is composed of some of the most humane of Irishmen.'[33]

The pace of executions continued to intensify, with thirty-four in January 1923 alone, and there were no further killings of government TDs. The same month Liam Deasy, deputy chief of staff of the IRA, was arrested and avoided execution by appealing to the IRA to agree to a ceasefire. Deasy had been a good friend of Seán Hales and he was struggling with the hopelessness of the anti-Treaty cause. His appeal failed; it had caused fury and accusations of treachery from some in the IRA. But it also enabled him to live until 1974, to the age of eighty. Deasy was of the view that state executions prolonged rather than shortened the war but was frank in admitting various shades of militancy among anti-Treaty republicans and in wondering whether what little popular support the IRA did receive in numerous parts of the country existed only 'because of who we were or because of our success in earlier times'.[34]

As he contemplated the new year in January 1923, Cosgrave hand wrote a letter of exceptional vehemence to Seán Mac Eoin denouncing talk of peace proposals. If his opponents had had enough of war, 'let them say so and be honest about it. We will meet them again as brothers, but this squealing is dishonourable and unIrish and we are not going to risk another Four Courts. We are going to establish a people's peace which will last.' A minority had made war and now, 'when they are beaten they squeal ... it is easy for them to try and win the peace now when they have lost the war'. They needed to 'act like men and admit the authority of the ballot box'; if not, 'they will have to submit to stronger force ... we don't want office for its profits, but our duty is to show we are a nation which will not allow bandits, gunmen or rebellion while there are men brave enough to work life, limb and property for the good of the country'.[35] The next month he met members of the neutral IRA who were searching in vain for a truce and insisted, 'I am not going to hesitate if the country is to live and if we have to exterminate ten thousand republicans, the three millions of our people is bigger than this ten thousand.'[36]

Neutrality, as seen by him and O'Higgins, was moral cowardice. Stances were cemented by personal loss. O'Higgins's father Thomas was shot dead by republicans in his house the following month in front of his twenty-one-year-old daughter Patricia, who told an inquest: 'My father had told them at the door that he had a copy of the document which said that fathers of members of the Dáil were not to be responsible for what their sons did. He said "this is from your own HQ," but in vain; 'the brain was lacerated. The wound was sufficient to cause instantaneous death.' His wife was then distraught and confined to bed, 'completely prostrated by the realisation of her fears'.[37] The family had to temporarily move to Wales for safety, while the three men tried by a military tribunal in relation to the killing were released due to lack of sufficient identification evidence.

There was unlikely to be 'another Four Courts', in 1923. De Valera's correspondence with Mary MacSwiney in early 1923 reveals that, despite her urging of him in September 1922 that 'we are going to win out. You must have the faith that moves mountains', there was a continuing gulf between him and 'all you diehards'. Liam de Róiste was wide of the mark in characterising both MacSwiney and de Valera as sharing a 'frenzied hatred', a reminder of the tendency not to distinguish between anti-Treatyites despite them exhibiting various shades.[38] In any case, as MacSwiney had told Mulcahy, even if de Valera was on the other side, 'we should still fight on'.[39] By May 1923 it was about, in de Valera's words, the need to persuade 'the remnant of our forces out of this fight' to prevent ultimate ignominy, and the following month he told Frank Aiken of the necessity 'to shepherd our men back to employment in civil life'.[40]

For those on the ground the civil war had become ugly, earthy and visceral: 'The West in winter is the last word and that word is MUD.'[41] John Judge, a Dairy Society clerk from Leitrim, died in Peamount sanatorium in July 1925 at the age of twenty from pulmonary TB; this was, according to officialdom, not attributable to his National Army service and operations in the Arigna Mountains; although 'frequently employed as a dispatch rider' and likely 'he often became heated up and had no opportunity of changing his clothes ... he was subjected to no greater hardship than the remainder of the troops similarly engaged'. His father was under no illusions in labelling his eldest son's cause of death as 'TB: wettings while serving in the army'. As he served, his mother died, leaving his father with eight children to rear on fourteen acres of poor land ('one small cow') and he was £19 in debt for John's funeral.[42] Ellen Carroll of Cumann na mBan was constantly on Cork roads during the civil war and 'soaked to the skin on many occasions'; her health had failed within a year and she was diagnosed with pulmonary TB: 'at the end of the civil war she was a complete wreck' according to her closest confidante.[43]

Jeremiah O'Neill, in the Cork IRA, was one of many who

never really recovered from the continual drenching; he could 'only move about with the aid of a stick' in 1937 at the age of forty-nine: 'In October 1922 I spent three days in water at Timoleague Bridge in an effort to recover [the] body of comrade who was lost there. Afterwards I spent several nights around the coast watching for the remains to be washed up.'[44]

CHAPTER TEN

THE PEASANT MIND

For some of the IRA members' former overlords, the burning down of mansions was an indication of more than civil disarray and there were more 'big houses' burned during the civil war than the War of Independence – an easier form of warfare as 'mansion burning was an exact science'.[1] James Hogan, the Jesuit educated historian and general officer in charge of inspection at National Army HQ in Dublin, recorded in his diary in his imperious style in March 1923 that the burnings were 'done by neighbours in order to consolidate their chances of getting the land. This is the peasant mind ... set against all possessing more worldly things than himself.'[2] Yet only about 4 per cent of the total number of these mansions were burned and the structures of 'purely religious difference' such as churches, schools and parish halls remained 'largely untouched'. Some Protestant middle-class supporters of the Treaty remained relatively undisturbed during the transition and R. B. McDowell concluded that 'hardships sustained by the Southern Loyalists were on the whole not excessively severe', but perception on the ground of what was happening was also a relevant factor.[3]

Brian Inglis was aware that his great uncle in Meath with his family 'were held up one night by masked men, told to collect what possessions they could carry and headed out on to the lawn to watch their house go up in flames'. But for some grand unionists in Malahide, suggested Inglis, 'there was no need for heroics; their social world remained stable; like a prawn in aspic it gradually began to go stale, but it did not disintegrate'. Some of the servants of his grandparents carried on as if the 'Treaty made no difference'. Landowners loved these workers 'because they knew their place and stayed in it, but we did not think of them as people; pets rather'.[4] If that was a common sentiment, it is surprising so few big houses were burned. Some of the propertied unionists 'thought they were loved ... it was only by sticking up their blinkers that they could keep going.'[5]

Terence de Vere White's Protestant father saw it differently; in his eyes the battle was fundamentally about class as 'the hewers of wood and drawers of water were attacking their masters', but despite the revolution, 'a residuum of the mighty still remained in their seats.'[6] The grand edifices could also be deceptive; some were, in the words of Molly Keane, whose family home was the eighteenth-century Ballyrankin House, 'down at heel grand people ... poor food, bad wine and no heat' and it is unsurprising that writers such as Keane became preoccupied with what the ruins represented in a wider sense.[7] The civil war had reinforced the idea that something fundamental divided the Anglo-Irish from the Irish, what novelist Elizabeth Bowen, whose family owned Bowen's Court in Cork, described as 'an affair of origin'. By the early 1920s, the Big House 'seemed to be pressing down low in apprehension, hiding its face ... It seemed to gather its trees close in fright and amazement at the wide light, lovely, unloving country, the unwilling bosom whereon it was set.'[8] Contrast that genteel decline with the fate of Thomas Brennan, a Limerick gardener who worked in one of the big houses and was shot through the head in September 1922, his body publicly dumped with a placard declaring his treachery – 'Convicted Spy' – and discovered in a pool of blood by passers-by on their way to Mass.[9]

As was evident in the diary of Hogan, class was also relevant away from the Anglo-Irish battle; in March 1923, in the army mess, Hogan discussed national teachers: '70% of NT's positively bad influence. Half-educated peasants, full of small vices, mean-minded, lazy, lying, spiteful.' In contrast, believed Hogan, Kevin O'Higgins had a 'thoroughbred quality of mind'.[10] Social status was a key component of friction and there was bilious sermonising about misguided republican youth, 'foolish young men', 'young hot bloods' and the 'attraction of the wild life'. These characterisations dovetailed with the lambasting of the women deemed to be neurotic and hysterical ('most of these women are unmarried – for a very good reason' was the response to female hecklers at one rally).[11] The emergence of labels such as 'city scum', 'corner boys', 'brigands' and 'blackguards' to describe those in arms against the Treaty suggested deeper snobberies and a 'degree of internal colonisation'.[12]

There was even a 'politics of appearance': resentment towards 'pencil pushers' in 'striped pants' and 'sartorial affectations' the republicans came to associate with the pro-Treaty elite at banquets and champagne lunches, a way, perhaps, of the diners distinguishing between their old revolutionary selves and their new positions.[13] The Free State's ministers and (paid) soldiers were accused of self-seeking materialism (Cosgrave was on an annual salary of £2,500, his ministers £1,700), in contrast to the self-sacrifice of the unpaid republicans.

There was also deep antipathy on the part of some republicans to the very idea of politics and they did not hold back in criticising those involved in the Labour Party for their supposed aspirations in the direction of 'respectability'.[14] Whether that antipathy made republicans anti-democratic as opposed to ademocratic is debatable; perhaps they saw themselves as above the political process, 'but they never sought to change it or to end it in the name of a Fascist, communist or militarist alternative'.[15] Yet they also made it clear they understood democratic politics. Con Moloney, adjutant general of the anti-Treaty IRA, was explicit in writing to Ernie O'Malley that 'questions of democratic politics, etc., are not for us'.[16] Liam Lynch, however, was also keen to use the Dáil to get the IRA's perspective heard; in reacting to killings by the National Army he urged 'having particulars given to some Labour TD to have these matters raised and exposed in the Dáil', and he complained when this was not done to his satisfaction.[17]

There were compelling economic reasons for enrolment in the National Army and service in it was certainly not the preserve of the better-off, but neither was the IRA solely fuelled by have nots. In Sligo, limited means 'did not produce more anti-Treaty activists or government army recruits', and there was an evenness of representation in class terms. Nor were republican internees more likely to come from poorer land holdings.[18] In Cork, 40 per cent of IRA men were farmers' sons and 26 per cent the sons of skilled workers.

National army recruits in Cork 'were mostly urban and unskilled ... almost none described themselves as farmers' sons'.[19] Where lay the 'stake in the country people'?[20] According to Peter Hart, 'the 1922–3 campaign did not follow the geography of poverty'. Perhaps not, but social factors cannot be discounted; contemporary observers made a clear correlation between land hunger and 'Irregularism', and class rhetoric was frequently employed.[21]

In his memoir, Limerick IRA man Mossie Hartnett noted the Free State soldiers were paid 'the then generous wage of 25 shillings per week and their keep. It had a staggering impact on poor needy labourers and ex-British soldiers, all without money or work. So it was goodbye to republicanism which most [of them] did not understand anyway.'[22] Government circulars suggest a weekly payment of £1 was initially offered to reservist recruits (who formed one of three kinds of volunteers, the others being the regular army and Truce Volunteers), though maintenance would also be provided. For their wages they were expected to 'flabbergast those who would protract things indefinitely in the country'.[23]

There was ongoing resentment that parts of the country perceived as too quiet during the War of Independence were now facing intense republican activity. During the War of Independence fifteen people in or from Kildare died, for example, compared to forty-five during the civil war.[24] A National Army complaint from Castlebar in January 1922 noted, 'they didn't fire a shot at the enemy during the Trouble. Tuesday night was the first time blood was spilt in that area.'[25] National Army members were, however, far from cherished by the new state; when Michael Rynne spent twenty weeks visiting injured soldiers his reports suggested satisfactory conditions in some parts but also uncovered conditions in, for example, Richmond Hospital, that were 'nothing short of scandalous', in relation to neglect and clothing. He was also aware of the failure to adequately deal with some prisoners' dependents.[26]

CHAPTER ELEVEN

GIVING IT TO THE BASTARDS

For the bereaved, details of civil war death could be laid painfully bare. Twenty-one-year-old labourer Laurence Sweeney of the South Dublin Brigade of the IRA was shot dead by the National Army in July 1922 in Kildare and his father was told there were 'about 40 Lewis gun bullets in stomach'.[1] For others, precisely what happened to cause death could remain vague or unread if there were literacy issues. Alice Crabbe, living in poverty in Dublin, was the mother of Edward Crabbe, killed in September 1922 at Glenamoy County Mayo, one of six National Army soldiers killed during an attack by the IRA, and noted, 'we can only give account of details of his death what was in newspapers'. Her husband John, a former seaman, had also served in the National Army, while Alice noted at the end of 1923 'the boy that's killed was very good to his brother. When he got wind of [the] boy's death his brother took it to heart and fretted and died 5 months after him, so we had 2 sons dead in 5 months'. Demobilised, John, with severe varicose veins, had 'no prospects of work'. They had two daughters, one sickly, and were also facing eviction from their rented property. The dependent's allowance of £4.8s. per month ceased in March 1924.[2]

Women in particular were also charged with the harrowing task of preparing mutilated bodies for burial; according to officialdom there did 'not appear to be anything outstanding', in this kind of service.[3] The reality for these women had undoubtedly been more complex and traumatic. Was the preparing of land mine victims' bodies not active and essential service? Some were initially buried without even a coffin: a trap mine explosion at Tallow in Waterford in March 1923 killed Thomas Greehy, aged nineteen; the mine had been planted in an IRA arms dump by National Army forces. A comrade of Greehy 'searched for the body and found that of Volunteer Greehy with head and right arm partly blown away. I tied the body up in his trench coat and put it on my back and brought it to [the] graveyard and buried it without any coffin.'[4]

Writer Liam O'Flaherty, co-founder of the tiny Communist Party of Ireland and involved in agitating on behalf of the unemployed in Dublin in January 1922 before fleeing to London a few months later, described the nature of some of the civil war killings in barely disguised fiction. Lieutenant Jim Dolan, a slim young man of twenty-two; a clerk in blue suit, was 'all torn and covered in dirt, his white young face haggard and blotched with terror of death and with want of sleep ... waiting with desperate hatred'. His hatred was well matched as he was cornered and then surrendered with his arms above his head: 'two cruel, cold faces staring coldly at him. Gradually he saw the faces growing colder and more cruel, the lips curling into a snarl and the eyes narrowing. Then one man said, "Let's give it to the Bastard". They both fired point blank into his head.'[5]

The Criminal Investigation Department (CID) was particularly keen to 'give it to the bastards'. An armed, plain-clothes counter-insurgency police unit organised separately from the unarmed Civic Guard and based in Oriel House on Westland Row in Dublin, its shadow hung over grisly brutalities. During the civil war it was responsible for the arrest of many anti-Treaty forces, used violence during interrogation and executed republican suspects and prisoners. Thomas Derrig a member of the IRA Army Council, had his eye shot out while in CID custody; in his own understated words, 'bullet wound causing loss of left eye. Shot fired at me in Oriel House, Dublin, subsequent to my arrest on 6 April 1923.'[6] Ten years later there was a 'scar from outer canthus extending for two inches horizontally across the temple ... leaving a marked depression'.[7] It was, according to medics, a 45 per cent disablement.

He was one of the lucky ones and went on to become a long-serving government minister from the 1930s to the 1950s, unlike three teenage republicans whose bodies were dumped in west Dublin in October 1922; one of the bodies had sixteen wounds, including three to the head, and it was strongly suspected those involved in National Army intelligence networks were to blame. IRA man Bobby Bonfield, who had killed Séamus Dwyer, a pro-Treaty grocer suspected by republicans of intelligence work, was taken in the general direction of Oriel House in March 1923 and his dumped body discovered the following day.[8] Another victim of Oriel House, Joseph Clarke, recounted his experience in November 1922: his interrogators 'twisted my arms and kicked me on the legs and body, tore my moustache off with a scissors, razor and some other torture instruments ... They also twisted my ears with a pliers. They also threatened to use a hot iron if I did not give them information ... I was told I would be taken to the torture room again in an hour's time if I did not give the information wanted.'[9]

Republican polemicists were quick to point the finger at the CID's political masters (the CID was under the control of the Department of Home Affairs): 'How do the CID earn their pay? Mr Cosgrave makes the people of Ireland pay £50,000 for the "secret service", the nature of which he refuses to disclose.'[10] The CID also viciously beat and tortured journalist Patrick John Lynch, who had joined the republican publicity bureau. He was then interned, only to succumb to insanity, and he died in Grangegorman mental hospital in 1934, 'one of the many unremembered tragedies of the extra-legal brutalities of the civil war'.[11] The IRA also demonstrated increased ruthlessness. Liam Lynch maintained that, up to November 1922, 'we have honourably stood by the rules of law ... this state of affairs will now end ... harassing tactics must be constantly adopted.'[12] Revenge attacks included the luring of four unarmed National Army soldiers to a Wexford pub; three of them were dragged to a remote townland and machine gunned to death.[13]

Women were also subjected to 'the ignominy of a complete stripping' to see that they hid 'no treasonable articles', as in the case of Mary Carey, a Cork newsagent whose house was a key location and lodging space for republicans.[14] Sexual assault was another reality, but the fact of it being widespread has not been adequately proven, a situation not helped by 'omissions and obscure language' and a cultural taboo against acknowledging rape.[15] What is clear is that some women suffered 'serious and traumatising interpersonal violence – often on account of their gender', but there were cultural and religious restraints that militated against 'the need for sexual violence as warfare'.[16]

When Ernie O'Malley declared that the anti-Treaty IRA were engaged in a 'just and holy war', Desmond FitzGerald retorted that 'the murder of Red Cross attendants and the rape of a Protestant lady by 4 men of Séamus Robinson's command are eloquent tributes to the claims of the sanctimonious O'Malley'.[17] This was a reference to the gang rape of Eileen Biggs in Tipperary in June 1922, a young married woman from the Protestant landowning class, who described how 'I was outraged by different men in turn, one after the other ... I believe I was outraged altogether on 8 or 9 different occasions.'[18] The rape devastated the family for decades and Eileen ended up in psychiatric care: 'we cannot hold up our heads amongst friends and acquaintances', she said afterwards.[19]

Home attacks were likely to generate a particular type of violence that impacted especially on women, and sometimes it is necessary to read between the lines in relation to testimony about 'rough handling' of women and 'shattered nerves' on account of nocturnal events, though the accounts of hair shaving were more explicit. In April 1923 Anne White, a priest's 'aged' housekeeper in Crookstown, County Cork, was seized from the house and 'dragged by force into the yard where they assaulted her ... forced into a motor car by the raiders and taken away to an unoccupied house 5 or 6 miles distance. She was detained there for some time, during which her hair was cut off.'[20] The following month, Margaret Doherty from Foxford in Mayo, a Cumann na mBan activist, was 'dragged from her bed and stripped naked'. Her hands were tied; she was held at gunpoint and then 'outraged' (raped) by three men in succession. Prior to that night 'she was in perfect health and had never been ill. After that date she gradually failed, physically and mentally.'[21]

Another rape victim, who became pregnant as a result of her ordeal in January 1923 in a house in Westmeath that she shared with her blind aunt and uncle, turned in desperation to Archbishop Byrne of Dublin ('I appeal to your charity to listen to my pitiful tale and beg your forgiveness'). In January 1923 a party of men, armed to the teeth & calling themselves republicans, forced their entrance into our house ... The object of their visit was money or lives and they were furious when they did not get money ... One brute satisfied his duty passion on me. I was then in a dangerous stage of health and thro' his conduct I became pregnant. Oh God could any pen describe what I have gone thro?

Dissuaded from suicide by a Franciscan, after the birth of her son, her prayers that he be taken to heaven 'fell on deaf ears'. She had to steal from her aunt to pay a rescue agency to mind her baby and received money from the archbishop to pay for an adoption to be arranged to avoid the stigma of public unmarried motherhood.[22]

Ernest Blythe, dripping in misogyny, was nonplussed about the Kenmare Case, when senior officers of the National Army's Kerry Command assaulted two young women in June 1923. Flossie and Jessie McCarthy were daughters of a local pro-Treaty doctor, Randall McCarthy, who had apparently run afoul of Paddy O'Daly because of McCarthy's concerns about the behaviour of the Kerry Command. The sisters were seized from home in the middle of the night, flogged with belts by three soldiers, including O'Daly, and had motor oil or grease rubbed into their hair; 'there was also the implicit suggestion of a [worse] sexual assault'.[23] A court of inquiry found one soldier guilty of the charges but the other two, including O'Daly, were declared innocent.

Judge Advocate General Cahir Davitt was adamant the matter could not be 'hushed up' on the grounds that 'One of the main reasons justifying the commencement of the Civil War was the necessity to stop unlawful interference by force with the rights of ordinary citizens.' Was it, he wondered, going to be tolerated in the Army itself?[24]

It was – despite the fury of Kevin O'Higgins, himself the son of a doctor.[25] The attorney general, Hugh Kennedy, did not take the case seriously, and as for Ernest Blythe: 'I did not agree with O'Higgins in feeling particularly revolted at what seemed to be merely a case of a couple of tarts getting a few lashes that did them no harm.' O'Higgins, he suggested, was 'almost hysterical about the affair', no doubt partly because it was 'a crime perpetrated against O'Higgins' own caste'.[26]

The confidential military reports of the National Army for February and March 1923 indicated that in some parts of the country there was 'nothing worth reporting', but there were pockets of trouble in, for example, Waterford ('Callan: Garrison was heavily attacked this morning with rifle and machine gun fire. Attackers estimated at 100 men'). Lies pervaded other accounts: 'Claremorris: prisoner named Corcoran accidentally shot near Ballina while removing mines.'[27]

Remoteness helped to prolong the resistance in some parts, though not so much in the east, including in Wexford where because of the flatness of the terrain it was 'not possible to keep a big column'.[28] The reports from Tralee underlined the disturbed state of Kerry; by the autumn the county accounted for almost one in five deaths of Free State forces and nearly 15 per cent of those wounded.[29] Members of the Dublin Guard led by Paddy O'Daly were determined to achieve a rout in Kerry, setting the scene for vengeful excess. March 1923 became the ultimate 'terror month', but April was awful too. At Knocknagoshel in rural north-east Kerry on 6 March, eight National Army soldiers investigated a tip-off about an IRA arms dump, which was an IRA trap, and when a mine exploded body parts were 'strewn in all directions'.[30] Five soldiers – Paddy O'Connor (who was decapitated), Michael Galvin, Laurence O'Connor, Michael Dunne and Edward Stapleton – died and Joseph O'Brien was so maimed both his legs were amputated below the knee and he was almost blinded. His wife Annie subsequently struggled to find suitable accommodation, as he was 'living in a top room' and had to plead for a wheelchair, which took six months to be provided, his brother stating 'it is a shame for him to be treated in such a way'.[31]

The Knocknagoshel explosion represented the highest daily death toll for the army in six months. O'Daly announced that henceforth republican prisoners would clear barricades in case of further booby-trap mines. Over the next fortnight such was the lust for revenge that nineteen republicans were killed. The day after the Knocknagoshel carnage nine republican prisoners in Tralee were taken to nearby Ballyseedy to supposedly clear rubble blocking the road and it has been suggested they were chosen as they had no known links to the Catholic clergy or hierarchy.[32] Tied together, they were told to smoke their last smoke, say their prayers, and called 'Irish bastards' before the pre-planted bomb was detonated. The scene was horrendous: 'mangled almost beyond recognition; portions of their limbs and flesh, with pieces of clothing, were found adhering to trees and strewn along the roads and fields over a hundred yards' from the scene, according to a contemporary newspaper.[33]

Astonishingly, Stephen Fuller survived: 'I was tied up in three places. The explosion cut all the ropes. I was about two feet from the mine – it would not be three feet. All the rest were killed – eight of them ... I recovered my senses when I went up in the air but I lost them again when I hit the road. I went straight up and must have been blown up fairly high. All my clothes were blown off ... all the skin was burnt off my hands and the skin burnt off the back of my legs.'[34] He retained afterwards 'several fine foreign bodies embedded in the musculature of his back', contracted TB and was 'profoundly neurasthenic [one description for post-traumatic stress disorder]'.[35] Further indignities awaited the bereaved families: such was the horrendous condition of the remains, hurriedly and improperly coffined, that 'the collective response was possibly a mental breakdown verging on temporary insanity'.[36] Angry crowds stoned members of the army.

The army inquiry into the Ballyseedy slaughter, presided over by O'Daly, 'even though the conduct of his own men was the sole issue', was a travesty and the families of the dead were not even notified of it.[37] The resultant report praised the discipline of National Army soldiers and contended that the IRA had placed the mine. Mulcahy made a point of reading it into the Dáil record: 'the court is of opinion that, in view of the abnormal conditions which have prevailed in this area, and of the inordinate and malignant nature of the fight carried out against the Army in their effort to restore peace, the discipline by the troops is worthy of the highest consideration'.[38] Once again, it was left to Labour leader Thomas Johnson to demand non-military answers to troubling questions, in vain. Nor was there an inquest.

Four more prisoners were killed in the same way the following day at Countess Bridge near Killarney, and on 12 March five more were killed at Cahirciveen. The cover-ups were blatant; in relation to Cahirciveen, for example, a query from the Department of Home Affairs noted the absence of testimony from relevant parties and discrepancies in army testimony.[39]

Even as Mulcahy read deep lies into the official Dáil record, another dark drama was playing out in the form of a cave siege at Clashmealcon in north Kerry below a steep cliff, where on-the-run IRA members were being 'starved out' by National Army men. In an attempt to reach the cave, one National Army soldier was killed and another wounded, later dying from his injuries. One of the IRA men, Tim Lyons, having agreed to surrender, died while scaling the cliff, falling from the rope lowered by the soldiers and then shot several times as he lay on the rocks; it is likely the rope was cut as he climbed, a matter reputedly boasted about afterwards by the cutter, who was 'never brought to book'.[40] There was of course, no need for rope cutting; as recorded in military reports, 'there is no means of escape ... prisoners in an exhausted condition and had been drinking sea water for days'.[41] Lyons's three comrades were later executed. By that stage, O'Daly 'must have thought he was invincible'.[42]

Chapter Twelve

THE MIND'S EXHILARATION

By the spring of 1923 there was little wind in the republican military sail. War weariness was apparent but that did not mean there was stability; there was still much reference in police reports to 'complete lawlessness'.[1] In various places advantage was taken of the disturbances to withhold rates, while preventing land seizure involved both the Department of Agriculture and the Department of Defence. Such was the tumult that a special infantry corps (SIC) of the National Army to tackle trouble spots was authorised in January, but even as the civil war faded 'land snatching has again broken out in Clare'.[2] With up to 4,000 men in eight units, the SIC lasted for a year, seizing livestock in lieu of unpaid debts and arresting agrarian suspects; it was also a product of politicians' warnings about imminent social collapse.[3] One of the most famous utterances during the civil war, by Kevin O'Higgins – 'we were the most conservative minded revolutionaries that ever put through a successful revolution' – was made amid a debate about the seizure of cattle by Free State troops and was enveloped by commentary about 'checking anarchy' and the insistence of O'Higgins that there was a 'desire to get rich quick on the part of people who think they have a vested interest in disorder'.[4]

There was a certain revival of tactics in Munster associated with the ranch war in the first decade of the century while the term 'Grazier' came to have a 'heightened currency as a derogatory label during the civil war'. While 76 per cent of the total acreage of Limerick had been purchased under land acts from 1881 to 1909, the figures for Tipperary and Waterford were only 61 and 56 per cent respectively; cattle drivers were very busy in parts of south Tipperary in early 1922 and there were reports of gruesome attacks on animals. There were an estimated 114,000 unpurchased tenancies remaining in the Free State in 1923 and 295,000 lived on uneconomic holdings.[5] The agricultural labourers in Waterford faced the considerable power of the Waterford Farmers Association headed by Sir John Keane, senator, landowner and promoter of farmers' vigilante groups, who admitted £1.10s for a six-day week, a reduction of 8s., was 'not a generous wage, but it is as much as the industry can stand'. Fifteen hundred labourers struck and the SIC was told to 'use your own discretion re action to be taken. Use no half measures. Make an example of the place.' The strikers retaliated with arson and other attacks; it was to last until December 1923, when the Irish Transport and General Workers' Union ran out of strike pay funds and the labourers were left at the mercy of the farmers.[6]

Unrest among internees and the resort to hunger strike was also creating waves. The allegations of bad treatment in a report of the International Committee of the Red Cross mission in Ireland from April to May 1923, were, suggested the government, 'entirely unfounded'. There were 7,369 in the 'principal camps' and 'the treatment of these prisoners is devoid of all hostile spirit', the government argued, suggesting they were being treated as prisoners of war. The Red Cross committee had been received by the minister for external affairs, Desmond FitzGerald, and, amusingly or revealingly, according to Mulcahy, 'A mutual understanding was arrived at as to the nature of the facts to be investigated, and as to the character of the intervention of the International Committee of the Red Cross so as to determine the exact lines in which the activity of the Delegates should be directed.'[7] That was convenient indeed.

A delegation of concerned senators that included the poet W. B. Yeats was more circumspect; oversight and improvements were needed, Yeats averred in May 1923, but he also accepted 'many statements' by critics could not be relied upon as to their accuracy.[8] This was probably true; FitzGerald was keen to highlight extracts of monitored letters from republicans expressing satisfaction ('we have nothing to complain about and the food is good'), but upbeat messages from prisoners were also likely for other reasons including the desire to prevent family worry and to appear mentally undefeated.

The same collection contained a letter from North Union internee Annie Hogan to her mother detailing sixty women 'sleeping out on mattresses on grass surrounded by armed soldiers'.[9]

Yeats and Cosgrave had first discussed prisoners in late 1922, but Yeats was keen not 'to embarrass the government'.[10] Yeats had a long history with Maud Gonne, the mainstay of the Women's Prisoners Defence League, who had rejected his proposal of marriage. He told Cosgrave in April 1923 that Gonne, who was twice imprisoned in 1923, had told her confessor she was not in favour of armed rebellion: 'it puts her in a different position from an avowed republican', maintained Yeats, chancing his arm, and he complained that 'she is 57 and cannot be expected to carry the same strain as a younger woman'.[11] Gonne was well able for that strain and more; her drive and energy made for a life of eighty-six years that ended in 1953, in contrast to some of the other younger female prisoners of that era who succumbed to premature deaths as a consequence of 1922–3. Yeats had fallen out with Gonne, but he thanked Cosgrave for an 'act of clemency' when she was released later that month.[12]

Tyrone native Patrick McCartan, a medical doctor and, as a TD in 1921, a very reluctant voter for the Treaty, also pleaded at length that month for the government not to allow these 'misguided' prisoners to die: 'we are now practically at the end of this hideous struggle and magnanimity will do more to heal the sores opened by it than any show of strength'.[13] Magnanimity was in short supply, however, and McCartan soon became so disillusioned that he left Ireland for almost fifteen years to focus on medicine in New York. Cosgrave's reply was notable for the bile directed towards women, who, he insisted, associated any act of grace as a weakness and were 'the mainstay of the trouble we have had ... I fear that it is not possible to consider these women as ordinary females.'[14]

A profile of some of the female prisoners that month, including Nell Ryan, Gonne and Mary MacSwiney, acknowledged 'no charge has been preferred' against them.[15] Ryan was a sister-in-law of Richard Mulcahy and Mulcahy refused clemency despite family pleas; like others, the civil war split the Ryan family, with one sister, Jo, a nun at Loreto convent, keeping the peace between them ('political discussion was suspended on summer holidays').[16] Two women who had completed twenty-seven days of hunger strike in April noted they had just received the last sacraments and wrote with a firm dignity to Archbishop Byrne: 'so apparently there is no longer any theological objection to our receiving the consolations of the Church. We, therefore, request your Grace to grant us the privilege of receiving Holy Communion till our death.'[17]

The same month Cosgrave insisted in a letter to Byrne that success had not attended the government's efforts 'until particular attention was directed to women, who operated with impunity in every way'; this was his explanation of his refusal to grant Byrne's request for releases.[18] He was still writing to Byrne on this matter in October, a reminder that Byrne was consistent in seeking more clemency: 'I believe each minister would prefer ... to leave public life altogether than to yield ... we have offered on more than one occasion a clean slate.'[19] Byrne had also composed private notes: 'hunger strike is against the inhumanity of the treatment ... no open air for 4 or 5 weeks ... acts of violence.'[20]

Embarking on hunger strike meant long-term health consequences. Mary Commins, a Cumann na mBan member from Kilkenny, endured thirty days on hunger strike in Kilmainham and a decade later was being treated for 'chronic gastritis, flatulence and rheumatic pains. She also suffered from chronic anaemia.'[21] The government deliberately gendered the idea of the hunger strike as a 'women's weapon', inflicting on themselves the hurt they could not inflict on a man.[22] Cumann na mBan's Ellen Walsh, arrested in April 1923, experienced prison in Kerry and Dublin and was briefly on hunger strike; she was also taken by the legs and pulled down stone stairs, hitting her head. She was dead within four years.[23]

A telling report on wounded prisoners by the end of 1923 reasonably and sadly concluded that such men could not be considered a danger to public safety: 'It will be years before any of them will be fit for military service – most of them will never be fit again.'[24] One of them was Ernie O'Malley, who had been captured and badly wounded after a dramatic shoot-out at a Dublin house in November 1922. He corresponded at great length with Molly Childers, who had a long history of anti-imperialist activity and was the widow of Erskine. Molly was a sort of surrogate mother to O'Malley, who admitted to her, 'I hardly know my family ... there was very little love in the family.'[25]

He certainly found more than a substitute mother in Molly, with whom Ernie could be remarkably intimate ('my bowels have just moved and I feel in good form, thank God, to write').[26] He was far from enduring a torrid, hellish prison experience: 'I'm just as well off in here – no one to bother me. I feel in my bones I could never live at home ... I have my books and plenty of time to think.'[27] This was a reminder that some republican prisoners found prison a calm, even enjoyable environment. Out of the fray, some went into themselves deeply, including Frank O'Connor in Gormanstown, who 'took advantage of enforced solitude to listen to his interior voices'. He did not want martyrdom and 'didn't want to die ... I wanted to live, to read, to hear music', as too many mythical abstractions reduced life to 'a tedious morality'.[28] Republicans, of course, claimed imprisonment as part of 'active service', but for all the difficulties endured, incarceration made some less vulnerable and prolonged their careers.

For Peadar O'Donnell, who went on to become a prolific author, internment prompted both political and personal reflection in relation to his republican socialism – how it might be progressed and how he could find expression for it:

> I know that I know the insides of the minds of the mass of the folk in rural Ireland: my thoughts are distilled out of their lives. Therefore, it is not my task to say anything new but to put words on what is in confused ferment in their minds. How would I say it? Write? I could try and I did ... If I could say their lives out loud to these remnants of the Irish of history until they would nod their heads and say 'this is us!' ... A powerful, vital folk, but they are too blasted patient.[29]

Confinement also gave some prisoners a chance to grow up a bit, or in some cases mature a lot, as they came to terms with the death of friends and comrades.

A mass hunger strike of internees began in October 1923 and lasted for forty-one days, spreading to over ten prisons and camps. There was extraordinary depth to O'Malley as he poured out his inner thoughts and sustained and then sought to recover from the hunger strike ('I think the main pain of hunger strike', noted Peadar O'Donnell, 'must be the apprehension of death ... the greatest sensation of a hunger strike is the exhilaration the mind achieves.')[30] O'Malley was, due to his literary abilities, 'the historian's ideal guerrilla'.[31] He was imprisoned until July 1924 but remained contemptuous of the failures of both his enemies and his allies ('I absolutely distrust our own propaganda').[32] While preoccupied with the spirituality of what he regarded as a pure republican mission ('the spirit of the race was warped until it could express its type of genius') it was a challenge he felt few could rise to, but like others, he was not to explicitly define 'the spiritual expression of nationhood'. He had no interest in politics or policy; he was also strangely detached from those fighting for his cause and had never been to several of the key areas under his command.[33]

O'Malley was intensely self-centred and demanding of Molly:

> could you please send me a dozen pears and a pound of grapes twice a week? I think the best biscuit is thin arrowroot but I also think there are other good unsweetened biscuits ... also please forward me a pot of strawberry jam ... I told our friend to ask you for a bottle of wine ... could you please send me some cigarettes.

He always wanted more books and magazines, though he did sometimes acknowledge his overly long lists: 'please pardon my wanting the moon'.[34] These pleas came when he was recovering from the called-off hunger strike, a failure he abhorred while telling doctors 'they have to reckon with the spirit and not the body'.[35] He was overtly pious and glad his sacrifices brought him 'closer to God ... one felt it impossible to have carnal thoughts or to sin'.[36] He was also crassly insensitive; how extraordinary it was that of all people, he would write to Molly, who had lost her husband, to impress upon her how imperative it was that her two young sons 'take a big part. The country has not had, as yet, sufficient voluntary sacrifice and suffering.'[37]

O'Malley was ecstatic when Denis Barry died on hunger strike ('so happy ... I felt strengthened') and as for executions: 'it seems such an easy matter to us'.[38] Barry had been in Newbridge internment camp and died in the Curragh military hospital in November 1923; the government initially refused to release his body to his family, as, according to Mulcahy, advantage would be taken of his funeral 'to prejudice the safety of the state'. His family took a high-court action and retrieved his remains, but the Catholic Bishop of Cork, Daniel Cohalan, refused him a Christian burial and forbade diocesan priests from officiating at his funeral because of 'the course' he had taken during the civil war.[39] This was the same Cohalan who had supported the hunger strike of Terence MacSwiney in 1920.

Barry's remains were taken instead to the headquarters of Sinn Féin in Cork city and the funeral took place in the republican plot at St Finbarr's cemetery where anti-Treaty TD David Kent recited prayers and sprinkled the grave with holy water. Cohalan explained his stance in a letter to the newspapers: 'I knew the deceased ... I knew him to be a very good man, but if it were my brother who had taken the course that Denis Barry chose to take I should treat his burial in the same way ... it is well to consider the general political situation.'[40] This was blatant politicisation; Barry, it seemed, had good morals, but bad politics.

The pledge signed in Mountjoy by hunger strikers had declared: 'what I am about to suffer I offer to the glory of God and for the freedom of Ireland'. As Peadar O'Donnell saw it, this involved 'a sort of moral conscription' owing to group loyalty, though plenty knew it was launched, in Seán O'Faoláin's words, 'in despair'. O'Donnell's parents were locked out of their parish chapel where they had gone to pray for him, and others walked out of churches. Cardinal Logue deemed the hunger strike foolish and 'of very doubtful morality', but also urged the government to release all non-convicted internees and his private contacts may well have been a factor in it being ended.[41]

Archbishop Byrne was 'besieged by requests' when there were 8,207 prisoners in custody and 7,003 on hunger strike, but Kevin O'Higgins preferred to focus on those 'conducting the hunger strike from outside'.[42] By early November the numbers on hunger strike had dramatically dropped to 3,067 and by mid November to just 315. The collapse of the hunger strike also began to erode the former discipline 'which had held the prisoners together'.[43] There were also manifold pleas from the US and a ten-page letter from Cosgrave to Cork-born Dr Daniel Mannix, the Catholic Archbishop of Melbourne, a champion of de Valera feared by Britain and hugely influential in Australia, seeking to correct his anti-Treaty sympathies. Cosgrave remained 'your Grace's obedient servant', but not before sharply criticising Mannix's 'injudicious and inaccurate pronouncements'.[44]

In August 1923, indemnity legislation was introduced that protected the Free State side from civil or criminal responsibility for actions taken since the end of June 1922 to suppress 'armed rebellion, created by the attempt to overthrow by force the lawfully established government'. By the start of December 1923, more than six months after the end of the civil war, there were still 5,774 prisoners in military custody.[45] By June 1924, in relation to sentenced prisoners who had been recommended for release but against whom charges were pending, it was decided sensibly that 'as a general rule prosecutions for these charges should not be gone with'.[46] At that stage there were 237 'political prisoners in military custody', a private bestowing of a recognition unavailable the previous year, but the government retained a veto over the release of imprisoned TDs, including Austin Stack and Patrick Smith. Stack's health deteriorated due to imprisonment and hunger strike and he died in 1929, less than four years after he married. Smith, in contrast, lived until 1982.

De Valera was still deemed to be 'solely responsible for the recent destruction in the country', a wild exaggeration.[47] A measure of the dubiousness of the state's claim was that after de Valera's arrest and imprisonment in August 1923 it was decided by the Executive Council 'that a charge should be brought against him with the least possible delay', but the attorney general, when interviewed by David Neligan of the Office of Director of Intelligence in the National Army, 'could not inform me under what statute he would be tried or the nature of the charge ... he was not clear as to what charge could be put against him ... I promised to hunt up some other original documents with de Valera's signature.'[48] The search was in vain, but de Valera remained in prison until July 1924.

Chapter Thirteen

FIZZLING OUT

On 10 April 1923 IRA chief of staff Liam Lynch – who exactly a year previously had been working hard to prevent civil war but who became dismissive of the people he insisted in early 1923 'were merely sheep to be driven anywhere at will' – was shot in the Knockmeal-down Mountains in Tipperary and died from his wounds. Yet the lust for reprisal was still strong; the day after, despite it being known that Lynch was dead, six men were executed at the old workhouse in Tuam in Galway ('shot against the oratory wall'), five of them members of an IRA column ambushed by the National Army in February.[1]

Lynch was eulogised in time for his 'simple patriotism', which he 'set above everything in his life and finally above life itself', his spirit a bridge to 'a self-replenishing heritage'.[2] But that was of little material use to his widowed mother, Mary, who was dependent on him, or his sister Mary, who almost forty years after his death was inquiring about a dependents' pension.[3]

The IRA executive assembled in Tipperary on 20 April and agreed peace should be negotiated, but that notion was never going to be contemplated by the Free State, and by 27 April, while de Valera defiantly declared the 'sovereign rights of the nation are indefeasi-ble and inalienable', Frank Aiken, the new chief of staff of the IRA, simultaneously ordered a suspension of IRA offensives and on 24 May ordered the IRA to dump arms. It was perhaps appropriate that it was Aiken who issued that command, as he 'hated' the civil war, was under severe emotional strain and was less dismissive of politics than some of his anti-Treaty peers, despite O'Higgins's labelling of him in the Dáil in February 1923 as a 'mad dog', a reminder of what the civil war had done to perspective.[4]

The defiant response to Liam Lynch's death from Ernie O'Malley – 'You who were a living force/ Are now a battle cry' – was wildly misplaced. O'Malley too had shared the arrogant conviction that it was unnecessary to 'consult the feelings' of the people: 'if we gave them a good strong lead they would follow'.[5] But as was recorded by a National Army military report, by then the IRA could only manage 'spasmodic incursions of small parties of 10 or 15 Irregulars who have so far evaded arrest by lying low in remote and difficult districts along the western seaboard'.[6]

By May the intention was 'to allow the fight to fizzle out ... the gunmen will go behind the scenes to allow the politicians to take the field'. In Dublin, the enemy's morale had 'gone to pieces' with only an estimated '170 in all ranks' but could not count 'upon more than 10% of their forces for active service', and by June, 'it is no exaggeration to say that, on the whole, the morale of the prisoners is far higher than that of the men on the hills'. Armed robberies and postal disruption were common right up to the end of the year with 'a disquieting increase', in them by November, while for the state side, 'it is becoming more and more apparent that the government will be judged by the conduct of the army'.[7]

There was no agreed or negotiated peace to end the civil war; no church bells pealed to celebrate its conclusion and there were no grand gestures of reconciliation. De Valera proclaimed to the 'Soldiers of the Republic, Legion of the Rearguard: The Republic can no longer be defended successfully by your arms. Further sacrifice of life would now be in vain ... military victory must be allowed to rest for the moment with those who have destroyed the Republic. Other means must be found to safeguard the nation's right.'[8] That exhausted legion, though still defiant, just 'hid their arms and went home'.[9]

Violence did not cease; it dribbled away, and that was as much as was possible, but making the transition from war to peace was not going to be straightforward for either side, especially in a small country where 'there was a horrible intimacy about the war' and when the following challenges loomed large: 'how do you preach law and order when for the last three years you have counselled your best men to kill; how do you get men to stop killing when it is possibly the one thing that they are good at, when it is, for some, the only thing that they now really enjoy, the only thing that sets them apart from everybody else?'[10] They were questions that lingered; guns were not surrendered but neither did concerted and serious anti-state violence last on a grand scale.

Despite the ceasefire, however, the violence and brutality did not stop, with a continuation of 'freelance acts of revenge'. Noel Lemass, brother of Seán and once an intelligence officer for the anti-Treaty side, escaped from custody and briefly sojourned to England before arriving back to Dublin in summer 1923, where he was then abducted and disappeared. His mutilated body was found in the Dublin Mountains in October, shot three times, the head detached from the body, some fingers cut off. When his parents were brought to the scene they could only identify him from his cigarette case, rosary beads and gold tie clip; 'later, the family would clash with the government over having these items returned to them'.[11] Even though witnesses at the Lemass inquest were intimidated, the jury still concluded he had been 'brutally and wilfully murdered' and that 'the armed forces of the State have been implicated'. The Coroner had told them that 'it would appear that the teeth were torn from the jaw and that in conjunction with the fact that hairs were found beside the body, suggested a barbarism of which the most pitiless savage would be ashamed'.[12]

How many died overall during the war? There has been no definitive answer. Estimates have varied too widely, from 1,200 to 4,000.[13] It is likely more National Army soldiers were killed than republicans, but there is no conclusive figure. Some have settled on the assertion 'less than 1,500' and sought to compare that to Finland's civil war dead of perhaps 36,000, of whom 8,700 were killed in battle and the remainder of whom were executed or died in prison camps.[14] County studies have suggested 220 civil war fatalities in Cork, 170 in Kerry, 130 in Tipperary and 258 in Dublin, the most violent counties. An overall estimate of 730 National Army and 350 IRA dead would seem reasonable; that does not tally exactly with figures given by the government in 1924 (800 National Army), or by the IRA that decade (400), but is not far off.[15] Up to 200 civilians were also killed.[16] The financial cost has been estimated at £47 million (about £2.7 billion today); such was the scale of the infrastructural damage that £10 million of £26.5 million spent on public services in 1922–3 was devoted to security and reconstruction.[17]

Kevin O'Higgins was at least able to recognise in July 1923 that 'the things that had been said in blame and praise of the government were probably equally extravagant and would be tempered in time', but propaganda from both sides endured strongly.[18] For the IRA it was necessary to counteract 'the base lie that the Irish people have, of their own free will, chosen to become a partitioned British province'. Those same republicans, who 'obeyed their nobler instincts' in 1922 and 1923 had to continue their task, as 'the world, once more, is looking on. Shall it be said that this generation has turned renegade to the national faith?'[19]

The world, however, was doing no such thing, and had not been for some time. In late 1923 Michael Rynne, now resigned from the army and in Italy, told the minister for external affairs, Desmond FitzGerald, of his frustration with having to explain 'that a country called Ireland exists ... that its capital is not London ... so I generally say "Terence MacSwiney" and everyone choruses "Il Sindaco di Cork" [The Lord Mayor of Cork] and we all become very Simpatico'.[20] It had been easier to capture international interest and imagination when fighting British imperialism than when fighting internally. For his part, FitzGerald noted that his department was coming in for some stick: 'many people failing to see that it serves any useful purpose'.[21] For all his lofty ambitions about it being the vehicle through which post civil-war Ireland could assume its place among the independent nations of the world, and notwithstanding the Free State's admission to the League of Nations in 1923, FitzGerald was well aware diplomatic feet would have to remain firmly on Anglo-Irish ground: 'England is our most important external affair.'[22]

Meanwhile, internally, dealing with the end and legacy of the civil war presented acute challenges and the lines between political and military affairs were still blurred. As far as the chief of staff of the National Army, Eoin O'Duffy, was concerned (although 'strictly speaking this matter should find no place in a military report'), in late

1923 there were two things to be worried about: 'Irregular activity' and 'labour troubles'. He was perturbed that the successes of anti-Treaty Sinn Féin in the general election of August 1923, when it won forty-four seats in the 153-seat Parliament, though only 64 per cent of the electorate voted, suggesting a certain exhaustion or apathy, 'have undoubtedly given a fillip to their military activities'. He was also concerned that 'the idea is being created insidiously in the public mind that there can be no peace until the gaol gates are open'. Republicans' fighting morale may have ebbed, but their political morale was extant, helped, according to O'Duffy (blinded as usual by his own prejudices), by Cumann na mBan, national teachers and post office officials as well as those who had evaded taxes and rates and have 'a selfish interest in promoting a state of lawlessness', while 'extensive unemployment during the winter months must only result in extensive irregularism'.[23] In relation to that election, class cleavages were certainly relevant to voters' preferences: 'the highest percentage of first-preference anti-Treaty votes were concentrated in the poorest, highest-emigration and heavily subsistence-farming regions of the south and west, whereas pro-government support predominated in the comparatively more prosperous east and midlands'.[24]

Ernie O'Malley had to acknowledge later that year, 'our movement is seemingly built on hope and not on faith', and that what was needed was 'the proper pitch of spirituality'.[25] What was really needed, as de Valera saw it, was a sustainable electoral pitch, not out of the question, given Sinn Féin's continuing appeal, which Ernest Blythe, now minister for finance, dismissed as of 'no undue importance ... the foundations are being cut away from Irregularism'. Yet as master of the state purse Blythe maintained current rates of expenditure could not continue, and 'the pruning hook will be diligently applied'.[26] It certainly was; salary cuts for public servants and a cut of 1s. to the 10s. weekly old-age pension were quickly implemented.

This was likely to help Sinn Féin, but as avowed abstainers from Parliament, their strategy was limited. Cumann na nGaedheal, the new name for the pro-Treaty Sinn Féin after April (and who won sixty-three seats in the August election), had watered down an earlier draft of the party's constitution, which focused on child welfare and access to healthcare and education. Trade unionist William O'Brien described its 1923 budget as a 'rich man's budget' and a farmers' party won fifteen seats in the election, suggesting it was not sufficiently satisfying them either.[27] While Liam de Róiste was struggling mentally 'to keep one's soul, to look calmly at the wild tempests of others', he was accurate in recording in his diary in March 1923 that, while there may have been considerable loathing for republicans, 'I do not say that "the people" may not cheer them again.'[28]

PART TWO

AFTERLIFE AND LEGACY

'The grass of 2 cows'

CHAPTER FOURTEEN

POTATOES, WATER AND PENSIONS

On his release from prison in July 1924 Ernie O'Malley received some money from the Irish White Cross to travel to Spain, but still had to request more to keep him abroad: 'could you please let me have £30? ... I still have 8 pieces of lead in me and my funds are rather limited.'[1] Republican emigrants – a 'lost legion', according to writer Frank O'Connor – were plentiful, and given that in the region of 220,000 people left the Free State for the US in the 1920s, and another estimated 185,000 relocated to the British dominions or Great Britain, the civil war disillusioned and impoverished were part of a very broad exodus.[2] For IRA members, permission to leave the country was required; chief of staff Frank Aiken made the absurd assertion in 1924 that 'even if our men have to live on potatoes and water for a year it is their duty to stay' as Ireland was still unfree, though that absolutism was unsustainable and perhaps up to 600 IRA men had left the country by mid 1924.[3] Up to 40 per cent of west Kerry IRA men had emigrated by the late 1930s: at that stage, of 87 IRA veterans from the Brandon Company, 44 were living abroad; for the Ballyduff Company veterans it was 23 out of 53 and for Dingle, 42 out of 168 while of 257 recorded west Kerry Cumann na mBan veterans, 106 were overseas in the 1930s, including 31 out of 65 from Annascaul and 25 out of 36 from Ventry. Nominal rolls of Cumann na mBan members collected in the 1930s included the names of 2,182 women who had emigrated, representing almost 13 per cent of the total registered membership in 1921.[4] Some travellers, like Ernie O'Malley, returned, while Aiken stayed and adopted the political route, prompting expulsion from the IRA. In 1928 he bought a dairy farm in South Dublin; he was to remain a politician for nearly fifty years.

Thousands of demobilised National Army soldiers faced a bleak vista; the government in December 1923 appealed to business owners to employ them.

The inevitable reduction in the size of a bloated army after the civil war's end created a whole new layer of impoverished men. Archbishop Byrne of Dublin was made aware, through the Association of Ex-Officers and Men, National Army, in 1925:

> The circumstances of many of our members are so pitiable, some practically in a state of destitution, that between 80 and 100 of them find a night's shelter in the Phoenix and other public parks of our city and again many of them find no other means of sustenance for their wives and families but to resort to the Dublin Union ... our funds are almost exhausted ... these men on giving their services to the state in its hour of need, find on returning to civil life there is no work for them, with the result that thousands are in a state of semi-starvation.

The Archbishop donated £25.[5]

In the aftermath of the civil war female republican soul mates also became scattered and isolated. Some were forced to emigrate while others, like Charlotte Despard, found themselves in Northern Ireland championing new versions of the old causes, denounced by the establishment; she died, bankrupt, in 1939. The vitality of Constance Markievicz 'had snapped', while Alice Milligan found herself living as a mental 'internee', feeling at home 'nowhere'; she died in someone else's cottage in poverty in 1953. All her life Milligan had aligned herself 'with the remnant who stayed outside'.[6]

Patronage and access to jobs undoubtedly 'became political weapons'. The scale of the persecution is difficult to quantify, but blacklisting was an ugly reality. In the civil service, discrimination against anti-Treatyites arising out of the civil war was 'more piecemeal than systematic and certainly fell short of a wholesale purge', but it has been suggested there were over 700 cases of alleged political victimisation from 1922 to 1932. Local government employees, road workers and contractors were also impacted, though some discrimination went in the other direction.[7]

For most victims of the civil war, material compensation came dropping slowly and meanly, if at all. In April 1923 the Free State established a Compensation (Personal Injuries) Committee to assess injuries sustained by non combatants 'in the course of the belligerence' (a separate entity considered damage to property), which ultimately considered 6,616 applications and paid out £269,000, or £15 million in today's terms. Overall, government expenditure fell from just under £29 million in 1923/4 to £18.9 million in 1927/8. In 1923/4 30 per cent of national expenditure was devoted to defence, while as late as 1927, compensation absorbed 6 per cent of the total outlay.[8] Another initiative was the introduction of compensation and pensions for those bereaved or injured during the war, or who had lost breadwinners as a result of their relatives' military roles, and for those who had rendered significant 'active' military service in the decade 1913–23, which was facilitated by a succession of army pensions acts and military service pensions acts from the 1920s to 1980.

The process began with a decision of the Oireachtas in June 1923 to recognise and compensate wounded participants and deceased participants' dependents under the first Army Pension Act. This was followed by the Military Service Pensions Acts of 1924 (which excluded those who had fought on the anti-Treaty side in the civil war and female volunteers in Cumann na mBan) and 1934 (which rectified these exclusions). The various acts that followed in subsequent decades sought to expand, amend, clarify and define many issues to do with the pensions process, including crucial questions of what constituted 'active service' between 1916 and 1923, time limits for application, means below a prescribed sum and special rates of allowances for widows, parents and dependent siblings of deceased persons.[9] The administrative infrastructure necessary to implement the acts involved, over the decades, boards of assessors, referees and various overseeing committees (consisting of those from both sides of the civil war divide) and the service pensions that were awarded depended on rank and length of service and were graded A (maximum) to E (minimum). Cumann na mBan applicants were restricted to the two lowest grades, D and E, as they were deemed to have acted only as 'auxiliaries' to the IRA. By 1943, over 70 per cent of the pensions were paid at the lowest grade. Veterans could also apply for military service medals.

The Board of Assessors provided for under the 1924 Act was replaced under the 1934 Act by a Referee with significant powers, including 'enforcing the attendance of witnesses and examining them on oath ... and for compelling the production of documents', and an Advisory Committee of two former high-ranking members of the forces and two civil servants. To deal with difficulties of verification, the lapse of time since the military events and the expected increase in the volume of applications, former IRA brigades were requested to form brigade committees to assemble records of membership and activities and appoint verifying officers to assist the Referee.[10]

A government memorandum in 1957 revealed that 82,000 people applied for pensions under the 1924 and 1934 acts; of these, 15,700 were successful and 66,300 were rejected. Just over 18,000 pensions had been awarded by 1960, which were costing the exchequer over £500,000 (£11.6 million today) annually.[11] The administration of the pensions process generated a remarkably voluminous and textured archive, and while it indicates a noble effort to alleviate suffering and take into account the consequences of demobilisation, it is also a monument to disappointment and disillusionment.

As a result of the main acts of 1924 and 1934, veterans of the revolution had to provide detailed accounts of their activities to make a case as to why they were deserving of a pension. There was no easy or satisfactory definition of what constituted active service and it remained a contentious issue. Corroboration of claims was supposed to be given by 'persons in a position to know the facts', but there was much complaint of 'demand for proofs which are practically impossible to get'.[12] Few words were treated as gospel: 'I will not fill in any more forms', declared Seán Lyons TD in 1926: 'what is the use of a deputy going to the trouble of filling in forms when his word will not be taken?'[13] Undoubtedly there were some who sought to deceive and exaggerate; the farming father of an executed republican who in 1937 declared himself 'a poor man today' was found to own two farms totalling 160 acres ('better than that of the average farmer') and almost £1,600 in savings in two banks.[14] But such a case was not representative, and the reports of the investigation officers assessing the means of the pension applications provide, overall, a landscape of misfortune and meagreness.

The narratives being pieced together were retrospective, often partial and vulnerable to agendas and faulty memory, and they should not be viewed in isolation or as at all definitive, but the wealth of detail about past services and current conditions is remarkable in its scale. Unlike veterans who gave statements of their War of Independence service to the state-backed Bureau of Military History in the 1940s and 1950s, pension applicants had no idea their applications would someday become public. There is an intense intimacy to many of the files that humanise the conflict and its contested legacy. The process prompted many questions: How were contemporaries and their offspring to make sense of it all? What positions were they left in or removed from? Who were the winners and losers and what does that tell us about politics, status, atmosphere and competing narratives in the post-civil war period?

Former senior IRA officers throughout the country may have had their own axes to grind and they had survived to create narratives when others had not, but the bar of proof was set high, a reminder of the relevance and resonance of the words of William T. Cosgrave, the first head of government in the Free State, in 1924, when he made it clear the government 'does not intend there should be any soft pensions'.[15] This was, and remained, the case. In the 1924 Act there was a reference to 'active service in any rank' in the eligible forces but it was not properly defined. The attorney general at that stage interpreted it as 'actively engaged on military service'. The 1934 Act did not add much greater definition: 'A person shall for the purposes of this Act be deemed to have been serving in the Forces while such person was rendering active service in any of the bodies which constitute the Forces.' It was a woefully inadequate and vague description and, as Marie Coleman has observed, it 'produced many myths about what it translated into in terms of volunteer actions', some believing that 'one major engagement and general service' was the benchmark, which seemed to be rejected by the minister for defence, Oscar Traynor, in 1953 when he suggested it was about the ability to prove 'continuous general Volunteer service'.[16]

Other complications for the pensions' administrators seeking to make the process manageable included resolutions from various Old IRA associations* seeking a 'liberal' interpretation of the term 'active service' and lobbying for free hospital treatment and increase in allowances. There were also complaints of party-political allegiances compromising verification processes and an acknowledgement from Referee Justice Eugene Sheehy, appointed in 1950, that there were cases 'where justice has not been done'.[17]

Whatever about difficulties of verification, an added value is the light the files shine on contemporary living conditions, attitudes to women, civil war politics, struggles for material survival and health and medicine and welfare; indeed, the pensions archive is a remarkable barometer of the physical well-being or otherwise of the civil war generation. If Cosgrave truly believed, as he asserted in 1927, that the kindly care of the poor was the best sign of true civilisation and 'that the condition of a Nation's poor indicated the character of the national mind', then his and subsequent governments in their treatment of impoverished civil war veterans fell badly short.[18]

Many had reason to get emotional because of the scale, not just of civil war animus that endured, but also of the fresh bitterness of post-civil-war betrayal as revealed in the pensions process. This is why it is necessary to move beyond the well-known personalities, interesting though they were, and the tendency to view the civil war through their lens, and their subsequent power bases or profiles, including those who during the civil war had 'stated again and again their contempt for politics and its power to corrupt the men in the field'.[19]

In opposition before 1932, Fianna Fáil, the new party established

---

*The term 'Old IRA' was widely used to describe War of Independence and civil war veterans who were not active in the post-civil war IRA. The Old IRA Men's Association was established in 1934; other representative bodies included the Federation of IRA, Old IRA Benevolent Association and the IRA Old Comrades' Association.

by de Valera in 1926 when he broke ranks with anti-Treaty Sinn Féin, sought to portray a bogus purity about the pensions process. As the party's defence spokesman, Frank Aiken in 1929 referred to members of the Board of Assessors as 'toadies of the government, men who would do anything they're told ... the Board will be influenced by considerations as to whether or not a man would in future give political service to the Cumann na nGaedheal party.' Dublin Fianna Fail TD Seán Lemass labelled Cumann na nGaedheal 'a government of pensioners, by pensioners for pensioners' and Con Ward, Fianna Fáil TD for Monaghan, accused the government of using the pensions process 'for the purposes of political graft' and to win votes.[20] When interviewed in 1967, Lemass recalled that part of Fianna Fáil's pre-election policy in 1932 was 'the abolition of military service pensions ... there was an enormous double crown poster with the list of all the pensioners and the amount they were getting published under the heading "What Price Glory" which was a very personal attack on the individuals concerned.'[21]

He did not elaborate on his party's quick volte-face on this issue by extending the pension to its own supporters after winning power in 1932, which Fianna Fáil backbenchers enthusiastically supported.[22] Lemass himself was awarded a pension for almost ten years' service, though during his sworn evidence he was taciturn and not for elaboration.[23] His award was for rank D (at a rate of £10 per year of service), amounting to £99.16s.5d. p.a., and like others he was often confused about the net amount payable when payment was activated in 1948 after he briefly left office, it being a requirement for those in receipt of public monies above a certain level to abate their pension.[24] By 1967/8, in retirement, the annual amount payable to him was £278 (about £5,000 today).[25]

That both Cumann na nGaedheal and Fianna Fáil embraced the pensions process prompted Fianna Fáil senator Séamus Robinson, who fought with the Tipperary IRA, to suggest the new act in 1934 would 'help us to forget the hatchet that we all believed has been buried for some time'.[26] For some time? Just eleven years after the end of the civil war? It was a reminder of the existence of a rhetoric that suggested healing had happened remarkably quickly, or else it was wishful thinking of just plain political pragmatism. Robinson had been one of the most ferocious speakers in the Dáil against the Treaty in 1922 and was in the Four Courts at the outset of the civil war. He was later appointed to the Military Service Pension Board and the Bureau of Military History in 1948, where he sat with civil war foes.[27]

The 1932 pensions poster was long remembered, especially by members of Fine Gael, the successor party to Cumann na nGaedheal established in 1933 by senior pro-Treaty figures. In April 1944, as minister for defence, Frank Aiken moved in the Dáil that a sum of £558,228 be voted to defray the cost of army pensions at a time when the pensions code for the army now consisted of fourteen different acts: 'This figure clearly shows that the State has made and is making generous provision for all those who have rendered military service.'[28]

Fine Gael's Seán Mac Eoin, the National Army GOC in western Ireland during the civil war, responded:

> The Fianna Fáil Party – and I charge them publicly with it and I want to have it on the records of the House – put out their posters saying: 'Here is the roll of honour.' They gave a list of every one of us in receipt of military service pensions … I accepted that designation that Fianna Fáil applied to us; it was a roll of honour because it contained the names of men who served this country faithfully and well in its hour of need but, in publishing that, Fianna Fáil appealed to the cupidity of every poor unfortunate devil in the country who had not got a living.[29]

Very lengthy exchanges ensued which underlined both the cross-party interest in the process and also the litany of disappointments, inconsistencies and still highly personalised exchanges it gave rise to, but also, in the use of the words 'cupidity', and 'every unfortunate poor devil', the blanket dismissal of those who were genuinely aggrieved and impoverished on both sides.

The 1932 election poster in question had been responded to by Cumann na nGaedheal under the title 'Roll of Dishonour' containing the accusation that if de Valera and his allies had 'refrained from making war upon the government, Dáil and people in 1922 … the question of military pensions would never have arisen'. More interestingly, it published an extensive list on the same poster of claims of compensation lodged within the courts in each county as a result of civil war damage, including The Gresham Hotel, O'Connell Street, Dublin: £102,905; *The Freeman's Journal*, Townsend Street, Dublin: £49,390 and Mitchelstown Castle, Cork: £46,475.

Some of the figures relating to compensation for property damage were certainly eye watering compared to those offered to individual civil war victims, and indeed, there was a glaring gulf between the lionising of 'heroes' and some of the humiliations they were subjected to. Class and material divisions meant that the rows of the 1930s were not just about raking over the hates of 1922 but also contemporary economic ideological debate. Fianna Fáil continued with its mantra that Cumann na nGaedheal represented government 'by the rich for the rich'.[30] Cumann na nGaedheal was adamant that '[Our] policy has been, and will be, to hold the scales even between all interests, to assist each without injury to the others', but Fianna Fáil was demonstrably able to illustrate this was not the case; when Cumann na nGaedheal accused it in 1932 of being the party of the gunmen and the communists, they failed to land the punch.[31] The previous year, even the conservative *Irish Times* was moved to decry that '4,830 tenement houses shelter 25,320 families in the heart of Dublin. It is almost a miracle that communism has not flourished aggressively in that hideous soil. What an irony it would be if the Free State having throttled sedition is killed by the cost of houses!'[32]

CHAPTER FIFTEEN

THE PRICE OF A LOST LIFE

Away from fiery civil war fuelled parliamentary exchanges, loss of loved ones was a personal cross being borne by the civil war bereaved, and their pension applications illuminated a broad social and economic canvas. John Tiernan in Cloone, Leitrim, whose son Thomas, a private in the National Army, was killed near Ballyhaunis in September 1922 ('the boy did not grudge giving his life for the dear old land nor neither would I if younger') was, in 1924, aged seventy, 'and looks it', with nine children, twelve acres of 'very bad land' and four cows. He was awarded a gratuity (a once-off payment, not a pension) of £80 (about £5,000 today) for his loss. The 'humble servant' Tiernan painted a bleak economic picture at a time when the crop and hay had failed: 'as you understand this is one of the worst years for small farmers come this long time and big taxes and high cost of living and to finish all the L[ocal]G[overnment] cut my old age pension to 1/= ... save me from the Sheriff.'[1]

Others settled comfortably into old and new grooves. Paddy O'Daly, so deeply embedded in the horrors of Kerry in the spring of 1923 as GOC of the National Army there, fared well after resigning his army commission in 1924 to return to his building contract business. At one point he was overseer for the Office of Public Works with accommodation in the Phoenix Park, ironically the former residence of the governor general, the Crown's representative in Ireland. By the 1950s his portrait adorned the walls of the Hugh Lane art gallery and he died at home in 1957. He was awarded fourteen years' military service for pension purposes in 1925 amounting to £280 per annum (about £17,000 today), and by July 1928 was earning £120 per year plus bonus of £198 and 'free residence', meaning a 20 per cent abatement of the pension.[2]

The elderly father of a victim of the March 1923 Cahirciveen outrage, however, when IRA prisoners were murdered by a mine explosion having been first shot in the legs at the time of O'Daly's commandership, was struggling. His son, twenty-year-old Daniel Shea, had been a labourer earning 15s. a week through casual work on neighbouring farms to help support the family of eight, but his father was refused compensation from the Personal Injuries Committee in 1925 and had to wait until 1933 to get a partial dependent's gratuity of £133 (about £9,500 today). As to the details of Daniel's killing: 'there is no need for me to relate here what would be for me a painful story. Dan was twenty-one years of age. He was lost to me when he had grown to manhood.' On official forms, he 'died by violence while a prisoner'.[3]

After his death, £12 had been raised from local subscription and the Irish White Cross gave £50. He was from 'a small farm of poor wet land, poor-law evaluation [a nineteenth-century creation to determine liability to pay rates] of £12'. By 1933, for the father, mother and four siblings who remained on the farm there was 'no income other than from [the] farm, which is the grass of about 8 cows'. The conclusion of local public officials who investigated the family circumstances was that there had been a partial dependency on Daniel.[4] The gratuity was used to pay off debt and provide a dowry for the deceased's sister.[5]

The victims of similar massacres also fared poorly. The depth of the abjectness that arose from the Knocknagoshel and Ballyseedy atrocities in 1923 is sobering to read, incorporating poverty, illness and anger at the paltry material value placed on the lives of the dead, though their families still often managed to remain dignified in their outrage. Margaret, the mother of Laurence O'Connor, killed at Knocknagoshel after only eight weeks in the National Army, was initially given 7s. a week from army funds and then a £100 gratuity under the Army Pensions Act of 1923. Laurence had been the eldest of nine children; he had earned 15s. a week and his father, John, a labourer suffering from sciatica, had no regular employment. Neighbours had managed to raise £11 in charity in 1924, but two of the children were stricken with fever and hospitalised. Margaret was initially offered £30: 'I refused to believe that you would estimate the life of a young Irishman as of less value than an Irish terrier for which I have seen larger compensation awarded.'[6]

After reconsideration the amount was increased to £100, but Margaret remained incensed; had he lived, she pointed out, he would have contributed £20 to £25 annually to the household. The £100 was the maximum amount permissible, however, and by 1927 his father John was £76 in debt and had 'no means to pay unless I go to jail'.[7] Margaret continued her appeals for more money, in vain, into the next decade, as a self-described 'poor and broken hearted mother'.[8]

Annie O'Shea, widowed mother of George O'Shea, a victim of the Ballyseedy explosion, who was a road worker for Kerry County Council and contributed £2 a week to the household, received a partial dependent's gratuity of £112 in 1935. At the time of George's death she was fifty-seven ('small farmer, 19 acres, 5 cows etc.'). George's sister Ellen was aged seven when he was killed, and was in 1959 'in a bad way', in a dilapidated house in Tralee and recovering from TB, having spent six months in a sanatorium. She was eventually awarded a special allowance in the 1950s of £208 monthly and she died in 1990 due to 'weight loss, self-neglect and personality disorder'.[9]

Michael Dunne, killed at Knocknagoshel, was a Dubliner and a fitter for a tramway company earning £3 a week and had a sister working in a chocolate factory earning £1 weekly; his asthmatic mother complained in 1924 that an army allowance of £1.10s. a week was 'scarcely sufficient to keep us in the necessities of life'. But this was actually an overpayment; the maximum payable to her under the 1923 Act according to her circumstances was £1 a week, and the excess had to be repaid even though the Army Finance Office had 'no wish to adopt measures which may appear harsh'. The mother was surely hoping beyond hope in feeling 'obliged to submit a claim for say, £3,000'.[10] She died in December 1924 and her daughter was refused a dependent's allowance.

Even more distressing was the shadow cast by the death of Edward Stapleton at Knocknagoshel; from Lower Gloucester Street in Dublin, he was a foreman at Eason's bookseller in the city. His mother, Julia, sixty-six, in poor health and having lost two other children to illness, wrote to local TD Alfie Byrne in November 1923: 'He was my only support ... he is now eight months killed and not one has come near me to see or know how I am living ... I had to rear him without a father from [when] he was three years old ... I am utterly worn out hoping every day that you would have some news for me.'[11] She was trying to survive on her daughter-in-law Mary's allowance and living with her and her two infant grandsons. In May 1924 Julia got a weekly allowance of £1 while Mary was awarded £90 per annum with a yearly allowance of £24 for each child until they reached eighteen. There was yet further tragedy in 1926 when Edward and Mary's youngest son died aged five. The Army Finance Office made sure to recoup the overpayment of £1.17s.5d. that had been made for the month after the child's death.[12]

Patrick Hartnett, killed at Ballyseedy, was an agricultural labourer from Listowel earning 15s. a week; the homestead consisted of '10 statute acres – bogland – 2 cows'. Patrick's brother John died in June 1923: 'this boy was practically an invalid and died as a result of being taken out of bed by Free State troops in that year'. His mother died in early 1924 'as a result of an injury to her knee sustained by her on a journey from Tralee after the death of her son', in March 1923. His father died in 1932: 'he suffered a complete breakdown after the death of his son and died practically of a broken heart'.[13] His sister was granted a partial dependent's gratuity in 1937 (£112, the maximum allowable). Her doctor deemed her totally dependent on her deceased brother owing to 'severe anaemia ... unable to earn her own living'.[14]

What to do with the remains and possessions of the civil war dead was another fraught question. Who, for example, had stolen Erskine Childers's gold watch, silver cigarette case, pipe and cuff links after his execution in November 1922? Sometimes it was the small cruelties that were most striking, when not money was lacking, but basic decency: 'it is quite obvious that the missing property is in the hands of various officers', concluded the army's adjutant general in March 1924 after 'every conceivable channel has been possibly explored'.[15] His widow Molly had been informed in November 1922 that 'the request of the delivery of the remains of your late husband cannot be acceded to'; but in reacting to the 'loss' of his possessions she carried a quiet and admirable dignity in July 1923: 'I have been deprived of other possessions of a special and sacred value to me and ... anxious not to add anything to the prevailing bitterness, I have not made their loss known'. The cigarette case had been engraved with her initials, while the gold cuff links 'had belonged to my father'.[16]

There were bodies that needed to be returned too. A government memorandum in June 1924 referred to the remains of seventy-five executed republicans, all coffined except for three. W. T. Cosgrave was 'disposed to hand over the remains to the relatives', but Eoin O'Duffy, by then GOC of the National Army, was opposed because such a move would facilitate 'the occasion for a demonstration ... at a time when the necessity for the executions has to a certain extent faded from the minds of the people'.[17] Recoffining was needed as the originals 'in many cases left much to be desired'. Government TD for Cavan, Patrick Baxter, appealed in a personal letter to Cosgrave for him to hand over the bodies to relatives; not to do so would 'do far more to add fuel to the flickering embers of hate' than a display over a burial ceremony, though Cosgrave would hardly have agreed with Baxter's assertion that the dead men 'could not by any stretch of the imagination be styled criminal'.[18] Galway TD George Nicholls was of a similar mind: the handing over would be 'a graceful act' and local authority resolutions added to the pressure.

Cosgrave wanted to move on this but minister for justice Kevin O'Higgins did not, fearful of military displays at a time when the IRA, on paper at least, still had a membership of about 15,000 and much militancy: 'The government can scarcely be expected to tacitly accept the idea of two armies in the country ... if military funerals and volleys over graves were to be permitted how long would it be before we should have an Irregular army marching with arms and in military formation through the country?'[19] There was recognition, however, that this would remain a festering sore and it was agreed there would be a handover on 28 October, but no firing parties would be permitted at burials.[20] Ultimately, eighty-one bodies were returned. Anne Dolan points out that for the families 'the discourtesies shown ... the year and a half that kept these bodies from them, the secrecies and the prohibitions, were at least alleviated by the promise of republican pomp and circumstance.'[21]

The promise was not to materialise in the way some republicans desired. Another Galway TD, Pádraig Ó Máille, had predicted in a letter to Cosgrave that if remains were returned 'there may be some demonstrations, but such demonstrations will not have much effect'.[22] He was correct. The director of army intelligence observed that at Athlone Barracks, 300 people gathered for the handover, and he complained of their drunkenness and disorderly behaviour as 'anything but a mark of respect to the dead', but 'nobody of note was present at the demonstration'.[23] The atmosphere at Glasnevin, however, was more charged and shots were fired at burials. As troops moved in 'a number of women present began to taunt the troops and struck at them with their umbrellas', while at St Patrick's cemetery in Dundalk there were revolvers, a grenade, shots fired and one Garda 'had his teeth knocked out', but it proved difficult to effect arrests.[24]

These disturbances resulted in the death of one man, Joseph Hughes: 'Immediately the shots had been discharged by the firing party the military rushed from all sides of the cemetery with fixed bayonets. The civilians [republicans] fired again and the military replied with fire from different points of the cemetery ... soon, nearly everyone was stretched in the wet grass, many hiding themselves behind tombstones.'[25] These scenes could have been even more explosive; it was difficult for republicans to make as much of the burials as they might have wished, due to both financial constraints and the sapping of morale as well as the need to remain at large if on the run and Church censure (Dr Michael Fogarty, the Bishop of Killaloe, forbade the use of Ennis Cathedral to five affected families), while some families wanted these occasions to remain private.

Glasnevin was also the location for a 'mean and dreary' plot for remembrance of National Army soldiers who died in 1922–3.[26] They were being referred to almost a century later as 'the forgotten fallen', perhaps up to 800 of them killed in action or as a result of accidental shootings, drownings and natural causes, the treatment of their memory derisory.[27] In 1923 the father of Edward Sheehy, a National Army soldier shot dead in Listowel in 1922, wrote to the Free State authorities looking for a headstone for his grave: 'His body lies in a nameless grave ... nothing to show how he died or what he died for ... twenty-two years of age and six foot two in height and an athlete of the first order ... it is not surprising that his mother's health should have suffered ... I am liable to lose her also.'[28]

While the 'conspiracy of silence' that was a part of the civil war legacy 'did not imply forgetting' and there were numerous memorials, 'ironically the winners of the civil war evinced far more ambivalence about the politics of remembrance'.[29] Memorials were clearly problematic from the outset: in 1925 the desecration of the grave in Castleisland of Patrick O'Connor, blown up at Knocknagoshel, was reported and regarded as a 'ghoulish outrage'. The inscription on the headstone, arranged by Patrick's brother, a priest, had been defaced with a chisel, the headstone displaced and wreaths ripped apart. The following year his father, whose targeting by the IRA through kidnapping and theft when looking for his son ('they came, they said, to look for his son. Not finding the latter, they proceeded to rob and plunder'), had been the subject of a compensation inquiry in 1923, was awarded £71 for malicious injury to Patrick's grave.[30] Was the gravestone simply deemed too ostentatious, at eleven feet six inches high 'of Durrow stone and Celtic cross design'? Judge Edward McElligott said he would not 'express my own view of this horrible outrage because it would do no good'.[31]

A life-size memorial statue of Seán Hales, the TD shot dead in 1922 and whose family had been divided by the civil war, was unveiled in Bandon in Cork in January 1930. While Michael Collins's brother Seán attended and spoke, the absences were more notable: 'letters of apology for non-attendance were received from, among others, President Cosgrave and all the Free State ministers'.[32] Since the first fundraising appeal for the monument, it had taken four years to pay for it. Were some civil war deaths still seen as 'a failure that no monument could be allowed to concede'? It seemed that 1930 was just too soon for the civil war victors 'to stand shoulder to shoulder with Seán's staunchly republican siblings'.[33]

CHAPTER SIXTEEN

INSULTING THE DEAD

Writers, politicians and former combatants fashioned contemporary and retrospective perspectives on the civil war. Seán O'Faoláin, the minor IRA solider who became a major literary talent from the 1930s, and a thorn in the side of revolutionaries turned conservative governors, chose at age seventy-six to define the post-civil war climate as a cold shower raining on warm revolutionary unity. The revolution was 'one of the most ecstatic periods of my life, during which all moral problems vanished in the fire of patriotism ... during those heavenly years I dreamed of liberty, equality, fraternity.' That was replaced by the 'end of the romantic dream', moral decay and 'a new, native, acquisitive middle-class intent only on cashing in on the change of governments'. The problem with nationalism was that 'sooner or later it ossifies the mind'; a romantic Ireland was replaced by a 'hard-headed and calculating Ireland'. The civil war, he maintained, 'woke us up from the mesmerism of the romantic dream. It set us asking questions ... about the pre-sanctified dogmas of our history. We were blessed by a series of writers who have had the courage to face experience and record it.'[1]

This characterisation was evocative and poetic but underestimated the fault lines within the republican movement prior to the civil war and his own prejudices as a young man. His daughter Julia remembered her parents cherished the idea of a 'national bond' that mirrored their own love, 'but bonds can chafe or fray and back in 1922 theirs did both'. They certainly did not elaborate on their civil war except for snippets ('your mother used to be fearless' Seán told his daughter). Nonetheless, their shared disappointment 'contributed to the glue which held them together'.[2]

It did not, however, stop his extramarital philandering and O'Faoláin was also apt to be as dismissive of republican women as some of the conservatives he derided: indeed, he was positively vituperative: 'the women I met were particularly disturbing – driven by that unfeminine animus which seems always to make the male constituent in women behave like the worse side of the feminine element in men. They were theatrical, self-dramatising, power-hungry, temperamental but with few warm emotions, ruthless, abstract in discussion and full of terrifying sentimentality.'[3] Neither could Seán Lemass cope with those women who were among the 'queer sort of cranks who were certainly confusing the public mood as to what Sinn Féin stood for'.[4]

As for writers who had the courage to face experience and record it, playwright Seán O'Casey was certainly one of them, recording events 'with that air of detachment and disillusionment which the historian aims at'.[5] O'Casey wrote his civil war play *Juno and the Paycock* (1924) while his mind was preoccupied with 'recent raids by the Free State army with scores to settle'; such brutality 'demoralises a country', he wrote at the time to Joseph Holloway, a champion of the Abbey theatre.[6] Not all those scores to settle were civil war related but audiences were jolted by 'O'Casey's removal of any barrier between reality and illusion'.[7]

Nor was O'Casey dismissive of women. The revolution had not been social or economic, an old social regime lingered, and O'Casey sought to depict, through the common sense of Juno, what that meant in 1922: 'when we got the makin of our own laws I thought we'd never stop to look behind us but instead of that we never stopped to look before us'.[8] O'Casey's sympathetic portrayal of strong women facing adversity, defying convention and creating discomfort for the products of a male social and political culture is particularly striking in *Juno and the Paycock*. Juno wondered: 'What can God do agen the stupidity of men?' The news of Mary's out-of-wedlock pregnancy is met by the declaration that such a discovery is worse than contracting tuberculosis, and Mary refers to her 'poor little child that will have no father', to which Juno responds witheringly: 'It'll have what's far better – it'll have 2 mothers.'[9]

Some chose fiction or pseudonyms to vent their crushing analyses; the mid 1920s produced a glut of narratives 'expressing disappointment with the revolution'. Frank O'Connor characterised his involvement as a sort of 'safety valve' for his own emotions as both he and the nation engaged in 'an elaborate process of improvisation' for an education 'I could not afford'.[10] P. S. O'Hegarty lamented the absence of 'reason and principle and morality', in favour of the 'mob', in his bilious book *The Victory of Sinn Féin* (1924), part of the European intellectual tradition of grappling with the definition of nationalism, but also the crises of post-First World War, post-revolutionary disputed boundaries and pessimism. Civil war militarism had become a 'fetish' and if the War of Independence was won, he concluded, it 'was won mainly by the civilians'.[11]

George Russell (AE) was also caustic about the militarists squandering 'a spirit created by poets'.[12] The moral basis for the revolution had been solid but he wished during the civil war for readers to 'imagine men opposed to each other listening with courtesy to the opinions of their political opponents'; the conflict blackened his conclusions as it was a 'moral ulcer'.[13] Desmond Ryan, author of *Remembering Sion* (1934) and who had supported the Treaty, was 'utterly repelled' by the civil war and by 1952 wanted, in a letter to Molly Childers, to represent the past 'in a new ecumenical light' to dilute the bitterness of the war. Childers was furious, and why wouldn't she have been? Ryan had earlier chosen to remove himself from the malignancy by going to London, where he was fragile; he did not want to speak of civil war but could not empty his mind of Ireland. Instead he looked back and eulogised the pre-civil war figures, 1916 martyrs Patrick Pearse and James Connolly.[14] But Ryan, as pointed out by Frances Flanagan, 'in his concern to leave aside the civil war and instead document the experiences of mental illness, mistakes, alienation and fluidity of revolutionary positions, divisions in the movement and the thesis that perhaps, the revolution had not been worth it, arguably articulated aspects of modern historiography more comprehensively than any other.'[15] The value of the Military Pensions Archive is that it also renders those same themes, not through fiction, but in the documented experiences of both soldiers and civilians.

When, from the vantage point of the 1950s, O'Casey looked back on the civil war he suggested 'civil war should be waged only for a deep and a great cause ... we should be careful of personal idealism; good as it may be and well meaning, its flame in a few hearts may not give new life and new hope to the many, but dwindle into ghastly and futile funeral pyres.'[16] O'Faoláin also came to a realisation of the glaring absence of civilians from the war's memorialisation in his revised biography of de Valera in 1939 to replace his first attempt, a hagiography in 1933: 'no monument will ever be erected to them, or ever is erected to the non-combatants in time of war, but they earned it hard.'[17]

In the absence of monuments, a decent monetary amount might have helped. Many of those who applied for pensions were far removed from the cultural elite who penned their versions of the civil war and its legacy; indeed, some were illiterate, signing 'X's as others filled their forms or wrote their letters. But most crafted their own words in letters that were elegant and dignified, if also at times suffused with desperation and disbelief that their losses and their physical, not moral ulcers, seemed to count for so little.

The rarefied prison world of Ernie O'Malley with his loyal servants of the Republic inside and outside the jail and his demands for grapes and literature met while he derided those weaker than he, was also divorced from what others impacted by the civil war were experiencing. Peter McCartney, the Leitrim-born solider shot dead during the capture of O'Malley at Ailesbury Road in November 1922, was the eldest of nine children aged from ten to twenty-three at the time of his death, born on a farm comprising thirty acres of poor land: 'with the exception of one daughter who is in America, they all work on the holding. Their earnings are nil except the girl in America, who sends about £1 per month.'[18]

Peter reportedly gave £1 of the £2.10s. a week he earned from painting before army enlistment to his father, Patrick, but not a portion of his army wages, though this could have been because of 'the numerous raids on post offices at that period and especially in that district'. The harsh conclusion was that his father was 'not totally dependent' on his son, only 'partially dependent'.[19] In 1924 Patrick was awarded a £40 gratuity for his son's death; as a 'poor man' he pleaded in 1925, 1926 and 1927 for more:

> I have six in family, no employment ... my appeals to yours for more compensation for the death of my son seems to be in vain so I apail once more if yous can do a little more. 5 pounds or less I would be satisfied. A government would not miss that trifle. I am a staunch supporter of your government ... his mother lost the sight in one eye from grief and trouble ... people having plenty of money seldom think of the poor ... my son left his employment for the freedom of the state.[20]

While political loyalties were cemented for many by the events of 1922, that brought no improvement for Patrick. As an eighty-six-year-old in 1955 he was still corresponding with the pension authorities to be told the £40 from 1923 'was in full and final settlement of your claim'. At that stage he was living with two of his sons, one of them, Thomas, aged twelve when his brother died, was an invalid ('nervous debility'), though not officially diagnosed, and three of the siblings were in the US.[21] Ernie O'Malley, carrying mental and physical scars, was awarded an annual service pension of £258 in October 1934 and an annual disability pension of £120.[22] That gave him considerable freedom and opportunity to indulge his creative spirit, and he excelled at it.

There was constant astonishment at the value that was placed on a dead National Army soldier's life, in contrast to the top brass who lived and in some cases flourished, or the fate of anti-Treaty republicans left to rot while their colleagues forged rewarding careers. Michael Kilroy, for example, a coachbuilder and hard man of the West Mayo Brigade who lived until 1962, was captured in an incident that killed five National Army soldiers at Newport in November 1922. He was badly injured and subsequently went on hunger strike. Elected a Sinn Féin TD in August 1923 while still in jail, he was a Fianna Fáil TD from 1927 to 1937, chairman of Mayo County Council until 1945 and awarded nine years' military service for pension purposes in 1934, amounting to £225 annually. In 1956 he informed the Department of Defence, 'I am leaving for a holiday in the USA for a period of some months. Would you please hold my pension over until I return.'[23] Clearly the man described in 1921 as 'puritanical and ascetic' had mellowed.[24] His pension application was just a neat but partial listing exercise: 'fights at Tubbercurry, Ballina, Glenlossera, Glenamoy, Newport, Islandeady, Castlebar, Clifden and others too numerous to mention'.[25]

What was just one place name in Kilroy's pension application – Newport – represented enduring pain and poverty for others. In Westport, Thomas Ruddy, the labouring father of Joseph Ruddy ('I am an old man over 70 years ... I am only a casual labourer working wherever and whenever I can'), one of the Newport dead, was granted a partial dependent's gratuity of just £50. He wrote an impassioned twelve-page letter in 1925 rejecting this amount as 'grossly inadequate ... an insult to the dead and an injustice to me'. Thomas had been imprisoned for eighteen months after the 1916 Rising and insisted the unmarried Joseph had been his and his wife's sole support: 'I have 3 children living all of whom are married and having enough to do to support themselves and their families ... won't it be a great day for the Irregulars round here (and there are many) when Captain Ruddy's father and mother has to go to the Workhouse to end their days'. His son, he insisted, 'made West Mayo Free State territory and kept it such ... I fear no man and I neither accept charity or unearned recompense from anyone. I only wish my case to be dealt with justly.'[26] His wish was not granted.

Also killed that day was eighteen-year-old Austin Woods from Westport, who had worked as a casual labourer and whose aunt, Sarah Wood, a forty-four-year-old domestic servant, was also granted a partial dependent's gratuity of £50:

> This boy contributed his wages to me to support his 2 sisters and 2 brothers. The sisters work daily in a paper bag factory and earn about 8/– a week each ... their mother is an inmate for some years in the Castlebar Asylum and the father left here to work in England seven years ago and never sends anything. I am employed daily myself and my sister who is in charge of the house is partially disabled since her childhood.[27]

As if that was not enough, the Garda report into the circumstances of the family noted that the siblings who were still in school 'have no prospects of employment'.[28]

Patrick McEllin, another of the Newport fallen, had worked with the Congested Districts Board; his mother's partial dependency gratuity was increased from £60 to £100 on appeal: as she had two other sons she was not deemed wholly dependent on the deceased but 'she has only 3 acres of mountainous land', observed a National Army intelligence officer. When writing, aged sixty, to the minister for finance, Ernest Blythe, in 1925, she referred to 'the small patch of land I hold to try and eke out an existence for myself and another delicate boy ... I beg of you ... I haven't a penny. My son volunteered to save the state.'[29] She was only at the start of her begging journey; the letters continued to flow from the mountain, but to no avail. In February 1928 she declared she was on 'the brink of starvation ... It breaks my heart when I see my son's grave growing weeds ... God will put more in your way if the widow's prayer is heard.' Her final letter was sent in 1941, when she was seventy-four, still looking for 'a few shillings to help. It's hard on me to put this application before you. I am hard hit.'[30]

Killed in the same engagement was Patrick Murphy, a baker from Galway; his mother was another who looked in vain for more than her £40 partial dependent's gratuity: 'is this the price of a Free State Soldier who has died for his country ... his poor old mother go to the County Home?' His two sisters were in England, his mother serving the state as a servant at Loughrea Garda Barracks.[31] Another fatality that day in Newport was Westport tailor Michael Joseph Walsh. There were nine children in the Walsh family in 1924, of whom four were in America.[32] His sister was seventeen at the time of Michael's death and ended her days in Castlebar's mental hospital 'suffering from manic-depressive psychosis ... slowly sinking into a sate of secondary dementia ... a non-paying, non-voluntary patient'.[33]

Thomas Rawl was a victim of the Glenamoy fighting in September 1922; he was a labourer with Leitrim County Council and his father received a partial dependent's gratuity of £30: 'I hope this is not all you are going to give me for my great loss ... he died for you'. He lived on twenty-four acres of poor land but had another son a rate collector who earned £95 a year, half of which went to the household.[34] More than thirty years later the deceased's brother Michael was still looking for justice, meeting Seán Mac Eoin, who by now was minister for defence and under whose command Thomas had served. Michael told him 'he fought for you and died for you'. Michael still found it within himself to wish Mac Eoin well politically but his request was rejected. His brother James, aged fifty-one, a schoolboy when his brother was killed, who lived with Michael, was a permanent invalid ('a thin, cadaverous subject and mentally he appears subnormal, somewhat of a simpleton'). They farmed thirty acres with '3 cows, 1 donkey, 7 fowl, 2 calves'. Eventually, in 1964 a pension of £166 p.a. was granted to James on the grounds that he was a permanently invalided relative, a resolution Mac Eoin had pushed for.[35]

Cork republican veterans also had many crosses to bear, including the family of Denis O'Neill, the man reputed to have killed Michael Collins. In 1953 Cork Fianna Fáil TD Seán MacCarthy maintained 'there was not a better family or one which suffered more'.[36] What constituted a superior family in relation to 1922–3 was, of course, subjective and coloured by political affiliation. Suffering, too, was relative, but it is amply documented in relation to the O'Neills.

There were five O'Neill brothers active on the republican side during the civil war. For decades between them they faced death (Michael was killed in April 1922), disability, life on the run, emigration and drink abuse. Denis, a native of Timoleague in Cork, had originally served with the RIC and the Royal Irish Regiment in France and was awarded a British pension as a result of disability caused by a gunshot wound to an arm, before joining the IRA, where he was involved in intelligence work in Dublin. By June 1922 he had returned to west Cork to take charge of a cavalry column.[37]

In the aftermath of the civil war he was living in Nenagh, County Tipperary, having married Mary Rohan, who owned a boarding house there and was described in an intelligence report as having 'advanced political views with a considerable amount of money, at whose house prominent Irregulars have from time to time been put up'. The suggestion was that 'O'Neill seems to be living on his wife's money'; furthermore, that he was 'a very unscrupulous individual. A most aggressive enemy of the present government.'[38] Some sense of the nature of post-civil war life on the run is also provided by intelligence reports; in September 1924 he had made 'a flying visit to the mountains' and avoided staying longer than one night in a house: he was also regarded as 'a first class shot and a strict disciplinarian'.[39] Denis was angered by the Grade D pension of £52 p.a. for 5¼ years' military service he was granted (he was also in receipt of an RIC pension of £101.8s. p.a.):[40] 'I am entitled to greater service and to a higher grade ... I am now the only officer who held the rank of O/C 3rd S/Division during the civil war,' and he insisted equivalent officers had 'been graded variously A, B + C'.[41]

Having applied for his pension in 1934, he was not awarded it until 1939 and, frustrated, he made an empty threat in July 1937: 'If there is any further delay I must consider the advisability of withdrawing my application.'[42] The slowness was to do with establishing the veracity of his claims about intelligence work during the War of Independence, the details of his RIC pension, the delay in getting evidence from Liam Deasy and the uncertainty of some of his peers as to whether he was a significant figure ('To be candid I don't remember him at all').[43]

The Béal na Blá ambush that killed Michael Collins was played down significantly in his own evidence: 'we accidentally ran into the Ballinablath thing'.[44] Despite his unhappiness, O'Neill accepted his award; his RIC pension was adjusted under the 1934 Act, leaving him with a final annual pension of £135.13s.6d. Active in Fianna Fáil politics in Tipperary, he died of coronary thrombosis/cardiac failure in June 1950 at the age of sixty-two.

His brother Daniel had also served in the RIC and was awarded a pension for five years' military service Grade E in 1953, at £37 p.a. He too had been on the run until December 1923, and was in receipt of an RIC pension of £128 p.a. but did not co-operate in completing the paperwork and choices necessary in relation to which pension option to choose; it would have been financially more favourable for him to forgo his military service pension rather than his RIC one.[45] Daniel referred in his evidence to 'a terrible financial loss' due to the civil war and claimed his RIC pension had been halted by the minister for finance in the 1920s 'on the grounds of my Irregular proclivities'.[46]

Another brother, Jeremiah, awarded a Grade E pension in 1938 for just over three years military service at £15.9s.5d. p.a., applied unsuccessfully for a disability pension; by 1937 at the age of fifty, he was disabled by rheumatism. His disability claim was rejected despite medical claims that seemed to partially vindicate his assertion that 'I am disabled for life owing to my activities in the IRA'. He claimed he contracted pleurisy but some doctors maintained he did not have that; nonetheless one doctor's testimony in 1941 was that he had been treated for pleurisy and rheumatism in 1923: 'This was, I believe due to his time out with the "boys". He is now a cripple with 2 sticks.'[47]

Yet he lived a lot longer, dying aged seventy-three, than his brother John, who had served with the IRA's 3rd Cork Brigade, though there was some confusion over the extent of his responsibilities and leadership of a column resisting Free State troops in West Cork in the summer of 1922. In 1942, the list of the current positions of John's fellow 1922 column members made for stark reading:

'Dead'
'Dead'
'Dead'
'USA'
'USA'
'USA'
'USA'
'Dead.'[48]

He was awarded a Grade D military pension for almost eight years' service (£79.11s.8d. p.a.) after an appeal and eventually a disability pension of £150 p.a. He was still engaged in correspondence over an appeal the year before his death at the age of just forty-nine. In 1935 he reminded fellow civil war veteran Tom Hales, elected a Fianna Fáil TD for West Cork in 1933, that

> From 1916 on I was never able to sleep one night in my own home until 1923 ... what vexes me most Tom is you know some of the men that have got their pensions were up against us in '16 ...

you understand all about my health and you know I cannot rob the state of too much (I hope I will).[49]

When he gave evidence to the Advisory Committee John noted that he had been arrested just before the 'dump arms' order; he was part of the 'last batch released from Tintown no. 2 … I was 18 or 20 days on hunger strike.'[50]

Ten years after the end of the civil war and only seven years after his marriage, now a father of three children, John was suffering 'breathlessness on exertion, weakness, spitting of blood and inability to do work of any kind' and had 'severe heart disease'.[51] But he still had to engage in tortuous correspondence with the minister for defence: 'I am a complete wreck, living with 3 children in 10 acres of ground and If I do a hands turn of work I get terrible vomiting of blood … I ask you in the name of honour, in fair play and as far as charity sake.'[52] Fourteen months after a medical examination that had established 100 per cent disability a decision had still not been reached and he wondered 'How in God's name can I pay my doctor?'[53] Some of the delay was attributable to divided evidence from medics, a reminder that there was no unanimity of opinion as to whether diseases such as rheumatic fever or cardiac weakness had been contracted as a result of active service or were pre-existing conditions exacerbated by active service; these distinctions mattered hugely. A further complication was elaborated on by Dr Dorothy Price, who had offered medical assistance to Cork IRA men in the early 1920s: 'it was impossible to keep notes of these cases at the time as my papers were constantly being read during raids'.[54] John O'Neill died of 'chronic endocarditis, cirrhosis of liver. Disease attributable to service in IRA' at the age of forty-nine. When his widow applied for a gratuity the Pensions Board desired to know what had caused his cirrhosis.[55]

CHAPTER SEVENTEEN

BROKEN LIVES

Some on the republican side received assistance from a sympathetic network in Irish-America. Michael Leahy, in the 1st Cork Brigade of the IRA during the civil war, contracted TB during the conflict and travelled to the USA where he worked collecting funds for the IRA and speaking at Clan na Gael (originally the Irish-American equivalent of the Irish Republican Brotherhood) meetings. While in San Pedro, California in 1935 he was awarded a military service pension of £175 p.a. and in his application noted of his departure from Ireland: 'December 1922, left for USA to collect funds. I think I am still on duty'; active service 'was and still is USA ... I had to go west of Denver otherwise I thought I had about six months to live.'[1] His doctor in Long Beach, who had treated him since 1923, 'at which time he was ill indeed', noted in 1935, 'he is at present feeling pretty well. My advice to him is to stay in a mild and fairly dry climate the rest of his life.'[2] He certainly did not take that advice, returning a few months later to damp Cork, where he was employed with the Office of Public Works; he lived until 1973.

Leahy's experience was also interesting because he was one of a number of infirm veterans who travelled to the US for medical treatment. The Los Angeles chapter of the American Association for Recognition of the Irish Republic 'offered unconditional aid to individual IRA members sent to the US for rehabilitation', including in sanatoria, and after 1926 the IRA and Clan na Gael worked together; at the Clan's convention in 1928 there was a reference to 'raising funds for disabled IRA men' and it managed to secure assistance from republican sympathisers with connections to medicine. But sanatorium care was expensive and the great economic depression complicated matters; at least with the military pensions opened to that group after the change of political guard in 1932 there were new options for some, including Leahy and Michael Newell, the IRA veteran from Galway who in 1932 returned from the US, where he had spent years recuperating in TB wards.[3]

The experiences and memories of many of those who left for the US have, until recently, been 'a compelling footnote'.[4] As Gavin Wilk has observed, it was often a complicated transition for IRA veterans, due to the harrowing impact and after-effects of hunger strikes, TB and disabilities, and they also experienced employment difficulties. Joe McGarrity, the Clan na Gael leader, referred to 'the sick and broken men from Ireland', and they had a need for what Jeremiah Murphy referred to as 'the security of greener pastures'. As Murphy wrote to his mother, however, the reality could be 'an awful place far beyond my imagination' for those who in one contemporary description were referred to as 'partial refugees', having come to the USA under cover.[5]

For Moss Twomey, IRA chief of staff from 1927 to 1936, the Clan was lacking 'an aggressive outlook', though the boycotting of British shipping lines and mailing campaigns against Free State coercion breathed further life into the organisation and the triumph of Fianna Fáil in 1932 created hope, or, as Joe McGarrity put it then, 'The opportunity of 1921 is present in Ireland.' That was unduly optimistic, and tensions remained between the Clan and the IRA about how to manage the post-civil war dispensation with some Clan members drawn instead to trade union activism.[6]

Some IRA veterans who stayed long-term became considerable players in US politics. John Keating, an internee during the civil war, was resident in Long Island by 1935 and could not prove his civil war service to the satisfaction of the Army Pensions Board (he had claimed 'bi-weekly sniping of Free State outposts at Kanturk', in June 1922 and distribution of arms to active service units). He had moved to New York in 1927 and often engaged in tetchy correspondence about difficulties being put in the way of pension applications being made from the US. There were often problems with the signing of warrants and multiple changes of address and the idea that they would have to return to Ireland to give evidence before the Advisory Committee, he insisted in 1937 'is a grave injustice as most of us are not financially able to make such a trip'.[7]

Keating had shown remarkable drive in the US and worked washing cars and as a clerk, took night classes, trained as a photolithographer, set up his own insurance business and in 1950 was appointed deputy director of commerce for New York City. Subsequently, as a supporter of President Kennedy, he became regional director of the US Post Office Department with responsibility for New York, the 'first native-born Irish person to hold such a senior federal appointment in the twentieth century'. He supported Fianna Fáil and in retirement orated at various republican funerals and commemorations.[8] The considered verdict of historian Patrick Maume is a reminder of triumph against the odds which sat alongside the broken lives never fixed:

> [Keating] represents an emigrant political and social milieu which is often treated dismissively by later, more cosmopolitan Irish commentators, but his career reflects not only his own considerable talents but the ways in which his milieu sustained a generation of immigrants and the contribution of Irish-America to Irish development in the post-war decades.[9]

Michael Flannery, another civil war veteran who endured imprisonment and emigrated with IRA assistance in 1927, did not, however, reconcile himself to the independent Irish state. He established NORAID in 1970 to raise funds for the republican campaign in Ireland and this organisation was much influenced not just by the Troubles in Northern Ireland but also American ethnic politics. In its early years it was mostly made up of Irish-born republicans and some felt initially it was 'just a bunch of Irish civil war vets' before it expanded with second- and third-generation Irish-Americans in the early 1980s.[10] Flannery always regarded the Irish state as illegitimate; he was put on trial in the 1980s for IRA gunrunning and acquitted. In some respects, the older NORAID activists were repeating the civil war charge of betrayal and indifference from the south of Ireland when it came to the republican demand for Irish unity.

Not all the post-civil war emigration was forced. The turmoil of 1922–3 generated an incurable restlessness, an inability to plant roots and a compunction to wander. Many of the emigrants were no doubt haunted and traumatised. George Lennon, born into a middle-class family in Waterford and who was barely out of his teens when he co-founded the west Waterford flying column active service unit of the IRA in the War of Independence (during which he suffered beatings and imprisonment and was on the run), found himself in the evacuated military barracks in Waterford at the start of the civil war. A reluctant presence there, he abandoned both it and the civil war in July 1922 (see Chapter 4), later referring to a complete nervous breakdown at that point. Almost fifty years on, he was back for a holiday in Ireland, still 'searching for lost times'.[11]

His pension file includes over ten changes of address; by 1925 he informed the Pensions Board he was 'unable to get continuous employment ... and my private resources are now exhausted'.[12] Lennon emigrated to New York and returned in the late 1930s to Ireland, where he tried various jobs, including with the Irish Tourist Board, only to leave again. He received both a military service pension of £120 and a disability pension after appeal. He had informed the Department of Defence from Bermuda in 1939 that it was necessary 'to come to this climate to spend the winter months'.[13] By 1945 he told the Department of Finance 'it is essential for me to live in the US for at least some years for health and business reasons'.[14] In 1940 a medical assessor noted he 'has no confidence in himself', and this was traced directly back to the civil war: 'feeling generally nervous and in particular that he does not feel able for responsibility since 1922. He states that he has suffered from several nervous breakdowns in the intervening years and that he has not been employed since 1935.'

An updated medical report in 1944 suggested he was suffering from 'reactive depression (psychasthenia) and pulmonary disease attributable to military service in IRA', and he was estimated to have an 80 per cent disability. He had 'recurrent depression, occasional bouts of insomnia and feeling of constriction and nervousness in upper abdomen'.[15] He could only do work of 'limited responsibility', such as cashier jobs.[16]

What was most interesting about Lennon's application was that it included substantial testimony on post-traumatic stress disorder, absent from many other applications. Ironically, it took the evidence of a former British army captain to impress on the Army Pensions Board the debilitating nature of a condition that was not widely understood at that stage. Dr Herbrand Ingoville wrote in 1943:

> in my opinion, both as a specialist in mental nervous diseases and as a captain in the British regimental army in receipt of disability retired pay and wound service [with 3 years of front line service during the First World War] ... Mr Lennon is suffering from traumatic neurosis ... which appears to have been the direct result of his war service.[17]

Lennon's application is riddled with trauma, though he was eventually to marry aged thirty-nine, start a family and find secure employment in Rochester, New York. Materially, Lennon found security, but the search for inner peace was a lifelong quest, and Lennon lived a very long life, dying aged ninety-one. He flirted briefly with communism, protested against the Vietnam War and finally embraced pacifism and Zen Buddhism in the late 1960s, having also been attracted to the Quakers. Perhaps his comment after the siege of Waterford and its abandonment was a summary of both the wider military dilemma for republicans and of much of his own life: 'we were not at all sure where we were going to next'.[18]

Emigration to America was not just the preserve of the losing side. Tipperary-born John Prout was particularly interesting because in 1919 he resigned his commission in the US Army (a member of the famous 69th Regiment) to return home to join the IRA, and during the civil war was the National Army's commanding officer in Kilkenny. His demobilisation in June 1924 was controversial and criticised by his contemporary champions as 'enforced retirement ... an act of the basest ingratitude'.[19] He received a £250 supplementary grant on demobilisation and then an annual pension of £100.

Prout's case highlighted the difficulties of adjustment to civilian life, the desire for status and the links between the military and politics. From 1925 to 1926 he had a well-paid job (£500 p.a.) as an assistant under-sheriff with the Department of Justice. He helped to establish a Cumann na nGaedheal branch in Fethard in Tipperary in 1927 and at that time he 'instanced the case of the USA which had taken 11 years to settle down after the civil war'.[20] He also rented Moneyguneen House, an early Georgian mansion in Offaly on 150 acres of fine agricultural land, from the Land Commission (some senior National Army figures received the option to rent these large allotments), but by February 1928 he owed rent arrears of over £219 and had left for the US, leaving his penniless family behind: 'I get no money from my husband ... as I am a stranger I find it very hard to get credit', wrote his wife Mary, who was left with their four children: 'Major General Prout is not doing well in America'. A Tipperary grocer was owed nearly £19 and demanding payment from Prout's pension.[21]

Prout eventually granted his wife power of attorney for his pension, but given the various debts she was 'only saved from absolute destitution by the charity of a few of her friends'.[22] The Land Commission repossessed the house and Mary was told she would have to pay £5 monthly to clear the rent arrears: 'this would leave me with £40 yearly to support my husband's mother, myself and five children'. She also stated her husband was alive 'as far as I know', underlining the lack of communication. By September 1930, now living in Kilmallock in Limerick before moving to Dublin, she was 'crazy ... with worry and trouble'.[23] John Prout was not co-operating in relation to the signing of life certificates to ensure payment of the pension and this saga dragged on until the early 1940s; the Department of Defence noted it did 'not even know his address'.[24] Eventually Joseph Brennan, the Irish minister in Washington, tracked Prout down and went to see him personally 'to persuade him to sign an authorisation for the payment of his pension to his wife'.[25] A few years later, in 1947, Mary Prout died at Dublin's Crooksling Sanatorium 'and the present address of her husband is not known'.[26]

Prout, meanwhile, had become quite the US nomad; he was reported in 1929 to have attended a dinner in New York in honour of Seán Mac Eoin, who was on a 'good will' visit to the US. Prout joined a real estate firm and campaigned in 1934 for Joseph McGoldrick, an unsuccessful 'fusion' candidate for the position of Comptroller of New York City. In 1940 Prout wrote to an Irish-American news-paper from Hollywood, where he was 'supervising and staging the production of a great screen picture of the famous "Fighting 69th" regiment in which he was a captain during the world war of 1914–18'. Stars of the picture included Jimmy Cagney, and Prout immodestly declared, 'in my honest opinion this is one of the finest war pictures ever made'.[27] That film, *The Fighting 69th*, came out in 1940.

For his champions, Prout was a gallant hero of the Free State side with 'exemplary character' and an 'engaging personality'.[28] He was also a great survivor; in 1968 he applied, on headed paper from New Hampshire, for arrears of his pension, which had not been paid since December 1944, stating he was entitled to £3,729. He had not applied during that period because 'it did not suit my circumstances'.[29] He died in 1969 at the age of eighty-eight in Vermont. His reputed gallantry, however, did not extend to the treatment of his wife, who was left to pick up the civil war pieces, compromising her own health and life in the process.

CHAPTER EIGHTEEN

THE UNCERTAINTY OF A SOLDIER'S LIFE

The wider consequences of demobilisation led to crisis by 1924, when it appeared the government was struggling to control the National Army, which by the civil war's end included 3,000 officers and 52,000 other ranks and had to be drastically downsized, necessitating the demobilisation of 37,000 members. Less than 9,000 of them secured employment.[1] For those who remained in the army after the conflict there was much tedium. Hugo (Aodh) MacNeill, an officer during the civil war (and nephew of Eoin MacNeill), who was appointed major general in 1924, complained to Michael Rynne in October 1923 that there was

> simply 'nuffin doin' in this little old isle. Everything is dull as ditchwater. The army is gradually ebbing away ... we are all tied up with acts of Parliament, defence force regulations, statutory orders etc. et-bloody-well-cetera ... of course it is all very well to be nicely legalised, get the status of a regular army etc., but there is too much red tape – a Prussianism about it for my taste. It's all heel clickery 'yes sir' and 'no sir' and 'all correct stuff' these days. 'Oh, have we got e'er a chance of a fight' as the song puts it ... no more sweeping the hills for elusive columns. No more tearing through the sleepy streets with a Crosby ... demobilisation is in full swing. God knows where that will leave us. It will mean a queer old scattering of the clans and general smash up of war comradeships. However, such is the glorious uncertainty of a soldier's life I suppose.[2]

But MacNeill, who had reached the rank of colonel during the civil war, had a promising military future, unlike thousands of his comrades. He was awarded a military service pension of £166 p.a. in 1927, payable from 1951 when he retired, along with retired army pay of £650, meaning 60 per cent of the military pension was abated.[3]

As GOC of the army, Eoin O'Duffy's reports to the government in April 1924 in light of the 'recent demobilisation of 1,000 army officers' were full of his customary self-importance, stridency and alarm ('I fear the constant strain is too much for me' he wrote to Cosgrave).[4] The strength of the army by the end of March 1924 was 'only 13,306 ... 510 are in hospital ... 800 are unfit ... officers have no sense of security in their positions'.[5] They also faced a hostile civilian population in areas such as south Leitrim, Ballinasloe and parts of Cork while in the west 'an aggressive attitude is being adopted towards the troops by released internees'. There was also 'leakage of munitions', including demobilised soldiers who took their arms with them and sold them, while 'Communism may hold out attractions for many of the restless type.'[6] The officer body in particular was problematic, being composed of War of Independence pre-Truce (July 1921) IRA members and officers recruited after the start of the civil war, including some ex-officers of the British army, whose promotion had generated resentment. There were officers 'who, if not politicians, may be designated as diplomats. They work in little circles and while their intentions may be good, their actions are unsoldier like and unhelpful.' Their courting and misleading of soldiers of lesser rank was 'indiscipline of the grossest type ... I will not tolerate such conduct.'[7]

In March 1924 two of the officers, Major General Liam Tobin and Colonel Charles Dalton, voices of the Old IRA, gave an ultimatum to the government demanding that it do more to achieve an Irish republic or face mutiny: 'We can no longer be party to the treachery that threatens to destroy the aspirations of a nation.'[8] It was a remarkably audacious move by those in the army who considered themselves keepers of the flame of Michael Collins, regarded ex-British army officers and post-Truce recruits as being given preferential treatment, and maintained that Irish Republican Brotherhood members within the army had undue sway over promotion and retention of army personnel. While the death of Collins 'ended any authority the IRB enjoyed', there were attempts to reorganise it, both within and outside the army.[9] The ultimatum from Tobin and Dalton – removal of the Army Council, suspension of demobilisation, an inquiry and a say in the reorganisation of the army – was quickly depicted as a challenge to the democratic foundations of the state. The minister for defence, Richard Mulcahy, responded: 'two army officers have attempted to involve the army in a challenge to the authority of the government. This is an outrageous departure from the spirit of the army. It will not be tolerated.'[10] That was only part of the story, as Mulcahy had had discussions with the putative mutineers, about fifty strong, leading them to believe his was a sympathetic ear.

In response to this crisis, Kevin O'Higgins asserted that never again would the institutions of the state 'take their stride from a soldier's boot'.[11] It was a good soundbite, but it deflected attention away from his own agenda and determination to sideline Mulcahy.[12] Initially, Tobin and Dalton went on the run as the government held firm. Mulcahy became isolated when he ordered the apprehension of some of the mutineers, as this was regarded as unauthorised by the government and they called for the resignation of the Army Council. Mulcahy resigned in protest at this demand and the army malcontents were treated with kid gloves, being allowed to resign rather than face courts martial, while their demand for an inquiry was acceded to.

Mulcahy had presided over the difficult scheme of demobilisation, and as historian Ronan Fanning saw it his 'selfless and dignified response to his own humiliation averted the prospect of a mutiny, and copper-fastened the primacy of civilian over military authority as well as the democratic legitimacy of the infant state'.[13] But that too is what was claimed of Mulcahy's nemesis in cabinet, Kevin O'Higgins, by his champions.

This was not just about the high politics and drama of the elite characters. What of Mulcahy's approach to those singled out for demobilisation? Those who refused to sign demobilisation papers were refused discharge grants. James Corbett from County Clare, with 4½ years' pre-Truce service, who joined the National Army in March 1922, refused to sign demobilisation papers 'on the grounds that we would not accept the same terms as ex-British and Truce officers, a principle which of course we still adhere to', and referred to his four years' service in the IRA and joining of the National Army before the civil war. As he was absent for so long from home he forfeited his farm inheritance: 'I have now no means of livelihood or nothing whatsoever to fall back on.'[14] Although 'there was nothing specific against him, his services were such that he would not warrant retention'.[15]

Peter Leavy from Roscommon had given seven years' service and refused to accept a demobilisation gratuity on principle as he had done nothing wrong: 'I am just now on the verge of starvation. I have a wife and 5 small children and no hope only the workhouse.'[16] His appeal, like all others, was dismissed as Mulcahy deemed him 'an officer surplus to requirements'. Many cattish comments were appended to these case files, such as the one attached to that of Patrick Gibbons from Newport, who claimed 'I was one of the first to join the Volunteers [which evolved into the IRA] in Mayo in 1913'. The retort was, 'He had a good record before the Irregular campaign began, but he lived and drank on his reputation.'[17]

Patrick Beirne from Castlerea declared, 'I have 8 years of the best of my life spent in the country's causes and have no means of living whatsoever to fall back on'; Mulcahy dismissed him as 'surplus to requirements and below average ability'.[18] Joseph Rooney averred 'my case is typical of that of many officers – old IRA men dismissed summarily, although ... there were no grounds for complaints against me.'[19] Martin Nolan, who had joined the Volunteers in 1914 and the National Army in February 1922, had taken charge of the Four Courts after its surrender in June 1922:

> I know certain men who have been kept on in the army who did not take half the interest or have half the results to their credit that I have ... now I am in the ranks of the unemployed. No work available and no chance of any in the future makes me wonder how I am going to support my wife and child. The nation thanks me for my good work, but that is not enough to keep my family.[20]

Thomas Corcoran had joined the Volunteers in 1917 and served as an engineering officer until joining the National Army: 'I then gave up a civilian position and a salary of £7 a week to join up with the rank of captain.' He served until March 1924, 'when I was demobilised after 2 days notice. I am 28 years old, a teetotaller and have had a fairly decent education.'[21]

The more senior mutiny characters and their opponents had other considerations, mostly reputational but also in relation to promotion. It was decided in April 1924 that it was necessary for an Army Inquiry Committee to 'inquire into the facts and matters which have caused or led up to the indiscipline and mutinous or insubordinate conduct lately manifested in the army'.[22] Those terms were expanded on subsequently, suggesting the mutineers were not the target, as seen by references to whether their actions were due to 'muddling, mismanagement and incompetence in the administration of the army'.

Lawyers were at the ready and retired veterans made their declarations, including James Hogan: 'so long as you have an army with a political mind you can have no state'.[23] Joe McGrath, another government minister involved in overseeing demobilisation from late 1923, had resigned in sympathy with the old-IRA members (as did eight TDs) and was not prepared to give evidence. McGrath had also served as director of intelligence for the National Army during the civil war, having been seconded from government, during which 'he presided over some of the more grisly aspects of the Treatyites' counter-insurgency policy'.[24] Richard Mulcahy was understandably particularly defensive, while the secretary of the Department of Defence claimed his 'knowledge of these matters on which you want information is almost nil'.[25]

The chief of staff, General Seán MacMahon, whose commission had been withdrawn – one of a number of IRB leaders in senior positions in the army and an ally of Mulcahy – felt 'a sting of degradation' at proceedings suggesting he had damaged the army; he was eventually reinstated.[26] Kevin O'Higgins suggested that 'some members of the Executive Council came gradually to the view that the army was breaking up into factions, societies or combinations'. He had privately met an army officer without Mulcahy's knowledge: 'it did not occur to me', he said, to meet the officer in the presence of Mulcahy. The officer spoke to O'Higgins of 'rival combinations tearing the army to pieces and rotting discipline and morale ... a resurrected IRB he said, was under the direct auspices of the HQ staff.'[27]

O'Higgins piously declared that in 1923 he had been 'profoundly dissatisfied with the condition of the army and the working of the army', with conspirators 'sent through the commands harnessing any elements of discontent they could discover and creating suspicion and discontent where previously there was none'. The question of ex-British officers was

> used by the old IRA as a stick to beat the new IRB with ... ex-British officers finding themselves menaced ... there was no lack of 'plugging' threats and in the matter of their future careers were tending to draw together to form still another clique ... within this state organisation for which the people were paying close on eleven million pounds in one financial year.

His informant also told him of 'drink, vice, disease and waste on the ascendant'.[28]

That was a frequent complaint: the Catholic Bishops were keen to ensure the 'creation of a good Catholic tradition' in the army, which had been severely compromised during the civil war.[29] By June 1923 there were eleven army chaplains; the head chaplain, Fr Dominick Ryan, took up duty in January 1923 and a year later reported to the Bishops that 'on the whole the religious standard is good', but that there was a post-war 'listlessness in military discipline' brought on by uncertainty of tenure and pending demobilisation,

> which exhibits itself in want of religious consistency. A careless atmosphere has created a spirit of discontent which the habit drink has converted into restlessness. This is the root of the prevailing immorality ... your Lordships should mark there is a number of demobilised soldiers who have been treated but are not cured from venereal disease and they will be a menace to the purity of your flocks.[30]

Considerable attention had been given to this; a VD map of Ireland illustrated that in April 1923, 124 cases were admitted to hospital, which was 'alarming'; there was a need for 'moral prophylaxis', but that 'by itself is insufficient ... in the British army their rate is decreasing; in our army it is increasing and that with fearful rapidity'.[31] Debauchery and fornication were encouraged by soldiers as 'a prevalent saying in the army is that a soldier is not "blooded" until he has contracted VD'. Lectures on self-restraint and chastity were needed but for those guiding them 'the question of prophylaxis is intentionally omitted. It is a dangerous one to discuss in such audiences.' Avoidance of drink, immoral talk and books, plenty of exercise and wet dreams ('they form nature's relief') provided the hoped-for solution.[32]

O'Higgins's close friend Paddy Hogan, the minister for agriculture (both were critics of Mulcahy), told Judge James Meredith, chairman of the army inquiry, 'there existed in the army not only the mutiny of the officers for whom Maj Gen Tobin and Col Dalton spoke but another mutiny ... a secret society [the IRB] had been revived within the army by the army council', though he conceded, 'the evidence which I have is largely circumstantial'.[33] Meredith did not want second-hand testimony or 'mere hearsay' but evidence 'as would be admissible in a court of law', although for the measurement of the extent of influences 'we may be justified in considering hearsay evidence ... none of the evidence on which we shall have to act is strict legal evidence'.[34] His instructions were hardly a model of clarity.

Another minister, Desmond FitzGerald, told Meredith his dissatisfaction with the army was a 'moral certainty' due to various civilian statements from around the country, but 'I had nothing that could be called evidence'.[35] Evidence was heard that until December 1922 there were no guidelines as to discipline in the army issued by the minister for defence: 'up to that time, we were proceeding under a state of war with no regulations'. Those officers who sought to probe into problems were 'generally choked off', and 'some of the best officers on the Inspection Staff were demobilised' according to Cahir Davitt, the first judge advocate general in the National Army, who produced *The General Regulations as to Discipline* at the end of 1922. The director of army intelligence from October 1923, Michael Joe Costello, who had been intelligence officer in the National Army during the civil war, said of those with responsibility for who was joining the army 'our duties were never fully defined'.[36]

As Colonel Charles Russell saw it, Tobin and his followers had been told by Collins, 'you will be alright and I do not think they ever doubted it, but they were just a little impatient. Here they were now without anybody who knew what they had done, and they were just a little blue'. GOCs were powerful men who 'lived in castles all over the country, each with his little army ... poor Tobin and Company could not get a look in with them.'[37]

Mulcahy's own tone when giving his statement to the inquiry was imperious, born of his anger at 'national humiliation'. He acknowledged that in 1923 he should have done more to forbid membership of secret societies to army members, but he took aim at those who set themselves up as 'people's ministers', publicly charging 'the men who have done the heaviest portion of that work with being mutineers'. Known members of the IRB 'were not challenged to sever their connection with it' on enrolment, but he did not believe the IRB should have been scrapped after the Treaty as it was never intended to be a counterbalance to the Old IRA.[38] Ultimately, the IRB was wound up by the end of 1924, on both sides of the Treaty divide.

Meredith annotated Mulcahy's statement: 'easy to lie when M/HA [Minister for home affairs, O'Higgins] disagrees with you', but also: 'IRB+appointments: no influence: no bona fide feeling in army that appointments due to IRB influence ... GOC held the influence'.[39] Mulcahy provided information on a meeting between Tobin, Cosgrave and Mulcahy in June 1923, where it was maintained by Tobin 'that the army was rotten: 40% of it were ex-IRA men, 10% ordinary civilians who were never anything but hostile to the IRA and 50% were ex-British soldiers [a serious exaggeration]'. Furthermore, it was claimed Cumann na nGaedheal was intent on reorganising the IRB with the aim 'of undermining the old republican tradition'.[40] They had a series of demands and Tobin was 'very hard and bitter' whereas Dalton had 'nothing to say'. There was another meeting with Mulcahy in early July 1923 in which Tobin spoke of 'the fulfilling of Mick's hopes', underlining the remarkable grip of Collins's ghost.[41] Meredith wondered 'was anything of this reported to Ex[ecutive] Council?' a question he asked repeatedly. He was also perplexed at Mulcahy's contention that the post-civil war army could unite the country by leading a cultural resurgence, which Meredith thought a 'dangerous idea'.[42] What Mulcahy was most sore about was the 'interference and encouragement of certain politicians' when it came to the malcontents.

The committee held thirty-nine meetings and heard from twenty-seven witnesses and agreed its report on 7 June 1924. It found that the mutiny had been engineered by Collins loyalists resentful of the demobilisation process; it was critical of the army for allowing the IRB to be reorganised but did not accept membership of it influenced appointments. It asserted the Army Council had not been guilty of 'muddling, mismanagement and incompetence'. Meredith signed the report 'subject to a reservation relative to which he stated he would send an addendum' to Cosgrave.[43]

That was quite an understatement. His report, which remained unpublished, did not extend the exoneration to Mulcahy and was much longer than the committee's report; he had his own sympathies, and they were emphatically not with Mulcahy. As far as he was concerned

> there is always an element of danger in the post of Minister for Defence being held by a person who is not a civilian or is only technically a civilian and General Mulcahy was actually commander in chief as well as Minister for Defence down to August 1923. In this dual capacity he was more in and with the army than in and with the cabinet.[44]

He thought the official report was 'silent on several points which I consider of vital importance'. He concluded Mulcahy had failed to deal with the problem of the Old IRA officers 'in a direct and straightforward way' and 'gave the impression he would go behind the back of the cabinet and join hands and assist the organisation in getting control of the army for a particular purpose' and therefore was not guiltless of mismanagement.

Mulcahy asserted he had dealt with the Collins loyalists 'at arm's length' and referred to 'childishness, insincerity and want of proper bona fides' on the part of these officers and claimed that, but for the interference of Joe McGrath, he could have dealt satisfactorily with the situation. This contention, maintained Meredith, was 'unproved and ungenerous ... well intentioned peace makers do not generally fare well in this country and Deputy McGrath seems only to have suffered the usual fate of those who try to throw oil on troubled waters'. Mulcahy was tactless and stubborn in wanting to deal with the problem his own way: 'there was nothing to prevent Mulcahy making the constitutional position of an officer in the army perfectly plain ... it was the notion that it was the mission of the gunmen to keep the country straight that led to the Irregular Campaign.'[45]

This seemed an endorsement of the idea that this was unfinished business from the civil war; that the mutiny episode represented that war's 'final echo' and the last vestiges of a mentality based on the idea of 'an independent political army'. But Meredith felt that 'the demobilisation of upwards of 30,000 men has been carried out without any reprehensible incidents ... as a military affair, the importance of the mutiny was much exaggerated ... taken as a whole the army is in a sound and healthy condition. The main repercussion was felt outside the army and in the political world'.[46] This would suggest Meredith was aware that some of the claims made in 1924 about the affair were outlandish, but what constituted reprehensible was subjective; it was understatement and avoidance of a difficult question to suggest, for example, 'the ordinary officer rightly or wrongly [feels] in a great many cases that sufficient care was not taken to assess each man's unique value before recommendations for demobilisation were accepted'.[47]

What was needed, Meredith concluded, was a minister for defence who was a civilian. That was what the government engineered with the appointment of Dundalk TD Peter Hughes in November 1924. That led to criticism that he was unequipped for the post but, of course, that was precisely the point; he had no military experience or baggage and in tandem with some of the military seniors being replaced it could be argued that this smoothing worked to contribute to the peaceful transfer of power in 1932 between Cumann na nGaedheal and Fianna Fáil.

With the departure of Mulcahy and McGrath, those who remained in core government roles 'were lawyers and UCD professors rather than old soldiers', men who personified what Mulcahy later called 'a Ballsbridge complex', Ballsbridge being an opulent suburb of Dublin.[48] Mulcahy was angry that O'Higgins, Hogan and FitzGerald 'had a superior feeling', in relation to the army men.[49] So straitened were his circumstances after his resignation that Mulcahy had to borrow £100 from Cosgrave.[50] Mulcahy felt that O'Higgins interfered far too much with the army and in reality did not know 'anything' about it; that his fellow ministers did not support his efforts in 'finding jobs for those who were discharged', in public works and housing, road building and forestry, although he acknowledged he could have pushed this more with his government colleagues and admitted to his son 'I fell down in not forcing them to realise that better.'[51] But it was interesting that Mulcahy felt he had never 'attempted to enter into detailed dissection of the O'Higgins mind'.[52]

Mulcahy, however, lived to resurrect himself politically, at least partially. As a man so closely identified with the draconian measures of 1922 he would have been deemed a likely target for republicans, but instead that was to be the fate of O'Higgins in August 1927 when shot dead on his way to Mass. Such was the nature of the survival lottery of that era that it was 'extraordinary', mused Mulcahy's son, that Mulcahy was able to 'walk the streets of Dublin and visit the four corners of Ireland from 1924–7 without guard or weapon'. He lived until 1971. O'Higgins, however, was as much targeted, Mulcahy recognised, not necessarily because of what he did 'but by his disposition that perhaps made him more vulnerable'.[53]

It was Eoin MacNeill who, by chance, came across the shooting and cradled the dying O'Higgins. MacNeill's subsequent evidence at the coroner's inquest helped to fashion the legacy of O'Higgins as the hard man of the pro-treaty 1920s government with the forgiving heart, reported under the headline 'Professor MacNeill's evidence of dying Minister's fortitude'. MacNeill told the inquiry 'when I stooped over him I thought he was on the point of death and I repeated close beside him some of the customary prayers. He then began to speak to me and the first thing he said was "I forgive my murderers."'

The veracity of that cannot be proven, but MacNeill, even as he held the dying O'Higgins, was still, in a sense, on the outside; it was minister for agriculture Patrick Hogan who then arrived to take charge of the papers O'Higgins had in his possession.[54] MacNeill had lost his Dáil seat a few weeks previously whereas O'Higgins was not only vice-president of the Executive Council but also minister for justice and minister for external affairs. MacNeill kept private his grief about the death of his IRA son Brian during the civil war, however; his refusal to publicly reflect or elaborate on it was one way of externalising the trauma of the war, but it was also the case that he had robustly supported the provisional government's policy of executions in 1922. Brian's coffin had been borne by his brothers from the opposite side of the civil war in Free State uniforms, the same brothers he had fought with in the Dublin IRA during the War of Independence, the same brothers he had wished well in correspondence five weeks before he died, but Eoin did not come to terms with the manner in which Brian was killed; nor did he visit the site of his death.[55] It was to remain a family, not a public tragedy.

For Mulcahy, his civil war past remained politically toxic and as leader of Fine Gael in 1948 he was not acceptable as a Taoiseach to replace his foe de Valera given that Seán MacBride, the leader of Clann na Poblachta, one of the putative coalition partners, was a former chief of staff of the IRA. Mulcahy graciously stood aside, having motorbiked around the country to revive his party's fortunes; it is hard to dispute the assertion 'he was not motivated by personal ambition'.[56] But perhaps he was also relieved that he was not taking on leadership of a disparate coalition: 'ending the Fianna Fáil hegemony was his only concern, and his goal had been achieved'.[57]

Some of those who had threatened army mutiny in 1924 were carrying their own personal traumas, while others rose above them. Liam Tobin resigned from his commission in March 1924.[58] From October that year he was awarded a pension based on fourteen years' military service, amounting to £280.[59] He was able to write positively to the minister for defence in 1926 on headed paper from his new business, Gresham Motor Hire Service ('only first class cars with uniformed drivers supplied') and in 1933 contacted the Army Pensions Board requesting payment of his pension to his wife as he was 'proceeding to the United States. I may remain there for 6 months or longer.' By then Tobin had joined the Irish Hospitals Trust established by Joe McGrath to raise hospital funds through a sweepstake, representing it in the USA. He remained in that job until 1939. He gave his address as c/o Seán Nunan, secretary to Leo McCauley, the Free State's consul in New York.[60] Nunan, who had served as secretary to de Valera in 1922 and opposed the Treaty, had been dismissed on political grounds in 1922 and was reinstated ten years later.

While Joe McGrath experienced financial difficulties after his resignation at the time of the army crisis in 1924, he struck gold with the sweepstakes and was paid an enormous salary. It was commonly asserted that the organisers made more money than was raised for charity and because of its charitable status the endeavour eluded proper investigation. Fifteen hundred people acted as agents for the sweepstakes in the US from 1934–40, and it ensured a steady flow of money into the country – not enough of which went to Irish health services – and was plagued by scandal, skulduggery, forgeries and gangsterism as the founding families amassed millions.[61] That Tobin was able to use an Irish diplomat's address highlights the networks and government connections that were used and the blind eyes that were turned. Tobin went on to be appointed superintendent of the Oireachtas (Parliament) in 1940 starting on a salary of £643, rising to £943 by 1947.[62]

Others central to the army mutiny coped less well. Tortured by the violence of the revolutionary era, Charles Dalton endured serious mental health problems and PTSD (leading to his wife's later assertion that 'I have 4 small children and am completely without income') and was eventually awarded a disability pension in 1941 of £200 p.a. 'in respect of delusional insanity'. He suffered from 'impressions and hallucinations' that 'referred back to those early years ... a constant state of fear – afraid of being shot at and that he is wanted by the authorities for various crimes etc.'. He was eventually discharged from court wardship, did his best to provide for his family (working for the Irish Hospitals Sweepstakes in a consultative capacity) and lived until 1974.[63]

His brother Emmet, in whose lap Michael Collins had died, and who was also a veteran of the Somme, became clerk of the Senate ('a pretty dull place'), where he lasted only three years, then fell on hard times and worked as a salesman. He also drank heavily and turned up drunk in 1932 at the Postmaster's Office demanding Department of Defence pension correspondence; the previous year solicitors on behalf of his wife, who was considering separation, feared that 'unless compelled to do so, he will make no effort to support them'.[64] Subsequently, he gave up alcohol for good, spent time working as a private detective and then moved to England to gamble on horses. This restlessness is hardly surprising given what he had experienced in combat, but he went on to become a force in the evolution of Irish filmmaking.[65] His own life was cinematic too.

Chapter Nineteen

IDEAL SPECIMENS OF WOMANHOOD

Post-civil war emigration was far from a male-only phenomenon. Ellen Carroll, active with Cumann na mBan in Cork during the civil war through intelligence and dispatch work which compromised her health due to regular soakings, was diagnosed with TB in 1924 and spent three months in a sanatorium. She was, by the end of the war, 'a complete wreck ... of her activities during that period a book could be written.'[1] She was turned down for a disability pension and eventually after appeal received a paltry Grade E service pension in 1943. She had told the Advisory Committee in 1938 'my nerves are very bad ... I am suffering from disability.'[2]

Working in a sorting office in Shepherd's Bush as London endured the Blitz, her letters to Nora Martin, under whose direction she had served in Cumann na mBan, depicted her mental demise:

> From hour to hour you are only waiting for death, it is just hell on earth. I must say I am very unlucky and think I am stuck over here for this, but I may thank the Irish government for that. I could be home now if they granted me that service pension. I suppose all the well off people of Cork got it ... I don't care what happens to me now.[3]

Another dilemma was that she could not take time off work to go to Dublin to be medically examined: 'If I take time off I will have to forfeit my job ... it would be very hard for me to get a job as I am 45 ... I have suffered hunger and want so you cannot blame me for sticking to my job.'[4] Carroll lived short term in various locations (six changes of address are included on her pension file), dying in Fulham in 1975, though she perhaps always retained the desire to return to Cork, informing the Pensions Board in 1965: 'I don't draw pension here; it goes back to the bank in Cork for my old age.'[5]

Carroll had a formidable champion in Nora Martin, who in 1942 highlighted the barriers that female applicants and Cumann na mBan veterans were facing in their dealings with the Pensions Board:

> From the very fact of being members of that militant organisation they were the butt of the jeers and insults of a large section of the community. They risked their jobs, their homes and their lives ... this bunch of women whose claims, written by themselves, appear so unpretentious ... in justice to them, one woman at least should be on that advisory board ... lawyers and civil servants, no matter how sympathetic, can never visualise the feelings of these women during the period 1920 to 1924.[6]

The overseer club, however, remained resolutely male.

Many of the pension sagas relating to women illuminate the veracity of Martin's assertions and the wider question of the cultural and social environment that was hostile to them. The civil war and attendant change in political discourse had emphatically underlined that, for the women, 'the political ground shifted under their feet'.[7] Consider, for example, the assertion of the *Irish Statesman* newspaper in January 1927: 'The activities of our wild women who were so much more extreme than any of our male intransigents in the preaching of militarism and violence ... excited disgust and a general dislike of political activities by women which has not yet subsided by any means.'[8] Sheila Humphreys was one of the civil war prisoners released after a thirty-one-day hunger strike, feeling no elation or appreciation: 'we were flattened. We felt the Irish public had forgotten us. The tinted trappings of our fight were hanging like rags about us.'[9]

Mary Commins, who had lasted thirty days on hunger strike, said her husband had been 'simply smashed through paying doctors ... to add to our plight we are boycotted because of our political views'. They had experienced 'days of plenty' but could not now get credit: her husband eventually abandoned her and their children: 'flew from his debts leaving all on me ... I have all belonged to me beggared.' Her anguished correspondence ran over three decades.[10]

Brigid (Bríd) Breen, wife of the famed Dan, had to battle to upgrade her pension from Grade E to Grade D in 1942; she did not, according to the advisory board, do herself any favours in 1940 when giving her evidence: 'This lady, who has an outstandingly good case, appears to be highly strung and was unable to give her evidence as connectedly as one would wish. This is particularly true of the civil war period.' She did have an advantage, however, in having well-connected verifiers, including junior Fianna Fáil minister Seán Moylan.[11] Her husband also weighed in. Dan was a master practitioner of the outraged missive, usually on behalf of himself, but as a TD in 1941 he took up the cudgels on behalf of his wife, writing to judge Thomas O'Donnell, appointed Referee under the Military Service Pensions Act 1934: 'I consider it an insult and I should expect better from you towards my wife ... I don't like writing or making a case for my wife, but I cannot allow your insult to go by.'[12]

Brigid, whose brother had been killed during the 1916 Rising, was more than capable of writing her own letters: 'I don't mean to appear dogmatic but with the record of myself and my family I feel I should be allowed to express an opinion.'[13] A Dublin IRA veteran writing to the Referee's Office noted curtly that history would do justice to Dan Breen, 'but justice will not be done to Dan Breen's wife' unless her slight was rectified, as it subsequently was after a successful appeal.[14] Brigid had to cope with other personal difficulties, including Dan and his injuries and drinking, and she was temporarily made a ward of court in 1947.[15] In 1953, Dan sidestepped questions as to whether he was separated from Brigid or if the marriage had been lawfully annulled or dissolved: 'Mrs Breen is in a private mental home and it would appear that the deputy is reluctant to make that statement in writing.'[16] In death, on her gravestone, was a pointed statement, lest there be any doubt: 'Brigid Malone Breen, 1897–1984. Member of Cumann na mBan (Active)', but she was more usually referred to after his death as 'Dan Breen's widow'.[17]

Even women with strong references struggled for recognition. Patricia Hoey, a journalist and suffragist who enlisted in the National

Army as assistant military censor under Piaras Béaslaí's staff, became disillusioned in the 1920s; at the front of her pension application lie the words 'Total Service for Pension: Nil.'[18] Her pension struggle underlined that the women, then, and during the civil war, were defined according to the men, Béaslaí writing in 1927 that during the civil war Hoey 'performed exactly the same duties as the male officers ... she was in fact in a position of higher trust and authority than most of them.'[19]

Hoey, who had turned down a permanent civil service position under British rule, which would have involved renouncing Sinn Féin, wrote that she instead 'went out to face starvation'. Now, she was reliant on 'any casual work I can get' and was suffering ill health and 'nerves' ever since imprisonment in Mountjoy during the War of Independence.[20] Despite being able to garner nine references (including one that insisted 'you certainly did a man's job at a very critical time')[21] and questions being asked by Dublin TD Alfie Byrne in the Dáil, her application was refused even though her service cost her a house, her livelihood and friends: 'you have done me a great injustice and I hate to feel that in connection with any government department ... no other woman in Ireland could have done the work because not one woman in a thousand had my knowledge of military matters ... censorship work for the army is military service.'[22] Her appeal was rejected in January 1928, and her final letter to the Pensions Board suggested an exhausted but not full resignation to her fate: 'of course if the opinion of the Board is that a woman was not eligible it is quite understandable. I am satisfied. But I feel at present that my case has been unfairly treated.'[23] She was dead less than three years later, aged forty-seven, from pulmonary TB; her funeral was attended by government minister Richard Mulcahy, a presence at odds with the bureaucratic cruelty she was subjected to by the state he represented.

Contested definitions of active service also went to the heart of other cases involving women. In 1939 John McCoy, formerly commander of the IRA's 4th Northern Division and a member of the Pension Board's Advisory Committee, was insistent that 'it would be unwise to adopt a standard of service for the women less exacting

than what will be applied to the men who are classed as "key men".
On the other hand, it would be most ridiculous to expect women
to have taken part under arms in engagement with enemy forces.'
McCoy stressed the value of women who had carried dispatches,
provided 'houses used for IRA services' and been involved in 'care of
arms and dumps'.[24] These were, it seems, only sometimes taken into
account and many women had to endure a belittling of their efforts.

The consequences for some women who went on hunger strike
during the civil war were devastating for them and their families.
The mother of Johanna Cleary from Ballymore in Dingle, who had
served with Cumann na mBan in Cork city, lodged a claim in 1933
for a gratuity arising from the death of her daughter in 1924, aged just
twenty-six, in an infirmary attached to Cork mental hospital, where
she had worked as a nurse and attendant. She had died from 'exoph-
thalmic goitre [Grave's disease]: exhaustion from excessive vomiting'.
Cleary had been involved in dispatch and intelligence work until her
arrest by the National Army in March 1923 and was interned at Kilmainham and the North Dublin Union. After a fourteen-day hunger
strike she was released in October 1923. She returned to work the
following month but became ill in September 1924. A doctor in the
hospital noted in 1920 she had been 'a young and healthy girl' and
ascribed her subsequent death to 'shock, strain, hardship of imprisonment and hunger strike during the period of civil stress'.[25]

At the time of her death, Johanna had been earning £72 p.a. (total
salary and emoluments £139) when 'the deceased applicant, husband
and 9 dependent children were living on a smallholding, the grass
of 2 cows'. It was greatly inadequate for their support and the family
were 'largely dependent on subscriptions from deceased and from 4
other members in the USA'. It was also revealing that the family's
circumstances now were not deemed to be abject, a reminder of how
relative the definition of impoverishment was in that part of the
country: 'presently, applicant, her husband, 3 sons and daughter live
on holding of poor or fair land. Circumstances: Fair.'[26] What those
circumstances would have been without emigration, however, is clear.

A partial dependent's gratuity of £100 was awarded in 1938, while
in 1953 an annual dependent's allowance of £180 p.a. was sanctioned.

The investigation officer's report in January 1937 noted that the poor-law valuation of the land in 1924 was £4; with the division of land by the Irish Land Commission in 1928 a further fifteen acres were added with six cows kept.

There were twelve surviving offspring, all over twenty-one, and the listing of their positions gives a succinct overview of the destinations and status of a large, small-farm family in the 1930s and the commitment to hard work:

'Mary: married in Dingle. Nell, Paddy and Julia married in USA. Kate nursing in England, Rita nursing in Dublin. Elizabeth, housework in England, Michael and John helping on holding, Owen in National Army. Seán, fisherman (staying at home). Bridget: at home.'[27]

This was also an interesting case as it revealed tensions within government. Seán MacEntee as minister for finance – who lived in comfort in the prosperous south Dublin suburb of Booterstown and was from a family with a penchant for fine dining, gold watch chains and expensive tailoring – told Frank Aiken (also comfortable in south Dublin) that he could not see his way to sanction any increase in the £100 gratuity. A scribbled note decried that 'this is the usual attitude of Finance'; surely, Aiken pleaded, it was evident that the Clearys were living in 'poor financial circumstances', but MacEntee insisted the mother's circumstances 'have improved considerably since the death of her daughter'.[28]

A further note added that 'four children in America who send her a few pounds each at Xmas, but who otherwise gave her no assistance. Deceased was the only one of the children in Ireland employed.'[29] It is difficult to avoid the conclusion that Johanna had been forced, through economic necessity, to return to work when she was seriously ill. Aiken was more explicit the following year in telling MacEntee 'the attitude of your department in dealing with disability cases is beyond understanding'.[30]

Johanna Cleary was not alone in experiencing such distressing final days, her future stolen by the combined harshness of civil war exhaustion, incarceration and starvation. Mary Carey from Cork died in November 1924, aged just twenty-six, from cardiac failure and pulmonary TB, which was deemed to have been due to her almost ten years' service with Cumann na mBan during which she carried arms and dispatches, while the family home and business, a tobacconist and newsagents in Washington Street that had once been profitable and provided a comfortable living, was used as an arms dump and safe house. The premises, described as the 'headquarters of the IRA in Cork city' from August 1922 to March 1923, were constantly raided and eventually had to close. Her mother, Mary Sr, received a partial dependent's gratuity in 1933 of £112 and subsequently a yearly allowance of £33.

Mary Jr had been arrested in February 1923 and was transported from Cork to Dublin by sea and then imprisoned in Kilmainham; she was hospitalised the following month, then released due to ill health. As a hunger striker she had contracted pneumonia, refused to accept conditional release and never recovered. Before 1923 she was described by her doctor as 'a healthy, vigorous, well-nourished girl'.[31] Republican sisterhood did not always extend to the pensions process; Mary MacSwiney refused to provide a reference in this case as she would not communicate with the Free State government. The report on the widowed Mary Carey Sr's circumstances in 1932 described her as 'in a very precarious state ... only the assistance of a friend whose resources are now exhausted has enabled them to survive thus far ... starvation stares them in the face.'[32] There was also an aunt residing in the family home.

Keen to stress the continuity of the family's republican politics and the possibilities for improved circumstances with the change of government, Carey also corresponded with Frank Fahy, who had been a less hardline anti-Treatyite but had topped the poll for Fianna Fáil in Galway in 1932 and was married to Anna Barton from Tralee, a metal artist and former Cumann na mBan member: 'as a friend of my daughter ... you remember that it was in your house that she came to stay when she came out of hospital ... it would be a great victory for our enemies to have us go down under a native government.'[33]

The Pensions Board initially was not satisfied that Mary's death was attributable to service, but additional evidence was provided to the effect that, while at the time of arrest she may have been 'confined to bed with Influenza', she had been 'taken from her home without sufficient time to fully clothe herself and was then driven through the streets of Cork in the cold'; and that was before the sea journey and harsh and cold imprisonment.[34] A local curate, Fr Dan MacCarthy, was also outraged, suggesting that seeking proof that she died from diseases attributable to service 'can only be compared with seeking proof of the cause of death of the late Terence MacSwiney'.[35]

There was no shortage of service and character references in this case, a reminder of the extensive reach of Cumann na mBan during the civil war. James Hickey, now a trade unionist, wrote to Frank Aiken that he had been a lodger in her home and arrested there: what he witnessed was that 'day after day she was raided and subjected to the ignominy of a complete stripping to see that she possessed no treasonable articles ... many men owe their lives to her attention.' Mary had also been exposed to 'many a wetting' as a result of being on duty: 'such was bound to tell on the physically strongest'.[36]

By 1937 her mother was living in a 'slum', in Cork and 'starving' herself to pay 15s. rent a week; she was being taken to court for debts owed and borrowed £15 from a money lender with a 100 per cent interest rate.[37] Those administering the pension, who had insisted that she had only been dependent on her daughter for help in the shop, went to much trouble to establish how many newspapers Carey was now selling in her new, austere premises. By 1940 she was aged sixty-five and wrote to the Department of Defence 'on the verge of starvation ... I fail to understand what the delay is about and what are ye looking for as my case is clear.' She feared she would be 'pitched in the street without a moment's notice'.[38] She was finally granted the annual allowance in March 1940 but died the following year.

Marian Tobin, another Cumann na mBan veteran and described by Dan Breen as 'our most trusted person in Tipperary ... there are few women and not many men who gave more help than Mrs Tobin', came late to the pensions process in 1949 when she was eighty years of age, because she was 'well off' previously: 'I never asked for anything for I didn't need it but now I'm in very poor circumstances ... I think I am more entitled to get something than many that got a pension.'[39] Her considerable abode, Tincurry House in Cahir, situated on ninety-six acres ('she was well provided for and had two farms'), had been burned by the Black and Tans in 1921 and was rebuilt in 1932; in 1928 she had sold some of the meadowlands and in 1942 her daughter put Tincurry up for auction.[40]

Tobin was widely known to IRA Volunteers who travelled south during the civil war. Ernie O'Malley had stayed regularly with her.[41] Tobin's husband, active in the Volunteers, had died in 1918 and she was left with three children and a large farm in Tincurry as well as another house, in Ballinalard.[42] Perhaps it was somewhat cruel that the telegram calling her to an interview about her application and evidence contained an advertisement for the Sweepstakes on its back ('some day you may get a telegram to say that you have won a £50,000 sweep prize') as Tobin was awarded a Grade E pension of £18.19s.2d. p.a. for just under four years' service. She ended up completely dependent on her son-in-law, referring at the end of 1951 to her old-age pension: 'I get £1 per week of which I have to give 10s a week to my son-in-law for my grubb.'[43] She died four years later aged eighty-six and after her death, it was suggested she felt it 'was her duty to carry on her husband's work'.[44] Only some newspapers mentioned that she had been the first female county councillor elected to Tipperary County Council in 1920, one of just forty-three across Ireland.[45]

Ellen Walsh, who had worked as a creamery maid in Kerry, was another Cumann na mBan veteran who fell between the cracks. Arrested in April 1923, she was imprisoned in Tralee and subsequently the North Dublin Union, where she went briefly on hunger strike and was viciously assaulted, sustaining a serious head injury (it being believed she had 'knowledge' of the instigation of the Knocknagoshel tragedy in 1923, which occurred near her home).[46] James O'Connor, who had been an IRA captain in Knocknagoshel, noted in 1938 'there was special animus directed against this family – subjected to persecution and personal abuse and hardships at the hands of Free State troops day and night'.[47]

Walsh's health deteriorated rapidly and she died in 1927. The medical officer who wrote about her as part of her mother Hanna's pension application, was keen to emphasise how a young healthy woman had been destroyed: he had examined her in 1920 and 'I then found her in perfect health, robustically so, with a fine genial disposition, an ideal specimen of womanhood.' But when examined in 1924 another doctor 'found her at that time in a very depressed and worn down condition of health which I attributed to hardship, exposure during the troubled times' (she, too, had often endured soakings when carrying dispatches). Her health by that stage was 'abnormal for an ordinary young girl' and the 'outlook for improvement was very doubtful'.[48]

Even more sadly, Walsh ended up dying in Lexington Avenue in New York, her mother attesting that 'she had to emigrate as she could not do any work' and had been advised to travel to a warmer climate to aid her recuperation. The mother was unable to get a death certificate from the USA, which meant the application for a dependency pension was unsuccessful: 'No death cert. No disease specified.'

The fallout for different families or even individual family members from the same event of the war generally highlighted class cleavages, luck, twists of fate and, repeatedly, trauma in its various guises. Mary Devins, the widow of Séamus Devins, a TD and one of six IRA officers, including Brian MacNeill, son of government minister Eoin, killed in disputed circumstances near Ben Bulben in September 1922 – it was likely they were shot after they surrendered, or at the very least were lured by deception and were killed in cold blood – was a national school teacher who was awarded an allowance in 1932 of £67 p.a. during widowhood and £18 p.a. in respect of their son Patrick. She did her best to educate Patrick privately to ensure he went to college (he later qualified as a solicitor and in the 1950s became county registrar). Mary witnessed the public veneration of her husband – a row of houses in Sligo on the site of a demolished military barracks named 'Benbulben Terrace' in honour of Devins and the five others, a pipers band named after him and an annual trophy for step dancing – but she died in 1936 as a result of 'poisoning by Lysol which she deliberately drank while suffering from mental depression'.[49]

The fiancée of Michael Collins, Kitty Kiernan, bereft and haunted, never really recovered from his death and carried a mix of genetic kidney problems and the distressing weight of 1922. While in 1925 she married a National Army civil war veteran, Felix Cronin, it was far from wedded bliss and Cronin lived with his own demons. In 1983 their son, also Felix, stated simply, 'I don't think she ever got over him [Collins] ... while those are harsh words for a son to say, I think my father accepted that when she married him. I think he always knew he was number two ... we grew up with an idolatry of Collins from both my parents.' Felix also maintained that when Kiernan died in 1945 his father bought the nearest available plot to Collins's grave in Glasnevin.[50]

The pension claim of Mary McNicholl, who had been the senior Cumann na mBan officer in Derry and East Tyrone, was originally rejected before she was awarded a modest Grade D pension for 2½ years' service at £22.10s. per annum. Active in transporting arms and dispatches, she highlighted in 1942, after rejection, a common frustration: 'I find it very hard to understand what you require as service or evidence of service ... I have done everything that a member of the CnB could do except actually fire a gun.'[51] Despite glowing references – McNicholl had been in charge of over a hundred members – she had to battle to be upgraded from the lowest Grade E. She was also requested to compile a complete 'nominal roll' of members, suggesting she was being treated as one of the 'key men', in terms of information gathering, but not akin to a key man in terms of pension.

McNicholl lived an exceptionally long life in Sandymount, dying in Dublin in 1995 at the age of ninety-eight, leaving an estate valued at £204,930.[52] She had outlived her husband Roderick by thirty years. Her gravestone does not mention her republican past, but it is likely that she and her husband had an acute sense of the trauma induced by conflict, as they fostered Liz O'Gorman, an orphan rescued by Irish aid workers as part of Operation Shamrock, an Irish Red Cross initiative to provide temporary homes (it became long term for some of them) and respite for children of war-ravaged Germany.[53]

McNicholl had applied from Dublin for her pension but her quest was compromised, it seemed, by the border, another potent and practical difficulty that had to be faced, as she highlighted in 1943: 'I am trying to get in touch with some of the old members who are still in the six counties to complete my list. As you are no doubt aware, I have to be careful how I go about this as there are at present some girls in jail in the North through their pension claims being caught in the post; several have been fined as well.'[54]

The complication of compiling information from Ulster for pension purposes emerged at various stages and veterans there clearly faced additional burdens; it was estimated in 1936 that 'about 250' of the IRA who were active in Belfast and district in 1922 'are now claiming pensions' and were enduring surveillance and raids and 'hindered in obtaining employment'.[55] Trying to organise their pension applications while keeping the contents private was problematic and they wanted them to be processed nearer to them than Dublin was.[56] They too faced depletion through emigration; twenty-seven of the thirty-six former members of the Meigh Company of the IRA in Armagh were listed as living outside Ireland by 1936.[57] James Gallagher wrote in 1937 of the Derry City battalion: 'I may state bluntly that the feeling amongst the men here generally is that obstacles are being placed in the way of members from this area. Men have been brought before the Board from every area in Ireland except Derry City.'[58]

Nonetheless, Gallagher persisted, while pointing out that those doing this work in Northern Ireland had to be more careful than their southern counterparts: 'the lists as enclosed are nearly as accurate as it is possible to make them in view of the fact that it is almost impossible to keep records here in the North'.[59] This was a point reiterated by one of his contemporaries, Patrick Shiels: 'owing to the activities of the RUC [Royal Ulster Constabulary] many lists, records etc. which had taken great trouble to gather had to be destroyed but the enclosed is a fairly true and authentic record.'[60] In one sense this was just a continuation of how Ulster republicans had felt sidelined by the prioritisation of southern objectives in 1922: 'we were sadly disappointed ... we had started something which we could not hope to carry out successfully alone', and the Antrim Volunteers in the midst of the civil war 'filtered back to be arrested or allowed to resume their ordinary lives under stringent enemy conditions' noted the Brigade Activity Report from Antrim, compiled in the 1930s.[61] Some were 'able to return to their homes later. But the majority were forced to find employment in other parts of Ireland or abroad'. Clearly, the civil war had compounded the sense of abandonment, captured in the stinging assertion 'We never knew if our position was clearly understood in Dublin.'[62] For some, the pensions process only exacerbated that, and for women it was even more difficult.

CHAPTER TWENTY

TWO TEETH

There were numerous families where siblings took opposite sides in the civil war, like Tom Hales and his brother Seán, the TD shot dead by the IRA in Dublin in December 1922 (though the brothers did not publicly criticise each other). Tom resigned from Fianna Fáil in 1936, the same year the government declared the IRA an illegal organisation, due to his opposition to the government's policy on internment, which he described as 'coercion and panicky action, applied in direct antagonism to a great and truthful ideal of the people.'[1] His perspective was undoubtedly honed by his own experiences: arrested in November 1922, he was detained in Cork prison and Hare Park Camp until December 1923. Whatever about political rows, there was little complication when it came to Tom's pension: he was awarded Grade B for nine years of service amounting to £180 p.a., having been O/C of the Bandon Battalion, and lived until 1966, aged seventy-four.[2] After his resignation from Fianna Fáil he contested subsequent elections unsuccessfully first as an independent republican and then with Clann na Poblachta, a new republican party formed in 1946, but ultimately opted out of politics and returned to farming.

Not all the Hales brothers fared so well. Tom and Seán's brother William only received a Grade E pension of £24.18s.7d. p.a. in 1935 for almost five years' service and unsuccessfully appealed for a higher grade. According to Liam Deasy, William 'would be better than Tom – I mean fighting activities', but 'he did not have a whole lot of civil war service'.[3] William was concerned that he be given recognition for his claim that he acted as an intermediary between Seán and IRA officers regarding the possibility of a peace agreement during the civil war ('other things happened in that period, some of which are not in my form'). He found this peace talk 'disagreeable', but he transmitted the messages: 'from that date forward I don't claim a pension'. He ceased being active in September 1922.[4]

William actually refused to draw his pension because he received no recognition for 1916 service. An unmarried farmer, he was still in correspondence with the Department of Defence over his pension in 1969; his case was complicated by Land Commission issues and transfer of property; as far back as 1940 he had been living in a 'large mansion' on forty acres, which 'does not suit me at all and is only fit for a large family'.[5]

By 1961 he felt the need to apply for a special allowance under the Army Pensions Acts and a social welfare report asserted 'there is no doubt applicant has been years in struggling circumstances' on land that was 'half good, half poor', but his yearly means still exceeded the limit set to qualify for an allowance.[6] Another brother, Robert, also a bachelor, was awarded a Grade E pension of £23.12s.3d. p.a. in 1937 for four years' service. Regarding the civil war, it was noted of Robert 'he was away with a rifle. Family feeling was pretty bad; he could not stay at home after Seán was shot. He went off anyway.' When asked if he was able to settle down after the civil war ended, he responded vaguely, 'I was not at home anyway. I was afraid to go home.'[7]

Robert had certainly lost none of his political trenchancy by the late 1930s: when asked if he had applied for a pension in 1924 he responded:

> No. I did not believe in applying for any remuneration under a constitution that was founded on the triumph of a mechanical murdering army inaugurated, dictated and financed by England which gave a preponderance of power and wealth to our Irish opportunists ... who broke their oaths to the Irish republic and found their faith and fidelity in a foreign king.

As to his own military activities: 'my payment for same was to finish up without home, money or family'.[8] By 1948 Robert had severe osteoarthritis and a sorry mouth: 'there are but two teeth, both affected with pyorrhoea'.[9]

In 1949 Robert complained to the Department of Defence that

> I got no fair play at all ... there were plenty men who never shot a
> gun got ... three times that amount ... as far as I could see the way
> the 1934 service pension was administered it would shock every
> sense of honour and every precept of morality in the breast of a
> monkey, much less a man who fought for the independence of
> his country ... the more a man did, the less he got ... I lost a grand
> job in England and was making all the money I wanted and had
> to give it up when I came home on account of rheumatism and
> only for staying with a friend I would be a sorry case ... what
> good is 28 pounds per annum at the present time when a man
> cannot earn his living?[10]

That special allowance of £28 p.a. came after the Army Pensions
Act of 1943, which granted allowances to veterans whose means did
not exceed a prescribed sum or were incapable of self-support. In 1952
the report of the Bandon social welfare division was that Robert,
whose unfitness for work due to rheumatism had already been veri-
fied, was 'in receipt of free board and lodgings' from his cousin in
Bandon 'in return for light assistance', in the farmyard.[11] He had to
spend a fortnight in hospital in 1955 and even then felt betrayed as
there was a payment demand for his treatment: 'the same amount as
if I were a farmer or a man of means ... surely the old IRA men in the
winter of their lives would expect some little prerogative?'[12] He died
in 1959 at the age of seventy-three with 'no will ... nothing to adminis-
ter'. His funeral cost £36.[13] Ten years later, his brother William wrote:
'four brothers RIP, only myself left'.[14]

Liam Deasy had been a good friend of Seán Hales and was distressed by his killing. Some former comrades were loath to forgive
Deasy for what they regarded as his betrayal when appealing to the
IRA to agree to a ceasefire in order to avoid execution in 1922, and
the impact his appeal for peace had on the morale of the anti-treaty
side. He had been court martialled and expelled by the IRA in 1924
for launching the appeal, but he was a key figure in the pensions and
verification process and frequently wrote frankly either on behalf or

to undermine the claims of some Cork veterans. By that stage he was a successful businessman dealing in waterproof textiles; he was also awarded a pension for 8¾ years' service in 1935 to the tune of £218.15s. p.a. While he was interned during the civil war he claimed active service because he was a 'prisoner of war' and 'had to fight authorities to maintain status of prisoners'.[15] He also enlisted in the Irish army in 1940 during the Emergency, after which he returned to business and wrote highly regarded memoirs in retirement, living until 1974.

Pension correspondence also highlighted the gulf between the fate of some of the veterans and their former comrades who had forged successful careers in politics and were seen as having abandoned their roots and empathies behind a bureaucratic wall of resistance or indifference. Some of those who made common cause with the republican martyrs and men of no property in the 1920s found themselves governing sternly and meanly in the 1930s. Laurence Sweeney, from Dundrum in south Dublin, a general hand at a hospital earning £2.5s. a week in 1922, of which he contributed £1.10s. to the household, was part of the South Dublin Brigade of the IRA and was killed in Kildare in July 1922 at the age of twenty-one. His father was aged sixty-five ('Rheumatism. Unemployed for a long time') and his invalided mother died in 1932, while a sister was afflicted with TB. His father's partial dependent's gratuity of £112.10s. was reduced to £100 following objections from minister for finance Seán MacEntee in 1934.[16] MacEntee insisted £112 was too much as the father had two other sons to assist him, even though it was pointed out that those sons were soon due to marry.

Ironically, a Celtic cross had been unveiled in Dundrum in July 1924 to honour the memory of Sweeney and the guest speaker was none other than MacEntee, who in his oration declared, 'Yes, Laurence Sweeney, you were not born to riches; you were not born to power, but you were born to immortality ... poor working boy, born to toil and hardship.'[17] MacEntee, who lived to the age of ninety-four and became one of Fianna Fáil's most prominent and powerful post civil-war politicians, told a journalist in 1974 that it was by then 'impossible for people to appreciate the Ireland of 1922–32', in relation to poverty, housing problems and lack of health services.[18]

Numerous pension applicants were not shy of pointing to what they regarded as the abject failure of the revolutionaries turned governors to honour the applicants' sacrifices, though their capacity to articulate their grievances was invariably affected by class, literacy, health, contacts and the extent of supportive political networks. Tom McEllistrim, a key figure in the IRA in Kerry during the War of Independence and civil war, when he commanded an IRA column, was proactive in pursuing the claims of Kerry veterans. Elected as a Sinn Féin TD in August 1923 at the end of the civil war, he served in the Dáil for forty-six years (he died in 1973) and he concentrated on assiduous and persistent letter writing and lobbying rather than publicly memorialising his own efforts. Unlike others, 'he never wrote a book about his exploits, nor was he prepared to talk about them publicly', and he eschewed parliamentary bombasticism.[19] His son and grandson also followed in his political footsteps in north Kerry.

McEllistrim had been part of the 'long' civil war in Kerry; he fought, he said, until September 1923: 'a few men in Kerry were killed after the "dump arms". At the time of the "dump arms" we put away our guns ... but we had to take them up again for protection.'[20] He was awarded a pension for 8¾ years' service at Grade C but this was increased to cover eleven years' service after an appeal; significantly, his case was reopened 'at minister's request' – a reminder of the advantage politicians held. Although there was concern about the 'very generous award he received on very slender evidence', in relation to some of the periods of conflict, his annual pension was increased from £131.5s. to £174.2s.2d.[21]

Even those well connected were not spared the repetitive strains of bureaucracy. McEllistrim's widow, Mary, complained in 1974 of 'my fourth letter in my endeavour to extract a reply' about a widow's allowance: 'to say I am hurt is to put it mildly and feel ashamed of the department for such gross indifference', despite constant interventions by her son, by then a TD.[22] Her correspondence in the 1970s was a reminder that some of the final battles of the veterans who lived long lives were for telephones. When informed that from July 1978 veterans would be eligible for free telephone connections, but not their widows, Mary was incensed, as she had been more than just a veteran's wife. She held a Cumann na mBan service medal and wrote sternly to the minister for finance, George Colley: 'I feel I am totally entitled ... were it not for the old IRA and Cumann na mBan we would not have the Ireland we have today. They were the builders ... I reside alone in the country – six miles from the nearest town and am eighty-two years of age.'[23] The Department of Defence had to apologise to her.[24]

Serving TDs who were veterans could be some of the most splenetic in their correspondence, none more so than Dan Breen, who suffered financial and employment difficulties after the civil war. As we have seen, the Breen family endured various traumas arising from their experience of conflict and post-war disillusionment, notwithstanding the success of his gung-ho memoir *My Fight for Irish Freedom* (1924). Although a TD for four years from 1923, he was rejected by the electorate as an independent candidate in 1927 and spent time in America running a speakeasy bar, returning to Ireland in 1932 and then elected a Fianna Fáil TD. After the civil war, Breen was often a coiled spring of antipathy. Having married fellow republican Brigid Malone in 1921 (a friend observed 'being a hero is a tricky business. Living with a hero must have been twice as tricky') and carrying considerable pain, he drank, gambled and fulminated.[25] He also made the significant decision to enter the Dáil in 1927 before the rest of Fianna Fáil had decided to, alienating him from some of the Fianna Fáil hierarchy; that and his 'lack of discretion' meant he was never part of the governing establishment.[26]

In the 1930s Breen maintained he could not work owing to loss of memory, and had one foot in the grave, though he was still waxing defiantly about the war in the 1960s: 'By that stage he was making something of a career of his revolutionary-era reminiscences, proving an arresting presence on TV.'[27] Having been shot on active service, he was regarded by 1925 as having '20% of total disablement', but his disability was 'not considered to be in a final and stationary condition'. One physician noted in 1932 that he had suffered a cerebral haemorrhage superinduced by previous injuries.[28] In 1933, when his disability pension was £150, a medical re-examination of Breen 'assessed his present degree of disablement at 75%' and 'not likely to improve'.[29]

Breen wrote to Frank Aiken in 1933:

> what use is £150 per year to me – what I want to get and I claim
> I am entitled to is my doctor's expenses and I am told by the
> best doctors in the world that I may not live another year and at
> the outside 2 years ... I don't want a pension, I want something
> for my wife and children when I pass out. I don't want to leave
> them to starve.[30]

Aiken agreed that Breen, suffering seriously not just from his
physical wounds but also from a bruised ego, 'has been rather harshly
dealt with' and gave the minister for finance a personal letter about
the case.[31] By 1935 he was awarded a Grade A pension of £225 p.a. for
nine years of military service and in 1937, the Army Pensions Board
found that he was '100% disabled'; the detailed medical reports on
Breen indicated 'continuous headaches, dizziness, loss of memory,
sleeps badly, lack of nervous control unduly affected by excitement',
and that he was 'in a highly nervous condition'.[32]

In 1939 Breen furnished particulars of expenses incurred by him
for treatment of his wounds in the US, to the amount of $12,208,
but when he was told it was not possible to facilitate reimbursement
through legislation, he decried the government hiding behind 'the
civil servants. It is a nice easy way for a government to get out of its
obligations ... how many men were wounded and suffered as much
as I did ... It is a bit hard on an old man like myself to get such treatment.'[33] He was then aged forty-five, and he certainly felt old, but
he was nowhere near death; as was pointed out by another medic
in 1943, he was physically robust and it was his mental condition
that was the problem: 'found him normal in every respect. Heart,
abdomen, lungs and central nervous system.' Attacks of unconscious-
ness were 'nervous in origin. He just needs reassurance about his
physical condition.'[34] In 1948 he was granted £3,000 from the army
pensions vote for his US medical expenses and in 1945 secured a final
disability pension of £200.

When Breen died in 1969 his death certificate referred to 'War
wounds: 50 years' as succinct an appraisal of the physical and mental

impact and legacy of the period of conflict as can be found. His wife Brigid received a widow's allowance of £322 p.a. and lived until 1984. An indication that the civil war wheel was turning full circle was that it was the leader of Fine Gael, Liam Cosgrave, son of William T., who made representations regarding Brigid's widow's allowance.[35] Cosgrave also communicated on behalf of the ninety-three-year-old sister of civil war IRA martyr Rory O'Connor in 1969, who was 'living in poor circumstances' and 'physically incapable of self-support'.[36]

CHAPTER TWENTY-ONE

POACHERS TURNED GAMEKEEPERS

Whatever about the range of correspondence and forms compiled for the purposes of military service pensions, many applicants spoke little of the events they covered. For David Andrews, growing up in middle-class Dublin comfort despite his civil war veteran father Todd liking to think 'that he was working class', his father and mother Mary Coyle's involvement in the civil war was not ignored, 'in fact, some of our neighbours, while remaining good neighbours, had very strong views on my parents' former activities'.[1] But Todd did not speak much to his children of his civil war experiences, despite being known as 'a man of direct and even violently held opinion'.[2] Remnants of the 1922 coldness remained: 'the deaths of certain other people didn't distress him. He told us that some of the things that were done during the conflict were horrendous.' Mary had also spent a year in Kilmainham during the civil war, 'much to the chagrin' of her respectable family who also disapproved of her relationship with Todd; she, however, unlike Todd, 'could forgive'.[3] Perhaps a middle-class existence and material comfort made it easier to relent.

Andrews's revolutionary fervour in 1922, when he was aged twenty, had been mainly based on 'emotionalism and enthusiasm. I rarely thought; I felt.'[4] He was injured in Dublin city during civil war fighting and retreated to Cork; unluckily, he was arrested 'about a week before the ceasefire' and remained interned until April 1924; he also partook in a hunger strike for fourteen days. He made his way back to UCD, graduating with a commerce degree and found a career path in the public service, becoming managing director of the Turf Development Board (which evolved into Bord na Móna) and later executive chairman of CIE, the semi-state transport body, and chairman of the RTE (the public service broadcaster) authority, as a champion of state intervention in the economy and semi-state enterprise. He also had a strong anti-clerical streak; indeed, it was more than that; after excommunication for his IRA activities he 'never attended church', was critical of the Catholic Bishops and 'remained upset throughout his life' about that issue.[5]

By the 1930s, he was 'in receipt of remuneration from public monies in excess of £600 p.a.'.[6] He was awarded a Grade D pension for 6½ years' service in 1941 at a rate of £61.13s.4d. p.a. His rank for pension purposes was important to him; although nominally a captain during the civil war he believed his duties and responsibilities entitled him to Grade C, and during the conflict, it had been 'impossible for me to pursue my ordinary avocation'.[7] This was true, of course, but the crucial point was that he was more than able to make up for that afterwards, unlike many others. By 1947 his salary as director of Bord na Móna was £1,700 p.a. and he also wanted full payment of his pension as he contended, regarding its abatement, 'that his remuneration as managing director of Bord na Móna is not public money as defined by the relevant section of the MSP Act 1934'.[8] The minister was 'disposed to accept this contention'. This was despite the fact that Bord na Móna was a semi-state company but Andrews saw peat development as a patriotic endeavour, 'as a way of life and as a crusade rather than a commercial project'.[9]

Contrast that profitable patriotic crusade and Andrews's salubrious south County Dublin homestead with the experiences of Edward Devitt, who, appropriately, lived on Fenian Street in Dublin in the 1930s and was a civil servant with the engineering branch of the Department of Posts and Telegraphs. He had made an unsuccessful application for a disability pension: 'I have a bad heart but I could not prove I got it through service' (according to his doctor he had 'a double aortic murmur and an enlarged heart'). He received a Grade E pension of £13.1s.1d. p.a. for 2½ years' military service but was rejected for a clerical officer post in the civil service on account of his poor health even though he passed the requisite exam. Like Andrews, Devitt had fought against National Army troops in Dublin during the civil war and kept 'an arms dump in a room of a tenement house which I called home'.[10] He lamented in 1936 that a '4/– per week pension is little use to me when I remember that I would have £2 a week more had I kept out of the war'.[11]

A hardly sympathetic fellow IRA veteran suggested 'his whole growl is that he had never been made permanent in the civil service', though he acknowledged that he 'finds it very hard to rear family in one room'.[12] Devitt, who was paid £224 for his services to posts and telegraphs in 1937, plaintively outlined that difficulty; as a husband and father of five, 'one has to live and keep six more ... when I followed the dictates of my heart instead of my pocket in 1922 I little thought my country would still keep me living in a single room in a tenement 12 years afterwards and the prospects are still the same'.[13] In relation to his disputed disability claim he not unreasonably pointed out that his heart disease was revealed by a medical examination in 1924, six years after he had joined the service in 1918: 'If I were medically fit when I started the PO service and was not so in 1924 it stands to reason that it must have occurred during that time.'[14]

He had endured drenching when working externally on the telephone network during the day, then doing IRA duties at night ('I wasn't a funeral procession Volunteer'). He also referred to the strain of lifting sandbags for Dublin barricades during the civil war:

> through your fault I am placed in the unconscionable position of always remaining an unestablished servant of the state, liable to be dismissed at a moment's notice without pension rights or anything else although I have 25 years' service in the post office ... the most important years of a man's life, between the age of 21 and 26, I let slip without thinking of <u>my</u> future, depending on my country to look after me in case of need ... I am to rot in the gutter with those for whom I am responsible.[15]

These implorations from the tenements came in a steady stream, partly because the chasm between those doing well and those floundering was so blatant. A £13 annual pension in the 1930s was a pittance (the equivalent of roughly £900 in today's purchasing power). In 1943 *The Bell* magazine estimated that a £400 annual salary (about

£18,000 today) 'will buy only the bare essentials of living ... little more than bare subsistence', while the 'very poor' who had less than £100 p.a. were almost living 'on nothing'. An unemployed labourer with a wife and children was entitled to just 27s.6d. per week in home assistance in the early 1940s.[16]

Devitt noted in 1935 that a senior Department of Defence civil servant had recently

> attended a funeral of an old member of my [IRA] company. He died in poverty. The state sends a representative of the minister for defence [Frank Aiken] and the man's old comrades have to pay for his interment ... the man's old comrades had to subsidise to save him from a pauper's grave ... What a farce. I don't want the same thing to happen to me. If I cannot get the sympathy of the state when it is actually needed, I won't require it when I am dead ... perhaps it is Mr Aiken's idea for all old IRA to fade away.[17]

Devitt continued in the civil service and moved beyond the tenement to a Dublin southside suburb, dying in 1968.

The focus of Devitt's ire, Frank Aiken, was granted a military pension for just over 8½ years' service at Grade A, but he withdrew his application in 1942, reactivating it in 1955.[18] He had been keen to prevent civil war and was somewhat in the wilderness after its end, but as he wandered around, 'his private means cushioned him against the worst hardships experienced by other republicans' (Aiken's father had been a successful builder and farmer) and in 1928 Aiken bought the dairy farm at Sandyford, County Dublin, where he lived and farmed for the rest of his life while serving as a politician. Some of the 'austere republican founding fathers' seem to have made sure their residences were anything but.[19]

While the tenement republicans lived on the likes of Fenian Street, Aiken eventually had a housing development named after him in Sandyford and it became an opulent, desirable twenty-first-century address:

> set in a wooded area in the foothills of the Dublin Mountains,

Aiken's Village is a series of five enclosed groups of homes in what was once the residence of former Tánaiste [deputy prime minister] Frank Aiken ... perhaps the most impressive home type ... is the four-storey, four-bedroomed end of terrace town-house ... with 1,512 sq. feet of accommodation, it's priced at €529,000 ... there are two wrap-around balconies.[20]

Aiken held his Dáil seat for fifty years; as well as his closeness to de Valera, one of the reasons he was appointed minister for defence in 1932 was because 'his heart was not in the civil war and he ... was probably more acceptable to the Free State officers than any other possible appointment. He soon reconciled the army to the new regime.'[21]

That was a delicate and crucial ministerial appointment less than ten years after the end of the civil war, but it was also the case that his first visit as minister was to IRA prisoners in Arbour Hill, who were released the following day. Deeply Anglophobic, he became independent-minded and imaginative while remaining thick-skinned, gruff and insensitive, but ultimately made his mark as the state's longest-serving minister for external affairs. His biographer has argued that his predilection for politics was 'as much a part of his character as his propensity for violence'.[22] The civil war was a matter that distressed him long term, and in 2008 his son Frank broke down and said in Dublin, 'I still get emotional when I remember how much he hated it.'[23]

Some senior politicians were loath to engage with what they regarded as demeaning demands for proof of their military service or fulfil the administrative requirements of regular form filling. Gerard Boland, a founder of Fianna Fáil who served from 1939 to 1948 as a steely minister in the Department of Justice, where he took a hard line against the IRA, including internment without trial, had briefly been commander of the IRA's 3rd South Dublin Brigade active in Wicklow at the beginning of the civil war and was captured in July 1922. The following month his anti-Treaty TD brother, Harry, was killed. Gerard was in prison for two years, participated in the Kilmainham hunger strike (he attributed his self-discipline to yoga) and also spent time in the Curragh internment camp, not being released until July 1924. He withdrew his initial pension service application in 1942 (he was deemed to have had 11½ years' service) and reactivated it in 1954 after Fianna Fáil left office; he was entitled to £231 p.a. (the salary for a minister at that stage was £2,124 p.a.).[24]

Boland took issue with the pensions declaration required under the 1962 Pensions Act, involving a signed, witnessed declaration ('I declare that I am entitled to receive payment of the pension granted to me') and returned this form: 'I consider this an insulting letter. I was reluctant to apply for a pension but was persuaded to do so by my old friend Oscar Traynor. You can keep it from now on'. In this case, status won out; a senior civil servant cancelled the planned formal reply reiterating the terms of the Act: 'we need not reply to Mr Boland. The cert may be accepted as it stands without witness.'[25]

His friend Oscar Traynor had been the most senior IRA officer not in the Four Courts in June 1922; instead he was in Sackville Street before retreating to Wicklow. On his return to Dublin at the end of July he was arrested and imprisoned in Gormanstown internment camp until 1924, a reminder that, as with Boland, imprisonment during this period by default ensured a solid political future. Traynor was a Fianna Fáil TD from 1932 to 1961. Nor was he shy about his war claims and was quick out of the blocks in January 1935 to apply for a pension; in that year he styled his 1922 self as 'in virtual control of the republican army … a lone executive officer'.[26] He secured a Grade A, fourteen years' service pension, worth £350 a year (about £22,000 today), abated when he was appointed a junior minister in July 1936: full ministerial office quickly followed. He too was to serve as minister for justice and also had to wrestle with the issue of stringent measures against the IRA. His widow, Annie, in 1971 turned down an allowance she was entitled to under new pensions legislation, a significant sum, as 'I am in receipt of a pension sufficient for my needs'. It was noted that 'the allowance, if applied for, would be £591.12s. a year'.[27]

It was Charles Haughey who replaced Traynor as minister for justice in 1961. Twenty years previously, Traynor had been made aware of the dire circumstances of the Haughey family owing to the civil war and its aftermath, when Charles was just a teenager. In time,

Charles would become the most controversial politician of his generation, and exceptionally venal, acquisitive and ostentatious, but it is interesting that this future leader of Fianna Fáil and Taoiseach came from the opposite side of the civil war divide from many of his party colleagues, and biographers have linked his later greed at least in part to his family's impoverishment as a result of the events of that period.[28]

While Traynor was fighting with the anti-Treaty IRA in 1922, Haughey's father John (Seán) had been a member of the 2nd Northern Division of the IRA in Derry during the War of Independence and at one point seen by Crown forces as 'the most dangerous man in the county'.[29] Haughey then became a commandant in the National Army and served in Mayo during the civil war; he also married Sarah, a Cumann na mBan member, in Derry in August 1922. He retired from the army in 1928, was granted a Grade E pension for six years' military service (£90 p.a.) and acquired a 100-acre farm at Dunshaughlin, County Meath, but when he developed multiple sclerosis this was not a viable option and in 1933 the family moved to Donnycarney, County Dublin, and lived in straitened circumstances.

Haughey was suffering from some form of trauma during the civil war period, later referred to by his wife as 'a nervous breakdown [in] 1923 and 1924'. His second in command, J. J. Flynn, referred to the 'onerous and very often almost superhuman duties' of 1923 involving continuous raids, administrative work and inspection of outposts, frequently travelling for two or three days in wet conditions as OC of the 61st Infantry Battalion when 400 men had been transferred to Mayo. A medical officer who attended him in Castlebar in 1926 noted he 'frequently suffered from fits of marked moroseness and depression and now that the question of decimated sclerosis has arisen I can well recall that Comdt Haughey's gait was definitely "spastic" in character'.[30] This moroseness meant he was not well liked and 'not very sociable'.[31] His battalion's medical officer thought it was a form of

> mild hysteria ... he was a very hardworking, zealous and sober officer and it is quite likely that army work and especially the over zealous way in which he overworked himself, may fairly be

said to have facilitated the onset of DS [decimated sclerosis] ...
the question of trauma, or trauma due to active service or war
as an aetiological factor in the genesis of DS or Insular Sclerosis
is moot and debatable but the thesis of such traumatic origin
in the case of DS has not been disproved and it may be that the
board decide to give him the benefit of the doubt.[32]

This came two days after a note from the Pensions Board indicated some of its members were 'not satisfied ... Haughey's disease
was excited, accelerated or aggravated by service in the National
Army', but two others disagreed and found in his favour and it was
noted his disability was 'final'.[33] That was certainly the case, and the
letters of Haughey and his wife had become increasingly desperate in
the late 1930s; in 1938 Haughey wrote to Frank Aiken to tell him he
was resigning as a reserve officer:

I have devoted the best part of my life to the national cause and
fell into bad health as a result ... I am a married man with 7 children; the eldest who is 16 years of age is still at school. I have had
a very hard struggle to feed and clothe my family since I became
an invalid and now that I am to lose my reserve pay I am left
without any earnings or income.[34]

By July 1939 things were worse, and he told Aiken regarding his
children, 'I think the country owes them more than starvation.'[35]
In 1942 Sarah informed the Department of Defence that John was
now aged forty-three and had to be 'carried up and down stairs ... he
is not able to write owing to his sickness; his hands are very shaky'.
She also wrote to Oscar Traynor, 'The doctor told me last week that
he is sinking fast ... requires constant attention day and night. The
strain of caring for him over this long period has played up with my
own health ... our funds cannot afford a nurse.'[36] Sarah could not get
funded hospice or hospital treatment for him, despite requests, as
there were no provisions for that in the pensions legislation. That year
he was granted a disability pension of £100 p.a. The medical report
for 1942 was devastating: 'complains of complete loss of power of

arms and legs. Defective vision. Memory impaired. Slurring speech, tremor ... applicant is confined to bed and incapable of any co-ordinated movement.'[37]

John Haughey died in 1947; Sarah, who had been awarded a very small pension for just under two years' service in 1941, wrote to the Army Pensions Board in 1957: 'Since my husband's death I have no means of support but the widow's pension of 22/6 per week and a small Cumann na mBan pension of £13pa and I find it very difficult to live on this since my sons got married', though she subsequently benefited from allowances paid under new pensions acts.[38] She remained a widow for forty-two years, dying in 1989 when her son was Taoiseach; her most fervent wish remained 'to see Ireland united'.[39] After she died, her daughter Maureen Haughey donated the £300 funeral grant payable to service pension recipients to the army benevolent fund.[40]

CHAPTER TWENTY-TWO

VIRTUE AND ERIN, SAXON AND GUILT

In contrast to his earlier eulogising of revolutionary camaraderie Seán O'Faoláin acknowledged the civil war continued 'to oppress me traumatically for many years' and he was reluctant to write about it and the consequences of the actions of those 'self-crazed by abstractions'. Shattering the dreams of the poets was 'a miserable business ... the lovely and the noble and the proud was dragged through a shambles'. But he was berated by Mary MacSwiney when he suggested a switch in focus to confronting poverty and education or even acknowledging the 'noble qualities' of opponents.[1] Such exchanges underlined the challenge of taking the sting out of civil war enmities in the formative decades of the state. When he published his book *The Victory of Sinn Féin* in 1924, P. S. O'Hegarty highlighted why reticence about it was to become common. There would be limited appetite to recall 'that our deep rooted belief that there was something in us finer than, more spiritual than anything in any other people, was sheer illusion, and that we were really an uncivilised people with savage instincts. And the shock of that plunge from the heights to the depths staggered the whole nation'.[2]

O'Hegarty's was a sweeping overstatement and the extent to which he had his finger on the pulse of the thoughts of the 'nation' is doubtful, but the excesses of the conflict did induce preferences for avoidance of the subject. The silence had actually begun during the war; as Liam de Róiste recorded in his diary: 'both sides silent when the murder is committed by their own supporters'.[3]

Stephen Fuller, after he survived the Ballyseedy mine, was 'on the run up to March 1924' and was even assisted by Free State supporters who sheltered him for a week. He applied for a wound pension under the 1932 Army Pensions Act and was granted £150 a year, based on '100% disablement' as a 'chronic neurasthenic [disabling fatigue, weak nerves, PTSD] ... dates back directly to the Ballyseedy outrage' and he also suffered from pulmonary tuberculosis due to exposure.[4] Fuller was dissatisfied with his Grade D pension (£52.10s. p.a. for 5¼ years' service) but withdrew his appeal in 1936: 'I do not wish to trouble the Board further.'[5] He married in 1931 but his first wife died two years later from TB; he subsequently remarried. He later served as a Fianna Fáil TD from 1937 to 1943 and lived to the age of eighty-four, but shunned interviews about the conflict with one exception, when he spoke on historian Robert Kee's 1980 Irish history television series at the age of eighty.[6]

According to his son Paudie, 'He held no bitterness against those who tried to blow him up; in fact, he was full of forgiveness ... my father once said to me that the Civil War divisions should not be passed on to the next generation.'[7] He was a humble man of few words who, according to some, 'never held any bitterness'.[8] Fuller's political career was short lived and, given his style, he was not going to be trading civil war insults across the Dáil floor; he opted out of politics to return to the farm, his departure no doubt influenced by not only his health but also a reluctance to be a living civil war monument. It is difficult to dispute the assertion that 'his lack of bitterness was remarkable'.[9]

It was not a magnanimity shared by some of his contemporaries on either side as they ploughed civil war divisions in politics, some with relish and aggression, others through bogusly pious sermons. On 12 August 1927 Fianna Fáil TDs took their seats in the Dáil, having swallowed the bitter pill of the oath of allegiance to the Crown. Following the assassination of minister for justice Kevin O'Higgins the previous month, W. T. Cosgrave's Cumann na nGaedheal government changed the law to invalidate the election of any TD who did not then take their seat. Cosgrave's reaction to O'Higgins's killing underlined the continuation of the civil war narrative: 'the prestige and credibility of a country depend more upon its administration of justice than any other single act'.[10]

The Dáil was dissolved a few days later, followed by a general election in September that saw Fianna Fáil win fifty-seven seats and Cumann na nGaedheal sixty-one, and when the new Dáil met on 11 October, Fianna Fáil TD Seán T. O'Kelly rose to speak:

> I do not want to start on a bitter note, though God knows I could, and God knows I would have justification, in thinking of those who lie in cold graves – 77 of my comrades who lie in cold graves to-day – and the fathers and mothers, and the sons and daughters of these people expect us and look to us to vindicate them in some way.

Cumann na nGaedheal's Ernest Blythe responded to O'Kelly:

> There was a sort of suggestion in Deputy O'Kelly's speech that on their side was virtue and Erin, and on ours Saxon and guilt. That is all very well for an election platform, but it does not bear any relation to reality ... I do not want to see recrimination. I suppose I could take my part in the battle of recrimination just as well as anyone else. But what good will that do the country?[11]

The endurance of the civil war trenches in Irish politics ensured that there was much reiteration of the 'virtue and Erin' and 'Saxon and guilt' rhetoric and accusations for the next thirty years, though J. J. Walsh, as a former Cumann na nGaedheal minister, suggested people grew 'tired of abuse as a substitute for what had been expected from a native government'.[12] Seán Lemass credited Walsh with giving de Valera the idea that he could enter the Dáil by declaring the oath of allegiance was 'an empty formula'; that it could be just a technicality to secure entrance to the chamber: 'It was then that Dev said, "If that's so, if what you say is correct, then it's no problem for us either"', Lemass recalls de Valera telling Walsh.[13] That was a fanciful assertion from Lemass and not at all in keeping with de Valera's style; he had actually sought theological opinion on the validity of taking an oath under duress: 'fear does not invalidate the oath', Michael Browne, a moral theologian, told him, 'it does however justify the swearer in taking the oath in a qualified or restricted sense'.[14]

Retrospectively, Lemass presented himself as clear headedly utilitarian about this – 'I often felt that the taking of a decision was perhaps even more important than the soundness of the decision' – but he too had privately sought counsel from the Church, asking Archbishop Byrne if he was 'morally justified' in taking the oath, 'given that I am publicly pledged to my constituents and privately determined also to nullify ... the authority of the British crown and cabinet in Irish affairs'. Byrne, who supported Lemass's political opponents, was not going to fall into that trap; he indicated he could talk to Lemass personally in a pastoral capacity but would not reply formally as the Bishops agreed that 'whatever answer was sent would be used as a political weapon to the detriment of religion'.[15]

Lemass declared in March 1928 that Fianna Fáil was a 'slightly constitutional party ... if we can achieve our aims by the present [constitutional] methods we will be very pleased but we will not confine ourselves to them'.[16] The Dáil offered a platform to rake over the civil war detritus and as Lemass threw his shapes, listed for parliamentary discussion were the topics of resigned RIC men, army pension claims, seizure of a motor car during the civil war; compensation for a republican killed in Kerry in custody in 1923 and demands for a review of all cases relating to prisoners 'whose cases arise out of civil war'. Lemass asserted the need to 'draw a veil' over the events of the last few years: 'a lot of water has flown under the Liffey bridges since then'.[17]

But this was the same Lemass who in November 1928 insisted that Fianna Fáil TDs should not speak to Free State ministers in Leinster House ('unbecoming and demoralising'), and he proposed that 'it should be the rule of the party that members should not conduct any business with CnG ministers or deputies in a bar or restaurant and that fraternisation under any circumstances be not permitted'.[18] Furthermore, Cumann na nGaedheal, maintained Lemass, 'had no aims of any sort, they had no objective to realise, they had no clear policy to communicate. They were just carrying on government. Their only argument for being allowed to carry on government was that they had won the civil war ... there was nothing that they could rally people to'.[19]

In some of her last letters to her sister, Constance Markievicz, who joined Fianna Fáil and won a seat for the party a month before she died in July 1927, stood behind the decision to enter the Dáil: 'some unlogical persons are howling', she wrote, but the mantra 'The Republic lives' was self-righteous foolery as 'there is no work here at all'.[20] Likewise for Peadar O'Donnell, by 1935 it was 'now for the living', though as a socialist not a centrist.[21] But centrist was what civil war politics ultimately became, notwithstanding initial differences between the two parties as Fianna Fáil, promoting economic protectionism, successfully sought to court those with little stake in the country, while their opponents were more likely to secure the support of commercial interests that benefited from free trade.

J. J. Walsh also found himself advocating protectionist pro-tillage policies, and in September 1927 stated he would not contest that month's general election as Cumann na nGaedheal was indulging 'ranchers and importers'. In 1932 he publicly backed Fianna Fáil and his post-politics businesses benefited greatly from the protectionist policies of the party. Fianna Fáil's continuation of Sinn Féin's civil war era economic programme chimed with many: 'to make the resources and wealth of the country subservient to the needs and welfare of the Irish people' through housing, land redistribution and public health initiatives.[22]

The 1932 general election was a crucial turning point. Invective from both sides was colourful and voluminous, with Fianna Fáil lambasted as subversive 'Reds' and Cumann na nGaedheal as being a government 'for the rich by the rich'. Cumann na nGaedheal also wondered about the civil war dead 'who died for an empty formula ... was it worth it?' and the party 'tried to co-opt the Catholic Church as an honorary party agent'. Seán Moylan, victorious for Fianna Fáil in North Cork, hailed a triumph for 'the owners of the donkey cart over the pony and trap class', a reminder that its electoral pitch had been largely social and economic.[23]

Having won seventy-two seats to Cumann na nGaedheal's fifty-seven, de Valera was quick to declare on assuming office with the support of the Labour Party (who won seven seats), 'we have had a peaceful change of government'. Subsequently, there was a tendency to laud Cosgrave exaggeratedly for agreeing to transfer power

– in other words, for accepting the result.[24] De Valera also speedily announced that the abolition of the oath of allegiance was a prerequisite 'for the peace, order and good government of the state'. A snap election the following year gave him an overall majority.

Cumann na nGaedheal governments of the 1920s were often remembered for their failure to court popularity, pension cuts, neglect of social services and a poor record in providing housing, rather than for balancing the state's finances and state building under pressure. This had been done without the luxury of a blueprint for reform because of the circumstances in which they took power. Their foreign policy efforts that saw Ireland join the League of Nations in 1923 and use imperial conferences to push successfully for greater autonomy for the dominions were also significant. In relation to these, de Valera admitted in 1938, such advances had 'practically' achieved for the twenty-six counties what 'I was aiming at in 1921 for the whole of Ireland ... I am prepared to confess that there have been advances made that I did not believe would be made.'[25]

Fianna Fáil, insisting it was the duty of the state to provide work, delivered on many of its social and economic promises after taking power in 1932, a reminder that despite the desperate poverty revealed in the pension files, and the continuing pain of a social and economic degradation that was deep and sharp, there were welfare initiatives that secured a loyal base for them among the urban and working classes. These policies included modest widows and orphans pensions, unemployment assistance, conditions of employment legislation, sale of public authority cottages to labourers, grants for private houses, land redistribution and an urban housing programme, identified by economic historians as one of the party's most impressive achievements in the 1930s.[26] The longer it was in government, the more likely it was to gain the approval of a significant portion of the wealthier voters also, and warnings from senior civil servants of the necessity for fiscal conservatism were often heeded. Agricultural self-sufficiency remained elusive and an economic war with Britain over the withholding of land annuities owed under historic land purchase schemes lasted from 1932 to 1938 and created distress for dairy farmers because of the retaliatory imposition of duties, exacerbated by violence, intimidation and threats to freedom of speech and expression. As a result of the campaign to prevent the collection of annuities, there were 197 violent attacks in Cork between July 1934 and January 1935.[27]

These tensions and related constitutional and political controversies as Fianna Fáil began to dismantle the Anglo-Irish Treaty kept some of the civil war ashes smouldering. Some, however, were just going through the tribal motions and before too long de Valera saw fit to use the same measures to defeat the IRA as his civil war enemies had. As Lemass recalled, it was necessary for Fianna Fáil to 'come down from the heights to solid earth and some people travelled down faster than others ... but it was often easy to send us back up into the clouds again'. This was especially true of the 1930s:

> you could spend a week in the Dáil perhaps, doing the most routine, practical job of some piece of legislation ... and then on the eight day someone would be back into the civil war again and all the blood would be coursing through your veins as strong as ever. Seán T. [O'Kelly] was outstanding in this. At the drop of a hat he would proclaim the republic off every housetop and every mountain top ... in many ways I was the most pragmatic of them all.

Lemass's tone gave the impression he did not take it all that seriously, but he never, even in old age, missed an opportunity to belittle Cumann na nGaedheal and its successor party Fine Gael, and over the course of twenty-three interviews from 1967 to 1969 failed to credit them with a single achievement.[28]

Forging a third political way was hugely difficult. In late 1926 a new National League party, composed largely of supporters of the old Irish Parliamentary Party, declared its mission to 'break the civil war mould' and won eight seats the following year, but it struggled to cohere around policy or protest and faded quickly. The National Centre Party, led by Frank MacDermot and with a farmer support base, also sought to build momentum by protesting against civil war politics and won eleven Dáil seats in 1933 but merged with Cumann na nGaedheal (with whom it shared similar policies) in the febrile atmosphere after Fianna Fáil's ascent to power. James Hogan contested a by-election in 1936 for Fine Gael and advocated an alliance between Fianna Fáil and Fine Gael to 'recreate the conditions' of 1916–21, demonstrating why he was ill suited to 1930s-style politics. He lost the election but was on safer ground in praising an electoral system that resolved differences in a peaceful manner.[29]

There is no doubt, however, that the first governors of the state struggled greatly with the transition to Fianna Fáil dominance. In embracing extremism in the early 1930s, by supporting the Blueshirts, Ireland's diluted version of the continental fascist movements, which evolved from the Army Comrades Association seeking to protect the interests of ex-National Army men, some pro-Treaty civil war veterans were also attempting to find an outlet for their fear of and antipathy towards Fianna Fáil. Dismissed as Garda commissioner in 1932, Eoin O'Duffy, who had been so prominent as political, policing and military priorities fused from 1922 to 1924, now, as the Blueshirts leader, became one of the most divisive figures of a polarising 1930s, accentuated by de Valera's electoral triumphs, the release of republican prisoners and the economic war with Britain. The hatred found expression not just in political squabbling but through brawls between Blueshirts (with well over 40,000 adherents, some of them armed) and IRA members 'at meetings, dancehalls and on the roadside'.[30]

At leadership level the Blueshirts were not monolithic, with the bombastic O'Duffy following a different agenda from the likes of Kevin O'Higgins and Richard Mulcahy, whose primary allegiance was to party politics. Sympathetic academics did much to justify the movement by linking it to developments on the continent and the teachings of papal encyclicals, but marrying the various layers, particularly given O'Duffy's refusal to accept the wisdom of his political peers, was to prove futile. There were various elements of fantasy and contradiction to O'Duffy's career. A moralist, or 'preacher of national virility' as his biographer Fearghal McGarry put it, he was far from that privately and although an advocate of teetotalism was also an alcoholic. There were many factors that drove him towards extremism, including the cultural environment in which he grew up, Catholicism and anti-communism, his ideas on sport and masculinity, but also the civil war. After leading an Irish Brigade to fight under General Franco in the Spanish Civil War, O'Duffy eventually collapsed under the weight of his own contradictions, and died in wartime Dublin, a broken man.[31]

A burning sense of injustice and an acute class consciousness, as Fianna Fáil sought to embrace the dispossessed, became for some Blueshirts an insistence that party politics had failed, but they were successfully faced down, from within and without, including through use of a special Garda unit and the Public Safety Act, which was a creation of the previous government. The Blueshirt saga was also a spur to a fusion of various interests to form a new party in 1933: Fine Gael, originally called 'The United Ireland Party: Fine Gael', with O'Duffy briefly at the helm, Cosgrave stepping aside as he maintained, 'Divided forces cannot win a political battle.' O'Duffy resigned the following year and Cosgrave was leader again of a party that maintained one of its aims was 'the wiping out of party animosities arising from the Anglo-Irish war or from civil conflict'.[32]

In parallel, given the potency of the 'shadow of the gunmen' theme, de Valera did not want his plans for governance to be compromised by that cloud, or allow the Treaty divide to dictate all his decisions. He had to deliver on his promise to release republican political prisoners after 1932 but he also invited pro-Treaty civil servant Maurice Moynihan to tea in the Dáil restaurant and asked the shocked economist to become his private secretary. Moynihan told him he didn't agree with many of his policies, but de Valera told him that did not matter. Moynihan was later to recall, 'He didn't ask how I voted and never did.'[33]

De Valera was also canny enough to appoint barrister and Longford-Westmeath TD James Geoghegan, who had left Cumman na nGaedheal in 1930 to join Fianna Fáil, to the sensitive post of minister for justice: Geoghegan had taken no part in either the War of Independence or the civil war. While the release of IRA prisoners followed Fianna Fáil's assumption of government, the Department of Justice subsequently became preoccupied with facing down the Blueshirts, a reminder that the IRA held no monopoly on threats to the state's security.

By 1932 Fianna Fáil could also engage in its version of patronage in public appointments – 'where technical qualifications are about equal, it is possible to take into account the national service that has been rendered' – but that faded relatively quickly.[34] It deliberately courted the support of civil servants, promising arbitration to address their grievances. Public service pay cuts and a dragging of heels undermined such pledges; in 1937 the civil servants were still looking for an arbitration scheme. Fianna Fáil did not purge the civil service; instead 'it made sure it controlled it, integrating the civil service into the broader social, cultural and political quest for self-sufficiency. The resulting civil service was centralised and hierarchical under the control of politicians, something the British had tried but failed to achieve.'[35]

As to the question of religion, leading members of Fianna Fáil, too, had stressed their impeccable Catholic credentials, though some continued to harbour a certain disdain. Those leading the Catholic Church had vigorously sought to direct and influence the post-civil war dispensation and Catholic pronouncements and publications in the 1920s became ever more vitriolic, as traced through the pages of the resentful and wrathful *Catholic Bulletin*, a monument to 'the basest insecurities of a post-colonial society'.[36] The stridency on display was also defensive; a product of fears generated by the violence and volatility of 1922–3, prompting a constant preoccupation with perceived transgressors. Early in 1924 Cardinal Michael Logue informed clerical students at Maynooth they would 'have to meet a divided people ... who had lost much of their reverence for religion and the church.'[37] Long term, Seán Lemass was to conclude there was 'a political advantage in having a certain anti-clerical tinge', even going so far as to assert 'there is an anti-clericalism in the Irish people', but this view was not expressed publicly and was not common among his political peers.[38]

De Valera was long practised in squaring the circle of episcopal denunciation; his parting message to the papal envoy Salvatore Luzio in 1923 had been 'Please give to the Holy Father my dutiful homage. Though nominally cut away from the body of the Holy Church we are still spiritually and mystically of it and we refuse to regard ourselves except as his children.'[39] His cause was never entirely bereft of ecclesiastical backing; John Regan points out that 290,000 Catholic voters opted for anti-Treaty candidates in the 1923 general election, showing a capacity to side with the excommunicated.[40] At the time of his consecration as Bishop of Clonfert in June 1924 Dr John Dignan had caused quite a stir: 'I predict that the republican party is certain to be returned to power in a short time. Prepare for that day. Do your best for its quick approach.' Dignan defended his remarks, maintaining republicans had been poorly treated and deserved public endorsement.[41]

By 1929, during an ineloquent contribution to a Dáil debate, Fianna Fáil TD Seán T. O'Kelly, excessively pious, sectarian, critical of Cumann na nGaedheal for being too open to Protestants and de Valera's 'virtual minister for ecclesiastical affairs', asserted, 'We of the Fianna Fáil party believe that we speak for the big body of Catholic opinion. I think I could say, without qualification of any kind, that we represent the big element of Catholicity.'[42] During the glorious centenary of Catholic emancipation that year his party was not going to be found wanting in expressing the ferocity of its faith.

Less than ten years after the end of the civil war, the Eucharistic Congress in Dublin in June 1932, an international Catholic gathering, provided an opportunity for both church and state to emphasise what united the citizens of the Free State rather than their deep political divisions. The piety and devotion on display was extraordinary and the exaltation of faith unprecedented. The shared Catholic heritage – by 1926, when there were 2,971,992 people in the state, 2,751,269 of them were Catholic and the number of Protestants was 32 per cent less than it had been in 1911 – was clearly a stabilising factor. While 1922 was not forgotten – thirty years after the civil war the powerful Catholic Archbishop of Dublin, John Charles McQuaid, privately expressed a preference for Fine Gael, as 'in assessing the attitude of a Fianna Fáil government, one may never forget the revolutionary past of that party' – it was also a powerful binding agent: 'our people [are] ever firm in their allegiance to our ancestral faith'.[43]

Political tensions, however, were not completely forgotten in the midst of religious fervour. Fianna Fáil's determination to snub the governor general (the king's representative in the Free State), James McNeill, as part of its republican agenda to undermine the Treaty, meant that he was not invited to the government's own Eucharistic

Congress reception in St Patrick's Hall in Dublin Castle. By the end of the year, McNeill had departed his position, ground down by the government's crude determination to humiliate him.

Writer and former Irish Parliamentary Party MP Stephen Gwynn, whose house was destroyed by republicans during the civil war, continued well into the 1930s to wonder 'what is the cost of the victorious hate?'[44] But there were also shared spaces, including for those intent on cultural and sporting pursuits. The Gaelic Athletic Association (GAA), promoting, as a nationwide amateur organisation, native Irish sports since 1884, provided common ground. It was undoubtedly difficult for the GAA to weather the civil war storm, given the different political allegiances of its members, and there were limits to its 'powers of healing', but the determination to look forward was strong. Eoin O'Duffy, as the commissioner of the new civic guard in 1922, had urged his men to 'play their way into the hearts of the people'.[45] That was ultimately what was done and the GAA survived the civil war and thrived beyond it because it managed to transcend the divisions and limitations of the bitter upheavals.

CHAPTER TWENTY-THREE

SIDESTEPPING DIFFERENCES

The politics of enmity could also be laid aside in the interests of common humanity. Desmond FitzGerald's son Garret, Taoiseach in the 1980s, suggested animosities among the children of the protagonists dissipated in the late 1930s when they were in university together.[1] Seán MacEntee's daughter, poet Máire, referred to the civil war as 'Cogadh na gCarad' (war of friends); even when MacEntee was fighting in Sackville Street in 1922 and Desmond FitzGerald was holed up in government buildings, Desmond's wife Mabel and Seán's wife Margaret 'took turns at bringing their children to stay the night in each other's houses on either side of Marlborough Road'. Four years later Margaret stood as Garret's godmother ('the child of the reconciliation'). When Seán MacEntee was dying, Garret, then Taoiseach, visited him to be told how much Margaret had loved him and Seán expressed his regret at the civil war.[2]

It is also notable that W. T. Cosgrave and Seán Lemass, despite their lineage, were not the most pugilistic exponents of civil war politics. Eunan O'Halpin has identified that as something of a paradox; that within a political system defined by the revolutionary era and the civil war, 'two of the most senior figures to emerge were unwilling to trade on their revolutionary records and experiences, or revisit them, although those were what first brought them into the public realm as public figures'. Both were also regarded as 'effective rather than charismatic politicians, disciplined to grand gestures and rather reserved individuals'. Coming from relatively modest Dublin backgrounds, the pair were silent on their personal losses, and their experiences 'left no detectable psychological scars'.[3] Cosgrave got on much better with Lemass than he did with de Valera, whom he could not forgive, but it was an almost blanket pro-Treaty position that de Valera had put personal ambition above principle in opposing the Treaty – 'Other republicans could be forgiven ... de Valera was different' – and Fianna Fáil entering the Dáil only solidified that hostility: 'the Treaty oath, worth a civil war in 1922, was somehow transformed into an empty formula'.[4]

After Cosgrave's death in November 1965, however, Lemass, still Taoiseach, paid him generous tribute in the Dáil and referenced his 'distinguished' achievements in helping to create a stable democratic state after 1922, and 'the grace with which he relinquished power when the people so willed ... the readiness with which, even in retirement from active public life, he gave of his counsel in the sphere of national development which was dear to him, and finally, the exemplary character of his long life ... the work he has done for Ireland endures.'[5]

Notwithstanding, civil war grudges could endure with even greater vehemence for some of the next generation; William's son Liam, who served as Taoiseach from 1973 to 1977, was forceful in 2013 and 2014 in maintaining his father 'had to take very strenuous actions against the Irregulars'. The actions taken were severe, but they were effective. Liam did not believe his father and fellow ministers got sufficient credit for establishing the state and stabilising its institutions: 'ruthless and clear, he and his colleagues did an immense good'.[6] Liam's contributions were a direct endorsement of civil war executions. The strength of such sentiment was exacerbated by Fianna Fáil's extraordinary success, holding power during 1932–48, 1951–4, 1954–7, 1959–73, 1977–81 and on into the modern era, when they learned to share power as the dominant party in various coalition governments.

The Labour Party could perhaps make similar complaints about lack of gratitude; squeezed by civil war alignments, it operated 'in the shadow of the national question', and while it performed well in the 1922 general election (gaining 21 per cent of votes cast) and also did much to stabilise parliamentary democracy in the midst of civil war, it struggled in 1923 and witnessed the halving of its first-preference vote; only fourteen of its forty-four candidates were elected.[7] It was tame, too, in a conservative, clerical climate ripe for the 'Red scare' and the partitioned Ireland of the 1920s, when in the North 35 per cent of the working population was employed in industry but that figure was only 14 per cent in the Free State. It was reluctant to pursue a class politics aggressively, not helped by instructions to priests that 'care should be paid to the working class, lest lured by the promises and deceived by the fraud of socialists, it loses its ancestral faith'.[8] Splits, infighting and the stealing of many of its political clothes and welfare focus by Fianna Fáil also contributed to Labour's impotence; if it was true that its leaders thought that, rather than 'resolute class character', it was 'the middle group [that] would yield the greatest gains', this was an ineffective strategy.[9] Seán Lemass greatly enjoyed tormenting the party – 'as harmless a body as ever graced any parliament' – insisting it was irrelevant as Fianna Fáil was the real Labour Party.[10] It clung on, surviving rather than thriving, periodically sharing power with Fine Gael to get Fianna Fáil out of government only to be electorally punished for that too.

For decades, through its various iterations, Sinn Féin was even more on the periphery; its president in 1928, J. J. O'Kelly, said it had 'no prospects to offer but the old unrequited service to a deathless cause', and only fifty delegates attended its Ard Fheis in 1949.[11] It was primarily a mouthpiece for the IRA and that imbalance endured for decades: 'Sinn Féin should come under Army organisers at all levels', according to a directive in possession of IRA chief of staff Séamus Twomey in 1977.[12] It eventually repositioned and revised on a journey that included dropping parliamentary abstention in Ireland, acceptance of consent in relation to a united Ireland and a championing of popular left-wing causes.

In power in the 1930s, de Valera managed to dismantle the Treaty, including getting rid of the despised oath of allegiance. He maximised Irish sovereignty by essentially winning the trust or pragmatic co-operation of certain British politicians and diplomats and then reworking 'almost single-handedly the constitutional relationship between Britain and Ireland', including removing the British Crown from Irish affairs and moulding a constitution that in 1937 made southern Ireland a republic in all but name and strengthened fundamental rights but also incorporated aspects of the 1922 Constitution.

The deal to end the economic war with Britain in 1938 included the return of the ports retained under British control by the terms of the Treaty, a one-off £10 million payment to settle the land-annuities issue and freer Anglo-Irish trade.

De Valera also sidelined the IRA and kept Ireland out of the Second World War. What he could not do – and this is why he did not declare an Irish republic – was come up with a means to end the partition of Ireland; he settled instead on rhetorically beating the anti-partition drum and relying on what became 'his well-worn and plaintive theme of British culpability'. But the civil war also led to 'the weakening of anti-partitionist purpose' on both sides of the divide, with a lessening of solidarity with northern nationalists and strengthening of Ulster unionist resolve.[13] This was also enabled by the suppression of the Boundary Commission report of 1925 to prevent further instability and humiliation; the report's recommendation of modest alterations to the border had crushed the nationalist dream of a dramatic redrawing of it to make Northern Ireland untenable as an entity and deliver unity.

De Valera's vision was 'powerful but blinkered'. The skill and confidence he brought to the successful quest for sovereignty, however, meant Fianna Fáil came to be seen as essential in the making of the modern Irish state.[14] In doing this, the party also built on foundations that had been laid in the 1920s, meaning their diplomatic successes lodged stubbornly in the throats of their civil war opponents. What both parties agreed on, however, was the importance of Irish neutrality during the Second World War (labelled the Emergency) a reminder that the civil war divisions could be subsumed in a wider appreciation of the imperative of being able to implement an independent foreign policy.

Todd Andrews suggested that as a result of the civil war the 'nation suffered a psychological wound which was largely unhealed until the second world war'.[15] That juncture was picked partly because veterans from both sides of the civil war joined the Irish army during the Emergency. This chimes with Lemass's response to journalist Michael Mills's observation that it was 'remarkable' that the bitterness of the civil war 'disappeared so quickly' compared to other countries. His response was that the Emergency and the need to bring the Old IRA into the army helped significantly.[16]

Despite the almost complete political consensus about neutrality, some historians have characterised it as being bound up with 'the self-reverential culture of Irish nationalism that was ill-equipped to rise to the moral challenges of world war'.[17] This stern moralising underestimates the trauma that a split body politic on the issue of involvement in the war would have generated just sixteen years on from civil war and just seven from the transfer of power from pro- to anti-Treaty parties.

It has further been suggested the Emergency was a 'watershed', in the relationship between the children of the revolution and the state. Ruairí Brugha, for example, the son of Cathal, killed in 1922, joined the IRA in 1933 and was interned in the Curragh in 1940, but he was already growing disillusioned with the IRA and the feasibility of its campaign. While he said he had been 'taught no way of serving ... except by arms and sacrifice', he ultimately became a moderate Fianna Fáiler; he even went as far as to tell his dying mother that 'his father was wrong to leave his family behind as he went out all guns blazing from the Gresham Hotel in 1922'.[18]

Ruairí ultimately found his own path and encouraged North–South co-operation, but perhaps what was also significant was that, when on the run before internment in 1940, in various hideouts 'he saw, first-hand, how the poor had to struggle to make ends meet'.[19] This may have made him question what good a new IRA campaign would do. The Emergency was also significant because the civil war anti-Treatyites were now governing and were hard line when it came to executing republicans (six IRA men were executed by army firing squad during the war; another was hanged while three others died on hunger strike). Lemass reflected on that in 1968, relieved that he never experienced as Taoiseach the problem

of a political execution. I often wondered how Dev stood up to this. It must have been a real tough job – ordering someone to be shot and disregarding all the appeals that were made for leniency ... it must have been a real test of personal moral and spiritual strength ... I feel I would have given in to the last minute plea for mercy – and I would have been wrong.[20]

There was still a great deal of tribal compartmentalisation going on here; he did not consider the similar dilemma faced by his pro-Treaty peers in 1922. Not that they were shy the same decade in expressing righteousness. The older Seán Mac Eoin got, the more he praised the actions of himself and his colleagues in 1922 as 'the greatest example of patriotism'.[21]

There were other limits to consensus. Fianna Fáil was ousted briefly from power in 1948 and the new Fine Gael-led coalition government declared an Irish Republic, taking southern Ireland out of the Commonwealth and wrong footing and embarrassing de Valera. While he was not going to oppose it, de Valera sourly redrew the civil war dividing line and refused to embrace the shared heritage of the two parties. It was not an occasion for celebrating, he said, when rejecting an invitation to mark the occasion jointly with Fine Gael Taoiseach John A. Costello, as the quest for a united Ireland 'remains uncompleted'.[22]

That quest was largely a quiet and mostly rhetorical one (though the IRA did pursue a violent and failed 'border campaign' from 1956 to 1962) and few other successor states from the post-First World War era managed to achieve the level of political stability present in Ireland after its civil war, as evidenced by the experience of Estonia, Latvia and Hungary, for example. That Fianna Fáil ascended to power so quickly meant 'the danger of volatility created by the party was partially mitigated'. It was also about combining 'a personalistic ethos within democratic institutions'. The civil war remained a touchstone when it came to voters' solidarity with parties, but there were also much deeper roots to the sense of an Irish 'national community' that was autonomous, and when compared to other new nations this sense facilitated parliamentary democracy 'because the idea of a national political authority was not in question'.[23]

The civil war also created, on both sides, a quasi-authoritarian streak of thinking, an impulse for strong centralisation and weak local government (autonomy at that level was systematically eroded over the decades), most memorably encapsulated in the assertion by Seán Lemass that the Irish needed such a centralised style of government owing to their 'fissiparous tendencies'.[24] Dan Breen explained that he had 'nothing but respect' for his civil war enemy Kevin O'Higgins: 'any man in government who will govern will hurt. If he won't hurt, he won't govern.'[25]

Preoccupation with civil war politics did not completely drown out the memory of shared pre-civil war service and purpose, and it was that which could also see veterans from both sides working together, not just in the Old IRA associations, but also in relation to establishing crucial details about War of Independence service. This was reflected in the co-operation in 1941 of Dan Breen and Liam Tobin, for example, in trying to establish how many had been on active service between 1916 and 1921, but crucially, they also had 'a shared sense of grievance about aspects of the new Ireland'.[26] The minute book of the Old IRA Men's Association in Cork from 1934 highlights its aim to 'protect and defend the rights and interests of those who have suffered in establishing and defending the Republic and their dependents'.[27] What mattered most when lobbying for changes to pensions, allowances and hospital care was communal IRA heritage rather than the civil war split. What was desired was legislation 'to provide for all old IRA men in distress'.[28]

There were concerns too that there were 'various organisations in existence whose objectives were identical but not very practicable owing to the fact that they were scattered in various counties all over the country'; what was needed was 'one solid organisation'.[29] Particularly prominent in the National Association of Old IRA were Liam Deasy and Frank Thornton, from either side of the civil war divide. Thornton had been wounded in Tipperary in 1922 following an IRA ambush; he too, like Deasy, rejoined the army during the Emergency; he too, like Deasy, was successful in business.

Veterans were not generally in the business of denying references because they had taken opposite sides in the civil war, something that, while not suggesting bitterness had disappeared, 'goes against the cliché of civil war politics'.[30] Felicity Hayes McCoy also suggested that the messages were more mixed and the inheritances and memories more textured than blanket 'civil war divide' assertions allow for. Some relationships were shattered, but

> not every family divided by the conflict found healing impossible; that was a myth that took hold and became fixed in the national psyche as time went on. Actually, by talking honestly or by avoiding what was contentious, many families like mine who had different views on the Treaty, and in some cases were active nationalists on different sides, managed to reconcile or sidestep their differences and moved forward.[31]

They could share tables at weddings, or sometimes they attended funerals that some of the congregation would not have welcomed them at, like Richard Mulcahy going in 1938 to the funeral of Kathleen Cruise O'Brien, whose son Conor noted that Mulcahy was 'for republicans like my aunt Hanna [Sheehy-Skeffington] the leading hate figure in Ireland. I rather admired him for coming to that funeral which he knew would be attended by Hanna and some of her friends, all of whom hated him.'[32]

In Galway, while silence could predominate ('the son of one IRA volunteer learned about a major aspect of his father's past while reading a book in university'), bonds of loyalty and respect could endure for decades 'even across the bitter Treaty divide'.[33] The pension application of Denis O'Neill includes evidence on his behalf given by Frank Thornton, a close associate of Collins, whom O'Neill is believed to have killed and who himself was badly wounded outside Carlow by anti-Treaty forces in 1922.[34] Lemass also provided supportive information about Charles Dalton, whose brother Emmet was believed by the Lemass family to have been involved in killing Lemass's brother Noel, by sending a five-page handwritten letter to Dalton's wife eighteen years after the civil war elaborating compassionately on Charles's mental fragility during the War of Independence.[35] He was well aware, it seemed, how violence destroyed so much for both victims and perpetrators; indeed, as a sixteen-year-old, Lemass had accidentally shot dead his two-year-old brother Herbert.[36]

CHAPTER TWENTY-FOUR

CODOLOGY

While some never lost their appetite for civil war insults, by the 1950s there was a broader sense that they represented a tiresome, stale politics. Historian Robert Dudley Edwards in 1955 derided a sterile history of recent times presented as 'a one-sided justification of the roles played by our leaders in 1922 ... when will the survivors of the civil war – on both sides – be big enough to admit their failure of judgement? As long as they keep silent their followers are committed to justifying FF and FG in terms of mutual hate.'[1]

James Dillon, the inheritor of an older, pre-revolutionary constitutional nationalist tradition (his father John was the last leader of the Irish Parliamentary Party crushed by Sinn Féin in 1918), prided himself on rising above what he termed the 'codology' that pervaded Dáil business. As the outgoing minister for agriculture, speaking in June 1951 as a new Fianna Fáil government was about to replace the inter-party government, Dillon, who was then an independent TD and had opposed Irish neutrality during the Second World War but was soon to rejoin and later lead Fine Gael, posed this question: 'what ideological differences, if words retain their meaning, divide any two deputies on any side of this house?'

Dillon had just listened to TDs trading civil war insults, and the Labour Party was not immune; its Cork TD Seán Keane, reacting to the nomination of Eamon de Valera as Taoiseach, offered this barb: 'Deputy de Valera was spoken about this evening as being the one man who pulled this country out of every difficulty. I can remember conditions into which Deputy de Valera put this country!' The Ceann Comhairle (speaker of the House), Patrick Hogan, responded wearily: 'The Deputy is too strong on history ... the Deputy is discussing the Irish Civil War but I want him to discuss the motion before the House.'[2] They certainly liked their history, but as Dillon saw it, that was just a smokescreen to hide their essential sameness.

Nöel Browne, former Clann na Poblachta minister for health, and an independent TD from 1951 until 1953, when he joined Fianna Fáil, was struck by the 'prolonged parliamentary squabbles' about the civil war, with those outside of this frame of reference or without civil war pedigree considered 'irrelevant and tiresome interlopers ... with no wounds to display and no blood on our hands'.[3] When he first came into the Dáil in 1948 he was shocked by the 'white hot hate ... the trigger words were "seventy-seven", "Ballyseedy" ... and, above all "The Treaty"'. He too, saw it as a distraction from serious debate on policy issues.[4]

The tribalists had a particular dislike of independents or former independents. Lemass despised Browne, and while that was partly because Browne was often dislikeable, drearily long-winded and arrogant ('He regarded himself as superior', according to Lemass), it was part of a more general loathing of independents.[5] They were, declared Lemass, 'among the most pathetic phenomena in public life ... his personal interest is to survive ... self-interest every time ... the so-called independent deputy is a bloody nuisance ... that is all he will ever be in parliament.'[6] That was a misplaced detestation: between 1945 and 2016, 3,130 TDs were elected to the Dáil, of whom 137 were independents (4.4 per cent), fifty-nine times the proportion elected in the UK. Part of the explanation lies in the fact that for so long Irish politics was dominated by the two civil war parties and a centrist Labour Party, meaning 'many niche interests' were not represented by the main parties.[7]

Lemass's derision also elided the questions of what Fianna Fáil stood for and what Fine Gael did not. When Lemass was asked what the difference was by an American journalist after the 1957 general election, which saw Fianna Fáil replace the Fine Gael-led coalition that had been in place since 1954, he reputedly stumbled somewhat and then answered 'well, the main difference is: we're in and they're out'.[8] It was a reminder that, by then, what had historically put some water between them – attitudes to law and order, Anglo-Irish and international relations (some in Fine Gael more open to links with the Commonwealth, notwithstanding a Fine Gael Taoiseach declaring the Republic in 1949), free trade and Northern Ireland, coloured by their 1920s stances and heritage – had clearly faded, though not completely. Both came to embrace the idea of export-led growth for a small open economy and rowed about management of finances rather than complete economic remodelling.

In 1957 J. V. Kelleher, a well-known Irish American, writing in the American journal *Foreign Affairs*, argued that a hatred of intellectual and psychological freedom was killing the country: 'Every democratic politician has the right to be pushed. The sad truth is that there has been no push at all in the Irish political situation since before the war. Instead of vocal discontent, there is silent emigration; and in what emigration leaves behind there is apathy below and smugness above.' And what of those running the Irish political show? 'To a great extent this has been achieved by a round-robin process of politicians, clergymen, professional Gaels, pietists and other comfortable bourgeoisie looking into each other's hearts and finding there, or pretending to find, the same tepid desires.'[9]

Such acerbity suggested the very impulses that created stability and consensus in the earlier decades of independence also facilitated a fundamental neglect of civic morality and citizenship, and these gloomy prognoses were deepened by the scale of emigration in the 1950s, when over half a million people left. But were children of the veterans still 'fighting their father's fight'? There was scepticism in some quarters by the early 1950s that too many in politics, in the words of a political correspondent in the *Irish Times* in June 1954, 'seem to be the son or the widow of someone who mattered'. Surveying the new cabinet, including Liam Cosgrave, he suggested

> they are all estimable people, without a spark of fire or enthusiasm – all that seems to have died with the last generation ... they seem to be content to follow in father's footsteps, along the lines which may have been new in 1922, but are stale today. They have nothing fresh to offer and are not going to die before a firing squad ... of course, that is right and proper.

But he wondered if the ghosts of Irish republicanism would look down at them and 'laugh – or cry'.[10] The political inheritance, it seemed, left 'very little psychological space in which to manoeuvre'.[11]

While Fine Gael shared power in coalition governments during 1948–51 and 1954–7, it then endured a return to the opposition benches until 1973, and its organisational staleness was not helped by senior members who devoted much of their attention to more profitable jobs while they were also TDs. In the 1960s some younger party members, notably Declan Costello, urged an ideological repositioning in the direction of a 'just society' through economic planning and targets for the public and private sectors, credit policies for banks under government control, sustained public capital investment and full and effective price controls. This crisis of identity for Fine Gael was never fully resolved. Most revealing, and a reminder of the long reach of civil war politics, was the response of one of the party's stalwarts, Gerard Sweetman, that the country needed 'alternative governments rather than alternative policies'.[12] The party's leader, James Dillon, did not believe in the 'just society' document and at the same time it was being unveiled he declared Fine Gael to be a private investment party. The party gained no new seats in the 1965 general election on the back of it, but the main reason its backbenchers supported the change of direction was because they were desperate to distinguish themselves from Fianna Fáil.

The real problem, according to Niamh Puirséil, historian of the Labour Party, was that the 'just society' idea was 'an effort to turn Fine Gael into a slightly left-wing party for people who were too snobbish to join the Labour Party'. She justifies this assertion by pointing out that Garret FitzGerald, though he had toyed with the idea of joining the Labour Party early in his career, ultimately did not because of its ties with the trade unions.[13]

The parties remained wedded to a conservative model of politics and its benches continued to be filled with TDs who ideologically shared much more than divided them. This has been seen as positive by some, as the lack of political extremism was in contrast to the lurches and excesses seen elsewhere at various stages, including the 1930s. In 2002 journalist Mary Holland suggested, 'The fact that the political debate was rooted in whose grandfather shot who in the early years of the last century was a major factor in enabling us to escape the worst extremes of some of our most sophisticated neighbours.'[14] But as *Irish Times* political commentator John Healy saw it in the 1960s, it was also about the 'stability of stagnation' and a 'barren dialogue which the civil war spawned'. It was the civil war, he suggested, that bred 'contempt for the democratic processes and institutions' and devalued the science of politics due to the triumph of those who were 'peddlers of recriminatory politics'. The people, he suggested, had disposed of the Treaty, 'but it continued to dominate politics ... slogans were substituted for thinking and there was no need to think of sociological goals ... those men fossilised parliamentary politics, closing out the people by closing out problems with which the people were concerned.'[15]

This was a distorted and exaggerated summation, most striking for its disallowance of any agency to the voters themselves, who, by his logic, were dim and docile. Nor is there any mention of the survival of Irish democracy when it crumbled elsewhere in Europe. But he could hardly be accused of exaggerating the stagnation. Perhaps what was missing in some of the Healy-type analysis was the extent to which the battles of that generation had not just been political but also personal, before they became 'bald or grey, pouncing, tired or sceptical'.[16]

Yet the civil war animus did not die. In 1968, when Desmond O'Malley contested a by-election in Limerick for Fianna Fáil and was up against Fine Gael's Tom O'Higgins, a nephew of Kevin O'Higgins, O'Malley's election director, Neil Blaney, got into a rage at the name O'Higgins being daubed on footpaths. Blaney's volunteers retaliated by painting the figure '77', a reference to the commonly accepted number of republicans executed during the civil war, after O'Higgins's name. It caused widespread anger and the young Fianna Fáil candidate was disgusted by the stunt.[17] Notwithstanding, a year later, to mark the fiftieth anniversary of the first Dáil, surviving veterans after the commemorative event in Dublin 'diverged into two dinner groups'; six dined with Fine Gael leader Liam Cosgrave while two other survivors attended a separate dinner addressed by Fianna Fáil Taoiseach Jack Lynch.[18]

Nonetheless, Michael Hayes, appointed minister for education in the provisional government in January 1922 and who then served as speaker of the Dáil until 1932 and presided over the entry into it of Fianna Fáil, suggested the same year that the bitterness engendered by the civil war 'has been exaggerated, both as to depth and duration'. In university, he maintained, the sons of opposite sides conversed together.

Education and privilege undoubtedly oiled such processes, but there was also a stability to Irish politics and a shared respect for its processes that were advantageous. Hayes recalled that

> A Canadian, afterwards Minister for Finance, visiting Dáil Éireann, was astonished that I could ring Mr de Valera's room and bring my visitor up straight away. Such a thing, he said, could not happen in Canada in relations with the leader of another party ... The Dáil was an institution and was able to overcome those who opposed it. Later it absorbed internal opponents and still survives, the only democratic Parliament which remains of the many new ones which were set up after the 1914–1918 War.[19]

Pragmatism was also evident in the restoration of Kilmainham Jail in the 1960s. Dubbed 'the Bastille of Ireland', it contained bitter civil war memories (including the execution of republicans there) and the building had fallen into ruin after its closure in 1924. When restoration was mooted, the Old IRA Association offered support provided nothing relating to after 1921 would be identified with the project and in the early years the civil war was deliberately rarely mentioned.[20]

Others were faithful to the 1922 legacy in their own distinct way, noticeably Erskine Childers Jr. His father before his execution wanted him to make peace with those who ordered his death ('I forgive them and so must you') and told him if he ever went into politics 'you must not speak of my execution in public'. It was a promise he kept.[21] Erskine Jr was quite detached from tribal politics and regarded as a long-winded maverick, yet he was serious about honouring his father's request. In devoting himself to the theme of reconciliation, however, he departed from his father's ideology: Erskine Sr had written to his wife, Molly, just before his execution: 'dead, I shall have a better chance of being understood and of helping the cause'.[22] But similar to Ruairí Brugha, Erskine Jr, who became president of Ireland in 1973, came to question that, suggesting in a private letter to the Taoiseach Liam Cosgrave in 1974 that there needed to be a focus not just on those who died for Ireland, but those who 'worked for Ireland ... we do not do half enough to commemorate the lives of those who worked for Ireland in the social, political and cultural fields.'[23] Yet he was writing those lines to the son of W. T. Cosgrave and there was nothing but tension between them, suggesting the ongoing relevance of the 1922 divide, while in his own party, Erskine's lack of trenchancy made him an object of suspicion.[24]

CHAPTER TWENTY-FIVE

BLIND LOYALTY ERODED

Active discouragement of political theorising was also a feature of civil war politics. Political scientist Tom Garvin noted of Fianna Fáil in 1976 that 'ideological commitment of any kind is frowned upon in the party'.[1] Fianna Fáil senator Eoin Ryan, whose father James was a founding member of the party, insisted the differences between the rival parties were not ideological but boiled down to Fianna Fáil's 'close contact with the grassroots ... we have, you could say, an instinct for what people want.'[2] It was also more disciplined, better organised and had a self-proclaimed status as a 'national movement' rather than a political party; over the course of twenty-five general elections from 1927 to 2007 it secured an average of roughly 45 per cent of the vote. But that dominance and orderliness was not felt to be guaranteed as the civil war generation bowed out of politics. Lemass noted in 1968, two years after he retired, that 'between us old timers there was a comradeship that will be impossible in the more sophisticated type of government of the future'.[3]

Earlier that decade Lemass had to endure the ever argumentative minister for agriculture, Paddy Smith, and was relieved to see him resign in 1964 over disagreements about the government's relationship with trade unions and what he regarded as its urban bias, but Lemass also had the security of knowing 'he was one of us. I mean he was a civil war man ... it was just inconceivable that he could go anywhere else except FF and therefore there was no danger to party unity ... this helped me in my speedy decision to accept his resignation.'[4] He was correct; Smith, a founding member of the party, stayed on the back benches until 1977, by which time he was father of the Dáil, almost fifty years after he had been chosen as a Sinn

Féin candidate while interned during the civil war. Lemass surmised that, owing to generational change, this was the last era in which the Fianna Fáil leadership would be able to bank on such blanket loyalty:

> You wouldn't have that at all now. You'd have some fellow whispering to the opposite side ... we are in a new situation where new members are going to be far more independent and less amenable to party discipline ... it will cause more difficulties in the future ... older members are far more loyal basically to the party than the younger people are.[5]

Smith's resignation gave Lemass the opportunity to promote his son-in-law Charles Haughey, and the further Haughey rose, the more difficult it became to maintain party unity. In referring to Fianna Fáil members like Haughey whose parents had supported the Treaty, Lemass suggested, 'These people are there because of an intellectual position ... they didn't come there by inheritance', which would mean not unquestioning obedience, but 'this business of handling the party and bring[ing] them along with you. Then, we didn't have to work at it at all.'[6]

As a young politician Haughey had been surrounded in his party branch by the sons of civil war veterans on the other side to his father, including George Colley and Harry Boland, with whom Haughey ran a successful accountancy practice. Just before Charles's death in 2006 he referred to his father as 'a committed supporter of Cumann na nGaedheal ... very [Michael] Collins'. His father's allegiance to the Free State side was said to have enraged Frank Aiken, and 'this greatly influenced Aiken's detestation of Haughey's son whom he saw as a "Free Stater" opportunist in Fianna Fáil clothes'.[7] Haughey did, however, have more of a sense of northern republicanism, given his parents' background, northern visitors to the house and trips across the border.

Garret FitzGerald, who became Haughey's arch political foe in the 1980s, voted for Fianna Fáil in the 1961 general election, believing that Lemass was 'the best Taoiseach available for the purpose of initiating a long overdue process of economic growth'. FitzGerald did not want to join Fianna Fáil, however, when he decided to enter politics in 1964 as he felt the party was falling into the hands of 'conservative materialists and traditional nationalists'. Instead, he opted for Fine Gael because it had a tradition of 'less aggressive nationalism' and a 'strong tradition of integrity'.[8]

This emphasis on integrity, or what Tom Garvin described as the 'moralist' approach to politics, endured and indeed was stiffened by the arms crisis of 1970, when Taoiseach Jack Lynch sacked two ministers, Neil Blaney and Haughey, for not subscribing to party policy on Northern Ireland, having been informed by the leader of Fine Gael, Liam Cosgrave, of a subversive plot in his party. Haughey was charged with importation of arms for use by Northern nationalists and, though he was acquitted, the issue poisoned the politics of the period. It was a reminder of the destabilising impact of the Northern Irish Troubles on the politics of the Republic and it also allowed Cosgrave to invoke civil war ghosts; then, as now, contended Cosgrave, Fine Gael was in the business of rescuing the state from lawlessness: 'only for this party there would be a real danger of civil war'. As he saw it, Fianna Fáil was hamstrung 'by having built myths into its very foundation'.[9]

Cosgrave's colleague John Kelly carved a niche for himself that decade by castigating Fianna Fáil as a 'political dodo of boastful intransigence'. He also expressed the view that political partisanship was a 'good thing' for democracy: 'there should be, on each side, a hard core of people committed with their hearts rather than their heads'.[10]

Both parties, however, were back in unison when it came to the importance of Ireland joining the EEC in 1973. That there was consensus from both sides of the civil war divide on major foreign policy milestones and, ultimately, facing down the IRA (fear that the Troubles would lead to civil war for the island 'shaped the policies of the Dublin government during that period') was a reminder of the endurance of significant shared priorities. That both embraced democracy even during times of convulsion meant there was shared purpose about the political order, Garvin concluding that, 'despite their mistakes and sins the Irish revolutionaries turned politicians got it more right than wrong'.[11]

A difficulty for both parties, however, was the changing behaviour of voters and the gradual erosion of blind loyalty. For decades it was unthinkable for many of both parties' supporters to transfer votes to each other under Ireland's single transferrable vote system, or to actually switch party preference from election to election. When, eventually, Irish electoral behaviour was first professionally analysed in 1969 it was discovered that Fianna Fáil managed the extraordinary feat of receiving equal support from all social classes, an achievement no other party could match, helped by its historic organisational spread and Lemass's courting of the labour movement in the 1960s. The same year, 90 per cent of voters indicated a preference for the same party as in the previous election, but by 1981 the proportion had fallen to 75 per cent. Thereafter, the electorate became more promiscuous. When he was interviewed by political scientist Peter Mair about this trend after he resigned as Taoiseach in 1979, Fianna Fáil leader Jack Lynch observed: 'In the old days ... one was either pro-de Valera or anti-de Valera, or pro-Lemass or anti-Lemass, or neither and then one supported Labour.'[12]

That he could sum up Irish electoral behaviour in such a way was an indication that Fianna Fáil believed the political world revolved around it; although adapting its techniques and modernising from the 1970s onwards, it still stuck to that mindset, despite the unprecedented challenge of a revitalised Fine Gael under Garret FitzGerald's leadership from 1977, an energy that propelled it to within striking distance of Fianna Fáil and to coalition government with Labour in 1982–7. The Fine Gael revival also involved the practical building up of the party's national network, the centralisation of power and the ruthless imposition of decisions from above.

Whatever doubts existed about the manner in which he ran the party, his colleagues recognised that FitzGerald was by far their greatest electoral asset in taking on Haughey, who had become leader of Fianna Fáil in 1979. FitzGerald had a penchant for occasionally radical rhetoric about social justice, redistribution and a more pluralist national identity, including getting rid of the Irish Constitution's territorial claim over Northern Ireland. Therein lay his dilemmas, both as a party leader – his Fine Gael contained a traditional and a modernising wing – and as a national leader attempting to be a reformer at a time of recession and strife.[13] FitzGerald's leadership galvanised the party's grassroots, but did not solve the Irish economic crisis of the 1980s which Fianna Fáil had done much to generate.

John Kelly dramatically changed his stance on the differences between the two main parties in the 1980s, suggesting Fine Gael could contemplate an 'arrangement' with Fianna Fáil, 'the other half of the old Siamese twin'. By 1989 he was privately arguing that it was not 'possible to fault Fianna Fáil convincingly on any of the old grounds'.[14] Fianna Fáil, he believed, was behaving more responsibly and showing less irredentism in relation to Northern Ireland. Retrospectively, Kelly seemed to regard the mid 1970s as the golden age for Fine Gael (it served in government with Labour from 1973 for four years before Fianna Fáil galloped back to power in 1977) precisely because it had what he regarded as a completely different identity:

> When Liam Cosgrave was leader it was easy to see Fine Gael, sincerely, as the one rational and moderate and more or less honest political option for the country and correspondingly easy to detest and oppose Fianna Fáil. In 1973 and thereafter they were arrogant, bullying, often corrupt, opportunistic, irresponsible about both the North and the economy. When Liam went out in 1977 his party could hold its head high.[15]

There was little appetite within Fine Gael for Kelly's sentiment, despite the decision of FitzGerald's successor, Alan Dukes, to announce in opposition in 1987 that 'When the Government is moving in the right direction, I will not oppose the central thrust of its policy ... any other policy of opposition would amount to a cynical exploitation of short-term political opportunities.'[16] It could be argued that this was the beginning of the end of civil war politics, and Dukes even went as far as suggesting coalition with Fianna Fáil after the 1989 general election, for which there was no enthusiasm on either side. Ten years later, Garret FitzGerald, while accepting the differences between the parties had not for a long time been socioeconomic, but 'on degrees of intensity of nationalism' and 'sensitivity to issues of probity', believed a merger of the two would be unwise, creating a 'monster' party with the capacity to govern indefinitely instead of alternating governments offering choices about 'distribution of national resources'.[17] Notwithstanding the efforts of the modernisers, the Dáil also remained bereft of gender balance; indeed, even at the very end of the century it stood out 'as a patriarchal fortress, where women, with only 12% of seats, were not even half way to constituting a quarter of its membership ... Ireland lay twelfth among European Union nations for women's election.'[18]

Meanwhile Fianna Fáil dissidents led by Desmond O'Malley, who abhorred Haughey, broke away to form a new party, The Progressive Democrats, in December 1985, maintaining the 'old loyalties on which the civil war parties had been founded were no longer enough to sustain them'.[19] Advocating tax reform, support for private enterprise, separation of church and state and a peaceful approach to Northern Ireland, it briefly soared, but then declined, surviving as a very small party that ironically ended up in coalition with Fianna Fáil before dissolving in 2009. It won the tax-cuts argument, and forced Fianna Fáil in 1989 finally to accept the option of coalition government, but did not break the dominance of the civil war parties.

While portraying Fine Gael as a party for the privileged, Fianna Fáil continued to maintain it was classless, something it had insisted on right from its foundation. It did not accept the validity of 'class politics' as suitable to Ireland. Fine Gael, which had a traditional reliance on wealthy professionals and large farmers, by this reckoning was 'un-Irish', while Fianna Fáil insisted, directly and indirectly, there was no need for the Labour Party because *it* was the real party for the working classes. Many trade union members seemed to agree and voted for Fianna Fáil; one of the ITGWU leaders in the 1980s maintained none of the other parties 'could talk to the Unions as well as Fianna Fáil'.[20] But the Labour Party also experienced a resurgence in the early 1990s, only to find itself, with an unprecedented thirty-three seats, in coalition with Fianna Fáil, the party it had so regularly castigated. At the time of its seventieth birthday in 1996 Fianna Fáil's historical approach to winning and keeping power was encapsulated by historian Joe Lee as a pragmatism that enabled them to 'square the economic and social circles'.[21] That was a hugely successful strategy but the party could not square circles indefinitely.

In time, a Fianna Fáil that prided itself on post civil-war welfarism, skilful wielding of power and the common touch was exposed by an accumulation of revelations, financial scandals, cover-ups and incompetence in government. These problems began in the 1960s as some of the younger generation of Fianna Fáil ministers began to cultivate links with the business world, but the extent of the corruption of individuals associated with the party was laid bare for all to see by the early twenty-first century.[22] It brought Fianna Fáil full circle. The party of self-proclaimed 'men of no property' came to power in 1932 deriding Cumann na nGaedheal's patronage of wealthy backers. The party that thrived on marshalling discontent, and promised, in the words of de Valera in 1926 to promote 'a programme for the common good, not a class programme' and who crushed the Labour Party in the process, came to be seen as a party that contributed to the economic collapse by indulging the men of property.

As to its historic swagger – the kind political correspondent Dick Walsh in 1990 described as 'like an overbearing heavyweight in late night company who cannot see how anyone can take a different view and in certain circumstances, why anyone should be allowed to do so'[23] – by 2011, that lay in tatters. This was a result of the financial crash, its egregious mismanagement of the economy and the exposure of a corruption that was referred to in a tribunal report that examined allegations of payments to politicians, as 'systemic and endemic', a venality not exclusively confined to Fianna Fáil.[24]

CHAPTER TWENTY-SIX

NOT CARING WHO DID WHAT

Modern scepticism of how civil war politics developed also meant the fallen of that war – the lost leaders – were elevated and exaggerated for their purity and potential, especially Michael Collins: 'the name rises immaculate and bright as a sovereign from the mire of events that muddy all normal men'.[1] Collins, insisted former Fianna Fáil minister David Andrews in 2001, could not be claimed by any contemporary party and would have disapproved of Cumann na nGaedheal's conservatism in the 1920s because he had written in 1922 about the need to avoid 'destitution or poverty at one end and at the other an excess of riches'. There was, Andrews further suggested, a 'Collins side of Cumann na nGaedheal' concerned with 'republicanism and social justice' whose adherents by 1932 had 'crossed to Fianna Fáil'. Had Collins lived, a 'repressive law and order agenda' would have been resisted and opposition to republicanism and social justice overcome.[2]

While it is true that there were different wings within Cumann na nGaedheal, the idea that Collins, who was undoubtedly exceptionally able and talented, would have been a uniquely progressive, unifying force is not rooted in any solid basis and there is no reason to believe that he would not have found common cause with the steeliness of his colleagues in late 1922 in the face of what was regarded as the outrageous defiance of the anti-Treaty side. Neither is there evidence Collins admired socialism or that he subscribed to a particular social or economic ideology. While he rhetorically criticised excessive capitalism and emphasised the necessity of a 'sound economic life in which great discrepancies cannot occur', with labour free to take its place as 'an element in the life of the nation', he was equally anxious, in his own words, to 'safely avoid State Socialism ... which has nothing to commend it in a country like Ireland'.[3] Class politics was in his view, 'a lower form of politics and beyond centrist sentiment'.[4]

Collins's civil war-era vision was filled with clichéd meanderings about the restoring of what he characterised as an ancient, glorious and democratic Gaelic civilisation. This was the kind of indulgence in myth beloved of many of that era, including de Valera. The idea was that the male patriots would restore what Collins referred to in his collected articles and speeches, *The Path to Freedom*, published in 1922, as an epoch when

> the people of the whole nation were united, not by material
> forces but by spiritual ones ... the Irish social and economic
> system was democratic. It was simple and harmonious. The
> people had security in their rights and just law ... their men
> of high learning ranked with the kings and sat beside them in
> equality at the high table.[5]

There were many instances of the Collins legacy being played out in terms of the myth of the great lost leader, as he became a blank canvas on to which his champions could paint whatever idealised image they wished. Authors of books, plays and memoirs as well as filmmakers, notably Neil Jordan in his 1996 film *Michael Collins*, which, in venerating Collins, made de Valera almost a cartoon villain, posited the Collins they needed, and he 'endured in all the ways we wanted him, far more than any other figure from that time'. Part of the need to understand him 'is to accept that the imagined Collins matters as much as the real one'.[6] De Valera, because of his survival and political dominance, eclipsed Collins, but also vindicated Collins's 'freedom to achieve freedom' view of the Treaty.[7]

Dramatic claims and exaggerated conclusions abounded at the annual gathering at Béal na Blá to commemorate Collins, and while they reflected the high esteem in which he continued to be held, the cross that marked his death was also 'a monument to grief' and to 'a past before civil war'.[8] The annual orations often represented misty-eyed and selective indulgence, a simplifying of what was a complex life, and overlooked the anger and confusion of Ireland in the early 1920s. It was very convenient, for example, for the attorney general, Declan Costello, during the intensity of the Northern Ireland Troubles, to assert at the annual commemoration in 1973 that rather than his military or organisational strategies it was Collins's 'remarkable moral qualities' that 'raised him to a position of pre-eminence'.[9] By the early twenty-first century there was a fairly desperate scraping of the barrel to come up with new ways to divorce Collins from his era. The Collins 22 Society, established in 2002, asserted that Collins 'offers us a vision of a healthy society based on our God-given human dignity', a curious assertion about the former director of intelligence for the IRA.[10]

It was not until 2010 that a Fianna Fáil politician was invited to address the Béal na Blá gathering. Minister for finance Brian Lenihan focused on the economic crash and banking crisis and the challenges faced by Collins, suggesting that they had given him perspective and encouragement as minister for finance facing the current crisis. He also addressed the theme of reconciliation, and his presence was regarded as historic and cathartic. The context for Lenihan's speech was the extent of the calamitous economic and banking meltdown that meant international lenders stopped lending to Ireland and the state was forced to accept an EU/ECB/IMF bailout at the end of 2010 which eventually amounted to over €60 billion. A humiliating milestone, indicating an effective loss of sovereignty, as massive private debt became a public one, it carried a particular charge, given the history of the Irish battle to achieve independence almost one hundred years previously.

This crisis led to considerable reflection on the nature of Irish decision making, political leadership, lack of distribution of power, financial regulation and links between business and politics. Garret FitzGerald suggested the same year that, in contrast to more recent leaders, the civil war generation through its 'unselfish patriotism' had provided a barrier 'to the spread to politics of the socially inadequate value system that we, as a people, had inherited from our colonial past'. This may be too sweeping an assertion, but there is some truth in it.[11]

The following year, in the context of the looming decade of centenaries of events central to the Irish revolution, thirty-two-year-old Fine Gael minister Leo Varadkar, six years later to be Ireland's youngest Taoiseach, in a clear break with his predecessors, made no bones about events such as the Ballyseedy mine outrage in 1923: 'people killed without trial by the first government were murdered'.[12] But passions never fully burned out; three years later a monument to the dead of the Knocknagoshel atrocity in 1923 was vandalised; it had been unveiled the previous year and in the audience was the son of the sole Ballyseedy survivor, Stephen Fuller.[13]

Reconciliation, piety, vandalism and posturing were still a living part of the civil war legacy, but what had changed dramatically was the political landscape. Some Fine Gael strategists had urged the party under the leadership of Enda Kenny not to wallow in its history and focus instead, especially after a disastrous general election in 2002 which left it with thirty-one seats to Fianna Fáil's eighty-one, on the idea of the 'progressive centre' by marrying facets of Fianna Fáil's populism with 'the great ideals which Fine Gael stands for'. It recovered to win fifty-one seats in 2007.[14] Given the gravity of the subsequent economic crisis, it merely needed to profit from its great rival's inevitable demise by, in the words of one of its TDs, 'feasting over the carcass of Fianna Fáil', which it did by winning seventy-six seats in 2011 in a Dáil of 166 while Labour won thirty-seven and Fianna Fáil just twenty.[15] The resultant government was a coalition of Fine Gael and Labour that had an unprecedented parliamentary majority.

Swapping Fianna Fáil for Fine Gael was hardly a revolutionary act by the electorate, given that the two parties' shared heritage and relative ideological compatibility, but Fine Gael was now the biggest party in the Dáil for the first time since 1927 (as Cumann na nGaedheal), and Kenny was proposed as Taoiseach by his youngest party colleague, who announced, 'Today, we hang out our brightest colours and together, under Deputy Kenny's leadership, we move forward yet again as a nation.' This was a reworking of words used in a letter by playwright George Bernard Shaw to Michael Collins's sister Hannie after Collins's death in 1922, a reminder that civil war touchstones were still deemed of use in the party 'after eighty years of playing second fiddle to Fianna Fáil'.[16] Kenny, too, sought to draw dubious parallels between the task he faced and that which faced Collins in the early 1920s, suggesting he had equal determination, and later insisted his party had reinstated the 'values' of the state's founders.[17]

The Fianna Fáil leader from 2011, Micheál Martin, promised to take his party back to its roots ('a community party that's in touch with the people'), while Kenny managed to preside over economic recovery and political stability and won the next general election in 2016, albeit with a much reduced seat tally, while the Labour Party was trounced. From 2016 to 2020 Fianna Fáil, having spurned Kenny's offer of coalition, agreed to support a minority Fine Gael government in the form of a 'confidence and supply' agreement, another indication of the dilution of historic enmities. A shared desire from 1998 to protect the peace process that brought an end to the Troubles was also a part of the politics of consensus, while from 2016, when Britain voted to leave the EU, the tortuous Brexit drama also saw them on the same page in relation to protecting the by then soft border in Ireland. The Brexit process also generated a shared Irish nationalist distaste of English ignorance of the significance of that issue and the danger of Ireland once again being a pawn in a distinctly English power game. This was a point made strongly by new Fine Gael Taoiseach Leo Varadkar who was also keen to emphasise his awareness of the context in which the Irish state had emerged and the central role in that of his party's predecessors.

Also significant was that the priorities of a younger generation continued to be problematic for the successors of both the winners and the losers of the civil war. In 2019, as the planet continued to burn, one of the best-known young Green Party politicians, Mayo's twenty-nine-year-old Saoirse McHugh, declared, 'I don't care who did what during the civil war.'[18] But to achieve power, her party had to enter coalition with the parties of the civil war divide, a coalition agreed in 2020 that was historic due to it being the first time Fianna Fáil and Fine Gael shared power. It was also an indication of their decline; between them they had secured only 43.1 per cent of the vote in that year's general election in contrast to almost 82 per cent forty years earlier.

Sinn Féin, as the major beneficiary of the peace process, continued to advance by in many respects successfully replicating what Fianna Fáil had done in the 1930s through attention to grassroots organisation, the claim to champion those of little or no property, the demand for aggressive state intervention for welfare purposes and a persistent rhetoric about ending partition. It won thirty-seven seats out of a Dáil of 160 in the 2020 general election. The civil war parties were partly thrown together through a common determination to keep Sinn Féin out of government: 'We do not believe that Sinn Féin operates to the same democratic standards held by every other party in this House' was the response of Micheál Martin, a reference to its association with the IRA. It was a similar accusation that his new partner's predecessors had made of Fianna Fáil in the 1930s.

As Martin prepared to begin his term as Taoiseach, a rotating position to be shared with Leo Varadkar, it was Varadkar who declared, 'Civil War politics ended a long time ago in our country, but today, Civil War politics ends in our parliament.'[19] Martin let it be known that his office would include portraits of both Michael Collins and Eamon de Valera. This was a fusion that some, including *Dublin Opinion* magazine, had wistfully lamented the absence of in 1922 during the early stages of the civil war with a drawing of the two men reaching for each other's hands under the title: 'If Only ...'[20]

NOTES

Introduction: Faith, Reason and Betrayal

1   University College Dublin Archives (UCDA), Papers of Eamon de Valera, P150/1657, de Valera to Mary MacSwiney, 11 September 1922.

2   Liam Deasy, *Brother Against Brother* (Cork, 1982); Michael Hopkinson, *Green Against Green: The Irish Civil War* (Dublin, 1988).

3   Monk Gibbon (ed.), *The Living Torch: AE* (London, 1937), p. 191.

4   National Archives of Ireland (NAI), Department of Taoiseach (DT), S1322, Winston Churchill to Michael Collins, 12 April 1922.

5   Paul Bew, *Churchill and Ireland* (Oxford, 2016), pp. 113–31.

6   Ronan Fanning, *Eamon de Valera: A Will to Power* (London, 2015), p. 127.

7   Maryann Gialanella Valiulis, 'The Man They Could Never Forgive: The View of the Opposition: Eamon de Valera and the Civil War', in Joseph O'Carroll and John A. Murphy (eds.), *De Valera and His Times* (Cork, 1986), pp. 92–100.

8   National University of Ireland Galway Archives (NUIGA), Papers of Michael Rynne, P133/4/7/23, 'Extracts from Journal 1922', 18 January 1922, 13 March and 2 July 1922.

9   Ibid., P133/4/7/11, Rynne to 'M', 12 May 1922.

10 Frank Gallagher, *Days of Fear* (Cork, 1967), p. 41.

11 Charles Townshend, *The Republic: The Fight for Irish Independence, 1918–1923* (London, 2013), p. 19.

12 David Andrews, 'Collins has more in common with Fianna Fáil ideals', *Irish Times*, 18 August 2001.

13 Michael Laffan, *Judging W. T. Cosgrave: The Foundation of the Irish State* (Dublin, 2014), pp. 120–21.

14 Seán Enright, *The Irish Civil War: Law, Execution and Atrocity* (Dublin, 2019), p. 120.

15 Bill Kissane, *The Politics of the Irish Civil War* (Oxford, 2005), p. 97.

16 NAI, DT S1369/12, unsent letter of W. T. Cosgrave to Rev. R. Ayres, Holy Cross Prison, Tralee, 1 January 1923.

17 UCDA, Papers of Desmond FitzGerald, P80/287(3), 'Muriel MacSwiney in Washington, September 1922'.

18 David Armitage, *Civil Wars: A History in Ideas* (New York, 2018), pp. 238–9.

19 Stathis Kalyvas, *The Logic of Violence in Civil War* (New York, 2005), p. 209.

20 J. J. Lee, *Ireland 1912–1985: Politics and Society* (Cambridge, 1989), p. 77.

21 Townshend, *The Republic*, p. 452.

22 Anne Dolan, 'Killing in "the Good Old Irish Fashion"? Irish Revolutionary Violence in Context', *Irish Historical Studies*, 44(165), May 2020, pp. 11–25.

23 Ibid.

24 Bill Kissane, 'On the Shock of Civil War: Cultural Trauma and National Identity in Finland and Ireland', in *Nations and Nationalism: Journal for the Association of the Study of Ethnicity and Nationalism*, 26(1), June 2020, pp. 22–43.

25 Townshend, *The Republic*, p. 452.

26 Cork City and County Archives (CCCA), U271/A/47, De Róiste diaries, 18 April 1923.

27 Patrick Murray, *Oracles of God: The Roman Catholic Church and Irish Politics, 1922–37* (Dublin, 2000), p. 83.

28 Seán O'Faoláin, *Inishfallen: Fare Thee Well* (London, 1949), pp. 89–90.

29 Richard English and Cormac K. H. O'Malley (eds.), *Prisoners: The Civil War Letters of Ernie O'Malley* (Dublin 1991), Ernie O'Malley to Molly Childers, 23 November 1923.

30 Anne Dolan, 'The Papers in Context', in Cormac K. H. O'Malley and Anne Dolan (eds.), *No Surrender Here! The Civil War Papers of Ernie O'Malley, 1922–1924* (Dublin, 2007), pp. xliii–liii.

31 Ibid., and Brian Hanley, 'Terror in Twentieth-Century Ireland', in David Fitzpatrick (ed.), *Terror in Ireland, 1916–1923* (Dublin, 2012), pp. 10–26.

32 Richard J. Evans, *Altered Pasts: Counterfactuals in History* (London, 2014), p. 30.

33 R. F. Foster, *Vivid Faces: The Revolutionary Generation in Ireland, 1890–1923* (London, 2014) and David Fitzpatrick, *Harry Boland's Irish Revolution* (Cork, 2003), pp. 326–7.

34 Calton Younger, *Ireland's Civil War* (London, 1968), p. 506.

35 Eoin Neeson, *The Civil War in Ireland* (Cork, 1966).

36 Hopkinson, *Green Against Green*, p. xii.

37   Ibid.
38   Anne Dolan, review of Bill Kissane, *The Politics of the Irish Civil War*, in *Reviews in History*, March 2006, www.history.ac.uk/reviews/ review/502, accessed 21 January 2019.
39   Townshend, *The Republic*, p. 359.
40   Frank O'Connor, *An Only Child* (London, 1961), pp. 256–7.
41   Lennox Robinson (ed.), *Lady Gregory's Journals, 1916–1930* (London, 1946), entry for 12 December 1923, pp. 195–6.
42   Leeann Lane, *Dorothy Macardle* (Dublin, 2019), p. 183.
43   Margaret Ward, *Unmanageable Revolutionaries: Women and Irish Nationalism* (London, 1995), p. 176.
44   Ibid., p. 192.
45   Jimmy Wren, *The GPO Garrison Easter Week 1916: A Biographical Dictionary* (Dublin, 2015), pp. 389, 410–11.
46   CCCA, U271/A/147, De Róiste diaries, 10 November 1922.
47   Eunan O'Halpin and Mary Staines, '"Between Two Hells": The Social, Political and Military Backgrounds and Motivations of the 121 TDs Who Voted for or Against the Anglo-Irish Treaty in January 1922', in Liam Weeks and Mícheál Ó Fathartaigh (eds.), *The Treaty: Debating and Establishing the Irish State* (Dublin, 2018), pp. 73–83.
48   Ibid.
49   Ibid.
50   Peter Hart, *The IRA and Its Enemies: Violence and Community in Cork, 1916–1923* (London, 1998), p. 147, and Brian Hanley, '"Merely Tuppence Half-Penny Looking down on Tuppence?": Class, the Second Dáil and Irish Republicanism', in Weeks and Ó Fathartaigh, *The Treaty*, pp. 60–70.
51   Foster, *Vivid Faces*, p. 311.
52   Irish Military Archives (IMA), Military Service Pensions Collection (MSPC), Administration Files, SP G/10, Eddie McAteer to Army Pensions Board (APB) on behalf of Ex-IRA National Army men of Monaghan Town, 25 May 1926. Correspondence concerning pensions was also variously addressed to the 'Army Pensions Branch', the Department of Defence and/or the 'Army Pensions Department'. For the sake of economy, APB has been used throughout.
53   IMA, MSPC, MSP 34 REF 236, Oscar Traynor: evidence of 18 January 1935.
54   IMA, MSPC, MSP 34 REF 12617, John Higgins: pension application, 18 April 1935.
55   Michael D. Higgins, *The Betrayal* (Dublin, 1990), pp. 7–10.

56 Donald R. Pearce, *The Senate Speeches of W. B. Yeats* (London, 2001), Debate on Damage to Property Bill, 28 March 1923, pp. 25–6.

57 IMA, MSPC, Brigade Activity Reports (BAR)/A/A, 1 Cork Brigade: Michael Leahy to Office of the Referee (OR), 25 September 1935.

58 IMA, MSPC, W5D 77, Patrick Doyle: Bridget Doyle to APB, 18 September 1928.

59 John Horgan, *Seán Lemass: The Enigmatic Patriot* (Dublin, 1997), p. 28.

60 Kevin O'Higgins, *Three Years Hard Labour: An Address Delivered to the Irish Society at Oxford University* (Oxford, 1924).

61 Kissane, *Politics*, p. 65.

1: 'No one has ever defined a Republic'

1 Townshend, *The Republic*, p. 24.

2 Peter Hart, *Mick: The Real Michael Collins* (London, 2005), pp. 138, 155.

3 Diarmaid Ferriter, *A Nation and not a Rabble: The Irish Revolution, 1913–1923* (London, 2015), p. 154.

4 NAI, Dáil Éireann Files (DE) 2/262, Jan Smuts to de Valera, 16 July 1921.

5 Diarmaid Ferriter, *Judging Dev: A Reassessment of the Life and Legacy of Eamon de Valera* (Dublin, 2007), pp. 61–99.

6 Ibid.

7 Michael Laffan, *The Resurrection of Ireland: The Sinn Féin Party, 1916–1923* (Cambridge 1999), pp. 346ff.

8 Hart, *Mick*, p. 293.

9 Laffan, *Resurrection of Ireland*, pp. 346–86.

10 Francis Costello 'Lloyd George and Ireland 1919–21: An Uncertain Policy', *Canadian Journal of Irish Studies*, 14(1), July 1988, pp. 5–16.

11 Gavin Foster, 'Res Publica na hÉireann? Republican Liberty and the Irish Civil War', *New Hibernia Review*, 16(3), Autumn 2012, pp. 20–42.

12 Brian Heffernan, *Freedom and the Fifth Commandment: Catholic Priests and Political Violence in Ireland, 1919–21* (Manchester, 2014), pp. 240–46.

13 Murray, *Oracles of God*, p. 49.

14 Donal Ó Drisceoil, 'Irish Newspapers, the Treaty and the Civil War', in John Crowley, Donal Ó Drisceoil and Mike Murphy (eds.), *Atlas of the Irish Revolution* (Cork, 2017), pp. 661–5.

15 Mel Farrell, '"Stepping Stone to Freedom": Pro-Treaty Rhetoric and Strategy During the Treaty Debates', in Weeks and Ó Fathartaigh, *The Treaty*, pp. 18–32.

16 John Dorney, 'Republican Representations of the Treaty: "A Usurpation Pure and Simple"', in Weeks and Ó Fathartaigh, *The Treaty*, pp. 46–59.

17 Foster, 'Res Publica'.

18 Sinéad McCoole, 'Debating Not Negotiating: The Female TDs of the Second Dáil', in Weeks and Ó Fathartaigh, *The Treaty*, pp. 85–96.

19 Jason Knirck, 'Women's Political Rhetoric and the Irish Revolution', in Thomas Hachey (ed.), *Turning Points in Twentieth Century Irish History* (Dublin, 2011), pp. 39–56.

20 Michael Farry, *The Aftermath of Revolution: Sligo, 1921–23* (Dublin, 2000), pp. 11–35 and Hart, *IRA and Its Enemies*, p. 269.

21 Meda Ryan, *The Real Chief: The Story of Liam Lynch* (Cork, 1986), p. 9.

22 IMA, MSPC, BAR/A/51/2, 1st Brigade, 4th Northern Division: account of Michael J. Fearon, 6 May 1940, including Aiken memorandum from 17 July 1922.

23 UCDA, Papers of Ernest Blythe, P24/43, Report of informal meeting at house of Seán T. O'Kelly, 4 January 1922.

24 Parliamentary Archives, Westminster, London (PAW), Papers of David Lloyd George, LG/F/184/3/4, note of Tom Jones to Lloyd George, 2 January 1922, and LG/F/184/3/5, telegram of Andy Cope to Irish Office, n.d., early January 1922.

25 NUIGA, Papers of Michael Rynne, P133/4/7/23, extracts from private journal, 7 January 1922.

26 Hart, *Mick*, p. 356.

27 UCDA, Papers of Seán Mac Eoin, P151/131, 'Taking Over of Athlone Barracks', speech by Mac Eoin, February 1922.

28 *Dáil Debates*, S2, 26 April 1922.

29 *Irish Times*, 24 March 1922.

30 *Dáil Debates*, S2, 28 April 1922.

31 John O'Beirne-Ranelagh, 'The IRB from the Treaty to 1924', *Irish Historical Studies*, 20(77), March 1976, pp. 26–39.

32 John Borgonovo, 'Cumann na mBan in the Civil War', in Crowley et al. (eds.), *Atlas of the Irish Revolution*, pp. 698–703.

2: The Ulster Rock

1 Robert Lynch, *The Northern IRA and the Early Years of Partition, 1920–1922* (Dublin, 2006), p. 220.

2 Public Record Office of Northern Ireland (PRONI), Cabinet Papers (CAB) 4/30, Draft conclusions of cabinet meeting, 26 January 1922.

3 PRONI, CAB 9A/4/1, Conference between chancellor of exchequer and Craig, 9 February 1922.

4 Ibid.

5   UCDA, Papers of Kevin O'Higgins, P197/86, O'Higgins to his wife
    Bridget, 23 January 1922.

6   PRONI, CAB 9A/4/1, Conference between chancellor of exchequer
    and Craig, 9 February 1922.

7   PRONI, Papers of Ulster Unionist Council, D1327/18/53, James Clark,
    Donegal, to Ulster Unionist Council Standing Committee, July 1922.

8   The National Archives, Kew, London (TNA), CAB 21/250, Ireland:
    Provisional Government of, Churchill to provisional government, 12
    February 1922.

9   TNA, CAB 21/250, Ireland: Provisional Government of, Chamberlain's
    account of interview with James Craig, 10 February 1922.

10 PAW, LG/F/10/6/8, Collins to Thomas Jones, 8 February 1922;
    telegram from Collins to the Irish Office in London, 9 February 1922;
    Lynch, *The Northern IRA*, p. 100.

11 Lynch, *The Northern IRA*, p. 122.

12 Ibid., p. 121.

13 PRONI, Department of Home Affairs (HA) 32/1/28, Outrages in
    Belfast: complaint of Michael Collins; telegram from Collins to
    Churchill, 6 March 1922.

14 PRONI, HA 5/189, Raids by IRA in NI: Churchill to Craig 20 March
    1922 and reply 21 March 1922.

15 PAW, LG/F/184/3/9, 'Secret memorandum on present position of
    imperial government in Northern Ireland', 18 March 1922.

16 *Northern Whig*, 31 March 1922.

17 PRONI, HA 32/1/206, Spender to Northern Ireland ministers, 22 June
    1922.

18 Laura K. Donohue, 'Regulating Northern Ireland: The Special Powers
    Acts, 1922–72', *Historical Journal*, 41(4), December 1998, pp. 1089–1120.

19 IMA, MSPC, BAR/A/56 (2), 3rd Cavan Brigade, 5th Northern
    Division: list of activities, February 1922.

20 IMA, MSPC, MSP 34 REF 2088, Maurice Donegan: sworn statement
    before Advisory Committee, 15 March 1935.

21 PRONI, HA 5/956A, Internee: Cahir Healy: Healy to Kevin O'Shiel,
    31 July 1922.

22 TNA, Colonial Office (CO) 906/30, Belfast Reports: June 1920 – July
    1922, 15 July 1922 and, 'Note on the situation in NI, June 1922'.

23 PRONI, HA 5/151, Reports of City Commissioner, RUC, 29 June 1922.

24 Ibid., Divisional Commissioner's Office, Belfast, to minister for
    home affairs, 26 June 1922; A. Solly-Flood, military advisor to the

northern government, to minister for home affairs, 27 June 1922; HA memorandum, 29 June 1922.

25 Lynch, *The Northern IRA*, p. 165.

26 PRONI, D1327/18/52, From the Ulster Vigilance Committee, Belfast, 23 June 1922.

27 NAI Department of Justice (DJUS) 2018/86/1–18, Billeting of NI refugees, 1922–4, W. E. Wylie to Eamon Duggan, 17 April 1922 and reply 3 May 1922; E. O'Frighil to John Keenan, solicitor, Monaghan, 15 March 1923 and note from Department of Industry and Commerce regarding expelled Belfast workers, 4 June 1923.

28 John Dorney, *The Civil War in Dublin: The Fight for the Irish Capital, 1922–1924* (Dublin, 2017), pp. 50–59.

3: 'Only putting off the evil way'

1   Kissane, *Politics*, p. 68.

2   Ronan Fanning, *Independent Ireland* (Dublin, 1983), p. 12.

3   Patrick Murray, 'Obsessive Historian: Eamon de Valera and the Policing of His Reputation', *Proceedings of the Royal Irish Academy*, 101 C (2001), pp. 37–65.

4   *Irish Independent*, 20 March 1922.

5   TNA, CAB 21/250, Cabinet Provisional Government of Ireland Committee: Conference on Ireland with Irish Ministers, 26 February 1922.

6   Ibid.

7   TNA, CAB 21/250, Conference on Ireland with Irish Ministers, 26 February 1922.

8   Ibid.

9   TNA, War Office (WO) 35/182/A, Precautionary measures April–May 1922: handing over of barracks to Free State troops, note of Major General commanding Dublin district, 15 February 1922.

10 Ibid., James Masterson Smith to Murray, 12 April 1922.

11 Pádraig Yeates, *A City in Civil War: Dublin, 1921–4* (Dublin, 2015), p. 216.

12 UCDA, Papers of Ernest Blythe, P24/69, Report of Commission of Inquiry into the Civic Guard: Findings of Commission, August 1922.

13 Vicky Conway, *Policing Twentieth-Century Ireland: A History of An Garda Síochána* (London, 2014), pp. 25–44.

14 Pat McCarthy, *The Irish Revolution, 1912–23: Waterford* (Dublin, 2015), p. 101.

15 Hopkinson, *Green Against Green*, p. 67.

16   Florence O'Donoghue, *No Other Law: The Story of Liam Lynch and the Irish Republican Army, 1916–1923* (Dublin, 1954), p. 230.

17   Fintan O'Toole, 'A Portrait of Peadar O'Donnell as an Old Soldier', *Magill*, February 1982, pp. 25–31.

18   TNA, CO 739/3, Irish Free State 1922, vol. 3, District Intelligence Officer, Queenstown, to Rear Admiral M. S. Fitzmaurice, 6 April 1922.

19   *Dáil Debates*, S2, 26 April 1922.

20   UCDA, Papers of Ernest Blythe, P24/38, Report of Ministry of Home Affairs, April 1922.

21   UCDA, Papers of Hugh Kennedy, P4/251/4, Bank of Ireland, branches raided on 1 and 2 May 1922.

22   UCDA, Papers of Seán Mac Eoin, P151, Mac Eoin to J. J. Sheridan, 10 April 1922.

23   UCDA, Mary Spring Rice Papers, P235/12, Spring Rice to Dorothea Knox, 26 January and 28 January 1922.

24   Ibid., Spring Rice to Knox, 10 March 1922.

25   Mary McAuliffe, '"An idea has gone abroad that all the women were against the Treaty": Cumann na Saoirse and Pro-Treaty Women, 1922–3', in Weeks and Ó Fathartaigh, *The Treaty*, pp. 98–109.

26   UCDA, Mary Spring Rice Papers, P235/12, Spring Rice to Knox, 19 May 1922.

27   PAW, LGF/10/2/68, Cope to Churchill, 18 April 1922.

28   PAW, LGF/10/2/67, Cope to Churchill, 17 April 1922; Churchill to Cope, 19 April 1922.

29   PAW, LGF/10/2/68, Cope to Churchill, 18 April 1922.

30   TNA, PRO 30/67/50, Midleton Papers, Churchill to Midleton, 5 April 1922.

31   Ibid., Edmund Talbot (Viscount FitzAlan) Howard to Midleton, 17 April 1922.

32   Ibid., Midleton to King George V, 30 April 1922 and reply, 2 May 1922.

33   Ibid., Midleton to Major A. Belton, 4 May 1922.

34   Ibid., Midleton to Churchill, 13 June 1922.

35   Ibid., Lansdowne to Midleton, 10 May 1922.

36   Ibid., memorandum of Midleton, 28 July 1922.

37   Yeates, *A City in Civil War*, pp. 21–3.

38   Murray, *Oracles of God*, p. 57.

39   *Freeman's Journal*, 1 May 1922.

40   UCDA, Papers of Ernest Blythe, P24/45, Dáil committee on agreed election, 11 May 1922.

41 UCDA, Papers of Hugh Kennedy, P4/236/1, Hugh Kennedy to chairman of provisional government, 20 May 1922.

42 UCDA, Mary Spring Rice diary, P235/21, 27 May 1922.

43 Ibid., letters of 3 July 1922, 17 July and 22 July 1922.

44 PAW, LGF/184/3/12, Conference on Ireland at Colonial Office, London, 26 May 1922.

45 Ibid.

46 PAW, LGF/10/3/3, Lloyd George to Churchill, 8 June 1922.

47 Jonathan Bardon, *A History of Ulster* (Belfast, 1992), p. 447.

48 PAW, LGF/10/3/3, Lloyd George to Churchill, 8 June 1922.

49 Ibid.

50 TNA, CAB 27/154, Provisional Government of Ireland, memorandum by Churchill, 21 December 1921.

51 TNA, CAB 27/186, Provisional Government of Ireland Committee, Military Sub-Committee, 6 April 1922.

52 TNA, PRO 30/67/50, Midleton to Churchill, 13 June 1922.

53 Ibid., meeting in room of secretary of state for the colonies, 13 June 1922.

54 PAW, LGF/21/1–8, Lloyd George to Arthur Griffith, 1 June 1922, and Griffith's reply, 2 June 1922.

55 Hart, *Mick*, p. 389.

56 Kissane, *Politics*, p. 73.

57 Ibid., p. 363.

58 UCDA, Papers of Hugh Kennedy, P4/237/2, Michael Collins to Hugh Kennedy, 11 June 1922.

59 Kissane, *Politics*, p. 72.

60 PAW, LG/F/10/6/4, Lloyd George to Collins, 22 June 1922.

61 Peter Hart, 'Michael Collins and the Assassination of Sir Henry Wilson', *Irish Historical Studies*, 28(110), November 1992, pp. 150–70.

62 PAW, LG F/10/3/14, Curtis to Lloyd George, 23 June 1923.

63 UCDA, Papers of Hugh Kennedy, P4/194/1, Hugh Kennedy to Edward Shortt, secretary of state for home affairs, August 1922.

64 Hart, 'Michael Collins and the Assassination of Sir Henry Wilson'.

65 Anne Dolan and William Murphy, *Michael Collins: The Man and the Revolution* (Cork, 2018), pp. 122–3.

66 PAW, LGF/185/1/5, Conference of British ministers held at Downing Street, 22 June 1922, and LGF/185/1/6, 'Very Secret: Proclamation by General Macready', 24 June 1922.

67 Keith Jeffrey, 'Sir (Cecil Frederick) Nevil Macready', in James McGuire and James Quinn (eds.), *Dictionary of Irish Biography*, 9 vols. (Cambridge University Press, 2009) (*DIB*), vol. 6, pp. 181–2.

68   T. Ryle Dwyer, 'British army fire did not spark civil war', *Irish Examiner*, 1 November 2012.

69   Hansard, House of Commons Debate, 155, 26 June 1922, cols. 1693–1811.

70   Hopkinson, *Green Against Green*, p. 111, and Kissane, *Politics*, p. 75.

71   UCDA, Papers of Kevin O'Higgins, P197/88, O'Higgins to his wife Bridget, 27 June 1922.

72   IMA, MSPC, MSP 34 REF 60286, Kathleen O'Connell: copy of dispatch carried by O'Connell, dated 28 June 1922.

4: The Call to Arms

1   PAW, LGF/10/3/13, Churchill to Cope, 1 July 1922.

2   Ibid., F/185/2/5, memorandum from Colonial Office, October 1922; F/184/3/1, Curtis to Lloyd George, 18 December 1921.

3   Michael Fewer, *The Battle of the Four Courts: The First Three Days of the Irish Civil War* (Dublin, 2018), p. 278.

4   Ibid., pp. 44–5.

5   UCDA, Papers of Hugh Kennedy, P4/283/2+3 Notes of C. P. Curran, Clerk of Four Courts regarding Public Record Office and note by Hugh Kennedy, June and July 1922: provisional government to Royal Society of Antiquaries, 23 July 1922.

6   Fewer, *Battle of the Four Courts*, pp. 255–6.

7   John M. Regan, 'Kindling the Singing Flame: The Destruction of the Public Record Office (30 June 1922) as a Historical Problem', in Cormac K. H. O'Malley (ed.), *Modern Ireland and Revolution: Ernie O'Malley in Context* (Kildare, 2016), pp. 107–24.

8   Dorney, *The Civil War in Dublin*, p. 76.

9   UCD Special Collections Library, *Poblacht na hÉireann, War News*, 10, 6 July 1922.

10   James Quinn, 'Cathal Brugha', in *DIB*, vol. 1, pp. 951–4.

11   Fergus O'Farrell, *Cathal Brugha* (Dublin, 2018), pp. 85–8.

12   Ibid., p. 89.

13   Ibid., p. 91.

14   NUIGA, Papers of Michael Rynne, P133/4/7/23, extracts from private journal, 11 October 1922.

15   Dorney, *The Civil War in Dublin*, pp. 95–101.

16   *Irish Times*, 7 and 8 July 1922, cited in ibid., pp. 101–4.

17   Hopkinson, *Green Against Green*, p. 226.

18   IMA, Papers of Army Inquiry Committee (AIC), IE-MA-AMTY 03021: statement submitted by General Mulcahy to the AIC, 29 April 1924, including note by Michael Collins, 12 July 1922.

19 Kissane, *Politics*, p. 80.

20 John M. Regan, *Myth and the Irish State* (Dublin, 2013), pp. 126–9.

21 Ibid., pp. 87–94.

22 TNA, CO 739/6, Irish Free State 1922, vol. 6, note from Colonial Office, 20 July 1922.

23 Kissane, *Politics*, p. 88.

24 TNA, CAB 27/153, Cabinet Committee, Provisional Government of Ireland 1921–22, discussions of 14 July and 1 August 1922.

25 PRONI, HA 32/1/247, A. Solly-Flood to secretary, minister for home affairs, 22 July 1922.

26 UCDA, Papers of Hugh Kennedy, P4/259/2, Collins to acting chairman, provisional government, 31 July 1922.

27 Michael Hopkinson, 'Civil War: The Opening Phase', in Crowley et al. (eds.), *Atlas of the Irish Revolution*, pp. 675–88, and Gerry White, 'Free State versus Republic: The Opposing Armed Forces in the Civil War', ibid., pp. 691–7.

28 Padraig Óg Ó Ruairc, *The Battle for Limerick City* (Cork, 2006).

29 P. J. Ryan, 'Armed Conflict in Limerick', in David Lee (ed.), *Remembering Limerick* (Limerick, 1997), pp. 274–6, and Jim Kemmy, 'P. J. (Cushy) Ryan', *Old Limerick Journal*, 9, Winter 1981, p. 3.

30 McCarthy, *Waterford*, p. 106.

31 Memoirs of George Lennon, 1922: Waterford City, Parts 1 and 2. http://www.waterfordmuseum.ie/exhibit/web/Display/article/317/20/Memoirs_Of_George_Lennon_1922_Waterford_City_Part_1_.html, accessed 4 February 2021.

32 McCarthy, *Waterford*, pp. 109–21.

33 IMA, MSPC, MSP 34 REF 2091, Florence O'Donoghue: copy of letter from O'Donoghue to Liam Lynch, 3 July 1922.

34 Brian MacNeill to OC 4th Western Division, 2 July 1922, quoted in Farry, *The Aftermath of Revolution*, p. 77.

35 Marie Coleman, *County Longford and the Irish Revolution* (Dublin, 2003), p. 144.

36 John Borgonovo, *The Battle for Cork: July–August 1922* (Cork, 2011).

37 Ibid., p. 55.

38 Frank Geary, 'The Taking of Cork, July 1922', in John Horgan (ed.), *Great Irish Reportage* (Dublin, 2013), pp. 1–16.

39 Borgonovo, *The Battle for Cork*, pp. 36–7.

40 Dolan and Murphy, *Michael Collins*, p. 119.

41 Hart, *The IRA and Its Enemies*, pp. 286–8.

42 Gerard Murphy, *The Year of Disappearances: Political Killings in Cork,*

1921–1922 (Dublin, 2010) and Andy Bielenberg, John Borgonovo and James S. Donnelly Jr, '"Something of the Nature of a Massacre": The Bandon Valley Killings Revisited', *Éire-Ireland*, 49(3–4), Fall/Winter 2014, pp. 7–59.

43 *Irish Times*, 19 June 1922.

44 Lynch, *The Northern IRA*, p. 148.

45 Ian d'Alton, "A Vestigial Population?" Perspectives on Southern Irish Protestants in the Twentieth Century', *Éire Ireland*, 44(3–4), September 2009, pp. 9–42 and Andy Bielenberg, 'Exodus: The Emigration of Southern Irish Protestants During the Irish War of Independence and Civil War', *Past and Present*, 128 (February 2013), pp. 199–233, p. 232.

46 Tom Doyle, *The Civil War in Kerry* (Cork, 2008), pp. 110–13.

47 Fergal Keane, *Wounds: A Memoir of Love and War* (London, 2017), pp. 225–6.

48 UCDA, Papers of Hugh Kennedy, P4/292/7, Aodh de Blacam to Mrs Pegg, London, August 1922.

49 David Fitzpatrick, 'Henry James ('Harry') Boland, in *DIB*, vol. 1, pp. 635–7.

50 Yeates, *A City in Civil War*, pp. 224–5.

51 UCDA, Papers of Hugh Kennedy, P4/188/1, Francis Greer, Irish Office, London, to Hugh Kennedy 10 August 1922.

52 UCDA, Papers of Seán Mac Eoin, P151/161/5, Richard Mulcahy to Mac Eoin, 14 August 1922.

53 Borgonovo, *Battle for Cork*, p. 64.

54 Niall C. Harrington, *Kerry Landing: August 1922* (Dublin, 1992), p. 71.

55 John Boyne, *Emmet Dalton: Somme Soldier, Irish General, Film Pioneer* (Dublin, 2015), pp. 178–213.

56 Liam Lynch to Ernie O'Malley, 4 October 1922, in O'Malley and Dolan, *No Surrender Here!*, p. 255.

57 Seán Lehane to O'Malley, 19 September 1922, ibid., pp. 197–200.

58 O'Malley to Seán Lemass, 21 October 1922, and O'Malley memorandum, 2 November 1922, ibid. p. 148.

59 Con Moloney memorandum to O'Malley, 28 September 1922, ibid., p. 235.

60 O'Malley to Liam Deasy, 9 October 1922, ibid., p. 165.

5: Lost Leaders

1   PAW, LG/F/10/3/24, Cope to James Masterson Smith, 12 August 1922.

2   PAW, LG/F/10/6/55, Lloyd George telegram to Collins, 12 August 1922.

3   Ibid., Lloyd George to Mrs Griffith, n.d., *c.*12 August 1922.

4   George A. Lyons, *Some Recollections of Arthur Griffith and His Times* (Dublin, 1923); preface. UCD Special Collections Library, 39 K 28.

5   IMA, Bureau of Military History (BMH), Witness Statement (WS) 939, Ernest Blythe, pp. 152–8.

6   Pearce, *The Senate Speeches of W. B. Yeats*, 14 March 1923, pp. 22–3.

7   Anne Dolan, *Commemorating the Irish Civil War: History and Memory, 1923–2000* (Cambridge, 2003), pp. 114–19.

8   UCDA, Papers of Desmond FitzGerald, P80/303/8, Statement by Maud Griffith, 30 July 1923.

9   Dolan, *Commemorating the Irish Civil War*, p. 7.

10   Gerard Murphy, *The Great Cover-Up: The Truth About the Death of Michael Collins* (Cork, 2018), pp. 34–42.

11   Dolan and Murphy, *Michael Collins*, pp. 245–89, and Murphy, *The Great Cover-Up*, pp. 121–30.

12   Boyne, *Emmet Dalton*, p. 364.

13   Dolan and Murphy, *Michael Collins*, pp. 245–89.

14   Murphy, *The Great Cover-Up*, pp. 121–30.

15   PAW, LG/F/10/6/6, Lloyd George statement to *Evening Standard*, 23 August 1922.

16   PAW, LG/F/10/3/37, Cope to Curtis, 23 August 1922.

17   TNA, CO 739/6, Irish Free State 1922, vol. 6, Cope to Curtis, 26 August 1922.

18   Benjamin Kline, 'Churchill and Collins 1919–22: Admirers or Adversaries?', *History Ireland*, 1(3), Autumn 1993, pp. 38–44.

19   Bew, *Churchill and Ireland*, pp. 7–12.

20   Hart, *Mick*, pp. 294–5.

21   PAW, LG/F/10/3/37, Churchill to Cope, 24 August 1922.

22   Ibid.

23   Ibid.

24   UCD Special Collections Library, *Poblacht na hÉireann, War News*, 47, 24 August 1922, and 50, 31 August 1922.

25   TNA, CO 739/7, Irish Free State, 1922, vol. 7, Curtis to Churchill, 7 September 1922.

26   PAW, LG/F/10/3/4, Curtis to Lloyd George and Churchill, 17 September 1922.

27   Ibid., Churchill to Cosgrave, 8 September 1922.

28   TNA, CO 739/7, Irish Free State, 1922, vol. 7, Curtis to secretary of state, 31 October 1922.

29   Laffan, *Resurrection of Ireland*, p. 398.

30 PAW, Papers of Andrew Bonar Law, BL/117/7/3 'IFS Constitution', 27 November 1922.

31 PAW, LG/F/10/3/56, Cosgrave to Lloyd George, 20 October 1922.

32 PAW, LG/F/10/3/50, Churchill, Colonial Office, to Lloyd George, 22 September 1922.

33 PAW, LG/F/10/3/48, Cope to Curtis, 8 September 1922.

34 Ibid.

35 PAW, LG/F/10/3/48, Curtis to Cope, 7 September 1922.

36 Kissane, *Politics*, pp. 82–3.

37 UCDA, Papers of Ernest Blythe, P24/70, memorandum by Ernest Blythe on Northern Ireland policy, 9 August 1922.

38 Kissane, *Politics*, p. 83.

39 Lynch, *The Northern IRA*, pp. 131–7.

40 NAI, DT S1801A, Séamus Woods to Richard Mulcahy, 29 September 1922.

41 Regan, *Myth and the Irish State*, pp. 56–86.

42 NAI, DT S11209, 'Deputation from Northern Ireland to the Provisional Government', 11 October 1922.

6: Raw Lads and the New Black and Tans

1 UCDA, Papers of Desmond FitzGerald, P80/343/3, Frank Dorr, Foxford Woollen Mills, to Dan McCarthy, 18 July 1922.

2 Con Moloney memorandum to Ernie O'Malley, 28 September 1922, in O'Malley and Dolan, *No Surrender Here!*, p. 235.

3 Kissane, *Politics*, p. 76.

4 Keane, *Wounds*, pp. 216–46.

5 TNA, PRO 30/67/51, Desart to Midleton, 20 and 22 October 1922.

6 Ibid.

7 IMA, AIC, IE-MA-AMTY 03021, statement submitted by General Mulcahy to the Army Inquiry Committee, 29 April 1924.

8 Ibid.

9 UCDA, Papers of Desmond FitzGerald, P80/341/5, 'General Regulations as to Discipline', Gearóid O'Sullivan to Desmond FitzGerald, 22 November 1922.

10 NUIGA, Papers of Michael Rynne, P133/4/8, 'Special Order of the Day' from Richard Mulcahy, 3 April 1923 and P133/4/7/31, *Limerick War News*, from the Publicity department, GPO Limerick, 29 July 1922 and *South Western Command War News*, 2 September 1922.

11 UCDA, Papers of Seán Mac Eoin, P151/164/10, Frank Shouldice to

Mac Eoin, 6 November 1922 and CCCA, U271/A/147, De Róiste diaries, 13 November 1922.

12 UCDA, Papers of Seán Mac Eoin, P151/166, Intelligence reports for Mac Eoin's Command Area, 4 December, 11 December, 19 November and 13 November 1922.

13 UCDA, Papers of Desmond FitzGerald, P80/338/3, FitzGerald to Mulcahy, 2 December 1922 and Smiddy to FitzGerald 15 December 1922.

14 TNA, CO 739/3, Irish Free State 1922, vol. 3, Lionel Curtis to Colonial Office, 13 September and 2 October 1922, and secretary of Admiralty to Colonial Office, 16 September 1922.

15 Ibid., secretary of Admiralty to Colonial Office, 3 October and 26 October 1922.

16 Ibid., Macready to Masterson Smith, 15 November 1922.

17 Seán Lehane to O'Malley, 15 October 1922, in O'Malley and Dolan, *No Surrender Here!*, p. 282.

18 Farry, *The Aftermath of Revolution*, p. 101.

19 UCDA, Papers of Seán Mac Eoin, P151/200, Intelligence reports on 'Irregular Operations', January–October 1923, 5 May 1923.

20 Ibid., P151/180, Monthly Operational Report by General Lawlor on operations in the west for December 1922.

21 IMA, BMH, WS 1066, Manus Moynihan.

22 Seán Lehane to Ernie O'Malley, 15 October 1922, in O'Malley and Dolan, *No Surrender Here!*, p. 280.

23 UCDA, Mary Spring Rice diary, P235/23–25, 10 July and 25 July 1922.

24 Ibid., Spring Rice to Knox, 10 July and 14 July 1922 and diary entries for 3 July and 6 July 1922.

25 Ibid., diary entry for 13 July 1922.

26 Ibid., 8 July 1922.

27 Ibid., 29 July 1922.

28 Ibid., 22 July 1922.

29 Ibid., 6 August 1922.

30 Ibid., P235/30, Spring Rice to Knox, 28 September 1922.

31 Ibid., P235/31, Spring Rice to Knox, 7 October 1922.

32 Liam Lynch to O'Malley, 16 September 1922, in O'Malley and Dolan, *No Surrender Here!*, p. 105.

33 *Freeman's Journal*, 14 September 1922.

34 *Southern Star*, 20 September 2006; CCCA, U156/13, Papers of Roibard Langford, copy of Inquest into Kennefick shooting.

35 UCDA, Papers of Desmond FitzGerald, P80/326–7,

October–November 1922, and UCDA, Papers of Seán Mac Eoin, P151/160, Mulcahy to Collins regarding Aodh de Blacam, 11 August 1922.

36 UCD Special Collections Library, Publicity department IRA, *Poblacht na hÉireann*, 23 September 1922, and LP 221, Republican propaganda leaflets, 1922.

37 UCDA, Papers of Desmond FitzGerald, P80/281, Piaras Béaslaí to FitzGerald, 7 August 1922.

38 Ibid., P80/281, Field HQ Northern and Eastern Command to editor, *Freeman's Journal*, 28 October 1922 and C. S. Quinlan to editor, *Waterford News*, 16 August 1922; ibid., P80/282(12/2) Military Censorship: General Instructions, July–November 1922.

39 Ibid., P80/282, Edmund Downey, *Waterford News*, to W. T. Cosgrave, 19 August 1922.

40 Ibid., P80/283, FitzGerald to Michael Collins, 25 July 1922.

41 Ibid., Collins to FitzGerald 26 July 1922.

42 Ibid., P80/285, Béaslaí memorandum on Patrick Mannion case, 19 September 1922.

43 IMA, MSPC, W2D126, Thomas O'Connor and John O'Connor: application of 29 November 1923 and letter to APB from John T. Guihan, solicitor, 23 March 1924.

44 UCDA, Papers of Ernest Blythe, P24/38, Report of Ministry of Home Affairs, April 1922, and P24/40, Report of Local Government Department, April 1922.

45 Uinseann Mac Eoin, *Survivors* (Dublin, 1987), p. 358.

46 TNA, PRO 30/67/51, note of Lord Lansdowne, 25 June 1922.

47 NAI, Land Settlement Commission (LSC), Mayo, 8 March 1922 and LSC 2A13, Tipperary, 28 February 1922, Buckley Estate.

48 NAI, LSC, Tipperary (64), LSC Miscellaneous (24), Longford, letter to Hugh McLoughlin, n.d. early 1923.

49 NAI, LSC, Misc., 27–28, August 1922.

50 Dublin Diocesan Archives (DDA), Papers of Archbishop Edward Byrne (ABP), Lay Organisations, Box 4, John Collins, Evicted Tenants and Land Settlement Association, to Archbishop Byrne, 31 October 1922.

51 Ibid., p. 7.

52 Brian Walker, 'Darkest Nights: Mystery of the Dunmanway massacre', *Irish Independent*, 30 May 2014.

53 Gemma Clark, *Everyday Violence in the Irish Civil War* (Cambridge, 2014), pp. 115–25 and 131–53.

54 Ibid.

55   UCDA, Papers of Hugh Kennedy, P4/239/1, J. Lysaght, Cork, to Chief of Inspection, 16 August 1922.

56   UCDA, Papers of Seán Mac Eoin, P151/125/66, letter from adjutant general, Midland Division to Mac Eoin 16 February 1922, and 'special memorandum' from chief of staff, 27 February 1922.

57   DDA, ABP, Lay Organisations, Box 4, Mrs Austin Stack to Byrne, 11 November 1922.

58   Conor Kostick, *Revolution in Ireland: Popular Militancy, 1917–1923* (London, 1996), pp. 188–9.

59   Mel Farrell, *Party Politics in a New Democracy: The Irish Free State 1922–37* (London, 2018), p. 67.

60   J. J. Walsh, *Recollections of a Rebel* (Kerry, 1944), pp. 62–3.

61   *Irish Times*, 2 May 1925.

62   *Dáil Debates*, 1(2), 11 September 1922.

63   *Dáil Debates*, 1(4), 13 September 1922.

7: Escape Tunnels and Shit Buckets

1   Kissane, *Politics*, p. 85; and John M. Regan, *The Irish Counter-Revolution, 1921–1936: Treatyite Settlement and Politics in Independent Ireland* (Dublin, 2001), pp. 35–50.

2   David McCullagh, *De Valera: Rise, 1882–1932* (Dublin, 2017), pp. 287–98.

3   *Irish Times*, 5 October 1922.

4   UCDA, Papers of Hugh Kennedy, P4/542/1, Kevin O'Shiel to W. T. Cosgrave, 28 September 1922.

5   Kissane, *Politics*, p. 91.

6   NAI, DT S1369/1, handwritten note of Diarmuid O'Hegarty, 9 July 1922, and response of Joe Mac Kelvey.

7   Ibid., letter of Charlotte Despard 5 July 1922, and secretary, Department of Defence, to Arthur Griffith, July 1922.

8   IMA, BMH, WS 939, Ernest Blythe.

9   NAI, DT S1369/3, report of postmaster general, Drogheda, 2 August 1922.

10   NAI, DT S1369/1, note to each minister regarding Lambay Island, 18 July 1922.

11   Ibid., 19 July 1922.

12   Ibid., minutes of Executive Council, 19 September 1922; *Irish Times* 3 January 1923 and note of minister for external affairs, 18 January 1923.

13   NAI, DT S1369/2, Civil war prisoners 1922: prison diet, and DT

S1369/3, 'Dublin Municipal Council committee to inquire into treatment of prisoners', 7–14 November 1922.

14 Ibid., secretary, Department of Home Affairs to minister for defence, 20 November 1922.

15 NAI, DT S1369/3; *Freeman's Journal*, 27 November 1922.

16 White, 'Free State versus Republic', and John Borgonovo, 'IRA Conventions', in Crowley et al. (eds.), *Atlas of the Irish Revolution*, pp. 670–75.

17 CCCA, U421 A/1, Seán Hayes Papers, Governor's notebook, 7 October 1922.

18 Ibid., 18 February 1923.

19 Ibid., 16 October and 28 November 1922.

20 Ibid., 18 October and 3 November 1922.

21 James Durney, *The Civil War in Kildare* (Cork, 2011), pp. 109–17.

22 CCCA, U421 A/1, Seán Hayes Papers, Governor's notebook, entries for 6 November and 19 November 1922.

23 NAI, DT S1369/3, letter of Hanna Sheehy Skeffington, 11 September 1922, letter of Diarmuid O'Cruadhlaoich, 4 September 1922 and statement of James Kelly, Dublin Brigade, IRA.

24 NAI, DT S1369/7, Civil War Prisoners: 'Attempted escape from Mountjoy', 10 October 1922.

25 Durney, *Civil War in Kildare*, p. 111.

26 Cormac K. H. O'Malley and Cormac Ó Comhraí (eds), *The Men Will Talk to Me: Galway Interviews by Ernie O'Malley* (Cork, 2013), pp. 178–205.

27 Peadar O'Donnell, *The Gates Flew Open: An Irish Civil War Prison Diary* (Cork, 2013), p. 184.

28 *Irish Press*, 26 May 1976, Fianna Fáil Golden Jubilee edition, and O'Malley and Ó Comhraí (eds.), *The Men Will Talk to Me*, pp. 178–244.

29 Paddy Brennan, OC Dublin 2 Brigade, to Ernie O'Malley, 2 October 1922, in O'Malley and Dolan, *No Surrender Here!*, p. 252.

8: God's Law and Joans of Arc

1 NAI, DT 1369/2, memorandum of minister for home affairs, 8 September 1922; note from Richard Mulcahy to government, 19 September 1922, and minutes of executive council, 23 January 1923.

2 Ward, *Unmanageable Revolutionaries*, pp. 190–93, and Borgonovo, 'Cumann na mBan in the Civil War'.

3 NAI, DT, S1369/9, 'Mary MacSwiney: Imprisonment and hunger strike',

MacSwiney to Byrne, 6 November 1922 and Byrne to MacSwiney, 8 November 1922.

4   Ibid., MacSwiney to Byrne, 6 November 1922.

5   Ibid., Byrne to MacSwiney, 8 November 1922.

6   Ibid., report of Major General Hayes, 10 November 1922.

7   P. S. O'Hegarty, *The Victory of Sinn Féin: How It Won It and How It Used It* (Dublin, 1924), p. 104.

8   Laffan, *Resurrection of Ireland*, p. 376.

9   NAI, DT S1369/9, Cosgrave to Logue, 15 November 1922.

10 Ibid., Byrne to Cosgrave, 16 November 1922.

11 Ibid., Cosgrave to Byrne, 18 November 1922.

12 Ibid., De Róiste to Cosgrave, 17 November 1922.

13 George Gavan Duffy to Smiddy, 10 March 1922; Denis McCullagh to provisional government, 31 March 1922 and Smiddy to Gavan Duffy 28 April 1922; Gavan Duffy report on foreign affairs, 26 April 1922 and memorandum by Gavan Duffy on approach to foreign affairs, 21 June 1922; all in Ronan Fanning, Michael Kennedy, Eunan O'Halpin and Dermot Keogh (eds.), *Documents on Irish Foreign Policy*, vol. 1: *1919–1922* (Dublin 1998), pp. 408–514.

14 Joseph Connolly to W. T. Cosgrave, 7 December 1922, cited in Ronan Fanning, Michael Kennedy, Eunan O'Halpin and Dermot Keogh (eds.), *Documents on Irish Foreign Policy*, vol. 2, *1923–26* (Dublin 1999), pp. 18–21.

15 *Irish Times*, 9 November 1922.

16 UCDA, De Valera Papers, P150/658, MacSwiney to Tomás Mac Aodha, 20 November 1922.

17 Patrick Maume, 'Michael Curran', in *DIB*, online edition, www.dib. cambridge.org.

18 M. P. McCabe, *For God and Ireland: The Fight for Moral Superiority in Ireland, 1922–1932* (Dublin, 2013), p. 53.

19 DDA, ABP, Box 48, Government, 1922–39, Cosgrave to Byrne, 21 July 1922.

20 Ibid., letter from Kevin O'Higgins to Cosgrave, 20 December 1922, forwarded to Byrne.

21 Ibid., *c*. February 1923, 'List of sympathetic priests excluded by the government from visiting prisoners'.

22 Olivia Freehill, 'Republican Dissent Among Irish Jesuits During the Civil War, 1922–23', *Studies*, 107(425), Spring 2018, pp. 57–76.

23 UCDA, Papers of Desmond FitzGerald, P80/338/1, David Robinson to Gavan Duffy, 10 October 1922.

24 UCD Special Collections Library, 34 N 1/2, Proinnsias O Gallchobhair [Frank Gallagher], *The Bishops' Pastoral: A Prisoner's Letter to His Grace the Archbishop of Dublin* (Dublin, 1922), pp. 3–11.

25 Seán Cronin, *The McGarrity Papers: Revelations of the Irish Revolutionary Movement in Ireland and America, 1900–1940* (Kerry, 1972), p. 130.

26 IMA, Army Chief of Staff Reports, IE/MA/CREC/02, Confidential Military Reports, Tralee: Kerry Command, 12 March 1923.

27 Paddy Brennan, OC Dublin 2 Brigade, to O'Malley, 21 September 1922, in O'Malley and Dolan, *No Surrender Here!*, p. 205.

28 Tomás Kenny, *Galway: Politics and Society, 1910–1923* (Dublin, 2011), pp. 41–2.

29 O'Donnell, *The Gates Flew Open*, p. 157.

30 DDA, ABP, Box 466: Government: 1922–39, Byrne to Count Plunkett, 25 July 1922 and Plunkett to Byrne, 19 August 1922.

31 Ibid., Anna O'Rahilly to Byrne, 15 December 1922.

32 Murray, *Oracles of God*, p. 14.

33 NAI, DT S1369/1, 'Civil War Prisoners 1922', telegram of Bishop Hallinan to Cosgrave, 11 November 1922, and reply of Cosgrave.

34 Murray, *Oracles of God*, p. 24.

35 *Irish Times*, 7 August 1922, in NAI, DT S1369/3.

36 CCCA, U271/A/47, De Róiste diaries, 4 November, 6 November and 11 November 1922.

37 Ibid., 6 November and 11 November 1922.

38 Ibid., 13 November 1922.

39 UCDA, Murphy Family Papers, P141/95, Conn Murphy to Annie Murphy, 2 January 1923.

40 Ibid., P141/96, Conn Murphy to Annie, 14 January 1923.

41 Ibid., P141/221, Connie Murphy, Cork City Jail, to her parents, 30 January 1923.

42 McCabe, *For God and Ireland*, pp. 113–38.

43 Patrick Maume, 'Salvatore Luzio', in *DIB*, vol. 5, pp. 609–10, and Maume, 'Michael Curran'.

44 Cosgrave to Gaspari, April 1923, in Fanning et al., *Documents on Irish Foreign Policy*, 2, p. 88.

45 UCDA, Papers of Desmond FitzGerald, P80/413, memorandum of Joseph Walshe, secretary of Department of External Affairs, May 1923.

46 CCCA, U271/A/47, De Róiste diaries, 16 November 1922.

47 DDA, ABP, Box 48, Government 1922–39, Conn Murphy to Byrne, 26 January 1923.

48 Ibid., Kathleen Murphy to Byrne, 28 March 1923.
49 UCDA, Murphy Family Papers, P141/122, Annie to Conn, January 1923.
50 Ibid., P141/230, Connie to Conn, 17 April 1923.
51 Ibid., P141/234, Connie to Annie, 1 May 1923.
52 DDA, ABP, Box 48, Government 1922–39, letter from female prisoners, Mountjoy, to Byrne, 17 November 1922.
53 Lane, *Dorothy Macardle*, pp. 31–91.
54 Ibid.
55 NAI, DT 1369/18, Sir Thomas Macardle to J. Baker, 9 January 1923.
56 Lane, *Macardle*, pp. 31–91.
57 Ibid.

9: Public Safety

1   *Dáil Debates*, 1(30), 17 November 1922.
2   *Freeman's Journal*, 25 November 1922.
3   IMA, MSPC, DP 5824, Richard Twohig: application of Mary Twohig, 24 March 1933.
4   Ibid., note of D. O'Sullivan, 24 May 1933.
5   Ibid., Mary Twohig to APB, 10 June 1933.
6   Hopkinson, *Green Against Green*, pp. 228–9.
7   *Irish Times*, 25 November 1922.
8   NAI, DT 1369/14, *Daily Sketch*, 25 November 1922.
9   TNA, CO 739/6, Irish Free State 1922, vol. 6, Cope to James Masterson Smith, 7 August 1922.
10 UCDA, Papers of Desmond FitzGerald, P80/304: Execution of Childers: IRA statements, 15 November and 19 November 1922, and P80/307, Free State assertions about Childers.
11 Enright, *The Irish Civil War*, pp. 40–43.
12 Ibid.
13 NAI, DT 1369/14, *London Times*, 25 November 1922, letter of Douglas Hyde, 23 November 1922, and letter of Tom Johnson, Cathal O'Shannon and William O'Brien, 23 November 1922.
14 NAI, DT S1884A, telegram of Thomas Cassidy to provisional government, 17 November 1922, reply of 18 November 1922, and 'Personal view of the C-in-C', 17 November 1922.
15 Ibid., telegram of Robert Hackett, 18 November 1922.
16 Ibid., Thomas Johnson to W. T. Cosgrave, 22 November 1922 and reply.
17 *Dáil Debates*, 1(28), 15 November 1922.
18 Pauric J. Dempsey, 'Philip Bernard Joseph Cosgrave', in *DIB*, vol. 2, p. 880.

19 NAI, DT S3439, Diarmuid O'Hegarty to Eoin MacNeill, 31 October 1923.

20 IMA, MSPC, WC 2145, Seán Hales: inquest on Brigadier Seán Hales TD, 11 December 1922.

21 Kissane, *Politics*, p. 88; Enright, *The Irish Civil War*, p. 54.

22 *Dáil Debates*, 2(3), 8 December 1922.

23 Ibid.

24 UCDA, Papers of Desmond FitzGerald, P80/289, memorandum regarding captured republican documents, 29 August 1922.

25 Desmond Greaves, *Liam Mellows and the Irish Revolution* (London, 1971), p. 29.

26 O'Donnell, *The Gates Flew Open*, p. 132.

27 IMA, MSPC, DP 10200, Liam Mellows: Sarah Mellows to minister for defence, 25 January 1940.

28 IMA, MSPC, MSP 34 REF 16537, Herbert Charles Mellows: Mellows to Office of the Referee, 11 July 1938 and 22 April 1939, and WDP 9821, disability pension application, 18 March 1938.

29 IMA, MSPC, DP 6664, Rory O'Connor: account of family circumstances, December 1933.

30 Dolan, *Commemorating the Irish Civil War*, p. 143.

31 UCDA, Papers of Kevin O'Higgins, P197/108, Kevin O'Higgins to Tom O'Higgins, 30 December 1922.

32 McCabe, *For God and Ireland*, p. 155.

33 CCCA, U105, Republican and Free State Tracts, *A Painful Necessity*, 1923.

34 Cited in Clark, *Everyday Violence*, p. 161, and Deasy, *Brother Against Brother*, pp. 100–111.

35 UCDA, Papers of Seán Mac Eoin, P151/202, Cosgrave to Mac Eoin, January 1923.

36 NAI, DT S8139, interview between Cosgrave, M. J. Burke and Donal O'Hannigan, 27 February 1923.

37 *Irish Times*, 17 February 1923.

38 CCCA, De Róiste diaries, 21 November 1922.

39 UCDA, Papers of Eamon de Valera, P150/657, MacSwiney to de Valera, 10 September 1922, de Valera to MacSwiney, 4 March 1923, and MacSwiney to Mulcahy 24 April 1922, cited in McCullagh, *De Valera: Rise*, p. 275.

40 Earl of Longford and T. P. O'Neill, *Eamon de Valera* (London, 1970), p. 221, and de Valera to Aiken, 4 June 1923, cited in Matthew Lewis, *Frank Aiken's War: The Irish Revolution, 1916–23* (Dublin, 2014), p. 199.

41 NUIGA, Papers of Michael Rynne, P133/4/7/23, extracts from private journal, entry for 31 January 1922.

42 IMA, MSPC, 5D13, John Joseph Judge: M. Brennan, attorney general, to secretary, APB, 17 August 1928; application form by Michael Judge, 3 August 1928; Garda Report on family circumstances, 18 June 1928; APB to minister for finance, 6 March 1929.

43 IMA, MSPC, MSP 34 REF 39909, Ellen Carroll: Nora Martin to Mr Flinn, 12 October 1942, and Nora Martin to APB, 28 April 1937.

44 IMA, MSPC, MSP 34 REF 29692, Jeremiah O'Neill: statement to Advisory Committee, October 1937, and supporting letter of Humphrey O'Callaghan, 26 October 1937.

10: The Peasant Mind

1 Clark, *Everyday Violence*, p. 66, and Terence Dooley, *The Decline of the Big House in Ireland: A Study of Irish Landed Families, 1860–1960* (Dublin, 2001).

2 James Hogan, 'Civil War Diary Fragment', 5 March 1923, in Donnchadh Ó Corráin (ed.), *James Hogan: Revolutionary, Historian and Political Scientist* (Dublin, 2001), pp. 203–12.

3 Ian d'Alton '"No Country": Protestant "Belongings" in Independent Ireland', in Ian d'Alton and Ida Milne (eds.), *Protestant and Irish* (Cork, 2019), pp. 19–34.

4 Brian Inglis, *West Briton* (London, 1962), pp. 13–19.

5 Sally Phipps, *Molly Keane: A Life* (London, 2017), pp. 33–4.

6 Terence de Vere White, *A Fretful Midge* (London, 1957), pp. 8–25.

7 Phipps, *Molly Keane*, pp. xi, 33–7.

8 Elizabeth Bowen, *The Last September* (London, 1929), pp. 66–7.

9 Clark, *Everyday Violence*, p. 168.

10 Hogan 'Civil War Diary Fragment', 6 March and 9 March 1923.

11 Gavin Foster, *The Irish Civil War and Society: Politics, Class and Conflict* (London, 2015), p. 33.

12 Ibid., pp. 57–61.

13 Ibid., pp. 109–13.

14 Ibid., pp. 37–74.

15 Peter Hart, *The IRA at War, 1916–1923* (Oxford, 2003), p. 97.

16 Dolan, 'The Papers in Context'.

17 Liam Lynch to Ernie O'Malley, 16 September and 28 September 1922, in O'Malley and Dolan, *No Surrender Here!*, pp. 185–9.

18 Farry, *The Aftermath of Revolution*, p. 109.

19 Hart, *The IRA and Its Enemies*, pp. 155–63.

20 Gavin Foster, 'Class Dismissed? The Debate Over a Social Basis to the Treaty Split and Irish Civil War', *Saothar*, 33, 2008, pp. 73–86.
21 Peter Hart, 'The Geography of Revolution in Ireland, 1917–1923', *Past and Present*, 155 (May 1997), pp. 142–76 and Foster 'Class dismissed?'.
22 Cited in Brian Hanley, 'Moderates and Peacemakers', *Journal of Irish Economic and Social History*, 43(1), 2016, pp. 113–30.
23 Patrick Long, 'Organisation and Development of the Pro-Treaty Forces, 1922–1924', *The Irish Sword*, 20(82), Winter 1997, pp. 308–31.
24 Durney, *Civil War in Kildare*, p. 14.
25 NUIGA, Papers of Michael Rynne, P133/4/7/24, Seán Walshe, Castlebar, to chief liaison officer, 18 January 1922.
26 Ibid., P133/4/7/22, Rynne's reports on injured Free State Soldiers, 9 April and 4 February 1923 and 17 December 1922.

11: Giving It to the Bastards

1 IMA, MSPC, DP 8107, Laurence Sweeney: application of Joseph Sweeney, 24 April 1933, and evidence of Timmy Coughlan, 3 October 1933.
2 IMA, MSPC, 2D36, Edward Crabbe: Alice Crabbe to APB, 7 November 1923 and 8 March 1924.
3 IMA, MSPC, MSP 34 REF 25857, Katie Walsh: note of Advisory Committee, 16 October 1941.
4 IMA, MSPC, DP 1837, Thomas Greehy: letter of Maurice Roynane, 11 December 1923.
5 Liam O'Flaherty, 'Civil War', in A. A. Kelly (ed.), *The Collected Stories of Liam O'Flaherty*, vol. 1 (Dublin 1999), pp. 183–9.
6 IMA, MSPC, WPD 3021, Thomas Derrig: application form for wound pension, 30 May 1933.
7 Ibid., statement of case by the Medical Board, 13 January 1934.
8 Yeates, *A City in Civil War*, pp. 205–6.
9 An account by Joseph Clarke of the treatment of prisoners by the CID, 13 November 1922 (UCDA, Twomey papers, P69/250). Quoted in Timothy Breen Murphy, 'The Government's Executions Policy During the Irish Civil War', unpublished PhD thesis, National University of Ireland Maynooth, 2010.
10 CCCA, U254/J/23, Meade Papers: The Civil War, *Eire*, 18 August 1923.
11 Patrick Maume, 'Patrick John Lynch', in *DIB*, www.dib.cambridge.org, and *Evening Herald*, 3 May 1934.
12 Brian Hanley, *The IRA: A Documentary History, 1916–2005* (Dublin, 2010), pp. 52–3.

13 Enright, *The Irish Civil War*, pp. 97–8.

14 IMA, MSPC, DP 1503, Mary Carey: James Hickey to Frank Aiken, 7 November 1933.

15 Gemma Clark, 'Violence Against Women in the Irish Civil War, 1922–3: Gender-Based Harm in Global Perspective', *Irish Historical Studies*, Vol. 44(165), May 2020, pp. 75–91.

16 Ibid.

17 UCDA, Papers of Desmond FitzGerald, P80/312/4, response to claims of Ernie O'Malley, August 1922.

18 Clark, *Everyday Violence*, pp. 86–93.

19 Linda Connolly, 'Sexual Violence and the Irish Revolution: An Inconvenient Truth?', *History Ireland*, 27(6), November/December 2019, pp. 34–8.

20 Clark, 'Violence Against Women'.

21 Connolly, 'Sexual Violence'.

22 Lindsey Earner-Byrne, 'The Rape of Miss Mary M: A Microhistory of Sexual Violence and Moral Redemption in 1920s Ireland', *Journal of the History of Sexuality*, 24, January 2015, pp. 75–98.

23 Regan, *The Irish Counter-Revolution*, p. 173.

24 IMA, BMH, WS 1751, Cahir Davitt.

25 Regan, *The Irish Counter-Revolution*, p. 173.

26 IMA, BMH, WS 939, Ernest Blythe, and Regan, *The Irish Counter-Revolution*, p. 173.

27 IMA, IE/MA/CREC/02, Confidential Military Reports, February–March 1923: reports from Cork Command, 1 March 1923, Claremorris, 13 March 1923, and Waterford Command, 26 February 1923.

28 IMA, MSPC, BAR/A/65(2), South Wexford Brigade: additional evidence before Advisory Committee, 3 February 1936.

29 Doyle, *The Civil War in Kerry*, p. 190.

30 Ibid., p. 90.

31 IMA, MSPC, WP66, Joseph O'Brien: telegram of 13 March 1923 to Annie O'Brien, recommendation of APB, 3 June 1924; Annie O'Brien to Department of Defence, 20 March and 11 August 1925, and letter of John O'Brien, 22 September 1925.

32 T. Ryle Dwyer, *Tans, Terror and Trouble: Kerry's Real Fighting Story, 1919–1923* (Cork, 2001), p. 369.

33 *Cork Examiner*, 9 March 1923.

34 IMA, MSPC, MSP 34 REF 6759, Stephen Fuller: sworn statement before Advisory Committee, 29 October 1935; *The Kerryman*, 30 January 1981.

35   IMA, MSPC, W34 D448, Stephen Fuller: medical assessment of Edward Dunn, Peamount sanatorium, June 1933.
36   Doyle, *The Civil War in Kerry*, p. 274; Ernie O'Malley, *The Singing Flame* (Dublin 1978), p. 240.
37   Enright, *The Irish Civil War*, p. 105.
38   *Dáil Debates*, 3(3), 17 April 1923.
39   *Irish Times*, 31 December 2008.
40   Tim Horgan, *Dying for the Cause: Kerry's Republican Dead* (Cork, 2015), p. 106; Enright, *The Irish Civil War*, p. 109.
41   IMA, IE/MA/CREC/03, Confidential Military Reports, April 1923; Kerry Command, 17 and 19 April 1923.
42   Dominic Price, *We Bled Together: Michael Collins, The Squad and the Dublin Brigade* (Cork, 2017), pp. 222–65.

12: The Mind's Exhilaration

1   Kissane, *Politics*, p. 95.
2   NAI, LSC, Misc. 27–28, 18 May 1923.
3   Foster, *The Irish Civil War and Society*, pp. 131–4.
4   *Dáil Debates*, 2(35), 1 March 1923; *Irish Independent*, 2 March 1923.
5   Farrell, *Party Politics*, pp. 74–7.
6   McCarthy, *Waterford*, p. 122.
7   *Dáil Debates*, 4(1), 3 July 1923.
8   NAI, DT S1369/3, 9 May 1923.
9   UCDA, Papers of Desmond FitzGerald, P80/326, extracts from letters from republican prisoners, October–November 1922, and letter of Annie Hogan, 5 May 1923.
10   NAI, DT S1369/13, Yeats to Cosgrave, 14 December 1922.
11   NAI, DT S1369/3, Yeats to Cosgrave, 28 April 1923.
12   Ibid., Yeats to Cosgrave, 30 April 1923.
13   Ibid., McCartan to Cosgrave, 16 April 1923.
14   Ibid., Cosgrave's reply, undated, April 1923.
15   Ibid., profile of female prisoners, 23 April 1923.
16   Foster, *Vivid Faces*, p. 321.
17   DDA, ABP, Box 466: Government 1922–39, Nell Ryan, Annie O'Neill and Kathleen Costello to Byrne, 18 April 1923.
18   Ibid., Cosgrave to Byrne, 14 April 1923.
19   Ibid., Cosgrave to Byrne, 23 October 1923.
20   Ibid., Byrne to Cosgrave, 28 October 1923 and Byrne's corresponding private notes, n.d.

21 IMA, MSPC, MSP 34 REF 4873, Mary Josephine Commins: letter of Dr Peter Conlon, 9 February 1934.

22 Ibid.

23 IMA, MSPC, DP 9584, Ellen Walsh: statement of Tom McEllistrim, 31 August 1938.

24 NAI, DT S1369/3, report on wounded prisoners, 17 December 1923.

25 English and O'Malley, *Prisoners*, O'Malley to Childers, 26 November and 1 December 1923.

26 Ibid., O'Malley to Childers, 12 November 1923.

27 Ibid., O'Malley to Childers, 17 December 1923, and O'Malley to Sheila Humphreys, 21 February 1923.

28 James Matthew, *Voices: A Life of Frank O'Connor* (Dublin, 1983), pp. 29–33.

29 O'Donnell, *The Gates Flew Open*, p. 132.

30 Ibid., pp. 167–75.

31 Peter Hart, Review of *Prisoners: The Civil War Letters*, *Irish Historical Studies*, 28, May 1993, p. 336.

32 English and O'Malley, *Prisoners*, O'Malley to Childers, 6 December 1923.

33 Dolan, 'The Papers in Context'.

34 English and O'Malley, *Prisoners*, O'Malley to Childers, 27 November 1923.

35 Ibid., O'Malley to Childers, 15 November 1923.

36 Ibid., O'Malley to Childers, 15 November 1923.

37 Ibid., O'Malley to Childers, 12 November 1923.

38 Ibid., O'Malley to Jim O'Donovan, 7 April 1923, and O'Malley to Childers, 19 November 1923.

39 Anne-Marie McInerney, 'Denis Barry', *DIB*, www.dib.cambridge.org.

40 Letter of Bishop Daniel Cohalan, as reported in *Irish Times*, 28 November 1923.

41 James Healy, 'The Civil War Hunger Strike, October 1923', *Studies*, 71, Autumn 1982, pp. 213–26.

42 NAI, DT S1369/10, 'Civil War Prisoners: General Hunger Strike 1923': Archbishop Byrne to Cosgrave, 23 October 1923, and Kevin O'Higgins to Executive Council, 26 October 1923.

43 Durney, *Civil War in Kildare*, p. 166.

44 NAI, DT S1396/13, Cosgrave to Archbishop Mannix, 17 December 1923.

45 NAI, DT S1369/4, 'Prisoners from Each County in Military Custody', 1 December 1923.

46 Ibid., memorandum of 12 June 1924.

47 Ibid.

48 NAI, DT S1379/15, M. Mac Donnchadha to minister for defence, 16 August 1923; David Neligan to minister for defence, 23 August and 5 September 1923.

13: Fizzling Out

1 Enright, *The Irish Civil War*, p. 122.

2 Tom Garvin, *1922: The Birth of Irish Democracy* (Dublin, 1996), p. 43; O'Donoghue, *No Other Law*, pp. 289–307.

3 IMA, MSPC, DP 5482, Liam Lynch: Rev. T. Lynch to Frank Aiken, 12 July 1933, and Margaret Mullins to APB, 2 November 1962.

4 Lewis, *Frank Aiken's War*, pp. 183–99.

5 English and O'Malley, *Prisoners*, and O'Malley, *The Singing Flame*, p. 25.

6 IMA, IE/MA/CREC/03, Confidential Military Reports, April 1923, North Donegal, 6 April 1923.

7 IMA, CW/OPS/01/02/11, Weekly Intelligence Reports by GHQ Intelligence to C.O.S., 3 May, 7 May, 30 June, 5 October and 8 November 1923.

8 Fanning, *Eamon de Valera: A Will to Power*, p. 142.

9 Joseph M. Curran, *The Birth of the Irish Free State, 1921–1923* (Alabama, 1980), p. 276.

10 Michael Hopkinson, 'The Guerrilla Phase and the End of the Civil War', in Crowley et al. (eds.), *Atlas of the Irish Revolution*, pp. 703–15 and Anne Dolan, 'Ending War in a "Sportsmanlike Manner": The Milestone of Revolution 1919–23', in Thomas E. Hachey (ed.), *Turning Points in Twentieth-Century Irish History* (Dublin, 2011), pp. 21–39.

11 Foster, *The Irish Civil War and Society*, pp. 158–64.

12 Yeates, *A City in Civil War*, pp. 307–8.

13 Andy Bielenberg, 'Fatalities in the Irish Revolution', in Crowley et al. (eds.), *Atlas of the Irish Revolution*, pp. 752–62.

14 Kissane, 'On the Shock of Civil War'.

15 Dorney, *The Civil War in Dublin*, pp. 323–8.

16 Ibid., and Durney, *Civil War in Kildare*, p. 159.

17 Fearghal McGarry, 'Revolution, 1916–23', in Thomas Bartlett (ed.), *The Cambridge History of Ireland*, vol. 4: *1880 to the Present* (Cambridge, 2018), p. 293. For estimating current value of old money see www.measuringworth.com/ppoweruk/.

18 *The Nationalist* (Tipperary), 14 July 1923.

19 NUIGA, Sinn Féin pamphlets, PO/30, Sinn Féin election manifesto, 1927.

20 NUIGA, Papers of Michael Rynne, P133/4/10/2, Rynne to FitzGerald, 4 December 1923.

21 Ibid., Desmond FitzGerald to Rynne, n.d., November 1923.

22 Ronan Fanning, 'Small States, Larger Neighbours: Ireland and the United Kingdom', *Irish Studies in International Affairs*, vol. 9, 1998, pp. 21–9.

23 IMA, IE/MA/CREC/01–05, chief of staff reports, 'Monthly Report of the General State of the Country', September 1923, sent to minister for defence.

24 Gavin Foster, 'The Social Basis of the Civil War Divide', in Crowley et al. (eds.), *Atlas of the Irish Revolution*, pp. 665–7.

25 English and O'Malley, *Prisoners*, Ernie O'Malley to Sheila Humphreys, 25 December 1923.

26 *Irish Times*, 24 November 1923.

27 Farrell, *Party Politics*, pp. 69–74.

28 CCCA, De Róiste diaries, 1 and 15 March 1923.

14: Potatoes, Water and Pensions

1   Cormac K. H. O'Malley and Nicholas Allen (eds.), *Broken Landscapes: Selected Letters of Ernie O'Malley, 1924–1957* (Dublin, 2011), letters to Madge Clifford, 28 July 1924, and John Raleigh, March 1925, pp. 9–10.

2   Foster, *The Irish Civil War and Society*, p. 205, and Gavin Foster, 'Locating the "Lost Legion": IRA Emigration and Settlement After the Civil War', in Crowley et al. (eds.), *Atlas of the Irish Revolution*, pp. 741–7.

3   Foster, *The Irish Civil War and Society*, p. 212.

4   Noel Ó Murchú, *War in the West: The Struggle for Irish Independence on the Dingle Peninsula* (Kerry, 2020), p. 283, and Síobhra Aiken, '"Sinn Féin permits ... in the heels of their shoes": Cumann na mBan Emigrants and Transatlantic Revolutionary Exchange', *Irish Historical Studies*, 44(165), May 2020, pp. 106–31.

5   DDA, ABP, Lay Organisations, Box 4, Appeal by Association of Ex-Officers and Men, National Army, 17 September 1925, and J. Davis, treasurer, to Byrne, 6 November 1925.

6   Catherine Morris, *Alice Milligan and the Irish Cultural Revival* (Dublin, 2012), p. 291.

7   Foster, *The Irish Civil War and Society*, p. 182.

8   Clark, 'Violence Against Women'.

9   Patrick Brennan, 'Origins, Scope and Content of the Collection', in
      Catriona Crowe (ed.), *Guide to the Military Service (1916–1923) Pensions
      Collection* (Dublin, 2012), pp. 14–44.

10   Marie Coleman, 'Military Service Pensions for Veterans of the Irish
      Revolution, 1916–23', *War in History*, 20(2), 2013, pp. 201–21.

11   Ibid.

12   IMA, MSPC, Administration Files, WSPG/54/2, letter of H. Tierney, 2
      January 1925, and letter of Old Defence Union, 28 September 1926.

13   Ibid., Seán Lyons to Gearóid O Sullivan, 30 March 1926.

14   IMA, MSPC, DP 1898, James Parle: APB report, September 1937.

15   Patrick Brennan, '"Active Service": Changing Definitions', in Crowe
      (ed.), *Guide*, p. 67.

16   Coleman 'Military Service Pensions for Veterans'.

17   IMA, MSPC, Administration Files, MSP Act 1949, File 3/13070, South
      Mayo Brigade pre-Truce IRA resolution, 2 September 1953; letter from
      Richard Mulcahy, 9 April 1951; File 3/15/10, Part 2, Military Service
      and Disability Pensions: Old IRA Mansion House Committee 1951;
      minister for finance to minister for health, 28 August 1959 and letter of
      Justice Eugene Sheehy, 13 December 1956.

18   *Report of the Commission on the Relief of the Sick and Destitute Poor,
      Including the Insane Poor* (Dublin, 1927), p. 18.

19   Anne Dolan, review of Bill Kissane, *The Politics of the Irish Civil War*,
      Reviews in History, 502, March 2006; www.history.ac.uk/reviews/
      review/502, accessed 7 February 2021.

20   Coleman, 'Military Service Pensions for Veterans'.

21   UCDA, P311, Seán Lemass interviews, 2nd interview, 31 May 1967,
      pp. 50–55. Lemass recorded twenty-three interviews with Dermot Ryan
      between 1967 and 1969.

22   Coleman, 'Military Service Pensions for Veterans'.

23   IMA, MSPC, MSP 34 REF 2078, Seán Lemass: sworn evidence, 1
      October 1942.

24   Ibid., WD 34D2300, service certificate, 19 March 1943, and Lemass to
      secretary, Department of Defence, 19 March 1948.

25   Ibid., A. MacGiolla Phádraig to Lemass, 23 April 1969.

26   Coleman, 'Military Service Pensions for Veterans'.

27   Marie Coleman, 'Séamus Robinson', in *DIB*, 8, p. 549.

28   *Dáil Debates*, 93(11), 26 April 1944.

29   Ibid.

30   www.flickr.com/photos/yournlireland/6856080817, 'The Roll
      of Dishonour', Fianna Fáil election poster 1932, accessed 8

February 2021, and www.irishelectionliterature.com/2012/02/14/
the-roll-of-dishonour-and-a-hot-record-2-great-1932-posters-from-
cumann-na-ngaedheal/, accessed 8 February 2021; UCDA, Archive
of the Fianna Fáil Party, P176/1196, 1932 election poster 'What Price
Glory'.

31 Farrell, *Party Politics*, pp. 85–90.
32 'Bricks and Communism', *Irish Times*, 21 October 1931.

15: The Price of a Lost Life

1   IMA, MSPC, 2D194, Thomas Tiernan: John Tiernan to APB, 10
November 1924 and report of Sgt C. Murray, Carrick on Shannon, 22
February 1924.
2   IMA, MSPC, W24D2, Pádraig Ua Dálaigh: Ministry of Finance to
Army Finance Office, 26 January 1925; note of J. J. Hogan, 16 July 1928,
and note of T. L. Ryan, Office of Public Works, 19 September 1928.
3   IMA, MSPC, DP 2588, Daniel Shea: James Shea to minister for defence,
7 July 1932.
4   Ibid., report on applicant's circumstances by M. O'Ceacháin, Customs
and Excise, Cahirciveen, 22 June 1933.
5   Ibid., 26 June 1942, investigation officer report regarding Mary Shea
claim, Cahirciveen, 1 June 1942.
6   IMA, MSPC, 3D57, Laurence O'Connor: Margaret O'Connor to Army
Finance Office, 19 July 1924.
7   Ibid., John O'Connor to APB, 23 August 1927.
8   Ibid., Margaret O'Connor to Department of Defence, APB, 12
September 1934.
9   IMA, MSPC, DP 6572, George O'Shea: Ellen O'Shea to Department of
Defence, 2 April 1959; death certificate of Ellen O'Shea, 16 January 1990.
10 IMA, MSPC, W3D164, Michael Dunne: Catherine Dunne to APB,
16 January 1924; report of Dublin Metropolitan Police, 5 March 1924;
letter of APB, 21 May 1924.
11 IMA, MSPC, 3D70, Edward Stapleton: Julia Stapleton to Alfred Byrne,
17 November 1923.
12 Ibid., Mary Stapleton to Army Finance Office, 19 July 1926 and letter
from Army Finance Office, 11 August 1926.
13 IMA, MSPC, DP 9533, Patrick Hartnett: statement from Moran and
Clarke solicitors, 4 April 1933, and report of Customs and Excise officer,
Listowel, 2 November 1933.
14 Ibid., letter of Dr Joseph McGuire regarding Mary Hartnett, 29 October
1937.

15   IMA/DOD/A15296-E4 Intelligence, Childers, Erskine: Office of Adjutant General to secretary, minister for defence, 31 March 1924.

16   Ibid., Molly Childers to adjutant general, 26 July 1923.

17   NAI, DT 1884A, 'Executions by Provisional and Saorstát Éireann Governments': President's Office to Eoin O'Duffy, 20 June 1924, and reply of O'Duffy, 27 June 1924.

18   Ibid., P. F. Baxter to Cosgrave, 13 August 1924.

19   NAI, DT S1884, minister for home affairs to Joseph Dolan, Ardee, 3 November 1924.

20   Ibid., George Nicholls to Cosgrave, 25 August 1924.

21   Dolan, *Commemorating the Irish Civil War*, p. 134.

22   NAI, DT S1884, Pádraig Ó Máille TD to Cosgrave, 27 August 1924.

23   Ibid., T. Kileen to chief of staff, 30 October 1924.

24   Ibid., Report of Colonel McCorley, 1 November 1924.

25   *Freeman's Journal*, 31 October 1924.

26   Anne Dolan, 'Divisions and Divisions and Divisions: Who to Commemorate?', in John Horne and Edward Madigan (eds.), *Towards Commemoration: Ireland in War and Revolution, 1912–1923* (Dublin, 2013), p. 146.

27   James Langton, *Forgotten Fallen*, vol. 1: *National Army Soldiers Killed in Action During the Irish Civil War* (Dublin, 2020).

28   Keane, *Wounds*, pp. 225–6.

29   Gavin Foster, 'The Civil War in Kerry in History and Memory', in Maurice J. Bric (ed.), *Kerry: History and Society: Interdisciplinary Essays on the History of an Irish County* (Dublin, 2020), chapter 22.

30   IMA, MSPC, 3D58, Patrick O'Connor: letter of Rev. M. O'Connor, brother of Patrick O'Connor Jr, 30 April 1923.

31   *Kerry Reporter*, 31 October 1925; *The Liberator* (Tralee), 20 October 1925; *Kerry News*, 13 January 1926.

32   *Irish Times*, 20 January 1930.

33   Dolan, *Commemorating the Irish Civil War*, pp. 142–3.

16: Insulting the Dead

1   Seán O'Faoláin, 'A Portrait of the Artist as an Old Man', *Irish University Review*, 6(1), Spring 1976, pp. 10–18; Seán O'Faoláin, *Vive Moi: An Autobiography* (London, 1965), p. 169, and Seán O'Faoláin, 'Romance and Realism', *The Bell*, 10(5), August 1945, pp. 373–82.

2   Julia O'Faoláin, *Trespassers: A Memoir* (London, 2013), pp. 8–9.

3   O'Faoláin, *Vive Moi*, p. 169.

4   UCDA, P311, Lemass interviews, 1st interview, 12 April 1967.

5   P. S. O'Hegarty's assessment, cited in Frances Flanagan, *Remembering the Revolution: Dissent, Culture and Nationalism in the Irish Free State* (Oxford, 2015), p. 107.

6   Christopher Murray, *Seán O'Casey: Writer at Work: A Biography* (Dublin, 2004), pp. 147–51.

7   Ibid., p. 141.

8   Seán O'Casey, 'Juno and the Paycock', in Seán O'Casey, *Three Dublin Plays* (London, 1998), pp. 63–149.

9   Ibid. and Murray, *Seán O'Casey*, p. 177.

10 Flanagan, *Remembering the Revolution*, p. 23.

11 Ibid., pp. 88–97.

12 George Russell (AE), 'Lessons of Revolution', *Studies*, 12(45), March 1923, pp. 1–6, and Flanagan, *Remembering the Revolution*, p. 121.

13 Flanagan, *Remembering the Revolution*, pp. 121–46.

14 Ibid., pp. 163–77.

15 Ibid., p. 196.

16 Ferriter, *A Nation and Not a Rabble*, p. 259.

17 Seán O'Faoláin, *De Valera* (London, 1939), p. 81.

18 IMA, MSPC, W2D164, Peter McCartney: report of circumstances by Chief Superintendent J. J. Molloy, 21 June 1924.

19 Ibid., Garda report, 12 February 1924; J. J. Hogan, Army Finance Office, to Patrick McCartney, 6 April 1927.

20 Ibid., Patrick McCartney to Cosgrave, 7 February 1927; McCartney to Department of Defence, 14 December 1926 and 18 April 1927; McCartney to minister for defence, 20 May 1924.

21 Ibid., Charles McCartney to APB, 7 September 1964; letter of Dr S. Farrelly, 7 October 1959 and memorandum of 6 October 1960.

22 IMA, MSPC, MSP REF 34A6, Ernest Bernard O'Malley, Service Certificate, 11 July 1935.

23 IMA, MSPC, MSP 34 REF 839, Michael Kilroy: Kilroy to Department of Defence Finance Branch, 27 March 1956.

24 Michael Hopkinson, *The Irish War of Independence* (Dublin, 2000), p. 134, and Hopkinson, *Green Against Green*, p. 158.

25 IMA, MSPC, MSP 34 REF 839, Michael Kilroy: application form, 12 January 1935.

26 IMA, MSPC, 2D331, Joseph Ruddy: Thomas Ruddy to Army Finance Office, 31 July 1925.

27 IMA, MSPC, 2D162, Austin Woods: Sarah Woods to Joe McBride TD, 27 April 1923.

28 Ibid., Report of Chief Superintendent A. O'Meara, 25 February 1924.

29 IMA, MSPC, 2D166, Patrick McEllin: report of Lieutenant Tomás Mac Suibhne, 4 February 1924, and Mary McEllin to Ernest Blythe, 6 February and 29 June 1925.

30 Ibid., Mary McEllin to APB, 23 February and 23 April 1928 and 29 September 1941.

31 IMA, MSPC, Con. Ran. 251, Patrick Murphy: Delia Murphy to APB, 18 August 1925; Garda Report, 1 February 1925.

32 IMA, MSPC, 2D330, Michael Joseph Walsh: Garda report, 24 November 1924.

33 Ibid., medical report on Sarah Walsh by J. V. Kelly, 17 May 1955.

34 IMA, MSPC, 2D141, Thomas Rawl: Patrick Rawl to APB, 22 January 1924 and 12 September 1924.

35 Ibid., Michael and James Rawl to Seán Mac Eoin, 12 February 1957; medical report on James Rawl by Dr H. O'Carroll, 6 April 1963; Mac Eoin to secretary, Department of Defence, 1 December 1960.

36 IMA, MSPC, MSP 34 REF 4067, Denis O'Neill: Seán MacCarthy to Oscar Traynor, 12 March 1953.

37 IMA, MSPC, MSP 34 REF 4067, Denis O'Neill: letter to APB, 28 January 1939.

38 Ibid., W2 21085, intelligence notes, 7 November 1929.

39 Ibid.

40 Ibid., report of T. Ua Domhnaill, 14 July 1939.

41 Ibid., Denis O'Neill to APB, 19 May 1938.

42 Ibid., Denis O'Neill to APB, 24 July 1937.

43 Ibid., statement of Paddy Kennedy to the Advisory Committee, July 1936.

44 Ibid., Denis O'Neill's sworn evidence, 16 May 1935.

45 IMA, MSPC, MSP 34 REF 27833, Daniel O'Neill: note of attorney general, 10 April 1959.

46 Ibid., sworn evidence of Daniel O'Neill, 24 March 1938.

47 IMA, MSPC, MSP 34 REF 29692, Jeremiah O'Neill: letter of Dr Humphrey O'Callaghan, 28 October 1941, and Jeremiah O'Neill to Disability Board, 26 July 1943.

48 Ibid., list attached in the correspondence between the Office of the Referee and F. Begley, Bandon, 11 November 1942.

49 IMA, MSPC, MSP REF 9778, John O'Neill: F. Begley to Office of the Referee, 11 November 1942; John O'Neill to Tom Hales, 3 January 1935.

50 Ibid., John O'Neill's sworn statement before Advisory Committee, 12 September 1935.

51 Ibid., WDP 2828, medical report on John O'Neill, 3 March 1933.

52   Ibid., John O'Neill to minister for defence, 29 November 1933.

53   Ibid., O'Neill to Department of Defence, 5 April 1934.

54   Ibid., medical reports for John O'Neill, 3 March 1933, 9 November and 24 October 1944 (posthumous) and letter of Dr Dorothy Stopford Price, 19 March 1934.

55   Ibid., WDP 2828, letter of 17 October 1944.

17: Broken Lives

1   IMA, MSPC, MSP 34 REF 4588, Michael Leahy: application form, 14 December 1934.

2   Ibid., letter of Dr J. Bernard Wilson, 12 December 1934.

3   Gavin Wilk '"No Hope for him unless he can be got out of the country": Disabled Irish Republicans in America 1922–35', *New Hibernia Review* 18(1), Spring 2014, pp. 106–19.

4   Gavin Wilk, *Transatlantic Defiance: The Militant Irish Republican Movement in America, 1923–45* (Manchester, 2014), pp. 28–32.

5   Ibid., p. 37.

6   Ibid.

7   IMA, MSPC, MSP 34 REF 17135, John Keating: Keating to Department of Defence, 3 November 1937; Keating to Office of Revenue Commissioners, 5 February 1963.

8   Patrick Maume, 'Seán P. Keating', in *DIB*, www.dib.cambridge.org.

9   Ibid.

10   Brian Hanley, 'The Politics of NORAID', *Irish Political Studies*, 19(1), Summer 2004, pp. 1–18.

11   Terence O'Reilly, *Rebel Heart: George Lennon: A Flying Column Commander* (Cork, 2009), pp. 194–244.

12   IMA, MSPC, MSP 34 REF 11591, George Lennon: Lennon to APB, 21 October 1925.

13   Ibid., Lennon to secretary, Department of Defence, 1 February 1939.

14   Ibid., Lennon to secretary, Department of Finance, 1 May 1945.

15   Ibid., medical report of 30 September 1940 and report of Dr Lee Parker, 22 May 1944.

16   Ibid., Lennon's statement of appeal, 4 February 1944.

17   Ibid., Lennon to secretary, Department of Defence, 16 December 1943, enclosing evidence of Dr Herbrand Ingoville.

18   O'Reilly, *Rebel Heart*, pp. 194–244.

19   *Irish Independent*, 19 June 1924.

20   *The Nationalist* (Tipperary), 20 April 1927; *Nenagh Guardian*, 16 April 1927.

21 IMA, MSPC, 24 SP 1763, John Prout: Mrs M. G. Prout to J. J. Hogan, 11 July 1928, and letter of Commandant O'Hegarty, 23 February 1929.

22 Ibid., A. Heron to Desmond FitzGerald, 8 July 1929.

23 Ibid., statement of Mary Prout enclosed in Heron letter of 8 July 1929.

24 Ibid., Peadar MacMahon, Department of Defence, to Joseph Walsh, Department of External Affairs, 1 December 1941.

25 Ibid., Joseph Walsh to Peadar MacMahon, 21 January 1942.

26 R. A. Hinchy to secretary, Department of Defence, 19 September 1947.

27 *Kilkenny People*, 6 January 1940.

28 *Irish Independent*, 19 June 1924.

29 IMA, MSPC, 24 SP 1763, John Prout: John Prout to Department of Defence, 26 December 1968.

18: The Uncertainty of a Soldier's Life

1 Jason Knirck, *Afterimage of the Revolution: Cumann na nGaedheal and Irish Politics, 1922–1932* (Wisconsin, 2014), pp. 83–104.

2 NUIGA, Papers of Michael Rynne, P133/4/7/25, Aodh MacNeill to Rynne, 31 October 1923.

3 IMA, MSPC, REF 24 SP 11777, Hugo (Aodh) Mac Neill: application form 23 February 1925 and pension rate as stipulated by Department of Defence, 2 October 1951.

4 IMA, IE/MA/CREC/06, O'Duffy's personal note to Cosgrave, 15 April 1924.

5 Ibid.

6 Ibid., O'Duffy's 2nd army report, 14 April 1924 and 10th Report, 22 September 1924.

7 IMA, IE/MA/CREC/06, O'Duffy's army reports, 1924, and O'Duffy to president and Executive Council, 7 April 1924.

8 Maryann Gialanella Valiulis, *Almost a Rebellion: The Irish Army Mutiny of 1924* (Cork, 1985), p. 51.

9 O'Beirne-Ranelagh, 'The IRB from the Treaty to 1924', pp. 26–39.

10 Valiulis, *Almost a Rebellion*, p. 53.

11 Regan, *The Irish Counter-Revolution*, p. 197.

12 Valiulis, *Almost a Rebellion*, pp. 51–4.

13 Ronan Fanning, 'Richard Mulcahy', in *DIB*, vol. 6, pp. 746–52.

14 IMA, Papers of the Army Inquiry Committee (AIC), IE-MA-AMTY01-60, Box 1, Claims for reinstatement by demobilised officers: statement of James Corbett, 19 February 1924 and response from minister of defence, 3 March 1924.

15 Ibid.

16 Ibid., statement of Peter Leavy, Roscommon, 21 February 1924.

17 Ibid., statement of Patrick J. Gibbons, Newport, 5 January 1924, and assessment of GOC, 3 March 1924.

18 Ibid., statement of Patrick Beirne, Castlerea, and Richard Mulcahy to Department of Defence, 3 March 1924.

19 IMA, AIC, IE-MA-AMTY 03-070, Box 11, Army Inquiry Committee correspondence: letter to chairman from Joseph Rooney, 13 May 1924.

20 Ibid., Martin Nolan to AIC, 29 April 1924.

21 Ibid., Thomas Corcoran to AIC, 24 April 1924.

22 IMA, AIC, IE-MA-AMTY 04-002, 'Report of the Army Inquiry Committee' (Dublin 1924) and AIC, IE-MA-AMTY 04-004, minutes of meetings, 7 April 1924 to 7 June 1924.

23 James Hogan's letter to the AIC, 12 April 1924, in Ó Corráin, *James Hogan*, pp. 213–9.

24 Regan, *The Irish Counter-Revolution*, p. 93.

25 IMA, AIC, IE-MA-AMTY 03-002, 'Verbatim Report of Evidence of Mr C. B. O'Connor', 9 April 1924.

26 IMA, AIC, IE-MA-AMTY 03-027, statement submitted by General Seán MacMahon, 19 May 1924.

27 IMA, AIC, IE-MA-AMTY 03-070, Box 11, evidence of Kevin O'Higgins, 22 April 1924.

28 Ibid.

29 DDA, ABP, Box 467, Government and Politics, Bishop Cohalan of Cork to Byrne, 20 April 1923.

30 DDA, ABP, 'Army Chaplains, 1922–4', Fr Dominick Ryan report to Bishops, 7 January 1924.

31 Ibid., 'Recommendations re: Combating VD', from J. Donal Carroll to head chaplain, 23 October 1924.

32 Ibid.

33 IMA, AIC, IE-MA-AMTY 03-070, Box 11, Paddy Hogan to James Meredith, 23 April 1924.

34 Ibid., memorandum by chairman, 19 April 1924.

35 Ibid., Desmond FitzGerald to Meredith, 16 April 1924.

36 IMA, AIC, IE-MA-AMTY 03-007, Box 3, evidence of Cahir Davitt, 16 April 1924 and evidence of M. J. Costello, 16 April 1924.

37 Ibid., Box 7, evidence of Colonel Charles Russell, 10 May 1924.

38 IMA, AIC, IE-MA-AMTY 03-021, statement submitted by General Richard Mulcahy, 29 April 1924.

39 Ibid.

40 Ibid. and Mulcahy's memorandum of 8 May 1924.

41 Ibid.

42 Ibid., Meredith's annotations on Mulcahy memoranda.

43 Ibid., minutes, 7 June 1924.

44 IMA, AIC, IE-MA-AMTY 04-003, Meredith to Cosgrave and chairman's reservation to committee's report, 10 June 1924.

45 Ibid.

46 Ibid. and Maryann Gialanella Valiulis, *Portrait of a Revolutionary: General Richard Mulcahy and the Founding of the Irish Free State* (Dublin, 1992), pp. 202–19.

47 Ibid.

48 Fanning, *Independent Ireland*, p. 52; Tom Garvin, 'The Aftermath of the Civil War', *The Irish Sword*, 20(82), Winter 1997, pp. 387–96.

49 Regan, *The Irish Counter-Revolution*, p. 91.

50 Fanning, 'Richard Mulcahy'.

51 Risteárd Mulcahy, *My Father the General: Richard Mulcahy and the Military History of the Revolution* (Dublin, 2009), p. 163.

52 Ibid., p. 166.

53 Ibid., p. 175.

54 *Irish Times*, 12 July 1927.

55 Dolan, *Commemorating the Irish Civil War*, p. 3.

56 Mulcahy, *My Father the General*, p. 202.

57 Ibid.

58 IMA, MSPC, W24SP2764, Liam Tobin.

59 Ibid., Tobin to secretary, Department of Defence, 3 November 1925, and decision of 5 October 1926.

60 Ibid., Tobin to secretary, APB, 22 August 1933.

61 Marie Coleman, *The Sweep: A History of the Irish Hospital Sweepstake, 1930–1987* (Dublin, 2009), pp. 2, 172–224.

62 IMA, MSPC, 24 SP 2764, Liam Tobin: letter of appointment as superintendent of Oireachtas, 18 November 1940.

63 IMA, MSPC, 24 SP 1153, Charles Francis Dalton: Theresa Dalton to minister for defence, 6 May 1940, letter of Dr H. L. Barnville, 22 April 1941, letter and assessment of Dr Richard Leeper, 3 April 1941, and Department of Defence letters of 21 October 1941 and 28 January 1944.

64 IMA, MSPC, 24 SP 13470, Emmet Dalton: Horan and Devine Solicitors to Department of Defence, 18 September 1931.

65 Ibid., Emmet Dalton, account of J. T. O'Kelly, 31 May 1932 and Boyne, *Emmet Dalton*, pp. 330–59.

19: Ideal Specimens of Womanhood

1   IMA, MSPC, 34 REF 39909, Ellen Carroll: Nora Martin to APB, 28
     April 1937.
2   Ibid., Sworn statement of Carroll before Advisory Committee, 14
     October 1938.
3   Ibid., Ellen Carroll to Nora Martin, September 1940.
4   Ibid., Ellen Carroll to secretary, APB, 15 January 1940.
5   Ibid., Ellen Carroll to Department of Defence, 3 February 1965.
6   Ibid., Nora Martin to Mr Flinn, 12 October 1942.
7   Knirck, 'Women's Political Rhetoric'.
8   *Irish Statesman*, 29 January 1927.
9   Ward, *Unmanageable Revolutionaries*, p. 198.
10   IMA, MSPC, 34 REF 4873, Mary Josephine Commins: letter of Dr
     Peter Conlon, 9 February 1934; Commins to minister for finance, 9
     December 1940; Commins to Senator W. Quirke, 26 June 1934, and
     Commins to Department of Social Welfare, 25 May 1957.
11   IMA, MSPC, MSP REF 28100, Brigid Breen: note of sworn evidence
     before advisory board, initialled by 'MJG', 13 December 1940, and letter
     from Seán Moylan to Brigid Breen, 12 December 1940.
12   Ibid., Dan Breen to Thomas O'Donnell, 21 February 1941.
13   Ibid., letter of Brigid Breen to Department of Defence, 18 August 1941.
14   Ibid., M. Moran to Referee's Office, 7 March 1941.
15   Ibid., Patrick Ruttledge, solicitor, to secretary, Department of Defence,
     9 October 1947.
16   IMA, MSPC, 34 REF 171, Dan Breen: letter of secretary, Department of
     Defence, 16 November 1953.
17   *Irish Times*, 30 August 1984; *Cork Examiner*, 30 August 1984.
18   IMA, MSPC, 24 SP 13691, Patricia Hoey: note on application form, 30
     January 1928.
19   Ibid., Piaras Béaslaí to APB, 1 April 1927.
20   Ibid., Patricia Hoey, application and letter, 11 May 1927.
21   Ibid., W. M. Brophy to Hoey, 22 October 1927.
22   Ibid., letter of Patricia Hoey, 22 July 1927.
23   Ibid., Hoey to APB, 25 February 1928.
24   IMA, MSPC, CNM 163, 'Memorandum on interpreting qualifying
     service' by John McCoy, 21 June 1939.
25   IMA, MSPC, DP 1681, Johanna Cleary: Dr Cashman, Cork mental
     hospital, to APB, 15 July 1933.
26   Ibid.

27   IMA, MSPC, DP 1681, Johanna Cleary: investigating officer's report by
     L. De Barra, January 1937.

28   Ibid., Seán MacEntee to Frank Aiken, 1 January 1938, and note by Aiken
     in response. See also Tom Feeney, *Seán MacEntee: A Political Life*
     (Dublin, 2009).

29   IMA, MSPC, DP 1681, Johanna Cleary: note of J. O'Connell, January
     1938.

30   IMA, MSPC, DP 5017, Eugene Kelly: Frank Aiken to Seán MacEntee,
     20 April 1938.

31   IMA, MSPC, DP 1503, Mary (Máire) Carey: letter of Dr Thomas Blake,
     3 August 1933.

32   Ibid., case report of 8 October 1932 and report of D. M. Caráin, 26 May
     1933.

33   Ibid., Mary Carey to Frank Fahy, August 1933.

34   Ibid., Seán French, Lord Mayor of Cork, to Department of Defence, 18
     November 1933.

35   Ibid., letter of Daniel MacCarthy, curate SS Peter and Paul's, Cork, 31
     October 1933.

36   Ibid., James Hickey, ITGWU, to Frank Aiken, 7 November 1933.

37   Ibid., statement of Mary Carey, 9 October 1937.

38   Ibid., Mary Carey to Department of Defence, 1 February 1940.

39   IMA, MSPC, 34 REF 61176, Marian Tobin: Tobin to APB, 21
     December 1949 and 27 November 1950.

40   *Nationalist* (Tipperary), 14 July 1928; *Nationalist* (Tipperary) 3 January
     2019.

41   IMA, MSPC, 34 REF 61176, Marian Tobin: letter of Dan Breen, 26
     March 1950 and letter of Ernie O'Malley, 26 March 1950.

42   *Irish Press*, 21 September 1955.

43   Ibid. and IMA, MSPC, 34 REF 61176, Marian Tobin: Marian Tobin to
     APB, 13 December 1951.

44   *Irish Press*, 21 September 1955.

45   *Cork Examiner*, 19 July 1920; *Nationalist* (Tipperary), 3 January 1919.

46   IMA, MSPC, DP 9584, Ellen Walsh: statement of Thomas McEllistrim,
     31 August 1938.

47   Ibid., statement of H. James O'Connor, 3 October 1938.

48   Ibid., letter of J. Prenderville, medical officer, Brosna, 2 September 1934,
     and letter of John P. Rice, 22 September 1934.

49   IMA, MSPC, DP 2054, IRA Brigadier Séamus Devins TD: award of
     April 1932; letter of Mary Devins to secretary, APB, 25 June 1936; death
     certificate following death on 16 October 1936; *Irish Press*, 13 August

1932, *Sligo Champion*, 25 November 1933; *Irish Independent*, 18 April 1935.

50   Caroline Walsh, 'The sad and enduring love of Kitty Kiernan', *Irish Times*, 18 November 1983.

51   IMA, MSPC, MSP 34 REF 21507, Mary McNicholl: McNicholl to Office of the Referee, 29 May 1952.

52   *Sunday Independent*, 18 February 1996.

53   *Irish Times*, 8 July 2017.

54   IMA, MSPC, MSP 34 REF 21507, Mary McNicholl: McNicholl to Office of the Referee, 4 January 1943.

55   IMA, MSPC, Administration Files, SPG/10, 'Explanatory statement of special circumstances connected with the national struggle in the Belfast Area', 1936.

56   Ibid., 'Applicants resident in the six counties', 23 October 1924 to 17 February 1927.

57   Lewis, *Frank Aiken's War*, pp. 199–200.

58   IMA, MSPC, BAR, A/39, Derry City Battalion: James Gallagher to secretary, Office of the Referee, 25 May 1937.

59   Ibid., 16 July 1937.

60   Ibid., Patrick Shiels to secretary, Office of the Referee, 15 September 1939.

61   Fearghal McGarry, '"Living under an alien despotism", The IRA Campaign in Ulster', in Cecile Gordon (ed.), *The Military Service (1916–23) Pensions Collection: The Brigade Activity Reports* (Dublin, 2018), pp. 84–108.

62   Ibid.

20: Two Teeth

1   *Irish Times*, 26 June 1936.

2   IMA, MSPC, MSP 34 REF 2074, Thomas Hales.

3   IMA, MSPC, 34 REF 9786, William Hales: evidence of Liam Deasy, 9 September 1935.

4   Ibid., William Hales's sworn statement before Advisory Committee, 11 September 1935.

5   Ibid., William Hales to secretary of the Irish Land Commission, 7 June 1940.

6   Ibid., William Hales, social welfare report, 11 May 1961.

7   IMA, MSPC, 34 REF 26254, Robert Hales: sworn evidence before Advisory Committee, 23 September 1936.

8   Ibid., Robert Hale's pension application form, 15 August 1935.

9   Ibid., medical report on Robert Hales, 24 April 1948.

10   Ibid., Robert Hales to Department of Defence, 28 March 1949.

11   Ibid., WDP 16452, Bandon social welfare office report on Robert Hales, 7 April 1952.

12   Ibid., Robert Hales to Department of Defence, 22 May 1955.

13   Ibid., Robert Hales, W34 E1624, 'Payment of sums due at death', June 1959.

14   IMA, MSPC, 34 REF 9786, William Hales: letter of 28 May 1969.

15   IMA, MSPC, 34 REF 2087, Liam Deasy: application form, 23 February 1935.

16   IMA, MSPC, DP 8107, Laurence Sweeney: secretary, minister for finance to secretary, minister for defence, 4 April 1934.

17   Ibid., 'Late Laurence Sweeney, Dundrum: Commemoration Service', press clipping included in Laurence Sweeney file, undated and untitled, but July 1924, submitted with letter of Joseph Sweeney to Department of Defence, 11 September 1933.

18   Máire Cruise O'Brien, *The Same Age as the State* (Dublin, 2003), pp. 73, pp. 124–8.

19   Ryle Dwyer, *Tans, Terror and Trouble*, pp. 10–12.

20   IMA, MSPC, 34 REF 840, Tom McEllistrim: sworn evidence made before the Advisory Committee, 29 January 1935.

21   Ibid., agreed revised pension, 20 August 1941.

22   Ibid., W34C5, Mary McEllistrim to minister for defence, 8 April 1974.

23   Ibid., Mary McEllistrim to George Colley, minister for finance, 23 March 1978.

24   Ibid., Robert Molloy, minister for defence, to Mary McEllistrim, 17 May 1978.

25   Joe Ambrose, *Dan Breen and the IRA* (Cork, 2006), pp. 92–104.

26   Michael Hopkinson, 'Daniel Breen', in *DIB*, vol.1, pp. 796–7.

27   Ibid.

28   IMA, MSPC, 34 REF 171, Daniel Breen: letter of physician George Mehler, 17 November 1932.

29   Ibid., report of Medical Board, 20 February 1933.

30   Ibid., Breen to Frank Aiken, 18 March 1933.

31   Ibid., note of Aiken to Department of Finance and Aiken to minister for finance, 1 September 1933.

32   Ibid., 1P201C, medical report on Breen, 3 August 1937.

33   Ibid., Breen to minister for defence, 17 May 1940.

34   Ibid., medical report of Professor Henry Moore, 21 July 1943.

35   Ibid., note of 7 January 1970 regarding Liam Cosgrave's representations.

36   IMA, MSPC, DP 6664, Rory O'Connor: note of Deputy Liam
       Cosgrave phone call, 24 November 1969.

21: Poachers Turned Gamekeepers

1   David Andrews, *Kingstown Republican: A Memoir* (Dublin, 2007),
       pp. 1–5.
2   Ibid., p. 19, and Tom Garvin, 'Christopher Stephen (Todd) Andrews', in
       DIB, vol. 1, pp. 112–13.
3   Andrews, *Kingstown Republican*, pp. 19–23.
4   Ibid., pp. 90–95.
5   Ibid., p. 2.
6   IMA, MSPC, 34 REF 57554, Christopher Stephen Andrews, pension
       application form, 28 December 1938.
7   Ibid., Andrews to APB, 29 December 1938.
8   Ibid., 34D1920, secretary, Department of Industry and Commerce to
       secretary, Department of Defence, 26 January 1947.
9   Donal Clarke, *Brown Gold: A History of Bord na Móna and the Irish
       Peat Industry* (Dublin, 2010), pp. 70–108.
10   IMA, MSPC, 34 REF 2211, Edward Devitt: letter of Dr F. Warren,
       13 February 1933, and Devitt's sworn statement before the Advisory
       Committee, 4 December 1935.
11   Ibid., Devitt to Department of Defence, 22 May 1936.
12   Ibid., evidence of Joe O'Connor before Advisory Committee, 20 July
       1936, and Joe O'Connor to M. S. Sheppard, 21 September 1936.
13   Ibid., Devitt to APB, 21 September 1933.
14   Ibid., Devitt to APB, 29 January 1935.
15   Ibid., letters of Devitt, 17 March and 28 May 1935.
16   Compiled, 'Other People's Incomes', *The Bell*, 6(4), July 1943,
       pp. 290–98, 6(6), September 1943, pp. 467–73, and 7(1), October
       1943, pp. 55–63. For contemporary value of old money see www.
       measuringworth.com/ppoweruk/.
17   IMA, MSPC, 34 REF 2211, Edward Devitt: letters of Edward Devitt, 28
       May and 19 June 1935.
18   Ibid., T. S. Ó Coileáin to Office of the Referee, 2 December 1955.
19   R. F. Foster, *Luck and the Irish: A Brief History of Change c.1970–2000*
       (London, 2007), pp. 70–75.
20   *Irish Times*, 26 February 2004.
21   Lee, *Ireland 1912–1985*, p. 176.
22   Lewis, *Frank Aiken's War*, pp. 176, 200.
23   'FitzGerald recalls civil war healing', *Irish Times*, 13 November 2008.

24 IMA, MSPC, 34 REF 15471, Gerald Boland: Boland to minister for defence, 28 May 1954.

25 Ibid., note on draft reply to Boland and Boland's returned form, 30 June 1971.

26 IMA, MSPC, 34 REF 236, Oscar Traynor: sworn evidence, 18 January 1935.

27 Ibid., Annie Traynor to APB, 26 October 1971.

28 Patrick Maume, 'Charles James (C. J.) Haughey', *DIB*, www.dib. cambridge.org.

29 IMA, MSPC, 24 SP 9208, John Haughey: Daniel McKenna to the APB, 15 July 1927.

30 Ibid., E. White, medical officer to secretary, APB, 12 August 1942.

31 Ibid., letter of C. Maguire, Dispensary House, Wicklow, 20 February 1942.

32 Ibid., letter of Ger Coyne, MOH, Ballinasloe, to APB, 30 October 1942.

33 Ibid., note of Eamon Ó Hogáin, APB, 28 October 1942.

34 Ibid., John Haughey to minister for defence, 14 November 1938.

35 Ibid., John Haughey to minister for defence, 14 July 1939.

36 Ibid., Sarah Haughey to secretary of Department of Defence, 21 April 1942, and to Oscar Traynor, 13 May 1942.

37 Ibid., medical report on Haughey, 9 February 1942.

38 Ibid., Sarah Haughey to APB, 6 February 1957.

39 *Irish Times*, 14 September 1989.

40 IMA, MSPC, 34 REF 4944, Sarah Haughey: Maureen Haughey to John Daly, Department of Defence, 19 October 1989.

22: Virtue and Erin, Saxon and Guilt

1 Paul Delaney, *Seán O'Faoláin: Literature, Inheritance and the 1930s* (Dublin, 2014), pp. 15–17.

2 O'Hegarty, *The Victory of Sinn Féin* (Dublin, 1998; first published 1924), pp. 117–26.

3 CCCA, De Róiste diaries, 6 April 1923.

4 IMA, MSPC, W34 D448, Stephen Fuller: letter of Dr Shanahan, 18 February 1933 and letter of Edward Dunn, Peamount sanatorium, to APB, 13 June 1933.

5 Ibid., Fuller's sworn statement before the Advisory Committee, 29 October 1935, and Fuller to Office of the Referee, 18 May 1936; *The Kerryman*, 30 January 1981.

6 *Irish Examiner*, 14 March 2009.

7   Michael Regan 'Stories of the revolution: Ballyseedy and the civil war's worst atrocity', *Irish Times*, 11 December 2015.

8   *The Kerryman*, 2 March 1984.

9   *Irish Times*, 11 December 2015.

10   *Dáil Debates*, 20(9), 12 July 1927.

11   *Dáil Debates*, 27(1), 11 October 1927.

12   Walsh, *Recollections of a Rebel*, p. 72.

13   UCDA, P311, Lemass interviews, 1st interview, 12 April 1967.

14   UCDA, Papers of Eamon de Valera, P150/2110, Michael Browne to de Valera, 6 October 1927.

15   UCDA, P311, Lemass interviews, 1st interview, 12 April 1967, and DDA, ABP, Box 466, Government: 1922–39, Lemass to Archbishop Byrne, 8 July 1927, Lemass to Fr Dunne, secretary to Archbishop Byrne, 19 July 1927, and draft response of Standing Committee of Bishops, July 1927.

16   *Dáil Debates*, 22(14), 21 March 1928.

17   Ibid.

18   Eunan O'Halpin, 'Parliamentary Party Discipline and Tactics: The Fianna Fáil Archives, 1926–1932', *Irish Historical Studies*, 30(120), November 1997, pp. 581–90.

19   UCDA, P311, Lemass interviews, 2nd interview, 31 May 1967; 4th interview, 17 August 1967, 7th interview, 3 October 1967; 8th interview, 9 October 1967.

20   Esther Roper (ed.), *Prison Letters of Countess Markievicz* (London, 1934); letters of May/June 1926, p. 307.

21   Richard English, *Radicals and the Republic: Social Republicanism in the Irish Free State, 1925–1937* (Oxford, 1994), p. 66.

22   UCD Special Collections Library, 35 E 2/19: *Sinn Féin Economic Programme 1923: Issued by the Re-Organising Committee Sinn Fein* (Dublin, 1923).

23   Dermot Keogh, *Twentieth Century Ireland: Nation and State* (Dublin, 1994), p. 64; Lee, *Ireland 1912–1985*, pp. 168–71.

24   Lee, *Ireland 1912–1985*, p. 175, and Stephen Collins and Ciara Meehan, *Saving the State: Fine Gael from Cosgrave to Varadkar* (Dublin, 2020), p. 26.

25   Laffan, *Judging W. T. Cosgrave*, pp. 266–7.

26   Cormac Ó Gráda, *Ireland: A New Economic History, 1780–1939* (Oxford, 1994), pp. 439–41.

27   Mike Cronin, *The Blueshirts and Irish Politics* (Dublin, 1997), p. 149.

28   UCDA, P311, Lemass interviews, 3rd interview, 25 July 1967.

29   Alan Burke, 'James Hogan and the Irish Civil War', in Ó Corráin, *James Hogan*, pp. 39–51.

30   Brian Hanley, 'The Civil War Continued? The IRA versus the Blueshirts', in Crowley et al. (eds.), *Atlas of the Irish Revolution*, pp. 810–13.

31   Fearghal McGarry, *Eoin O'Duffy: A Self-Made Hero* (Oxford, 2005), pp. 343–51.

32   Ciara Meehan, *The Cosgrave Party: A History of Cumann na nGaedheal, 1923–33* (Dublin, 2010), pp. 218–21.

33   Deirdre McMahon, 'Maurice Moynihan (1902–1999) Irish Civil Servant: An Appreciation', *Studies*, 89(353), Spring, 2000, pp. 71–6.

34   Foster, *The Irish Civil War and Society*, pp. 195–9.

35   Martin Maguire, *The Civil Service and the Revolution in Ireland, 1912–1938* (Manchester, 2008), pp. 170–225.

36   Margaret O'Callaghan, 'Language, Nationality and Cultural Identity in the Irish Free State, 1922–7', *Irish Historical Studies*, 24(94), 1984, pp. 226–45.

37   John H. Whyte, *Church and State in Modern Ireland, 1923–1979* (Dublin 1980), p. 24.

38   UCDA, P311, Lemass interviews, 9th interview, 11 January 1968.

39   Enda McDonagh, 'Church–state relations', *Irish Press*, 26 May 1976, Fianna Fáil, Golden Jubilee supplement; see also UCDA, Papers of Eamon de Valera, P150/1809, March–June 1923.

40   Regan, *The Irish Counter-Revolution*, p. 285.

41   Diarmaid Ferriter, 'John Dignan', in *DIB*, vol. 3, p. 273, and Dermot Keogh, *The Vatican, the Bishops and Irish Politics, 1919–39* (Cambridge, 1986), pp. 97–122.

42   McCabe, *For God and Ireland*, p. 249, and Lee, *Ireland: 1912–1985*, p. 167.

43   Ferriter, *Judging Dev*, pp. 218–19.

44   Cited in Paul Bew, 'Rising was a Catholic revolt against Redmondite elite', *Irish Times*, 15 April 2006.

45   William Murphy, 'The GAA During the Irish Revolution, 1913–23', in Mike Cronin, William Murphy and Paul Rouse (eds.), *The Gaelic Athletic Association, 1884–2009* (Dublin, 2009), pp. 61–77.

23: Sidestepping Differences

1   'FitzGerald recalls civil war healing', *Irish Times*, 13 November 2008.

2   Garret FitzGerald, 'No mean era', *Irish Times*, 15 November 2000, and Cruise O'Brien, *The Same Age as the State*, pp. 73–6.

3   Eunan O'Halpin, 'Personal Loss and the "Trauma of Internal War": The Cases of W. T. Cosgrave and Seán Lemass', in Melania Terrazas Gallego (ed.), *Trauma and Identity in Contemporary Irish Culture* (Berlin, 2020), pp. 135–49.

4   Valiulis, 'The Man They Could Never Forgive'.

5   *Dáil Debates*, 218(11), 17 November 1965.

6   *Irish Times*, 5 October 2017.

7   Michael Laffan, 'In the Shadow of the National Question', in Paul Daly, Rónán O'Brien and Paul Rouse (eds.), *Making the Difference? The Irish Labour Party, 1912–2012* (Cork, 2012), pp. 32–43.

8   Fearghal McGarry, 'Catholics First and Politicians Afterwards: The Labour Party and the Worker's Republic, 1936–39', *Saothar*, 25, 2000, pp. 57–67.

9   Niamh Puirséil, *The Irish Labour Party, 1922–73* (Dublin, 2007), pp. 27–37.

10 Michael Gallagher, *The Irish Labour Party in Transition, 1957–82* (Manchester, 1982), p. 70.

11 Laffan, *Resurrection of Ireland*, pp. 433–66.

12 Ibid., pp. 456–7.

13 Garvin, 'The Aftermath of the Civil War'.

14 Fanning, *Eamon de Valera*, pp. 159–82.

15 C. S. Andrews, *Dublin Made Me: An Autobiography* (Dublin, 1979), p. 306.

16 Michael Mills, interview with Seán Lemass, *Irish Press*, 23 January 1969.

17 Paul Bew, *Ireland: The Politics of Enmity, 1789–2006* (Oxford, 2007), p. 473.

18 Máire MacSwiney Brugha, *History's Daughter: A Memoir from the Only Child of Terence MacSwiney* (Dublin, 2005) and Patrick Maume, 'Ruairí Brugha', *DIB*, www.dib.cambridge.org.

19 MacSwiney Brugha, *History's Daughter*, p. 191.

20 UCDA, P311, Lemass interviews, 10th interview, 22 January 1968.

21 UCDA, Papers of Seán Mac Eoin, P151/1812, notes for 1960s speeches.

22 NAI, DT S14440, de Valera to Costello, 7 April 1949.

23 Jeffrey Prager, *Building Democracy in Ireland: Political Order and Cultural Integration in a Newly Independent Nation* (Cambridge, 1986), pp. 50–67, 215–26.

24 Diarmaid Ferriter, *Lovers of Liberty? Local Government in Twentieth-Century Ireland* (Dublin, 2001), p. 17.

25 Ambrose, *Dan Breen*, p. 57.

26 Eunan O'Halpin and Daithí Ó Corráin, *The Dead of the Irish Revolution* (New Haven, 2020), pp. 1–25.

27 CCCA, U342/1, Old IRA Men's Association Minute Book, 18 February 1934.

28 Ibid., 14 April 1934.

29 Ibid., 9 November 1935.

30 *Irish Times* supplement on Military Service Pensions Collection, 3 October 2014.

31 Felicity Hayes-McCoy, *A Woven Silence: Memory, History and Remembrance* (Cork, 2015), p. 174.

32 Conor Cruise O'Brien, *Memoir: My Life and Times* (Dublin, 1998), p. 67.

33 O'Malley and Ó Comhraí (eds.), *The Men Will Talk to Me*, p. 63.

34 *Irish Times* supplement on Military Service Pensions Collection, 3 October 2014, and IMA, MSPC, MSP 34 REF 4067, Denis O'Neill: evidence of Frank Thornton given to the Advisory Committee, 8 July 1936.

35 IMA, MSPC, 24 SP 1153, Charles Francis Dalton: Seán Lemass to Theresa Dalton, 12 May 1941; and Bryce Evans, *Seán Lemass: Democratic Dictator* (Cork, 2011), pp. 34–5.

36 Eunan O'Halpin, 'Seán Lemass's silent anguish', *Irish Times*, 21 July 2013.

24: Codology

1   Evi Gkotzaridis, *Trials of Irish History: Genesis and Evolution of a Reappraisal, 1938–2000* (New York, 2006), pp. 45–9.

2   *Dáil Debates*, 26(1), 13 June 1951.

3   Noel Browne, *Against the Tide* (Dublin, 2007 edn), pp. 228–9.

4   Ibid.

5   UCDA, P311, Lemass interviews, 10th interview, 22 January 1968.

6   Ibid., 16th interview, 20 June 1968.

7   Liam Weeks, *Independents in Irish Party Democracy* (Manchester, 2017), pp. 1–15.

8   Diarmaid Ferriter, 'Fianna Fáil and Fine Gael may have to consider coalition' *Irish Times*, 1 February 2020.

9   J. V. Kelleher, 'Ireland ... And Where Does She Stand?', *Foreign Affairs*, 3, 1957, pp. 48–95.

10 'Akenfton', 'Following in Father's footsteps', *Irish Times*, 12 June 1954.

11 Senia Paseta, 'Fighting Their Father's Fight: The Post-Revolutionary Generation in Independent Ireland', in Senia Paseta (ed.), *Uncertain*

Futures: Essays About the Irish Past for Roy Foster (Oxford, 2016), pp. 148–61.

12   Stephen Collins and Ciara Meehan, *Saving the State: Fine Gael from Cosgrave to Varadkar* (Dublin, 2020), p. 102, and Ciara Meehan, *A Just Society for Ireland? 1964–1987* (London, 2013), pp. 41–62.

13   Puirséil, *The Irish Labour Party*, pp. 230–40.

14   Mary Holland, 'No appetite for politics of the right', *Irish Times*, 23 May 2002.

15   John Healy, 'Responsibility and the legacy of the civil war', *Irish Times*, 13 February 1968.

16   Delaney, *Seán O'Faoláin*, pp. 15–17.

17   Desmond O'Malley, *Conduct Unbecoming: A Memoir* (Dublin, 2014), p. 31.

18   Diarmuid Bolger, 'Housing protest and bitter divide saw Dáil's 50th birthday fall flat', *Irish Independent*, 19 January 2019.

19   Michael Hayes, 'Dáil Éireann and the Irish Civil War', *Studies*, 58, Spring 1969, pp. 1–23.

20   Rory O'Dwyer, *The Bastille of Ireland: Kilmainham Jail from Ruin to Restoration* (Dublin, 2010), pp. 29–59.

21   Leonard Piper, *Dangerous Waters: The Life and Death of Erskine Childers* (London, 2003), pp. 228–37.

22   Ibid., pp. 228–9.

23   Diarmaid Ferriter, *Ambiguous Republic: Ireland in the 1970s* (London, 2012), pp. 231–43.

24   Ibid., p. 150.

25: Blind Loyalty Eroded

1   Tom Garvin, 'Getting the vote', *Irish Press*, 26 May 1976, Fianna Fáil Golden Jubilee supplement.

2   Ibid.

3   UCDA, P311, Lemass interviews, 11th interview, 19 February 1968.

4   Ibid., 19th interview, 22 November 1968.

5   Ibid., 20th interview, 29 November 1968.

6   Ibid.

7   Stephen Kelly, 'Fresh Evidence from the Archives: The Genesis of Charles J. Haughey's Attitude to Northern Ireland', *Irish Studies in International Affairs*, 23, 2012, pp. 155–70.

8   Garret FitzGerald, *All in a Life: An Autobiography* (Dublin, 1991), p. 64.

9   Ferriter, *Ambiguous Republic*, p. 62.

10   Ibid., pp. 58–9.

11 Bill Kissane, *Nations Torn Asunder* (Oxford, 2016), pp. 1–18, and Tom Garvin, 'Revolutionaries turned politicians: a painful, confusing metamorphosis', *Irish Times*, 6 December 1997.

12 Peter Mair, 'Explaining the Absence of Class Politics in Ireland', in John Goldthorpe and Chris Whelan (eds.), *The Development of Industrial Society in Ireland* (Oxford, 1992), pp. 383–410.

13 William Murphy, 'Between Change and Tradition: The Politics and Writing of Garret FitzGerald', *Éire-Ireland*, 43(1), 2008, pp. 154–78.

14 Ferriter, *Ambiguous Republic*, p. 59.

15 Ibid.

16 Michael McLoughlin, *Great Irish Speeches of the Twentieth Century* (Dublin, 1996), p. 364.

17 Garret FitzGerald 'Our party system may be limiting party choices', *Irish Times*, 11 September 1999.

18 Frances Gardiner, 'The Women's Movement and Politicians in the Republic, 1980–2000', in A. Bourke et al. (eds.), *The Field Day Anthology of Irish Writing*, vol. 5: *Irish Women's Writing and Traditions* (Cork, 2002) pp. 228–37.

19 *Irish Times*, 23 December 1985.

20 Kieran Allen, *Fianna Fáil and Irish Labour: 1926 to the Present* (London, 1997), pp. 169–70.

21 Joe Lee, 'Squaring the Economic and Social Circles', in Philip Hannon and Jackie Gallagher (eds.), *Taking the Long View: 70 years of Fianna Fáil* (Dublin, 1996), pp. 54–65.

22 Diarmaid Ferriter, 'State now morally as well as economically bankrupt', *Irish Times*, 26 March 2012.

23 Dick Walsh, 'Making a statement about ourselves', *Irish Times*, 3 November 1990.

24 *The Final Report of the Tribunal of Inquiry into Certain Planning Matters and Payments* (Dublin, March 2012) https://planningtribunal.ie/wp-content/uploads/2016/11/sitecontent_1257.pdf, accessed 12 February 2021.

26: Not Caring Who Did What

1 Sebastian Barry, *The Whereabouts of Eneas McNulty* (London, 1998), p. 60.

2 Andrews, 'Collins has more in common with Fianna Fáil ideals'.

3 Dolan and Murphy, *Michael Collins*, pp. 187–8.

4 Ibid.

5   Michael Collins, *The Path to Freedom* (Cork, 1968 edn, first published 1922), pp. 95–106.

6   Dolan and Murphy, *Michael Collins*, pp. 289–329.

7   Dolan, *Commemorating the Irish Civil War*, p. 79.

8   Ibid., p. 68.

9   *Irish Times*, 20 August 1973.

10 Website of the Collins 22 Society, www.generalmichaelcollins.com, accessed 12 February 2021.

11 Garret FitzGerald, 'Apocalypse may yet spark the rebirth of civic morality', *Irish Times*, 16 October 2010.

12 *Dáil Debates*, 747(5), 24 November 2011.

13 *Irish Times*, 7 April 2014.

14 Collins and Meehan, *Saving the State*, pp. 303–4.

15 Ibid., p. 324.

16 *Irish Times*, 10 March 2011.

17 Collins and Meehan, *Saving the State*, p. 345.

18 *Irish Times*, 2 November 2019.

19 Collins and Meehan, *Saving the State*, p. 413.

20 *Dublin Opinion*, 1(6), August 1922.

BIBLIOGRAPHY

National Archives of Ireland, Dublin
Dáil Éireann
Department of Foreign Affairs
Department of Justice
Department of Local Government
Department of the Taoiseach
Land Settlement Commission

Irish Military Archives, Dublin
Papers of the Army Inquiry
    Committee
Bureau of Military History
Civil War Operations and
    Intelligence Reports
Chief of Staff Reports
Confidential Military Reports,
    1922–23
Military Service Pensions Collection

University College Dublin Archives
Papers of Ernest Blythe
Papers of Eamon de Valera
Papers of the Fianna Fáil Party
Papers of Desmond FitzGerald
Papers of Hugh Kennedy
Seán Lemass Interviews
Papers of Seán Mac Eoin

Papers of the Murphy Family
Papers of Kevin O'Higgins
Papers of Mary Spring Rice

University College Dublin, Special Collections Library
Poblacht na hÉireann War News
Republican Propaganda Leaflets,
    1922

Dublin Diocesan Archives
Papers of Archbishop Edward Byrne

Public Record Office of Northern Ireland, Belfast
Cabinet
Papers of Cahir Healy
Home Affairs
Ulster Unionist Council

National Archives, Kew, London
Cabinet
Colonial Office
Dominions Office
Home Office
Earl of Midleton Papers
War Office

Bibliography

Parliamentary Archives, Westminster, London
Papers of Andrew Bonar Law
Papers of David Lloyd George

National University of Ireland, Galway
Papers of Michael Rynne
Sinn Féin Pamphlets

Cork City and County Archives
Liam de Róiste Diaries
Papers of Seán Hayes
Papers of Roibard Langford
Minute Book of Old IRA Men's Association
Republican and Free State Tracts

Newspapers
Cork Examiner
Evening Herald
Freeman's Journal
Irish Examiner
Irish Independent
Irish Statesman
Irish Times
The Kerryman
Kerry News
Kerry Reporter
Kilkenny People
The Liberator
The Nationalist
Nenagh Guardian
Poblacht na hÉireann War News
Sligo Champion
Sunday Independent
Southern Star
Times (London)

Journals and Periodicals
The Bell
Dublin Opinion
Eire Ireland
Foreign Affairs
History Ireland
Irish Economic and Social History
Irish Historical Studies
Irish Political Studies
Irish Studies in International Affairs
The Irish Sword
Irish University Review
Journal of the History of Sexuality
Magill
New Hibernia Review
Past and Present
Saothar
Studies
War in History

Official Reports and Publications
Dáil Éireann Debates
Seanad Éireann Debates
Hansard Debates, House of Commons
The Final Report of the Tribunal of Inquiry into Certain Planning Matters and Payments (Dublin, 2012)
Report of the Army Inquiry Committee (Dublin 1924)
Report of the Commission on the Relief of the Sick and Destitute Poor, Including the Insane Poor (Dublin, 1927)

Reference Works

Quinn, James and James McGuire (eds.), *A Dictionary of Irish Biography: From the Earliest Times to the Year 2009*, 9 vols. (Cambridge, 2009)

Web Sites

www.dib.cambridge.org
www.generalmichaelcollins.com
www.irishelectionliterature.com
www.measuringworth.com/ppoweruk/
www.militaryarchives.ie
www.waterfordmuseum.ie

Books and Articles

Aiken, Síobhra, '"Sinn Féin Permits ... in the Heels of Their Shoes": Cumann na mBan Emigrants and Transatlantic Revolutionary Exchange', *Irish Historical Studies*, 46(165), May 2020, pp. 106–31

Allen, Kieran, *Fianna Fáil and Irish Labour: 1926 to the Present* (London, 1997)

Ambrose, Joe, *Dan Breen and the IRA* (Cork, 2006)

Andrews, C. S., *Dublin Made Me: An Autobiography* (Dublin, 1979)

Armitage, David, *Civil Wars: A History in Ideas* (New York, 2018)

Andrews, David, 'Collins has more in common with Fianna Fáil ideals', *Irish Times*, 18 August 2001

——*Kingstown Republican: A Memoir* (Dublin, 2007)

Bardon, Jonathan, *A History of Ulster* (Belfast, 1992)

Barry, Sebastian, *The Whereabouts of Eneas McNulty* (London, 1998)

Bew, Paul, *Churchill and Ireland* (Oxford, 2016)

——*Ireland: The Politics of Enmity, 1789–2006* (Oxford, 2007)

——'Rising was a Catholic Revolt against Redmondite Elite', *Irish Times*, 15 April 2006

Bielenberg, Andy, 'Exodus: The Emigration of Southern Irish Protestants During the Irish War of Independence and Civil War', *Past and Present*, 128, February 2013, pp. 199–233

——'Fatalities in the Irish Revolution', in Crowley et al. (eds.), *Atlas of the Irish Revolution*, pp. 752–62

Bielenberg, Andy, John Borgonovo and James S. Donnelly Jr., '"Something of the Nature of a Massacre": The Bandon Valley Killings Revisited', *Éire-Ireland*, 49(3–4), Fall/Winter 2014, pp. 7–59

Bolger, Diarmuid, 'Housing Protest and bitter divide saw Dáil's 50th birthday fall flat', *Irish Independent*, 19 January 2019

Bibliography

Borgonovo, John, *The Battle for Cork: July–August 1922* (Cork, 2011)

'Cumann na mBan in the Civil War', in Crowley et al. (eds.), *Atlas of the Irish Revolution*, pp. 698–703

'IRA Conventions', in Crowley et al. (eds.), *Atlas of the Irish Revolution*, pp. 670–75

Bowen, Elizabeth, *The Last September* (London, 1929)

Boyne, John, *Emmet Dalton: Somme Soldier, Irish General, Film Pioneer* (Dublin, 2015)

Brennan, Patrick, '"Active Service": Changing Definitions', and 'Origins, Scope and Content of the Collection', in Catriona Crowe (ed.), *Guide to the Military Service (1916–1923) Pensions Collection* (Dublin, 2012), pp. 64–84 and 14–44

Browne, Noel, *Against the Tide* (Dublin, 2007 edn)

Burke, Alan, 'James Hogan and the Irish Civil War', in Donnchadh Ó Corráin (ed.), *James Hogan: Revolutionary, Historian and Political Scientist* (Dublin, 2001)

Clark, Gemma, *Everyday Violence in the Irish Civil War* (Cambridge, 2014)

——'Violence Against Women in the Irish Civil War, 1922–3: Gender-Based Harm in Global Perspective', *Irish Historical Studies*, 44(165), May 2020, pp. 75–91

Clarke, Donal, *Brown Gold: A History of Bord na Móna and the Irish Peat Industry* (Dublin, 2010)

Coleman, Marie, *County Longford and the Irish Revolution* (Dublin, 2003)

——'Military Service Pensions for Veterans of the Irish Revolution, 1916–23', *War in History*, 20(2), 2013, pp. 201–21

——*The Sweep: A History of the Irish Hospital Sweepstake, 1930–1987* (Dublin, 2009)

Collins, Michael, *The Path to Freedom* (Cork, 1968 edn, first published 1922)

Collins, Stephen and Ciara Meehan, *Saving the State: Fine Gael from Cosgrave to Varadkar* (Dublin, 2020)

Connolly, Linda, 'Sexual Violence and the Irish Revolution: An Inconvenient Truth?', *History Ireland*, 27(6), November/December 2019, pp. 34–8

Conway, Vicky, *Policing Twentieth Century Ireland: A History of An Garda Síochána* (London, 2014)

Costello, Francis, 'Lloyd George and Ireland, 1919–21: An Uncertain Policy', *Canadian Journal of Irish Studies*, 14(1), July 1988, pp. 5–16

Cronin, Mike, *The Blueshirts and Irish Politics* (Dublin, 1997)

Cronin, Seán, *The McGarrity Papers: Revelations of the Irish Revolutionary Movement in Ireland and America, 1900–1940* (Kerry, 1972)

Crowley, John, Donal Ó Drisceoil and Mike Murphy (eds.), *Atlas of the Irish Revolution* (Cork, 2017)

Cruise O'Brien, Conor, *Memoir: My Life and Times* (Dublin, 1998)

Cruise O'Brien, Máire, *The Same Age as the State* (Dublin, 2003)

Curran, Joseph, M., *The Birth of the Irish Free State, 1921–1923* (Alabama, 1980)

d'Alton, Ian, '"No Country": Protestant "Belongings" in Independent Ireland', in Ian d'Alton and Ida Milne (eds.), *Protestant and Irish* (Cork, 2019), pp. 19–34

——'"A Vestigial Population?" Perspectives on Southern Irish Protestants in the Twentieth Century', *Éire Ireland*, 44(3–4), September 2009, pp. 9–42

de Vere White, Terence, *A Fretful Midge* (London, 1957)

Deasy, Liam, *Brother Against Brother* (Cork, 1982)

Delaney, Paul, *Seán O'Faoláin: Literature, Inheritance and the 1930s* (Dublin, 2014)

Dolan, Anne, *Commemorating the Irish Civil War: History and Memory, 1923–2000* (Cambridge, 2003)

——'Divisions and Divisions and Divisions: Who to Commemorate?', in John Horne and Edward Madigan (eds.), *Towards Commemoration: Ireland in War and Revolution, 1912–1923* (Dublin, 2013), pp. 145–54

——'Ending War in a "Sportsmanlike Manner": The Milestone of Revolution, 1919–23', in Thomas E. Hachey (ed.), *Turning Points in Twentieth-Century Irish History* (Dublin, 2011), pp. 21–39

——'Killing in "the Good Old Irish Fashion"? Irish Revolutionary Violence in Context', *Irish Historical Studies*, 44(165), May 2020, pp. 11–25

——'The Papers in Context', in Cormac K. H. O'Malley and Anne Dolan (eds.), *'No Surrender Here!' The Civil War Papers of Ernie O'Malley, 1922–1924* (Dublin, 2007), pp. xliii–liii

Dolan, Anne and William Murphy, *Michael Collins: The Man and the Revolution* (Cork, 2018)

Donohue, Laura K., 'Regulating Northern Ireland: The Special Powers Acts, 1922–72', *Historical Journal*, 41(4), December 1998, pp. 1089–1120

Dooley, Terence, *The Decline of the Big House in Ireland: A Study of Irish Landed Families, 1860–1960* (Dublin, 2001)

Dorney, John, *The Civil War in Dublin: The Fight for the Irish Capital, 1922–1924* (Dublin, 2017)

——'Republican Representations of the Treaty: "A Usurpation Pure and Simple"', in Weeks and Ó Fathartaigh, *The Treaty*, pp. 46–59

Doyle, Tom, *The Civil War in Kerry* (Cork, 2008)

Durney, James, *The Civil War in Kildare* (Cork, 2011)

Earner-Byrne, Lindsey, 'The Rape of Miss Mary M: A Microhistory of Sexual Violence and Moral Redemption in 1920s Ireland', *Journal of the History of Sexuality*, 24, January 2015, pp. 75–98

English, Richard, *Radicals and the Republic: Social Republicanism in the Irish Free State, 1925–1937* (Oxford, 1994)

English, Richard and Cormac K. H. O'Malley (eds.), *Prisoners: The Civil War Letters of Ernie O'Malley* (Dublin, 1991)

Enright, Seán, *The Irish Civil War: Law, Execution and Atrocity* (Dublin, 2019)

Evans, Bryce, *Seán Lemass: Democratic Dictator* (Cork, 2011)

Evans, Richard, J., *Altered Pasts: Counterfactuals in History* (London, 2014)

Fanning, Ronan, *Eamon de Valera: A Will to Power* (London, 2015)

——*Independent Ireland* (Dublin, 1983)

——'Small States, Larger Neighbours: Ireland and the United Kingdom', *Irish Studies in International Affairs*, 9, 1998, pp. 21–9

Fanning, Ronan, Michael Kennedy, Eunan O'Halpin and Dermot Keogh (eds.), *Documents on Irish Foreign Policy*, vol. 1: *1919–1922* (Dublin, 1998); vol. 2: *1923–26* (Dublin, 1999)

Farrell, Mel, *Party Politics in a New Democracy: The Irish Free State, 1922–37* (London, 2017)

——'"Stepping Stone to Freedom": Pro-Treaty Rhetoric and Strategy During the Treaty Debates', in Weeks and Ó Fathartaigh, *The Treaty*, pp. 18–32

Farry, Michael, *The Aftermath of Revolution: Sligo, 1921–23* (Dublin, 2000)

Feeney, Tom, *Seán MacEntee: A Political Life* (Dublin, 2009)

Ferriter, Diarmaid, *Ambiguous Republic: Ireland in the 1970s* (London, 2012)

——'Fianna Fáil and Fine Gael may have to consider Coalition', *Irish Times*, 1 February 2020

——*Judging Dev: A Reassessment of the Life and Legacy of Eamon de Valera* (Dublin, 2007)

——*Lovers of Liberty? Local Government in Twentieth-Century Ireland* (Dublin, 2001)

——*A Nation and Not a Rabble: The Irish Revolution, 1913–1923* (London, 2015)

——'State now morally as well as economically bankrupt', *Irish Times*, 26 March 2012

Fewer, Michael, *The Battle of the Four Courts: The First Three Days of the Irish Civil War* (Dublin, 2018)

FitzGerald, Garret, *All in a Life: An Autobiography* (Dublin, 1991)

——'Apocalypse may yet spark the rebirth of civic morality', *Irish Times*, 16 October 2010

——'No mean era', *Irish Times*, 15 November 2000

——'Our Party system may be limiting party choices', *Irish Times*, 11 September 1999

Fitzpatrick, David, *Harry Boland's Irish Revolution* (Cork, 2003)

Flanagan, Frances, *Remembering the Revolution: Dissent, Culture and Nationalism in the Irish Free State* (Oxford, 2015)

Foster, Gavin, 'The Civil War in Kerry in History and Memory', in Maurice J. Bric (ed.), *Kerry: History and Society: Interdisciplinary Essays on the History of an Irish County* (Dublin, 2020), chapter 22

——'Class Dismissed? The Debate Over a Social Basis to the Treaty Split and Irish Civil War', *Saothar*, 33, 2008, pp. 73–86

——*The Irish Civil War and Society: Politics, Class and Conflict* (London, 2015)

——'Locating the "Lost Legion": IRA Emigration and Settlement After the Civil War', in Crowley et al. (eds.), *The Atlas of the Irish Revolution*, pp. 741–7

——'Res Publica na hÉireann? Republican Liberty and the Irish Civil War', *New Hibernia Review*, 16(3), Autumn 2012, pp. 20–42

——'The Social Basis of the Civil War Divide', in Crowley et al. (eds.), *Atlas of the Irish Revolution*, pp. 665–7

Foster, R. F., *Luck and the Irish: A Brief History of Change, c.1970–2000* (London, 2007)

——*Vivid Faces: The Revolutionary Generation in Ireland, 1890–1923* (London, 2014)

Freehill, Olivia, 'Republican Dissent Among Irish Jesuits During the Civil War, 1922–23', *Studies*, 107(425), Spring 2018, pp. 57–76

Gallagher, Frank, *The Bishops' Pastoral: A Prisoner's Letter to His Grace the Archbishop of Dublin* (Dublin, 1922)

——*Days of Fear* (Cork, 1967)

Gallagher, Michael, *The Irish Labour Party in Transition, 1957–82* (Manchester, 1982)

Gardiner, Frances, 'The Women's Movement and Politicians in the Republic, 1980–2000', in A. Bourke et al. (eds.), *The Field Day Anthology of Irish Writing*, vol. 5: *Irish Women's Writing and Traditions* (Cork, 2002), pp. 228–37

Garvin, Tom, 'The Aftermath of the Civil War', *The Irish Sword*, 20(82), Winter 1997, pp. 387–96

Bibliography

'Getting the Vote', *Irish Press*, 26 May 1976, Fianna Fáil Golden Jubilee
    supplement
——*1922: The Birth of Irish Democracy* (Dublin, 1996)
——'Revolutionaries turned politicians: a painful, confusing metamorphosis',
    Irish Times, 6 December 1997
Geary, Frank, 'The Taking of Cork, July 1922', in John Horgan (ed.), *Great
    Irish Reportage* (Dublin, 2013), pp. 1–16
Gibbon, Monk (ed.), *The Living Torch: AE* (London, 1937)
Gkotzaridis, Evi, *Trials of Irish History: Genesis and Evolution of a
    Reappraisal, 1938–2000* (New York, 2006)
Greaves, Desmond, *Liam Mellows and the Irish Revolution* (London, 1971)
Hachey, Thomas (ed.), *Turning Points in Twentieth-Century Irish History*
    (Dublin, 2011)
Hanley, Brian, '"Merely Tuppence Half-Penny Looking Down on
    Tuppence?": Class, the Second Dáil and Irish Republicanism', in Weeks
    and Ó Fathartaigh, *The Treaty*, pp. 60–70
——'The Civil War Continued? The IRA versus the Blueshirts', in Crowley
    et al. (eds.), *Atlas of the Irish Revolution*, pp. 810–13
——*The IRA: A Documentary History, 1916–2005* (Dublin, 2010)
——'Moderates and Peacemakers', *Journal of Irish Economic and Social
    History*, 43(1), 2016, pp. 113–30
——'The Politics of NORAID', *Irish Political Studies*, 19(1), Summer 2004,
    pp. 1–18
——'Terror in Twentieth-Century Ireland', in David Fitzpatrick (ed.), *Terror
    in Ireland, 1916–1923* (Dublin, 2012), pp. 10–26
Harrington, Niall, C., *Kerry Landing: August 1922* (Dublin, 1992)
Hart, Peter, 'The Geography of Revolution in Ireland, 1917–1923', *Past and
    Present*, 155, May 1997, pp. 142–76
——*The IRA and Its Enemies: Violence and Community in Cork, 1916–1923*
    (London, 1998)
——*The IRA at War, 1916–1923* (Oxford, 2003)
——'Michael Collins and the Assassination of Sir Henry Wilson', *Irish
    Historical Studies*, 28(110), November 1992, pp. 150–70
——*Mick: The Real Michael Collins* (London, 2005)
Hayes, Michael, 'Dáil Éireann and the Irish Civil War', *Studies*, 58, Spring
    1969, pp. 1–23
Hayes-McCoy, Felicity, *A Woven Silence: Memory, History and Remembrance*
    (Cork, 2015)
Healy, James, 'The Civil War Hunger Strike, October 1923', *Studies*, 71,
    Autumn 1982, pp. 213–26

Healy, John, 'Responsibility and the legacy of the civil war', *Irish Times*, 13 February 1968

Heffernan, Brian, *Freedom and the Fifth Commandment: Catholic Priests and Political Violence in Ireland, 1919–21* (Manchester, 2014)

Higgins, Michael D., *The Betrayal* (Dublin, 1990)

Holland, Mary, 'No appetite for politics of the right', *Irish Times*, 23 May 2002

Hopkinson, Michael, 'Civil War: The Opening Phase', in Crowley et al. (eds.), *Atlas of the Irish Revolution*, pp. 675–88

——*Green Against Green: The Irish Civil War* (Dublin, 1988)

——'The Guerrilla Phase and the End of the Civil War', in Crowley et al. (eds.), *Atlas of the Irish Revolution*, pp. 703–15

Horgan, John, *Seán Lemass: The Enigmatic Patriot* (Dublin, 1997)

Horgan, Tim, *Dying for the Cause: Kerry's Republican Dead* (Cork, 2015)

Inglis, Brian, *West Briton* (London, 1962)

Kalyvas, Stathis, *The Logic of Violence in Civil War* (New York, 2005)

Keane, Fergal, *Wounds: A Memoir of Love and War* (London, 2017)

Kelleher, J. V., 'Ireland ... And Where Does She Stand?', *Foreign Affairs*, 3, 1957, pp. 48–95

Kelly, Stephen, 'Fresh Evidence from the Archives: The Genesis of Charles J. Haughey's Attitude to Northern Ireland', *Irish Studies in International Affairs*, 23, 2012, pp. 155–70

Kemmy, Jim, 'P. J. (Cushy) Ryan', *Old Limerick Journal*, 9, Winter 1981, p. 3

Kenny, Tomás, *Galway: Politics and Society, 1910–1923* (Dublin, 2011)

Keogh, Dermot, *Twentieth Century Ireland; Nation and State* (Dublin, 1994)

——*The Vatican, the Bishops and Irish Politics, 1919–39* (Cambridge, 1986)

Kissane, Bill, *Nations Torn Asunder* (Oxford, 2016)

——'On the Shock of Civil War: Cultural Trauma and National Identity in Finland and Ireland', in *Nations and Nationalism: Journal for the Association of the Study of Ethnicity and Nationalism*, 26(1), June 2020, pp. 22–43

——*The Politics of the Irish Civil War* (Oxford, 2005)

Kline, Benjamin, 'Churchill and Collins, 1919–22: Admirers or Adversaries?', *History Ireland*, 1(3), Autumn 1993, pp. 38–44

Knirck, Jason, *Afterimage of the Revolution: Cumann na nGaedheal and Irish Politics, 1922–1932* (Wisconsin, 2014)

——'Women's Political Rhetoric and the Irish Revolution', in Thomas Hachey (ed.), *Turning Points in Twentieth-Century Irish History* (Dublin, 2011), pp. 39–56

Kostick, Conor, *Revolution in Ireland: Popular Militancy, 1917–1923* (London, 1996)

Laffan, Michael, 'In the Shadow of the National Question', in Paul Daly, Rónán O'Brien and Paul Rouse (eds.), *Making the Difference? The Irish Labour Party, 1912–2012* (Cork, 2012) pp. 32–43

——*Judging W. T. Cosgrave: The Foundation of the Irish State* (Dublin, 2014)

——*The Resurrection of Ireland: The Sinn Féin Party, 1916–1923* (Cambridge 1999)

Lane, Leeann, *Dorothy Macardle* (Dublin, 2019)

Langton, James, *Forgotten Fallen*, vol. 1: *National Army Soldiers Killed in Action During the Irish Civil War* (Dublin, 2020)

Lee, J. J., *Ireland, 1912–1985: Politics and Society* (Cambridge, 1989)

——'Squaring the Economic and Social Circles', in Philip Hannon and Jackie Gallagher (eds.), *Taking the Long View: 70 years of Fianna Fáil* (Dublin, 1996), pp. 54–65

Lewis, Matthew, *Frank Aiken's War: The Irish Revolution, 1916–23* (Dublin, 2014)

Long, Patrick, 'Organisation and Development of the Pro-Treaty Forces, 1922–1924', *Irish Sword*, 20(82), Winter 1997, pp. 308–31

Longford, Earl of and T. P. O'Neill, *Eamon de Valera* (London, 1970)

Lynch, Robert, *The Northern IRA and the Early Years of Partition, 1920–1922* (Dublin, 2006)

Lyons, George A., *Some Recollections of Arthur Griffith and His Times* (Dublin, 1923)

Mac Eoin, Uinseann, *Survivors* (Dublin, 1987)

MacSwiney Brugha, Máire, *History's Daughter: A Memoir from the Only Child of Terence MacSwiney* (Dublin, 2005)

Maguire, Martin, *The Civil Service and the Revolution in Ireland, 1912–1938* (Manchester, 2008)

Mair, Peter, 'Explaining the Absence of Class Politics in Ireland', in John Goldthorpe and Chris Whelan (eds.), *The Development of Industrial Society in Ireland* (Oxford, 1992), pp. 383–410

Matthew, James, *Voices: A Life of Frank O'Connor* (Dublin, 1983)

McAuliffe, Mary, '"An idea has gone abroad that all the women were against the Treaty": Cumann na Saoirse and Pro-Treaty Women, 1922–3', in Weeks and Ó Fathartaigh, *The Treaty*, pp. 98–109

McCabe, M. P., *For God and Ireland: The Fight for Moral Superiority in Ireland, 1922–1932* (Dublin, 2013)

McCarthy, Pat, *The Irish Revolution, 1912–23: Waterford* (Dublin, 2015)

McCoole, Sinéad, 'Debating not Negotiating: The Female TDs of the Second Dáil', in Weeks and Ó Fathartaigh, *The Treaty*, pp. 85–96

McCullagh, David, *De Valera: Rise, 1882–1932* (Dublin, 2017)

McDonagh, Enda, 'Church–State relations', *Irish Press*, 26 May 1976, Fianna Fáil Golden Jubilee supplement

McGarry, Fearghal, 'Catholics First and Politicians Afterwards: The Labour Party and the Workers' Republic, 1936–39', *Saothar*, 25, 2000, pp. 57–67

——*Eoin O'Duffy: A Self-Made Hero* (Oxford, 2005)

——'"Living under an alien despotism", The IRA Campaign in Ulster', in Cecile Gordon (ed.), *The Military Service (1916–23) Pensions Collection: The Brigade Activity Reports* (Dublin, 2018), pp. 84–108

——'Revolution, 1916–23', in Thomas Bartlett (ed.), *The Cambridge History of Ireland*, vol. 4: *1880 to the Present* (Cambridge, 2018)

McLoughlin, Michael, *Great Irish Speeches of the Twentieth Century* (Dublin, 1996)

McMahon, Deirdre, 'Maurice Moynihan (1902–1999), Irish Civil Servant: An Appreciation', *Studies*, 89(353), Spring, 2000, pp. 71–6

Meehan, Ciara, *The Cosgrave Party: A History of Cumann na nGaedheal, 1923–33* (Dublin, 2010)

——*A Just Society for Ireland? 1964–1987* (London, 2013)

Morris, Catherine, *Alice Milligan and the Irish Cultural Revival* (Dublin, 2012)

Mulcahy, Risteárd, *My Father the General: Richard Mulcahy and the Military History of the Revolution* (Dublin, 2009)

Murphy, Gerard, *The Great Cover-Up: The Truth About the Death of Michael Collins* (Cork, 2018)

——*The Year of Disappearances: Political Killings in Cork, 1921–1922* (Dublin, 2010)

Murphy, William, 'Between Change and Tradition: The Politics and Writing of Garret FitzGerald', *Éire-Ireland*, 43(1), 2008, pp. 154–78

——'The GAA During the Irish Revolution, 1913–23', in Mike Cronin, William Murphy and Paul Rouse (eds.), *The Gaelic Athletic Association, 1884–2009* (Dublin, 2009), pp. 61–77

Murray, Christopher, *Seán O'Casey: Writer at Work: A Biography* (Dublin, 2004)

Murray, Patrick, 'Obsessive Historian: Eamon de Valera and the Policing of His Reputation', *Proceedings of the Royal Irish Academy*, 101 C, 2001, pp. 37–65

——*Oracles of God: The Roman Catholic Church and Irish Politics, 1922–37* (Dublin, 2000)

Neeson, Eoin, *The Civil War in Ireland* (Cork, 1966)

O'Beirne-Ranelagh, John, 'The IRB from the Treaty to 1924', *Irish Historical Studies*, 20(77), March 1976, pp. 26–39

O'Callaghan, Margaret, 'Language, Nationality and Cultural Identity in the Irish Free State, 1922–7', *Irish Historical Studies*, 24(94), 1984, pp. 226–45

O'Casey, Seán, 'Juno and the Paycock', in Seán O'Casey, *Three Dublin Plays* (London, 1998), pp. 63–149

O'Connor, Frank, *An Only Child* (London, 1961)

Ó Corráin, Donnchadh (ed.), *James Hogan: Revolutionary, Historian and Political Scientist* (Dublin, 2001)

O'Donnell, Peadar, *The Gates Flew Open: An Irish Civil War Prison Diary* (Cork, 2013)

O'Donoghue, Florence, *No Other Law: The Story of Liam Lynch and the Irish Republican Army, 1916–1923* (Dublin, 1954)

Ó Drisceoil, Donal, 'Irish Newspapers, the Treaty and the Civil War', in Crowley et al. (eds.), *Atlas of the Irish Revolution* (Cork, 2017), pp. 661–5

O'Dwyer, Rory, *The Bastille of Ireland: Kilmainham Jail from Ruin to Restoration* (Dublin, 2010)

O'Faoláin, Julia, *Trespassers: A Memoir* (London, 2013)

O'Faoláin, Seán, *De Valera* (London, 1939)

——*Inishfallen: Fare Thee Well* (London, 1949)

——'A Portrait of the Artist as an Old Man', *Irish University Review*, 6(1), Spring 1976, pp. 10–19

——'Romance and Realism', *The Bell*, 10(5), August 1945, pp. 373–82

——*Vive Moi: An Autobiography* (London, 1965)

O'Farrell, Fergus, *Cathal Brugha* (Dublin, 2018)

Ó Fathartaigh, Mícheál and Liam Weeks (eds.), *The Treaty: Debating and Establishing the Irish State* (Dublin, 2018)

O'Flaherty, Liam, 'Civil War', in A. A. Kelly (ed.), *The Collected Stories of Liam O'Flaherty*, vol. 1 (Dublin, 1999), pp. 183–9

Ó Gráda, Cormac, *Ireland: A New Economic History, 1780–1939* (Oxford, 1994)

O'Halpin, Eunan, 'Parliamentary Party Discipline and Tactics: The Fianna Fáil Archives, 1926–1932', *Irish Historical Studies*, 30(120), November 1997, pp. 581–90

——'Personal Loss and the "Trauma of Internal War": The Cases of W. T. Cosgrave and Seán Lemass', in Melania Terrazas Gallego (ed.), *Trauma and Identity in Contemporary Irish Culture* (Berlin, 2020), pp. 135–49

——'Seán Lemass's silent anguish', *Irish Times*, 21 July 2013

O'Halpin, Eunan and Daithí Ó Corráin, *The Dead of the Irish Revolution* (New Haven, 2020)

O'Halpin, Eunan and Mary Staines, '"Between Two Hells": The Social, Political and Military Backgrounds and Motivations of the 121 TDs Who Voted for or Against the Anglo-Irish Treaty in January 1922', in Weeks and Ó Fathartaigh, *The Treaty*, pp. 73–83

O'Hegarty, P. S., *The Victory of Sinn Féin: How It Won It and How It Used It* (Dublin, 1924)

O'Higgins, Kevin, *Three Years Hard Labour: An Address Delivered to the Irish Society at Oxford University* (Oxford, 1924)

O'Malley, Cormac K. H. (ed.), *Modern Ireland and Revolution: Ernie O'Malley in Context* (Kildare, 2016)

O'Malley, Cormac K. H. and Nicholas Allen (eds.), *Broken Landscapes: Selected Letters of Ernie O'Malley, 1924–1957* (Dublin, 2011)

O'Malley, Cormac K. H. and Anne Dolan (eds.), *No Surrender Here! The Civil War Papers of Ernie O'Malley, 1922–1924* (Dublin, 2007)

O'Malley, Cormac K. H. and Cormac Ó Comhraí (eds.), *The Men Will Talk to Me: Galway Interviews by Ernie O'Malley* (Cork, 2013)

O'Malley, Desmond, *Conduct Unbecoming: A Memoir* (Dublin, 2014)

O'Malley, Ernie, *The Singing Flame* (Dublin, 1978)

Ó Murchú, Noel, *War in the West, 1918–1923: The Struggle for Irish Independence on the Dingle Peninsula* (Kerry, 2020)

O'Reilly, Terence, *Rebel Heart: George Lennon: A Flying Column Commander* (Cork, 2009)

Ó Ruairc, Pádraig Óg, *The Battle for Limerick City* (Cork, 2006)

O'Toole, Fintan, 'A Portrait of Peadar O'Donnell as an Old Soldier', *Magill*, February 1982, pp. 25–31

Paseta, Senia, 'Fighting Their Father's Fight: The Post-Revolutionary Generation in Independent Ireland', in Senia Paseta (ed.), *Uncertain Futures: Essays About the Irish Past for Roy Foster* (Oxford, 2016), pp. 148–61

Pearce, Donald R., *The Senate Speeches of W. B. Yeats* (London, 2001)

Phipps, Sally, *Molly Keane: A Life* (London, 2017)

Piper, Leonard, *Dangerous Waters: The Life and Death of Erskine Childers* (London, 2003)

Prager, Jeffrey, *Building Democracy in Ireland: Political Order and Cultural Integration in a Newly Independent Nation* (Cambridge, 1986)

Price, Dominic, *We Bled Together: Michael Collins, The Squad and the Dublin Brigade* (Cork, 2017)

Puirséil, Niamh, *The Irish Labour Party, 1922–73* (Dublin, 2007)

Regan, John M., *The Irish Counter-Revolution, 1921–1936: Treatyite Settlement and Politics in Independent Ireland* (Dublin, 2001)

——'Kindling the Singing Flame: The Destruction of the Public Record Office (30 June 1922) as a Historical Problem', in Cormac K. H. O'Malley (ed.), *Modern Ireland and Revolution*, pp. 107–24

——*Myth and the Irish State* (Dublin, 2013)

Robinson, Lennox (ed.), *Lady Gregory's Journals, 1916–1930* (London, 1946)

Roper, Esther (ed.), *Prison Letters of Countess Markievicz* (London, 1934)

Russell, George, 'Lessons of Revolution', *Studies*, 12(45), March 1923, pp. 1–6

Ryan, Meda, *The Real Chief: The Story of Liam Lynch* (Cork, 1986)

Ryan, P. J., 'Armed Conflict in Limerick', in David Lee (ed.), *Remembering Limerick* (Limerick, 1997), pp. 274–6

Ryle Dwyer, T., 'British army fire did not spark civil war', *Irish Examiner*, 1 November 2012

——*Tans, Terror and Trouble: Kerry's Real Fighting Story, 1919–1923* (Cork, 2001)

Townshend, Charles, *The Republic: The Fight for Irish Independence* (London, 2013)

Valiulis, Maryann Gialanella, *Almost a Rebellion: The Irish Army Mutiny of 1924* (Cork, 1985)

——'The Man They Could Never Forgive: The View of the Opposition: Eamon de Valera and the Civil War', in J. P. O'Carroll and John A. Murphy (eds.), *De Valera and His Times* (Cork, 1986), pp. 92–100

——*Portrait of a Revolutionary: General Richard Mulcahy and the Founding of the Irish Free State* (Dublin, 1992)

Walker, Brian, 'Darkest nights: mystery of the Dunmanway massacre', *Irish Independent*, 30 May 2014

Walsh, Caroline, 'The sad and enduring love of Kitty Kiernan', *Irish Times*, 18 November 1983

Walsh, Dick, 'Making a statement about ourselves', *Irish Times*, 3 November 1990

Walsh, J. J., *Recollections of a Rebel* (Kerry, 1944)

Ward, Margaret, *Unmanageable Revolutionaries: Women and Irish Nationalism* (London, 1995)

Weeks, Liam, *Independents in Irish Party Democracy* (Manchester, 2017)

White, Gerry, 'Free State versus Republic: The Opposing Armed Forces in the Civil War', in Crowley et al. (eds.), *Atlas of the Irish Revolution*, pp. 691–7

Whyte, John H., *Church and State in Modern Ireland, 1923–1979* (Dublin, 1980)

Wilk, Gavin, '"No Hope for him unless he can be got out of the country": Disabled Irish Republicans in America, 1922–35', *New Hibernia Review*, 18(1), Spring 2014, pp. 106–19

——*Transatlantic Defiance: The Militant Irish Republican Movement in America, 1923–45* (Manchester, 2014)

Wren, Jimmy, *The GPO Garrison Easter Week 1916: A Biographical Dictionary* (Dublin, 2015)

Yeates, Pádraig, *A City in Civil War: Dublin, 1921–1924* (Dublin, 2015)

Younger, Calton, *Ireland's Civil War* (London, 1968)

ACKNOWLEDGEMENTS

Led by Cécile Gordon and Officer in Charge Daniel Ayiotis, those working in the Irish Military Archives to make the Military Service Pensions Collection accessible have done extraordinary work in recent years and my deepest gratitude goes to them all. I am also grateful to the staffs of the UCD James Joyce and Richview libraries, the staff of the UCD Archives, and those working in the National Archives of Ireland in Dublin, National Library of Ireland, Dublin Diocesan Archives, NUI Galway Library, Cork City and County Archives, the Public Record Office of Northern Ireland, the National Archives in Kew and the Parliamentary Archives at Westminster. Warm thanks also to Andrew Franklin and Penny Daniel of Profile Books, the gifted wordsmith Trevor Horwood, my colleagues in the UCD School of History, Catríona Crowe, my siblings Cian, Tríona and Muireann, and my parents Nollaig and Vera, to whom this book is dedicated. My deepest debt is to the great loves of my life: Sheila, Enya, Ríona and Saorla.

INDEX

Index

McCartney, Patrick 146–7
McCartney, Peter 146
McCauley, Leo 173
McCoy, Felicity Hayes 223–4
McCoy, John 178–9
McDonald, Fr Walter 82
McDowell, R. B. 98
McElligott, Judge Edward 142
McEllin, Patrick 149
McEllistrim, Mary 192–3
McEllistrim, Tom 53, 192
McGarrity, Joseph 83, 155
McGarry, Emmet 94
McGarry, Fearghal 212
McGarry, Seán 94
McGoldrick, Joseph 160
McGrath, Joe 165, 170, 171, 173
McHugh, Saoirse 243
McKelvey, Joe 92
McNeill, James 215–16
McNicholl, Mary 185–6
McNicholl, Roderick 185
McQuaid, Archbishop of Dublin, John Charles 215
Mellows, Herbert 93–4
Mellows, Liam 23, 42, 47, 92, 93
Mellows, Sarah 93
Michael Collins (film) 240
Midleton, William Brodrick, Earl of 36–7, 40, 64
Military Service Pensions Acts: (1924) 129–30, 131; (1934) 129, 130, 131–2, 133, 177
Military Service Pensions archive 11, 145
Milligan, Alice 128
Mills, Michael 13, 220–1
Ministry for Home Affairs 35
Moloney, Con 55, 63, 100
Moloney, P. J. 10
Monaghan 26, 47, 133
Mountjoy Prison, Dublin 75–6, 78, 87, 88, 91, 93, 116, 178
Moylan, Seán 177, 209
Moynihan, Manus 66
Moynihan, Maurice 213

Mulcahy, Richard 74, 178, 212; Ballyseedy slaughter and 108, 109; British Army departure from Ireland and 33; calls army convention 23; clamour for the arresting of women, on 79; Denis Barry and 116; de Valera meets 74; executions and 89, 91; Fine Gael leader 172; Hoey funeral, attends 178; International Committee of the Red Cross prisoners report and 111; MacSwiney and 96; minister for defence 41, 47, 64, 163, 169; National Army and 47, 54, 61, 64, 163–4, 165–6, 167, 168–72, 178; National Army mutiny/demobilisation and 163–4, 165–6, 167, 168–70; northern IRA efforts to destabilise Northern Ireland and 41; O'Brien, attends funeral of 224; political resurrection 171, 172; resigns as minister for defence 163, 171; Ryan and 112; War of Independence and 23
Murphy, Annie 87
Murphy, Conn 85, 86–7, 94
Murphy, Constance (Connie) 86–7
Murphy, Humphrey 53
Murphy, Jeremiah 155
Murphy, Kathleen 87
Murphy, Patrick 149

National Army: Army Comrades Association 212; Army Inquiry Committee 165–74; Association of Ex-Officers and Men 129; Ballyseedy atrocity and *see* Ballyseedy atrocity; Beggar's Bush Barracks headquarters 29; Black and Tans, comparisons with 64–5; Cahirciveen killings and 109, 137; call to arms 47; casualty numbers 120; Catholic Church and 82–3, 166; Clashmealcon cave siege and 109; Collins appointed commander-in-chief 47, 48; Collins death and 57, 61; commandeering 66; Constitution (1922) and 31; Countess Bridge killings and 108–9; creation